The Cruel Choice

DENIS GOULET

The Cruel Choice

A New Concept in the Theory of Development

CENTER FOR THE STUDY OF
DEVELOPMENT AND SOCIAL CHANGE
Cambridge, Massachusetts

NEW YORK *Atheneum* 1971

Portions of Chapter Three appeared originally in "Development for What?" by Denis A. Goulet in *Comparative Political Studies,* Volume 1, Number 2 (July 1968), and are reprinted by permission of the publisher, Sage Publications, Inc.

To Ana Maria, Andrea, and Sinane

PREFACE

The aim of this work is to thrust debates over economic and social development into the arena of ethical values.[1] I state my own values explicitly so as to elicit from others further reflection, criticism, and experimentation. The premise underlying this work is that, for developed and underdeveloped societies alike, basic questions are neither economic, political, nor technological, but moral. What is the good life and what is the good society in a world of mass technology and global interdependence? Is fullness of good compatible with abundance of goods? Is human development something more than a systemic combination of modern bureaucracy, efficient technology, and productive economy?

I have studied the ethics of development by allying empirical observation, and experiences as a planner and anonymous participant in underdeveloped communities, to reflection on the findings of social scientists and on the testimony of "simple folk" as well. This latter source is invaluable; indeed, I share Danilo Dolci's view "that no study from the outside can equal the value of self-examination by a population."[2] My theoretical analysis rests on two concepts: "vulnerability" and "existence rationality." Vulnerability is exposure to forces one cannot control. In the present context it is the inability of underdeveloped societies to determine the outcome of their own responses to pressing social forces. To state that "vulnerability" is the key to understanding underdevelopment and promoting development is to imply that the diverse worlds of experience, symbol, and social structure can be fruitfully integrated around this concept. Moreover, "vulnerability" provides a frame for viewing underdevelopment as an initial condition, and development both as change process and as terminal state. Vulnerability is expressed in the failure of many low-income countries to meet their development goals, and in the bitter harvest of mass aliena-

---

[1] For the meaning of terms, cf. Appendix I, "The Terms 'Ethics' and 'Development.'"
[2] Danilo Dolci, *The Man Who Plays Alone* (Pantheon, 1968), Introduction, p. x.

tion in certain societies where prosperity has already been achieved.

"Existence rationality," in turn, designates the strategies employed by all societies to process information and make practical choices designed to assure survival and satisfy their needs for esteem and freedom. These strategies vary widely and are conditioned by numerous constraints. "Existence rationality" is central to my claim that certain universal goals are common to developed and non-developed societies alike. Hence, under present constraints and levels of information, development is pursued or rejected depending on whether or not change is thought to enhance sustenance, esteem, and freedom.

Vulnerability and existence rationality are closely linked. To the extent that a society is vulnerable to worldwide ecological, symbolic, and social forces, to that same degree are the constraints surrounding its "existence rationality" increased. It is likewise with the ability to process information: groups which are technologically less vulnerable have greater capacities than others to process the information relevant to their survival and the satisfaction of perceived needs.

By centering his analysis on these two constructs one confers upon the development experience its full historical significance. Technological modernization, economic advance, and social transformation never occur in a historical vacuum. Centers of innovation, diffusion, and control exist whence flow certain stimuli; and it matters greatly at what time and in which space—geographical, political, and cultural—a society first launches its quest for "development." The present book, accordingly, analyzes diverse vulnerabilities and existence rationalities of societies in terms of a normative question which is central to development—namely: what are the requirements of the good life and of the good society in the modern world?

A dialectical rhythm courses through this study. Powerful countries must become vulnerable in order to achieve reciprocity with weaker partners suffering from structurally imposed vulnerability. Austerity can be imposed on the poor only if it is also assumed by the rich. A cultural revolution must take place inside developed countries if underdeveloped countries are to succeed in their own cultural revolution. My basic contention is that prevailing images of development are defective and that the standard view of its proper means and goals is erroneous. Not ethical theorists alone, but all those concerned with development must consider new possibilities.

The vulnerability concept is central to my critique of development's goals and to its presentation as a conflictual process. Since development experiences are rooted in history, the traumatic character of much initial change also needs to be explained. Any development ethic would be sterile, of course, unless it offered strategies for action. Ethics will be judged, finally, not on the elegance of its analysis, but on the realism of its prescriptions.

The specific ethical strategies for development here proposed conform to three regulative principals expounded in Chapter 6. Thereafter, the endless task is to thrust theory out toward the farthest frontiers of practice so as to generate critical conscience and the marriage of efficiency with justice.

This essay is neither a manual nor a textbook. Although numerous development problems raise ethical issues and call for appropriate strategies, no attempt has been made to be exhaustive. Accordingly, the reader will search in vain for a detailed population strategy, although the ecological implications of demography are discussed briefly in Chapter 12. The moral issues here are now evident: rational population policies must be tailored to differing needs of societies. Nevertheless, even massive birth control does not obviate the need for resource planning, selective investment, sound educational strategies, incentive strategies respectful of popular wishes, and, above all, for the elimination of structures of domination. Population control, in short, is no panacea. Similarly, no formal treatment is given in this book to other important questions such as: which levels of technology ought to be adopted by economies now entering an industrial phase—vanguard technologies, advanced, intermediate, or newly obsolete technologies? Or what is the content of good interdisciplinary pedagogy for "developers"? Each of these themes—and many others—would require a lengthy book.

Because of their urgency, however, illustrative strategies have been outlined in three domains: democratic planning, technical cooperation, and the creation of value change. Planning is democratic when it is controlled by, and responsive to, all persons affected by its decisions. Technical cooperation comes about when transfers of technological skills or information are achieved without producing or consolidating the dominant position of the more "advanced" partner. Finally, changes in value must be obtained in a certain manner and in a proper sequence. Discussion of these three issues comprises much of the middle portion of this book.

What kind of development would result from adopting these strategies? Certainly not existing models of "development," since much of what goes by that name is anti-development! What, then, constitutes authentic development? And how can world resources be used to meet the priority needs of all men? Finally, do ethicists have anything to say to revolutionaries who despair of all solutions short of guerrilla action? These are the questions treated in the book's final chapters. In three appendices the terms "ethics" and "development" are defined, the influence of moral values on political power is discussed, and a method for conducting research on value changes is outlined.

Development ethics borrows freely from the work of economists, political scientists, sociologists, planners, and spokesmen for other disciplines. Although each discipline supplies its own definition of development, ethics places all definitions in a broad framework wherein development means, ultimately, the quality of life and the progress of societies toward values capable of expression in various cultures. Along with the late L. J. Lebret, I view development as a complex series of interrelated change processes, abrupt and gradual, by which a population and all its components move away from patterns of life perceived in some significant way as "less human" toward alternative patterns perceived as "more human." *How* development is gained is no less important than *what* benefits are obtained at the end of the development road. In the process new solidarities, extending to the entire world, must be created. Moreover, cultural and ecological diversity must be nurtured. Finally, esteem and freedom for all individuals and societies must be optimized. Although development can be studied as an economic, political, educational, or social phenomenon, its ultimate goals are those of existence itself: to provide all men with the opportunity to live full human lives. Thus understood, development is the ascent of all men and societies in their total humanity.

This book was commissioned by the Center for the Study of Development and Social Change (Cambridge, Massachusetts), whose financial help from August 1968 through January 1969 is gratefully acknowledged. An evaluation session organized by Center Director James Lamb around the initial outline proved helpful. I take this opportunity to thank all participants, as well as Denise Dreher for secretarial help.

Later chapters of the manuscript were written during my stay as Visiting Fellow (February through July 1969) at the Center for the Study of Democratic Institutions in Santa Barbara, California. The Center provided a unique arena for stimulating dialogue on the book's major issues. Its secretarial staff aided cheerfully in typing several versions of the manuscript, but special thanks are due to Florence Givens for sustained attention to my typing needs. Financial assistance from the Research Institute for the Study of Man and the Sheinbaum Foundation enabled me to make extensive final revisions.

Valuable suggestions have come from many colleagues. I am especially grateful to João da Veiga Coutinho and to Sheldon Gellar for criticizing several versions of the manuscript. Helpful comments have also come from A. A. Fatouros, William Gorman, Allen D. Grimshaw, Everett E. Hagen, Benjamin Higgins, Albert O. Hirschman, Irving Louis Horowitz, Ivan D. Illich, H. Merrill Jackson, Neil H. Jacoby, Helio Jaguaribe, Ileana Marculescu, Francisco Suarez, Marco Walshok and Donald P. Warwick. Since all suggestions were received in the same spirit of independence with which they were made, I bear full responsibility for the text as it now stands.

CONTENTS

Introduction   3

    THE REBIRTH OF MORAL PHILOSOPHY   3

    THE CONTEXT OF CHANGE   13

I / *The Development Experience*

1 The Shock of Underdevelopment   23

    INERTIA AND COMPLACENCY   25

    THE RUDE AWAKENING   28

2 Vulnerability, the Key to Understanding and Promoting Development   38

    THE VULNERABILITY OF THE WEAK   38

    THE VULNERABILITY OF THE POWERFUL   51

    AN ILLUSTRATIVE CASE: ITAPARICA   57

3 Development Goals: Promise Versus Performance   60

    PLANS   61

    AID DOCUMENTS   66

    UNITED NATIONS DOCUMENTS   69

    WHY THE GAP?   73

    A CRITIQUE OF GOALS   85

4 Development as Dialectical Process   96

    THE MEANING OF "DIALECTICAL"   98

    THE DIALECTICS OF DEVELOPMENT   101

II / *Ethical Strategies for Development*

5 General Requirements   111

6   Three Strategic Principles   *123*

    FIRST PRINCIPLE: TO "HAVE ENOUGH" IN ORDER "TO
      BE MORE"   *128*

    SECOND PRINCIPLE: UNIVERSAL SOLIDARITY   *138*

    THIRD PRINCIPLE: BROAD POPULAR PARTICIPATION IN
      DECISIONS   *144*

7   Development Planning as Dialogue   *153*

    THE PLANNER'S OCCUPATIONAL HAZARDS   *154*

    AN ALTERNATIVE: THE CAILLOT FORMULA   *161*

    DEVELOPMENT POLES   *164*

    THE DIFFUSION OF RESPONSIBILITY   *167*

8   Technical Cooperation in a New Key   *170*

    THE NATURE OF TECHNICAL TRANSFERS   *171*

    DEFICIENCIES OF THE PRESENT SYSTEM   *174*

    WORLD DEVELOPERS   *178*

9   Existence Rationality and the Dynamics of Value
   Change   *187*

    EXISTENCE RATIONALITY   *188*

    THE REPRESENTATIVITY OF MARGINALS   *192*

    GYPSIES   *195*

    IMPLICATIONS FOR RESEARCH   *203*

    IMPLICATIONS FOR PLANNING   *206*

III / *What Kind of Development?*

10   Anti-Development and the Constraints upon Development   *215*

    ANTI-DEVELOPMENT   *216*

    SOURCES OF ANTI-DEVELOPMENT   *223*

    THE CONSTRAINTS   *225*

11   The Dimensions of Authentic Development   *235*

    A THEORY OF NEEDS   *236*

    DEVELOPMENT'S THREE DIMENSIONS   *249*

12   World Resources and Priority Needs   273

    ECOLOGICAL CONTROL   273

    THE REQUIREMENTS OF OPTIMUM RESOURCE USE   281

    TWO FORMS OF INCREMENTALISM   294

13   Despair's Dilemma: Ethics and Revolution   299

    THE ETHICAL DILEMMA   301

    CHRISTIAN ETHICS IN DISTRESS   309

    THE TRAVAIL OF MARXIST ETHICS   314

    THE MORAL STANCE OF REVOLUTIONARIES IN THE
    UNITED STATES   317

   Conclusion: The Cruel Choice   326

Appendixes

1   The Terms "Ethics" and "Development"   331

2   The Ethics of Power and the Power of Ethics   335

3   Research on Value Change   342

   Index   353

The Cruel Choice

Introduction

The Rebirth of Moral Philosophy

Contemporary moral philosophy is proving unable to answer normative questions raised by development economics. As David Apter writes, the study of modernization "brings us back to the search for first principles and rapid-fire developments in social theory and the breakthroughs in the biological sciences, not to speak of the retreat of philosophy into linguistics, have combined to render us philosophically defenseless and muddled." [1] It was not always thus, however, for moral philosophy is one of the ancestors of economics. Only gradually did economics gain autonomy as a separate branch of learning. Plato, in his ethical system, discussed but one properly economical question: the division of labor, which for him was simply an aspect of justice. According to George Wilson, Plato held that "each man should get enough, and no more, to enable him to perform the function that fate or the special educational system Plato outlines had chosen him to perform within the confines of the polis." [2] Like Plato, Aristotle endorsed Socrates' position that "to have few wants is godlike."

With hindsight, many regard this restraint as rationalization for the

[1] David E. Apter, *The Politics of Modernization* (University of Chicago Press, 1967), p. 6.
[2] George W. Wilson, ed., *Classics of Economic Theory* (Indiana University Press, 1964), Introduction, p. 12.

static gross product of Greek city-states operating at low economic levels. Perhaps, however, we are faced with nothing more than an early example of a tendency oft betrayed by philosophy to become, in the quaint words of two contemporary authors, the "handmaiden ready to provide a beautiful prospectus for a house of habit and custom in which society has long since been comfortably adjusting its goods and chattels." [3]

The Greek outlook on labor and wealth-getting prevailed in European thought until the advent of medieval scholasticism. By the thirteenth century, inquiry into the satisfaction of human wants had become part of a holistic theological system. Clearly, medieval theologians did not rely upon Greek wisdom as their only source of inspiration. On the contrary, their inherited tradition had "baptized" that wisdom in Christian waters. The central tenets of early Christian ethics as applied to economic life were: the existence of hierarchy and order in society, the providential origin of one's appointed station in life, and the obligation incumbent upon all to practice distributive as well as commutative justice. Albert the Great, Thomas Aquinas, and Antoninus of Florence elaborated guidelines to be obeyed by merchants, craftsmen, and noblemen in setting just prices, raising taxes, determining proper lending practices, and making proper use of superfluous goods. They stressed the ancient patristic doctrine of the common destination of the earth's goods to meet the needs of all men. They relied heavily on early texts such as this one from Chrysostom: "Everything comes from the earth, we all come from a single man, we all have the same sojourn [here on earth]. There are things which are common, such as baths, cities, public squares and promenades. Now you will notice that with regard to goods such as these, there is no dispute and peace is complete. But if, on the other hand, someone should attempt to usurp or appropriate a good to himself, quarrels immediately arise. It is as though nature itself revolted against men's attempt to divide things which God himself had united. This is the result of our efforts when we seek to have goods of our own, when we mouth these two insipid words 'yours and mine.' Remove these words, let us have no more quarrels, no more enmities. . . . The community [of goods] is far more suitable to us and is better grounded in nature than [private] property. God has given us the first goods in common so that we should know how to place the second

[3] Marquis W. Childs and Douglass Cater, *Ethics in a Business Society* (Mentor Books, 1963), p. 33.

kind in common." [4]

For several centuries thereafter, Europe professed doctrines formulated in a feudal setting characterized by little trade beyond the scope of neighboring manorial units, innumerable units of exchange and measurement, and, more importantly, generalized economic stagnation at low common levels. Nevertheless, the Biblical doctrine of stewardship continued to influence the morality of economic life. Long after mercantilists, physiocrats, and other theorists of "political arithmetic" (as knowledge about wealth came to be called) began discussing new doctrines, men found it hard to conceive of land, labor, and capital as abstract factors in a process whose overt aim was to produce wealth. Work and wealth-getting had not yet become proper subjects of independent analysis. The idea of the propriety (not to say the necessity) of a system organized on the basis of *personal gain* had not yet taken root. Nor had a separate and self-contained economic world yet emerged from its moral context. Heilbroner cites the trial of Robert Keane of Boston in 1644 to illustrate current practices before profit-seeking had obtained social legitimacy. Keane, a minister of the gospel, was charged with a heinous crime: he had earned over sixpence profit on the shilling, an outrageous gain! The court debated whether to excommunicate him for his sin, but in view of his spotless past it dismissed him with a fine of £200. On the following Sunday the local minister denounced "some false principles of trade," among them:

I. That a man might sell as dear as he can, and buy as cheap as he can.

II. If a man lose by casualty of sea, etc., in some of his commodities, he may raise the price of the rest.

III. That he may sell as he bought, though he paid too dear. . . . All false, false, false, cries the minister; to seek riches for riches' sake is to fall into the sin of avarice. [5]

In daily practice, of course, commerce had already acquired, by the seventeenth century, new dimensions and new legitimacy. Industry had begun to harness mechanical inventions to tasks of production, to concentrate a labor force, to abide by the law of capital accumulation,

[4] From *Patrologie Grecque,* ed. by Migne, Tome XIX, Homily 12 on Paul's First Epistle to Timothy, cited in L. J. Lebret, *La Montée Humaine* (Les Editions Ouvrières, 1958), p. 183, footnote 9.

[5] Cf. Robert L. Heilbroner, *The Worldly Philosophers* (Simon & Schuster, 1966), pp. 10–11.

and to adjust itself to the demands of what was in effect becoming a competitive "market." *Homo œconomicus* now existed; all he needed was a doctrine to explain him. In 1776 a rambling encyclopedic work was published by Adam Smith, a man of leisure who had abandoned a university career as professor of moral philosophy to tutor a young nobleman and later retired with a lifetime pension. *The Wealth of Nations* was in effect the Declaration of Independence severing economics from moral philosophy. With its publication, economics launched its career as a separate discipline. Rapidly, however, "Smith's followers lost sight of the fundamentally moral nature of human action. So much so that in atomizing economics they were led to object to Smith's introducing social dimensions into the economic domain. Smith's separations had been provisional; the systematic, methodical, and strictly deductive approach was the work of his followers." [6] The author of *The Wealth of Nations,* a treatise on man's propensity to barter for gain, was also a moral philosopher whose *Theory of Moral Sentiments* defended the sentiment of sympathy which held society together. For Adam Smith these two propensities were not in conflict, since all were governed by the higher regulative principle of justice. For this earnest Scotsman, the "invisible hand" that guided society was not a cynical apology for immoral economics, but rather the expression of its author's unshakable belief in Divine Providence. Nevertheless, a powerful thrust had been given to the separation of economics from the larger context of moral life. And long before 1776 "the equation between private vice and public virtue had become commonplace." [7] Great economists after Smith—Ricardo, Mill, Malthus, Marx, Jevons, Marshall, Keynes—remained moral reformers at heart, however, directing their analysis toward contemporary problems. But now that economics had acquired a life of its own, neither ethics nor theology any longer provided norms or direction.[8] Even Marx, a passionate moral critic in *The Communist*

[6] Ernest Becker, *The Structure of Evil* (George Braziller, 1968), p. 34.

[7] Wilson, *op. cit.,* p. 23, who adds: "The need to curb the acquisitive instinct is obviously less important in an expanding economy, and it slowly became perceived that the achievement of expansion might require a dismantling of feudalistic and mercantilistic restraints—or at least a drastic change in their form. The road to laissez-faire was a long and devious one, but when economic growth in general and a higher degree of economic security became established facts the entire attitude toward the national economy changed. It was then possible to reduce restraints against individual profit-seeking. *Economic thought thus became less ethical and more analytical"* (italics mine).

[8] This is not to ignore, of course, the role of the Puritan ethic in encouraging entrepreneurship. The statement refers to formal economic doctrine, which prided itself on analyzing inner workings of economic systems.

Manifesto, remains utterly detached from considerations of morality in *Das Kapital.* In Heilbroner's words, "The book describes with fury, but it analyzes with cold logic. For what Marx has set for his goal is to discover the intrinsic tendencies of the capitalist system, its inner laws of motion, and in so doing, he has eschewed the easy but less convincing means of merely expatiating on its manifest shortcomings." [9] The very style of Marx, even more than that of Mill, reveals how deep had grown the chasm between ethics and economics. The subsequent history of both disciplines has served to widen the gap still more. It is not true of economic doctrines today, as it had been in the distant past, that they have almost always been associated with moral codes about the manner of work and the division of the product. On the contrary, economics has now become the most abstractly mathematical and the most practically applicable of all social sciences. It has achieved great virtuosity in handling means, but is no longer competent to evaluate ends or ideals. Nevertheless, new teleological questions posed by development have re-awakened economists to their long-forgotten intellectual kinship with moral philosophers. As early as 1954 Adolf Berle wrote "that the really great corporation managements have reached a position for the first time in their history in which they must consciously take account of philosophical considerations. They must consider the kind of a community in which they have faith, and which they will serve, and which they intend to help construct and maintain. In a word, they must consider at least in its more elementary phases the ancient problem of the 'good life' and how their operations in a community can be adapted to affording or fostering it." [10]

Economics seems to have come full circle from finding a rationale for a small and static economic surplus, a state of affairs which led men to disdain most forms of wealth-getting and to emphasize just distribution. Now there is a new concern with economic surplus which leads some to de-emphasize growth and to study the composition and distribution of the gross national product and, more broadly, the quality of our wants. Economic growth doubtless remains the first order of

---

[9] Heilbroner, *op. cit.,* p. 130. On p. 142 Heilbroner adds that "shorn of its overtones of inevitable doom, the Marxist analysis cannot be disregarded. It remains the gravest, most penetrating examination the capitalist system has ever undergone. It is not an examination conducted along moral lines with head-wagging and tongue-clucking over the iniquities of the profit motive—this is the stuff of the Marxist revolutionary but not of the Marxist economist. For all its passion, it is a dispassionate appraisal and it is for this reason that its somber findings must be soberly considered."

[10] Adolf A. Berle, Jr., *The 20th Century Capitalist Revolution* (Harcourt, Brace and Company, 1954), p. 166.

business in much of the world, even within significant portions of affluent society. Nonetheless, economic thought itself is once again raising teleological questions long considered the special province of philosophy. Nothing has equipped economic science, however, to answer its own questions. More and more economists look to ethics. But ever since the separation of economics from the study of morals, ethics has had a dismal career. It too is presently incapable of answering development's normative questions.

Why is modern ethics so ill-prepared to answer the normative questions posed by development economics? The emancipation of economics from moral philosophy is simply one manifestation of a general trend toward specialization in knowledge. Major gains have been made by those branches of learning which became cumulative by relying on empirical investigation derived from revisable and nondeductible theories. Greatest methodological progress has come in the natural sciences. Such progress greatly facilitates observation and classification and has been the springboard for major breakthroughs in theory (evolution, relativity, astronomy). Later, borrowing freely from natural sciences, the "sciences of man" also reached impressive levels of generality in the theoretical order (systems theory, general theory of action). Social sciences deal with life, however, and even recent gains have not dissipated the growing malaise of social scientists in the face of life's complexities.

Ethics, in turn, once stripped of its effective role as society's norm-setter, strayed along diverse paths. Soon all philosophies gradually fell into disrepute. With each new success of the experimental method and the rising ascendancy of empirical science, philosophical speculation came to be regarded as an "armchair procedure" enjoying dubious value.[11] Many contemporary philosophers have taken highly individualistic existentialist routes, a jungle maze replete with meandering byways. Others have embraced Marxist prescriptive doctrine and become exegetes of a new scripture, that of dialectical materialism. A third group, few in number and limited in influence, maintains allegiance to "natural law" morality. Most ethical theorists in "developed" countries, however, have chosen the road of positivism. And it can be asserted without exaggeration that mainstream positivist ethics has abandoned normative prescription on grounds that it is pretentious, unscientific, or both. Instead, ethics now seeks to derive guide-

11 On this, cf. James K. Feibleman, *The Institutions of Society* (London: George Allen & Unwin, 1956), p. 61.

8

lines for action from social preferences, positive law, psychological conditioning, or the demands of efficiency. By its own admission, positivist ethics regards teleology as meaningless. Therefore, when economists ask what consumption is for or what kinds of goods foster the good life or what is the nature of welfare, positivistic ethics has nothing to say.

Marxist ethics supplies one set of answers to these questions. But, as its own contemporary spokesmen acknowledge, Marxist ethics has long been under the spell of its own dogma and refused to examine a whole gamut of profoundly meaningful questions on the grounds that such questions are vestiges of "bourgeois decadence." [12] Only in recent years have certain Marxist moralists begun to view ethical inquiry as an essentially open-ended process without pre-determined answers. For their part, existentialists have either rejected social ethics as unimportant or engaged in tortuous, self-analyzing (and self-justifying) efforts to build dialectical bridges from their quasi-absolute commitment to personal freedom as the ultimate value to the demands of social philosophy. Such commitments to personal freedom necessarily render the formulation of a social ethic difficult. Nevertheless, Camus and, in more explicitly critical terms, Sartre have laid a foundation for bridging the distance between personal and societal ethics. Yet their language and style are so strongly conditioned by their particular historical experience of World War II and postwar France that their "social" morality has experienced difficulty in gaining wide acceptance in "underdeveloped" countries.

This explains why many Latin American social philosophers find Marxism far more attractive than existentialism. For one Brazilian philosopher, "The philosophy of existence, among all contemporary doctrines, is the one which most clearly exposes its followers to the danger of alienation." He believes the reason is that "existential philosophy is the philosophy of the centers of domination over underdeveloped regions." [13]

[12] Cf., e.g., Adam Schaff, *A Philosophy of Man* (London: Lawrence & Wishart, 1963); the contributions of Roger Garaudy, Ernst Fischer, *et al.,* in *Dialogue,* an International Review published by Forum (Vienna), especially Vol. I, No. 1 (Spring 1968), pp. 104ff. Also Peter Smollett-Smolka, "Revisionist International," *New Statesman,* April 28, 1967, p. 570.

[13] Cf. Alvaro Vieira Pinto, *Consciência e Realidade Nacional* (Rio de Janeiro: Instituto Superior de Estudos Brasileiros, 1960), I, 65–66. One should not be absolute, however, about Sartre's acceptance in "underdeveloped" countries. He has, after all, written the preface to Fanon's *Les Damnés de la Terre* (1961). Cf. also A. A. Fatouros, "Sartre on Colonialism," *World Politics,* Vol. XVII, No. 4 (July 1965), pp. 703–720.

In short, development economists do not receive much normative help from moral philosophers even when they seek it. On issues of importance to policy-makers and development planners, available ethical systems provide little light. Existentialists are too individualistic and too complex, Marxists too deductively prescriptive and not sufficiently responsive to social and symbolic relativities.[14] Natural-law ethicians are increasingly viewed as defenders of a particularistic confessional doctrine in a world become increasingly secular and pluralistic. Positivists suffer from an overdose of success in description and analysis, resulting in the atrophy of their ability to engage in normative or evaluative inquiry. To put it bluntly, the mainstream of moral philosophy has run dry.

Nevertheless, as Gilson remarks, "the first law to be inferred from philosophical experience is: *Philosophy always buries its undertakers.*" [15] For over twenty-five centuries the death of philosophy has been regularly attended by its revival. The present moribund state of moral philosophy is possibly the harbinger of a new spring. Few contemporary philosophical systems attempt to provide a total explanation of reality. In part the reason is that philosophers know how difficult it is to reach a synthesis of realities which are themselves fluid and complex. Permanent inquiry into meaning goes on, nonetheless, and we may soon witness the birth of new philosophies whose hallmarks are non-dogmatism, a reaction against simplistic forms of relativity, and a genuinely self-critical spirit.

There is an "economic" law at work here. Human societies cannot long endure unless their need for meaning is met by adequate philosophies. Technology and mass demonstration effects presently challenge the values of all societies. United Nations documents, development plans, and aid manifestos talk about a "better life," "greater equity in the distribution of wealth," the need to assure "social improvement" for all. Here is clear proof of the existence of a "demand" for development ethics. It is the "supply" side which is wanting. If moral philosophers prove incapable of supplying answers, or if they take refuge in concepts alien to the real experiences which alone can provide raw materials for their ethical reflection on development, others will try to formulate an ethics of development. Economists, anthropologists, sociologists, and psychologists will attempt it. A more alarming possibil-

---

[14] There are exceptions of course, but the "exciting" Marxist social philosophers are precisely those who profoundly question orthodox Marxist ethics.
[15] Etienne Gilson, *The Unity of Philosophical Experience* (Charles Scribner's Sons, 1937), p. 306.

ity is that political demagogues, technological manipulators, or the high priests of ideological thought-control will do it. Notwithstanding the lateness of the hour, there may still be time for moral philosophers to stop "moralizing" and undertake serious analysis of the ethical problems posed by development, underdevelopment, and planning. In order to succeed, they must go to the marketplace with philosopher Eric Weill and to the factory with Simone Weil. Better still, they must go to the planning board and the irrigation project.

There are additional reasons why moral philosophy has become impotent to deal with economic issues. A full inquiry would perforce include a critique of Christian morality, the ethical matrix out of which the "developed" world has confronted the "Third" World. Twentieth-century men are fully conscious of the "mystification" wrought by moral values in the past. They know the long history wherein "developed" societies have "used" these values as a cover for the defense of their interests. In the light of such history, one is understandably skeptical about any development ethics. Even Marx's radical unmasking of the class nature of all morality leaves us doubting; the universal claims of the class morality he proposes in its stead enjoy dubious applicability at best to a rapidly changing technological milieu. Neither historical events since Marx nor the evolution of Marxist moral theory inspires much confidence in its ability to avoid substituting voluntarism for wisdom. Although we stand in urgent need of a "reconstruction of social ethics," no single mind can effectuate such reconstruction. Today's ethicians are forced by reality to renounce pretensions at "grand theory." Paradoxically, however, they must learn to think in new experiential and empirical modes without becoming ashamed of speaking prescriptively. Their prescriptions will have relative merit at best; and they must be tested. They may—indeed, they must—aspire to universality, not some universality *toute faite,* but rather *a tentative model of partial universality in the making.* Through examination of the very processes by which societies give different responses to the stimuli provided by technology, planning, the quest for new meaning, and the option among multiple alternative value systems, a normative system must emerge. Like every system, it will be ephemeral! But moralists must learn to glory in the ephemeral without abdicating their passion for the normative.

The reflections of any man, or any team of men, always carry the brand of ethnocentrism. Full liberation from ethnocentrism is impossible. Whatever be his formal intent, his cross-cultural sensitivity, or his sophisticated use of protective devices to safeguard objectivity, any philosopher or social scientist will propound truths derived from limited personal cognitive experience in given cultural modes. If he is North American, he cannot speak for Africans or Chinese. If he is Indian, he cannot speak for Arabs. Nevertheless, he might possibly— in his best moments of sublime, flashing intuitions—manage to speak as a man. Strip away his Western accent, his African costume, his Asian formula—and you may have something which can become universal. Literature supplies us with examples of great writers who have initiated their readers to the universal by plunging deeply into the particular reality they knew best. Shakespeare is so very English, but he has plucked heart strings outside the British Empire. So with Lao-Tze: his masterful essay on The Way is thoroughly rooted in Chinese sensibility, yet it strikes a responsive chord in African or Western minds. And Dante, so profoundly Italian, has won rightful acclaim as a "universal" genius. Ideally, it should be thus for ethicians who address themselves to the issues of development. Authors will be culture-bound, but if they are successful, they will attain a register of expression wherein values are *capable of becoming universal.*

The prospective development ethicist faces four tasks. (1) He must elaborate a consciously critical position as to the goals of development. (2) He must analyze development processes from the inside and "isolate," as a chemist isolates an element in a compound, the values and counter-values latent in those processes. (3) His third function is to prepare guidelines for different sectors of behavior whose importance to development processes is crucial. These guidelines will constitute, in embryonic form, normative strategies to be followed in a variety of domains. (4) The most important contribution of the development ethician, however, is to build a coherent theoretical framework in which partial and fragmentary ethical constructs can be unified around a few central and inter-related analytical concepts. The larger background against which this theoretical framework is to be understood reveals to the analyst a world in which a monumental quest for social purpose is going on, in which multiple cultural manipulations are taking place, and in which powerful forces thrust all human groups toward standardization. Concomitantly, however, the desire to assert cultural diversity operates even where it has long lain dormant.

The present book is one attempt to begin elaborating such an ethic. My propositions, taken jointly, constitute but one of many possible ethics of development. Unless research and debate among moral philosophers, social scientists, and practitioners of development become widespread, however, philosophers will lack the input and the feedback required to validate their own intuitions and experiences, to correct them, and, above all, to raise them to the level of authentic *praxis*.

Development is no abstraction, but a historical reality situated in time and place. Consequently, before analyzing its goals and its nature as a change process, one must identify the context or matrix within which change occurs.

The Context of Change

Development has captured the central stage of history. This ambiguous process is often depicted as the crucible through which all societies must pass and, if successful, emerge purified: modern, affluent, and efficient. But such a portrait is misleading: it confuses a part of contemporary history with the larger whole. History is made by the interaction of several broad change processes which touch all spheres of human life. These changes are, in their totality, far more comprehensive than development alone.

As a result of broad ecological, social, and symbolic processes, man's image of himself and of the world is transformed. His instincts, his mind, his genetic potential, his societies, and his symbols are all modified. The collective knowledge now possessed by the human species can transcend parochialisms of time and of space. A mere century and a half ago men ignored the existence of countless ancient civilizations. But with the advent of archaeology they overcame temporal as well as spatial provincialism. Their spatial horizons of knowledge, in turn, are now expanding as rapidly as the universe itself.

Man's altered relationship to time and space introduces new dimensions into his awareness. Moreover, psychic and social transformations are paralleled by unprecedented ecological changes as a result of which the total environment becomes increasingly man-made, not natural. Not surprisingly, he finds it necessary to redefine himself and his roles. Even man's psyche, to say nothing of his body, can no longer be viewed as part of nature or as a mere physiological entity. Like his environment, man himself has become a technically manipulable artifact.

According to most writers, relatively few of the changes now occurring constitute social change. Obvious examples include new patterns of population growth, work, and production, and revised models of life in community. Yet not all "social" change is development, since much of it takes place in societies already "developed." Certain kinds of social change can be called "modernization." "Development" in turn is regarded by many simply as one aspect of modernization— namely, movement toward economic and social modes of existence characterized by relatively high levels of material living and rational control over environment. Later in this work I shall attempt to refute this view. Nevertheless, I agree with its adherents that development is a process situated midway between complete indeterminism and total determinism. Its proper zone is the response individuals and societies give to massive new stimuli. Developed nations[16] are, manifestly, in a stronger position than others to respond with a sense of mastery to these stimuli.

If we wish to grasp the full significance of this inequality, we must distinguish two categories of change processes. The first processes concern production, mastery over nature, rational organization, and technological efficiency; the second concern structures of power and ideology. Historically, processes of both types have been launched and disseminated by societies now termed "developed." The two categories remain closely inter-related. Technologically advanced nations also wield dominant political power and ideological influence in the world. Consequently, entry into technological modernity can only be obtained on terms set by those who already master both series of proc-

[16] In this work I frequently employ the terms "developed" and "underdeveloped" nations without calling the reader's attention to obvious heterogeneities within both. Clearly, not every individual, interest group, or social class within a "developed" country exercises power or possesses wealth. Similarly, there are classes, centers of economic or political influence, and collective interests within "underdeveloped" lands which are not vulnerable, traumatized by demonstration effects, or victimized by prevailing structures. More importantly, certain entities, such as large trans-national corporations and powerful networks of information-processing, operate throughout the world with little regard for national boundaries or interests.

What I attribute to "developed" and "underdeveloped" *nations* is likewise intended to apply, in general terms and *mutatis mutandis,* to interest groups, classes, and influential strata within countries of both types, as well as to that larger arena where powerful agents pursue goals which are not coextensive with those of the country in which their headquarters are located or from which their personnel is drawn. It is assumed that the reader will infer from each context when my statements are meant to apply literally and exclusively to nations or entire societies and when, on the other hand, they must be understood analogically and applied to sub-systems or particular interests, both within national societies and beyond their boundaries.

14

esses—those relating to technology itself and those which pertain to power, political and ideological. Historically, colonialism has been an expression of the industrialized world's role in the second set of processes. But the industrialized world has also been responsible for the spread of the ideas of progress, political democracy, and a secular view of life. While professing a desire to share technology and abundance with less-developed nations, advanced societies (or sub-systemic units of decision-making) struggle to maintain their supremacy in domains relating to the second set of processes. That is to say, *power and ideological mastery are not to be transferred on the same terms and in the same manner as economic progress or scientific know-how.* The crucial problem arises precisely because low-income nations are often thwarted in their pursuit of goals implicit in the first processes by the prevailing structures which govern the second. As a result, their response to global change processes is qualitatively different from that observed in advanced countries, which enjoy greater relative strength and can influence international events in more decisive fashion. This is why the Third World's quest for "a place in the sun" must be analyzed at two distinct levels.

First, leaders in underdeveloped societies wish to lead their nations to economic prosperity and technical modernity. Second, they seek to alter existing power structures and influence substantive international decision-making. But how are these two impulses to be mutually related? One's ability to understand the profound dynamisms at work in development processes rests on a prior effort to situate these processes within the larger historical matrix of change just described. Failure to do so leads one to conclude that development is, above all, an economic, a technical, an organizational, or a political problem, a matter of "modernizing" institutions, attitudes, and behavior. But this is only half true, because development is also an excruciatingly painful effort on the part of vulnerable groups and societies to adapt themselves to interrelated processes over which they can gain only marginal control. At best, poor nations can count on the rich to help them advance within the first set of processes—those bearing on economic progress, technological improvement, and modernized institutions. But it is illusory to suppose that developed nations (or interests) will spontaneously resist the temptation to "domesticate" the development of the "have-nots." The greater likelihood is that governments will continue to dispense aid on geopolitical and ideological grounds and international firms will continue to pursue profit with little regard for priority needs. More importantly, however, any effort by Third World nations to gain power and influence over world ideological structures is likely to be resisted by those who wield that power. This creates serious tension inasmuch as the aspirations of the poor toward economic improvement are encouraged largely by those already developed. Yet, how can low-income peoples mobilize for "development" without also creating new capacities for cultural and political self-affirmation? In fact, prospects for success in responding to the first series of challenges are dim unless non-developed societies gain strategic freedom to redefine the parameters operative in the second set of processes.

It should be noted, parenthetically, that developed societies are also trapped in webs of determinism. They have not discovered how to exercise political and ethical control over the very technologies they have created. Notwithstanding impressive mastery over nature and inanimate objects, they have in the main failed to bring wisdom to their social structures and human relationships.

But let us return to the Third World's responses to stimuli produced by massive social forces around them. As they struggle to adapt, to defend themselves, and to master their own responses, their leaders strive to gain partial freedom to create for themselves some leverage with which to overcome ancient inertia as well as new determinisms. Planning is their main policy instrument; their faith in planning is based on the assumption that the human mind can know the agencies and dynamisms at work in the total processes of change. Nevertheless, as indicated above, men tend to mistake particular aspects of change for the whole series of change processes. Consequently, many experts continue to speak of development as if it occurred independently of the larger processes which constitute its very matrix. The truth is, however, that development has no meaning apart from the ecological and symbolic transformations which envelop it.

These wider changes not only disrupt the precarious "harmonies" enjoyed by all societies in the past, they also condition the manner in which societies and individuals can react to change stimuli. What, we may ask, are the consequences of these profound disturbances of "traditional equilibrium"? This term designates the secular tendency of all pre-modern societies to experience substantive changes only over long time spans (at the very least, over several individual lifetimes). Cultural and geographic insularity enabled them to minimize disruptive external threats to their vital institutions except when outright military invasion occurred. Even in cases of armed conquest, victors usually remained powerless to alter the core values of the vanquished except by destroying or repressing them. They rarely succeeded in challenging old values by cultural "seduction." Spanish *conquistadores* forcibly baptized heathen Indians, but failed to make Hispanic values "enticing" to them. And though Islamic warriors imposed the rule of the sword over a Christian Levant in the eighth century, they were unable to elicit mass defections of Christians to Islam. Today's transcultural contacts, on the contrary, are marked by their irresistible seductiveness. Societies on the "receiving end" of demonstration effects are threatened in their cultural virginity. Neither past purity nor present denunciation of the proffered pleasures' corrupting effects can exorcise the temptation. As the cynic has written of woman's virtue, "there are no impregnable fortresses, there are only poor strategies of attack." This dictum quite literally mirrors the situation today: no undeveloped society can fully resist the blandishments of "developed" suitors, for in their arsenal these suitors hold the weapons which enable men to conquer *time* and *space*.

Thanks to his scientific knowledge, reflective self-consciousness, and technological prowess, modern man need no longer endure time as a process of duration outside his control. On the contrary, he can tamper with time to suit his ends. He re-interprets the past to fit his conceptual frames, not those of actors in the past. He tampers with the present by prolonging human life, shortening the duration of pain, "capturing" time in photographs and motion film, and, in "advanced" economies, by liberating men from having to spend their time merely producing necessities. Finally, technological man tampers with time by programming and shaping, instead of passively awaiting, the future.

Shattering "time-consciousness," however, is a minor victory compared to man's triumph over space. Distance has, in fact, been annihilated, thereby breeding a new quality of interaction in which all particular human experiences and episodes can have universal repercussions. The converse is also true—each global happening can now touch local scenes and private lives. Indeed, victory over distance is *eo ipso* a triumph over time itself. For man, distance is equivalent to time: to suppress the one is to neutralize the other. One consequence of this "disturbance" is that pre-technological societies have lost their immunity to the example, when not to the direct pressure, of the technologically strong. Several asymmetries necessarily result—imbalances in the utilization of world resources, differential degrees of power exercised by societies, and inequitable distribution of wealth and influence.

Sociologically speaking, we are witnessing worldwide stratification; economically, a polarization between rich and poor nations. But poor and rich alike are struggling to find adaptive and defensive postures as they confront global ecological, social, and symbolic change processes. The common problem facing them all is: can they gain freedom to define their stance? At stake is the possibility of control over both the planned and the unplanned consequences of human responses to change.

It is here that ethics must play its twofold role of critique and prescription. In the face of such perplexing processes man gropes feebly to frame models of action which are neither fully determined nor totally undetermined. Perhaps, as Toynbee has written of chance and necessity, "though at first sight the two notions may appear to contradict one another, they prove, when probed, to be merely different facets of one identical illusion." [17] Ultimately, planning and every development policy rest on the assumption that life is precarious indeterminacy in domains lying midway between broad impersonal trends and incommunicable personal decisions.

At best, vulnerable human wills may exercise fragile choices in these middle domains by defining their goals, setting their policies, and evaluating their institutions in a critical spirit. Development must play out its options, and if these be cruel, the reason is that whoever seeks to regulate development must accept harsh constraints and bitter consequences. Because choices are made within narrow confines, powerful determinisms are felt. In a sense, developed countries cannot avoid dominating underdeveloped regions and these in turn cannot help being backward. We are well advised to remember, however, that historical determinisms are man-made, not natural. Past decisions and omissions have either widened or narrowed the present range of choice. The free agent may perhaps trace his own lines in history, but never on a blank page!

As employed in this book, the term "ethics" signifies that modicum of freedom which human wills are capable of within limits fixed by the

---

[17] Arnold J. Toynbee, *A Study of History*, abridgment by D. C. Somervell (Dell Publishing Co., 1965), I, 507. Toynbee views technical improvement not as a sign of genuine progress but as an index of a civilization's decline. Genuine growth, he states, resides in a process of overcoming material obstacles and releasing the energies of society to respond to challenges that are internal rather than external, spiritual rather than material. On this, see pp. 223–247.

workings of nature, the inherited past, and present social configurations. Development ethics, in particular, affirms the possibility of partial freedom and responsibility in those processes known as development.

When used normatively, "development" proposes images of the good society, prescriptions for obtaining it, and symbols for generating enthusiastic allegiance to it. Above all, however, it deals with power. I have spoken of the asymmetries flowing from the annihilation of time and space and of the differential utilization of the world's limited resources by competing societies. Those countries which have gained the victory over space and time have also won privileged access to the world's resources. This is why development ethics must cope with structures of differential wealth and power among societies. Were it otherwise, ethics would be reduced to mere preachments addressed to the "good will" and generosity of the powerful, and to the escapist sentiments of the powerless. It is, on the other hand, in the interstices of power and in the structural relationships binding the weak to the strong that development ethics must unfold itself.[18] Development processes, it is true, are themselves immersed in a larger matrix of changes, yet in most cases development is the sharp forward edge of change which impinges on poor societies to produce the shock of underdevelopment.

[18] The relations between ethics and power are discussed in Appendix II, "The Ethics of Power and the Power of Ethics."

PART I

The Development
Experience

CHAPTER ONE

The Shock of
Underdevelopment

Underdevelopment is shocking: the squalor, disease, unnecessary deaths, and hopelessness of it all! No man understands if underdevelopment remains for him a mere statistic reflecting low income, poor housing, premature mortality, or underemployment. The most empathetic observer can speak objectively about underdevelopment only after undergoing, personally or vicariously, the "shock of underdevelopment." This unique culture shock comes to one as he is initiated to the emotions which prevail in the "culture of poverty." The reverse shock is felt by those living in destitution when a new self-understanding reveals to them that their life is neither human nor inevitable. But why must those who are not destitute experience the reality of dehumanizing existence? Because the prevalent emotion of underdevelopment is a sense of personal and societal impotence in the face of disease and death, of confusion and ignorance as one gropes to understand change, of servility toward men whose decisions govern the course of events, of hopelessness before hunger and natural catastrophe. Chronic poverty is a cruel kind of hell; and one cannot understand how cruel that hell is merely by gazing upon poverty as an object. Unless the observer gains entry into the inner sanctum of these emotions and feels them himself, he will not understand the condition he seeks to abolish.

The dominant emotions of a development scholar, a technical expert, or an educator are totally opposed to those of his "subjects." They are fragile, he is strong; he has knowledge, but they are ignorant. He understands how decisions are made, while they suffer the consequences of decisions they have not reached. The "developed" man does not fear bad health unduly because he knows it can be cured. Hence, would-be developers must cross the threshold separating rationalist self-sufficiency from vulnerability if they are to comprehend underdevelopment as it truly is. They need to discover—by experiencing impotence and vulnerability—that what appears normal is abnormal, and that what appears aberrant is the lot of the common man. They must also learn that weakness is not something others have and strength something they have. They must discover that developed and underdeveloped men alike are imbued with strength and weakness.

In 1961 I spent three months in Rondônia, a federally administered territory in Brazil's sparsely populated Amazon region. This tropical zone was inhabited largely by *seringueros*—men living in virtual serfdom, whose occupation was gathering latex from wild rubber trees. One of their few pastimes was river fishing. *Seringueros* believed that mermaid-like creatures surfaced in the waters at dusk, and that fishermen should avoid them if they did not wish to be cursed. Although inclined to ridicule such superstition, I once found myself in a rowboat with a *seringuero* out fishing after sunset. As the latter hooked a mermaid, he emitted a shriek of unfeigned horror. I liked to think of myself as a cool-headed observer. Nevertheless, I had just spent several weeks of total isolation in the jungle. As I listened in alarm to the strange sounds of the Amazonian evening, for one compellingly real hour in my life I became *absolutely convinced* of the existence of the mythical creature and of the real danger confronting me and my companion. Because I believed and experienced genuine fear, I was able to help the uncritical and "superstitious" *seringuero* disengage his fishing line. The lesson is simple: emotions which are real for those who experience them are not real for those who merely observe them.

The central emotions of "underdeveloped" men are of this kind. To evoke Gabriel Marcel's well-known distinction, underdevelopment is more of a "mystery" than a "problem." A problem is a difficulty one encounters along his way; he can step back from it, measure it, devise solutions, and perhaps overcome it. In mystery, on the other hand, it is impossible to situate oneself outside the dilemma; a problematic

24

element is present, but the viewer himself is part of the problem. Indeed, the developed viewer is a large part of the underdevelopment problem. Therefore, if he chooses to treat the matter as a mere problem extrinsic to himself, he is condemned to misunderstand it and not solve it. He needs to be shocked into discovering the falsity of the certitudes he brought with him into the "problem arena." He must make the dramatic discovery that there exists an inherent structural paternalism in the very relationship between him as helper and the other as helpee, between him as "developed" and the other as "underdeveloped." The very existence of such nomenclature is evidence of cultural paternalism. To awaken to it experientially is to undergo the "shock of underdevelopment."

This revelation is no mere adventure of the spirit, however—some kind of transcendent empathy which humbles the sensitive man's soul but bears no consequences for his actions. The very opposite is true: this psychic transformation can revolutionize his technical and political dealings. If indeed relationships between developed and underdeveloped are structurally paternalistic, programs conducted within the boundaries of these relationships necessarily breed paternalism and domination. It is not the policies alone which are deficient but the attitudes as well. Nevertheless, attitudes also determine policies. But I contend that attitudes can be sound only if both parties to the relationship experience the shock of underdevelopment. In order to understand the importance of this shock, we must reflect on the prevailing state of unconsciousness which precedes it and on its consequences.

Inertia and Complacency

Men in backward and advanced societies alike labor under serious misconceptions. Until they are deeply shaken by outside demonstration effects and by impact strategies critical of their ordinary world view, underdeveloped populations ignore the existence of a state of "development" as possible *for them*. It is not that they have no notion of "development," but the notion is not relevant to their aspirations. With the new awareness that accompanies the shock, however, they no longer view themselves as men without culture, because now culture has been redefined in their minds in terms other than the mere possession of reading or writing skills. Moreover, they no longer view themselves as powerless because they can begin to think of themselves as potential agents of their own destiny. They stop regarding themselves as *naturally* poor, illiterate, badly housed, having ill health or poor employment chances, and begin to imagine themselves as possibly less poor and better housed, fed, and clothed. Once they have been shocked into considering their "normal" state of affairs as aberrant and reversible, men are psychically ready to begin playing political roles in society: they have become organizable.

The number of peasants, shepherds, fishermen, and poor urban workers who have undergone this shock is admittedly small. Were it larger, development would encounter both greater ease and greater difficulty in being accepted. Greater ease because more people would demand the goods promised by development, greater difficulty because they would perceive that these goods were being offered to them paternalistically. It is no accident, therefore, that effective pedagogies for awakening consciousness arouse the suspicions of political establishments. Indeed, such awakening augurs a veritable cultural revolution whose structural effects are monumental.

The shock of underdevelopment triggers a recognition in both parties to the relationship that subordinates have been stigmatized by superiors. According to one American black leader, the poor have largely subscribed to the prevailing man's view that "if you are nobody economically you are nobody, period." Recognition that one is "underdeveloped" is, upon analysis, the recognition that: (a) the terms of reference "developed" and "underdeveloped" have been defined by the stronger partner to the relationship; (b) one could be developed; (c) one should be developed. Underdevelopment is a humiliating condition because it reveals weakness or failure, lowers self-esteem in the face of the obvious triumph of the other, and leaves unanswered the question *why?*

Neither is the developed man who experiences the shock immune to disturbing emotions. Is it "right" for him to be developed while the other is underdeveloped? Does any causal link exist between his own development and the other's underdevelopment? Is he in any sense responsible or guilty for the other's underdevelopment? Is it correct to designate the other "underdeveloped" simply because he has fewer material possessions and lacks certain skills? What relationship, if any, is there between "having riches" and "being humanly rich"? Which institutions and interests does the developed man serve? What net effect do these institutions and interests have on the underdevelopment of the other? Must the developed man foster the active interests of the other even if this undermines his own privilege? Such thoughts are disturbing precisely because most development thinkers have uncritically assumed that underdevelopment can be treated as a "problem" to be solved. It turns out, however, that the "problem" transcends the limits of mere difficulties to be overcome and raises critical questions regarding the interactions at work. A realistic look at underdevelopment places developed and underdeveloped men alike in a common arena in which the values vital to both are radically challenged. Not only personal values but societal values as well are contested. Consequently, the shock of underdevelopment, once experienced, affects institutions and policies, not merely sensibilities. Thus, if "aid" is revealed to be a means of "domesticating" the other's development, it follows that no aid technician or administrator can continue to approve the fundamental premises upon which his programs rest. If one understands that his technological superiority is but a relative benefit and that a man who is materially poor and technologically inferior may be humanly, esthetically, and spiritually superior to him, he may feel compelled to question the value priorities of his own society and contest the legitimacy of his own institutions.

Since most people engaged in "development work" have not experienced this shock, they remain ill-prepared to understand underdevelopment at its deepest level and to devise appropriate policies for eliminating it. The position here defended clearly thrusts empathy to the forefront of analysis; it then becomes not only a psycho-biological disposition, but a conceptual tool as well. Predictably, individuals and societies resort to all kinds of defense mechanisms to avoid undergoing the shock of underdevelopment. This is true of the needy poor and of the helping rich, since both risk losing much by accepting reality. The experience disenchants a man, destroys his confidence in the familiar images he has of underdevelopment. An Indian villager, for example, may have grown accustomed to identifying acquisitiveness with greed, a trait he is taught to reprimand in moral terms. It is deeply upsetting for him to learn that "greed" may at times prove to be quite an effective, perhaps even a praiseworthy, motor of human and social improvement. Conversely, it is discomforting for a sophisticated technical expert from a rich country to learn that men who live on the margin of subsistence and daily flirt with death and insecurity are sometimes capable of greater happiness, wisdom, and human communion than he is, notwithstanding his knowledge, wealth, and

27

technical superiority. At the very least, the shock alerts men to the massive ethnocentrism latent in their "normal" views of life.

The Rude Awakening

Development has become a matter of survival for the Third World and a problem of conscience for rich nations. Three important consequences follow from the generalized emergence of a new consciousness.

I. *The poor demand rapid development.* Whatever their prior state, poor nations now demand rapid development. Although illiterate masses are still largely indifferent to the prospect of change, leaders have condemned inertia and committed their societies to the pursuit of development. Velleities usually originate among intellectuals, labor leaders, budding politicians, nationalist entrepreneurs, and civil servants. But the masses are accustomed to acquiesce in decisions taken by leaders. And since they are unfamiliar with the complex mechanisms of modern decision-making, they cannot veto the elite's commitment to development on their behalf. Without a doubt, most leaders want development now.

In 1956 Nehru declared: "We are not going to spend the next hundred years in arriving gradually, step by step, at the stage of development which the developed countries have reached today. Our pace and tempo of progress has to be much faster." [1] And Raúl Prebisch speaks as a typical Latin American when he asserts that "profound transformations of our economic and social structure are necessary to facilitate the appearance of means suited to accelerating the rhythm of economic and social development . . . these transformations are urgent." [2]

Realistic or not, declarations made by Third World leaders are deeply voluntaristic. They *will* development and believe their act of will can help them obtain it. Among them widespread admiration exists for the development achieved by the Soviet Union within forty

---

[1] Cited in Gunnar Myrdal, *Asian Drama* (Pantheon, 1968), II, 716. On the same page Myrdal also quotes U Nu, then prime minister of Burma: "We have been in a hurry. . . . We have waited for a long time and we feel we must accomplish a great deal in a short time."

[2] Raúl Prebisch, "Aspectos Econômicos da Aliança Para o Progresso" in *A Aliança Para o Progresso,* ed. John C. Dreier (Rio de Janeiro: Editora Fundo de Cultura, 1962), p. 55.

28

years: a huge feudal society has become a world economic, industrial, scientific, military, and political power. The Soviet performance has made them think that rapid success is possible. It is but an imperceptible step for them to conclude that no country, including their own, need evolve slowly over a century or two in order to become industrialized.

In reality, rapid development is impossible for many low-income countries. Their demographic increase, limited resource base, insufficient capital, shortage of skilled managerial, entrepreneurial, and technical personnel, and limited maneuvering room in the world political arena constitute obstacles to rapid gains. Investment capabilities are often so limited, and initial levels of living so low, that even heroic efforts over the next twenty-five years would not raise conditions to levels presently enjoyed by advanced countries. Heilbroner asserts "that economic development over the next decade or two cannot substantially better the lot of the world's *misérables.* . . . It is only self-deception which pictures economic development leading *within our lifetime* to any large and continuous human betterment. That lies still in the distant future. In the meantime this generation of the backward lands will have no alternative but to bear the burdens of the past as they labor for a future they will not live to enjoy." [3]

National planners sometimes recognize this limitation and try to persuade their countrymen that the goals of national efforts, even over the long term, cannot be to reach the affluence now enjoyed by rich countries, but must be simply to abolish mass poverty. Nonetheless, most Third World spokesmen are impatient and do not resign themselves to development's "slow unhurried pace." This impatience is not confined to political leaders and technical experts; it extends to the people at large. Increasingly, peasant leaders, union organizers, adult educators, religious spokesmen, community mobilizers, and other influential men tell their people that change is needed rapidly! Thus, Brazilian Archbishop Helder Câmara exhorts the youth of his country "to accelerate the march of history, for it is necessary that your generation lead the Third World to sit, not as a beggar but as a brother, at the world's round-table where dialogue finally becomes possible." [4]

2. *The poor blame the rich for their own poverty.* Because of de-

[3] Robert L. Heilbroner, *The Great Ascent* (Harper Torchbooks, 1963), pp. 120–121.
[4] Helder Câmara, "Carta a los Jovenes," in Centro Intercultural de Documentación (Doc. 68/99), Cuernavaca, Mexico, p. 2.

velopment's exasperatingly slow pace, there is a growing tendency on the part of the poor to blame rich classes and nations for their own backwardness. There is not always an explicit accusation of guilt for past exploitation, but rather a stress on the interference of rich nations with the poor's present efforts to overcome underdevelopment. Myrdal summarizes this state of affairs as follows: "(i) the peoples in the underdeveloped countries are becoming increasingly aware of these huge international inequalities and the danger that they will continue to grow; and (ii) these peoples and their spokesmen show an inclination to put part of the blame for their poverty on the rest of the world and, in particular, on the countries which are better off—or, rather, they attribute the inequalities to the world economic system which keeps them so poor while other nations are so rich and becoming richer." [5]

One need not endorse any simplistic "scapegoat" theory of underdevelopment to accord some plausibility to this interpretation. Development writers in growing numbers now attribute the *perpetuation* (if not the creation) of underdevelopment to the voracious nature of the "development" of those already wealthy.[6] Similarly, the notion of "internal colonialism," in which the maintenance of privilege explains the continuation of misery within national borders, is gaining credence.[7] Causal analyses of past development no longer rely solely on technological innovation and entrepreneurial activity as explanatory categories, but appeal to such dominant structures as: privileged access to raw materials, freedom for industrializing nations to "impose" their products on fragile Third World markets, the power of strong countries to control world market mechanisms to their advantage, their ability to disrupt internal efforts at industrialization by poor countries through dumping and other means,[8] and their capacity to attract trained personnel away from the underdeveloped world.

What is germane to this discussion is not some judgment of the

[5] Gunnar Myrdal, *Economic Theory and Under-Developed Regions* (London: Duckworth, 1959), p. 7.
[6] For a detailed review of these theories, cf. Jacques Freyssinet, *Le Concept de Sous-Développement* (Paris: Mouton, 1966), pp. 177–242.
[7] The concept of "internal colonialism" is analyzed in Rodolfo Stavenhagen, "Seven Fallacies About Latin America," in *Latin America, Reform or Revolution?* ed. James Petras and Maurice Zeitlin (A Fawcett Premier Book, 1968), pp. 13–32.
[8] The disruptive effects of U.S. aid to Vietnam, for instance, are described in J. M. Albertini, *Le Programme de Sécurité Mutuelle et le Développement du Sud Viet-Nam,* unpublished Ph.D. thesis, Université de Grenoble, January 1965, pp. 244–270.

rightness or wrongness of these sentiments, but the recognition of their existence and influence. Quite generally and at present levels of consciousness in the world, representatives of underdeveloped nations attribute their own unsatisfactory state, at least in part, to the way rich countries behave. On these grounds the seventy-seven signatories of the Charter of Algiers have pleaded for non-parity treatment, and Fidel Castro has sought to justify expropriation without indemnization, alleging redress for past "exploitation." On similar grounds other Third World spokesmen argue their "right" to receive assistance from the rich world, independently of the latter's inclination to be "generous" or not. One cannot understand the tensions operative in the present world, therefore, without adverting to this by-product of heightened consciousness: the poor, by and large, hold the rich responsible for their underdevelopment.

3. *The rich world discovers its own underdevelopment.* A third consequence of growth in consciousness is the discovery by the rich world that it too is "underdeveloped." I do not refer primarily to the acknowledgment by advanced countries of the existence of poverty within their own borders. What is more important is that the values of "developed" countries are now being challenged in the light of quite different values observed in "backward" countries. To illustrate, large numbers of Peace Corps volunteers, upon returning to the United States, have examined their own society with critical new eyes. After their experience in Africa, Asia, or Latin America, they can compare the treatment accorded old people in the United States with that dispensed to the aged in societies where the extended family provides satisfying roles for grandparents. Not surprisingly, many judge treatment of the aged in the U.S. to be cruel: "like throwing obsolete people on the junk heap." A similar reappraisal occurs in attitudes toward leisure. As American society automates more fully and creates ever more "spare hours" for larger numbers, it becomes painfully evident that neither the educational system of the United States, its mass media, nor other instruments of socialization have prepared people to make joyful use of leisure. Comparisons are inevitable between the United States and "underdeveloped" African or Latin American societies where group rejoicing and celebration are ingrained traditions. Likewise, in the face of increasing bureaucratization of life in "developed countries," there is a growing readiness to entertain the possibility at least that rich countries are emotionally, esthetically, communally, and spiritually underdeveloped. The rebirth of pride in

31

indigenous history taking place in countries now asserting their national identity has awakened men in "developed" countries to values obscured by the ethnocentrism implicit in the use of terms such as "developed" and "underdeveloped." Especially for educators, technicians, and administrators who have "experienced the shock of underdevelopment," growth in awareness poses fundamental challenges to the values of all civilizations and the quality of life. The issue is no longer "making good" in the sense of "getting more goods." [9] Throughout the world and in all domains of human endeavor, it is now true, as one Indian specialist writes, that "the problem is not merely one of developing resources in a narrow technical sense but of improving the quality of human life and of building up an institutional framework adequate to the wider ends in view." [10]

The shock of underdevelopment has shattered the apathy of people who had been resigned to their own secular poverty, and the complacency of those who had judged themselves to be superior because they were wealthier than others. Knowledge about the developed world has made the Third World painfully aware of its own "underdevelopment." Conversely, probes into the deeper meaning of the economic and technical backwardness of the Third World have led developed peoples to suspect that they too are "underdeveloped" in certain basic human dimensions. This common disenchantment gives rise to the further suspicion that the "development" of both rich and poor may well require that the entire world alter its values.

Ironically, this very perception is fragmentary and leads to new tensions. Few members of the "developed" world fail to perceive that the values, practices, and structures of the "underdeveloped" world must change if development is to take place there. In parallel terms, there is wide consensus among Third World spokesmen that the rich world must alter its values, practices, and structures if the poor are to have a chance to develop. One looks in vain, however, for evidence that the two visions will converge. Modest progress is nonetheless being made: lucid observers from both groups acknowledge the need for total change. Barend de Vries, an economist at the World Bank, sheds light on these issues by insisting that the ability to relate and integrate the backward with the advanced sectors of a country, and not the

[9] Barbara Ward, *The Rich Nations and the Poor Nations* (Canadian Broadcasting Corporation, 1964), p. 21.

[10] Baljit Singh, "Institutional Approach to Planning," in B. Singh, ed., *Frontiers of Social Science* (London: Macmillan [no date]), p. 369. Cited by Myrdal, *Asian Drama*, II, 711.

achievement of the highest per capita income, is the true test of development. He also argues that "those of the richest communities which demonstrate awareness of their own internal development needs also show most understanding of the needs of other communities. This is not merely a question of essential balancing of domestic against foreign objectives. *Rather, a country's attitude toward the development problems of others, and toward what is commonly called development assistance, is closely akin to its attitude toward its own development needs.*" [11]

For several years reform-minded Latin American leaders have asserted that the United States is powerless to deal equitably with them unless it first undertakes a "revolution of values" within its own borders.[12] If this country proves incapable of responding in enlightened fashion to the demands of its own underprivileged blacks and *Chicanos,* it can never view advocates of basic developmental changes inside the Third World except as subversives or irresponsibles. There is doubtless a dialectical oversimplification at work on both sides of the debate. At times backward countries are unwilling to change themselves, and they seek convenient refuge in a scapegoat explanation of their own underdevelopment. On the other hand, government spokesmen, business officials, and assistance administrators from rich countries often refuse to examine the broad international contexts within which the Third World must deploy its development efforts. As a result, they are prodigal with advice to the poor countries to undertake reform, but remain silent regarding the need to alter their own value system, their own trade and policy practices, their own power and wealth structures, their own relations with the Third World.

Not unexpectedly, therefore, realism gives way to pessimism. The occurrence of change on a scale commensurate with needs appears ever more unlikely. This is the reason why many students of the revolution of rising expectations privately declare "the Third World will never make it." The obstacles are monumental and the slow pace of progress is discouraging. One serious obstacle to satisfactory development on a world scale is the prevalent idolatry of national sovereignty. Powerful states grant themselves the luxury of spending enormous sums on destructive activities and wasteful consumption, and there-

[11] Barend A. de Vries, "New Perspectives on International Development," *Finance and Development*, No. 3 (1968), p. 26. Italics mine.

[12] I have discussed this in Denis A. Goulet, "Lebret's Thought and the U.S. Presence in the Third World," *Développement et Civilisations*, No. 30 (June 1967), pp. 44–55.

after proceed to plead inability to pay (even one percent of their GNP) for development assistance to the poorer nations. Their governments are quick to bend development needs to their geopolitical strategies. Yet, paradoxically, they are prone to denounce the "exacerbated nationalism" of such countries as mainland China, Ghana under N'Krumah, Indonesia under Sukarno as xenophobic and disruptive of world order. The most serious anomaly of all is that nation-building (which requires a powerfully nationalistic myth) is one of the most potent instruments for mobilizing development efforts within impoverished countries. Trans-national solutions, however, are indispensable for many of their major problems. Therefore, the likelihood of their accepting "good" solutions to the issues they face is minimal. Furthermore, rich nations will not allow the development of the Third World to "get out of hand"; they must domesticate it. At the same time, however, the Third World needs to affirm itself nationalistically in order to unite its own populace and galvanize it to act and to accept sacrifices. No *laissez-faire* economic policy will produce development in the world. Similarly, no global arena of unbridled nationalisms can create suitable conditions for a worldwide plan of resource use—a meaningful harnessing of productive energies in all countries according to a strategy of priority needs. One of the unhappy by-products, therefore, of the shock of underdevelopment is pessimism over the Third World's chances of "making it."

The requirements of worldwide development may prove incompatible in the long term with economic nationalism and even with the essence of a national economy. French economist François Perroux believes that no single nation, if left to its own resources and habitual economic procedures, possesses the means to create a human economy on the basis of greater need instead of greater solvency. He does not advocate worldwide socialization of economic life but the "supranational organization and globalization of economies which would remain flexible, retain great plasticity and openness one to another." [13] If nations energetically pursue a substantial, lasting, and progressive increase of general well-being in real terms, they must just as energetically accept the dissolution of the borders which nationalize their economies. The prospects of such "denationalization" doubtless appear remote. But perhaps we can invoke here the operation of what Hirschman, with great imaginativeness, has called the "principle of

[13] François Perroux, *L'economie du XXième Siècle* (Presses Universitaires de France, 1964), p. 358.

the Hiding Hand."

He believes it may be a general principle operative in development projects. Projects are usually undertaken because they appear possible. But nearly always they reveal themselves to be more difficult than anticipated—in fact, so difficult that they might not have been undertaken at all had difficulties been realistically anticipated. To offset these obstacles, on the other hand, there often lie in hiding behind appearances a set of unsuspected strengths or remedial actions that can be taken once a project is in trouble. While studying projects in several continents Hirschman has, he believes, detected a benevolent ruse of reason which mercifully leads "ignorant" project-planners to undertake tasks before which they would flinch were they to suspect all the difficulties inherent in them. As they progressively meet these difficulties, however, they are challenged to salvage their investment and effort. Surprisingly often, they discover unsuspected allies or alternative solutions to their dilemmas. To use Hirschman's own terms, "since we necessarily underestimate our creativity, it is desirable that we underestimate to a roughly similar extent the difficulties of the tasks we face so as to be tricked by these two offsetting underestimates into undertaking tasks that we can, but otherwise would not dare, tackle. The principle is important enough to deserve a name: since we are apparently on the trail here of some sort of invisible or hidden hand that beneficially hides difficulties from us, I propose 'the Hiding Hand.' " [14]

The relevant point here is that the Hiding Hand may be at work to lead the world surreptitiously to the kind of supra-national economic system necessary for successful development. The rich nations of the world would probably not have undertaken the task of aiding the Third World had they known initially how complex the task would turn out to be. After two decades of trial and error, however, it is now becoming apparent that profound changes will have to take place in the basic ground rules of nations' economic and political behavior if development is to result in the world at large. As with Hirschman's projects and development aid, this may prove to be more than the rich nations bargained for. During the early euphoric years of capital transfers and technical missions, many experts believed that great improvements in levels of living could be obtained without completely restructuring the world's value systems, institutions, and international

[14] Albert O. Hirschman, *Development Projects Observed* (The Brookings Institution, 1967), p. 13.

relationships. Now they know better. That developer is naïve indeed who does not understand that the "revolution of rising expectations" must either fail or turn to destructive vindictiveness against its authors unless the foundations of the world's entire political and social thought are questioned and, eventually, replaced. Viewed in the light of the various processes described in the Introduction to this essay, the Hiding Hand may be our only hope of success.

As mentioned above, processes of two opposite types are at work in the world. Taken in their totality, these processes constitute the matrix within which developmental responses occur. The first series of processes affects men's control over nature and their wealth-producing efforts; we may conveniently group them under the label "technological mastery." The second series of processes refers to the patterns of control exercised by some nations in the world over others in virtue of their wealth, power, and ideas. General agreement exists in the world over the need to disseminate the first processes so that poor nations can become capable of mastering nature rationally and generating greater wealth for themselves. Sharp antagonism arises, on the other hand, over the distribution of power and ideological influence. Like Black Power militants within the United States, an increasing number of Third World spokesmen now demand, in addition to initiation to technology and a share of its benefits, effective participation in decisions governing world structures of wealth, power, and "images" of life. The developed world is far less inclined to relinquish control over processes in the second category than it is to "share" the advantages accruing from those in the first. Developed countries, however, are gradually discovering that changes in their own value systems and changes in their world role become mandatory *if development is to succeed*. Inasmuch as it is crucial to their own security, their continued prosperity, and their good conscience that development succeed, they may themselves be forced into initiating the kinds of changes required in the second set of operative processes. Stated differently, the Hiding Hand may be at work benignly disguising both the difficulty of the total development enterprise and unsuspected sources of strength with which to meet that difficulty. For this reason one need not resign himself to absolute pessimism. The task of achieving "human" development is in truth more arduous than "developers" bargained for. It may even prove impossible unless the Hiding Hand, with an assist from the wisdom born of failure, leads nations to "minimize their losses" if not to "maximize their gains" in ways compatible with genuine development on a worldwide scale. Neither optimism nor pessimism is in order, but rather that kind of creativity which, according to Hirschman, men are constantly underestimating in themselves. Hope might just barely be justified if the ultimate consequence of the "shock of underdevelopment" is to give birth to such creativity.

Yet creativity must be the joint accomplishment of partners enjoying reciprocity in their mutual relations. In the absence of reciprocity, relationships are structurally exploitative. New relationships cannot be defined, however, until we understand what is wrong with the old ones. The main defect of these is that they institutionalize, for the weaker partner, a condition of vulnerability which makes reciprocity impossible. It is the task of the following chapter to analyze vulnerability in relationships among partners of unequal strength.

CHAPTER TWO

Vulnerability, the Key to Understanding and Promoting Development

The Vulnerability of the Weak

Throughout Latin America, Africa, Asia, and the ghettos of the United States, poor people experience underdevelopment as vulnerability.

Etymologically, the term "vulnerability" means the inability to defend oneself against wounds. An individual is vulnerable when he is exposed to injury, societies when they have no adequate defenses against the social forces which propel them into the processes of change.

Underdevelopment is not merely the lack of development or a time lag in achieving industrial strength, productive agriculture, or universal schooling. Underdevelopment is an historical by-product of "development." This statement must not be understood in a simplistic mode. Raymond Aron warns that "the state of high development of some countries is neither a cause nor a condition of the underdevelopment of other countries."[1] Nevertheless, the condition of underdevelopment in its totality is a consciously experienced state of deprivation rendered intolerable because of newly acquired information regarding the development of other societies and the existence of technical means for abolishing misery. Inequalities have always existed, to be sure, among national and regional economic units. But their scope was relatively modest, and general optimism prevailed regarding the ability of the less favored to match at some future time the condition of those enjoying temporary advantages. At a given moment in history, however, in the words of Freyssinet, "the Industrial Revolution of Western capitalist economies not only accentuated the spread and aggravated the lag, but actually propelled industrial economies, on the one hand, and non-industrialized economies on the other, into divergent paths."[2] As a result, over long periods industrial economies sustained rates of economic growth far higher than those previously registered anywhere in the world. Technical progress was rapid and led to the speedy accumulation of productive wealth. After two centuries of industrial growth, gaps of unprecedented magnitude were discernible between industrialized and non-industrialized nations. More significantly, the logic of the capitalist system which presided over the industrial revolution led expanding economies to establish economic relations marked by a new kind of imperialism *vis-à-vis* non-industrialized nations. Powerful nations in the past had always imposed unequal exchange systems on weaker neighbors and at times even engaged in outright pillage. But even in such extreme cases their impact on the internal economic structures of dominated countries had been relatively slight. The opposite proved to be the case with pioneer capitalist powers: they reaped something more than incidental profits in non-industrialized zones. They created instead "partners" whom they needed both as suppliers of raw materials and as outlets for semi-manufactured or finished products. Their dominant economy altered the structure of the weaker partner so that it might play the dual role of supplier and demander required for the progress of the stronger partner. A modern sector was created and traditional economies (whether autarchic or operating within limited exchange circuits) were disrupted. In the process, indigenous "development" was

---

[1] Raymond Aron, *The Industrial Society: Three Essays on Ideology and Development* (Simon and Schuster, 1968), p. 1.
[2] Jacques Freyssinet, *Le Concept de Sous-Développement* (Paris: Mouton, 1966), p. 334.

blocked. Not that development, as we now conceive it, would necessarily have taken place had the stronger economy been absent, or that industrializing powers deliberately interfered with the execution of some plan clearly formulated by the weaker partners to industrialize themselves. Rather, historical structures and forces were launched which tended, of their own accord, to perpetuate the "backwardness" of the one partner in the very process of contributing to the advance of the other.

There is no need to condemn the process as morally bad or to imagine that developed nations are necessarily "guilty" of the backwardness of others. An illustration of what is meant by the impersonal workings of structures, independently of the moral intentions of economic agents, is contained in a speech delivered by Fidel Castro in 1965. After noting that one third of the Cuban population, that living around Havana, receives nearly 50 percent of the national revenue, Castro explained that, although the distribution was unfair, "nobody would ever think of blaming the workers and the people of Havana for this problem; they are in no way to blame." [3] It is an "economic deformity" and not the favored group, he added, which is at fault. An analogous argument applies in the larger case: the British, for instance, were not "guilty" of keeping India underdeveloped. Nevertheless, their colonial operations seriously disjointed Indian social structures and helped create conditions which would have made it impossible for India to develop even if its leaders had systematically sought to mobilize the nation's resources to this effect. Britain's development was "exogenous" and to a considerable degree parasitical, relying heavily on the workings of an enclave economy in the colonies. The "modern" enclaves introduced profound disruptions into old resource ecology systems and bred powerful domination effects rendering self-adjustment to these disruptions virtually impossible.

It is also incorrect to imply that people in underdeveloped lands were too apathetic or unimaginative to launch the dynamic processes capable of generating their own industrial revolution. Their underdevelopment cannot be adequately explained by appealing either to scapegoat theories which lay blame exclusively on the exploitation of outsiders (in alliance with internal privileged groups) or to a conspiracy of inertia within. The phenomenon of underdevelopment

[3] Fidel Castro, *Apply Theory to the Particular Conditions of Each Country* (Republic of Cuba, Ministry of Foreign Relations), text (in English) of a speech delivered on January 2, 1965, p. 7.

cannot be explained in these terms because they ignore historical mechanisms and structures. There is no historical evidence for regarding underdevelopment as the stagnation of economies which, for mysterious reasons, are somehow deemed unfit to promote their own development. "Underdeveloped" economies are not stagnant or stationary. For more than a century they have been undergoing profound change—the disintegration of traditional economic practices and circuits and the implantation in their midst of a modern sector controlled by and serving outside interests. Demographic trends as well as the size and nature of productive structures have also been altered. But that small dynamic nucleus of progress known as the modern sector has not operated as a force for diffusion of progress throughout the economy. On the contrary, it has served as a way-station for flows originating and terminating in foreign economic centers.[4] The development of any economy is possible only under the dynamic influence of the leading sectors or the modernizing poles of progress. Poles are physical centers which attract people, capital, and innovations.

Within underdeveloped economies, however, the existence of a modern nucleus or "pole" of development[5] does not guarantee the spread of innovations within the country itself. On the contrary, the pole tends of necessity to buttress the favored position of those who control it: although it is a "vanguard sector," the pole itself is at the service of interests residing outside native economic circuits. These structural limitations have generated collective psychological attitudes which differ according to the type of country observed. Industrialization in advanced countries has had the effect of diffusing rationality, the ideal of productivity, and the value of "progress." In non-industrialized nations, on the other hand, industrialization has frequently been associated with economic exploitation or political domination, at times even with military intervention. This is why mechanical inventions readily evoke in many populations images of forced labor, agricultural unemployment, or the expropriation of lands. Not surprisingly, therefore, psychological resistance to "modernization" appears. Even overt behavioral resistance to "progress" may take place. His-

---

[4] The workings of the modern nucleus in a non-industrialized economy are well described in J. M. Albertini, *Les Mécanismes du Sous-Développement* (Les Editions Ouvrières, 1967), pp. 47–149.

[5] The development "pole" and the conditions under which progress is diffused have been studied in detail by François Perroux. A statement of his position may be found in *L'Economie du XXième Siècle* (Presses Universitaires de France, 1964), pp. 123–295 and 585–657.

41

torical events after World War II have added new sophistication to what was formerly a naïve consciousness of colonial-type relations.

Mass demonstration effects, the diffusion of new "myths" (such as a better life for all), and the breakdown of old political hegemonies are some of the events which have contributed to a new consciousness. A whole generation of nationalists has been instructing people from former colonies to regard allegedly "normal" economic situations as abnormal, bad, and exploitative. Within a few years Latin American countries, long since politically independent, began to see parallels between the political colonization observable in Africa and Asia and their own economic servitude. Inside many "underdeveloped" countries themselves, opinion became increasingly more sensitive than heretofore to the "internal colonialism" governing relations between privileged and deprived classes or regions. Massive technological progress in transportation and communication assured the wide diffusion of the objects, symbols, and images of a "better life." These objects were such things as transistor radios, bicycles, sewing machines, canned foods, bottled beverages, factory-made clothes and cigarettes. The symbols took the form of displays of military or technological prowess, native industrial complexes, especially those on the grand scale: dams, steel mills, or modern airports. The images could also be viewed in films depicting an abundance of goods, or in the presence of tourists with insatiable wants and unlimited means of satisfying them. The messengers of progress—technicians, educators, community organizers, doctors—would appear with greater frequency even in remote outposts of backwardness to preach the new message of salvation. Every man could have a better life if he were better educated and worked more productively. Slowly at first, more rapidly thereafter, the awareness of the masses was transformed. They now began to perceive their state as one of "underdevelopment." This perception quite rapidly led to reaction, in some cases even to aggression. On rare occasions, the latent dynamisms unfolded to their limits and produced rebellion.[6] This is not the place to examine the psychology of revolution, however. It must nonetheless be noted that much of the imagery employed by revolutionary mobilizers is simply a more sharply honed expression of sentiments shared by the Third World as a whole. Once they become conscious of the meaning of their situa-

---

[6] The progression from awakening consciousness to reaction, to aggressivity, to rebellion is described in L. J. Lebret, *Suicide ou Survie de l'Occident* (Les Editions Ouvrières, 1958), pp. 141–157.

42

tion of deprivation, masses throughout the world begin thinking in explicitly political terms. This happens in all serious efforts at cultural mobilization.

One representative example of such effort is the "pedagogy of the oppressed" employed by Paulo Freire, first in Northeast Brazil, after 1964 in rural Chile. Working through adult-literacy programs, community-development projects, or land-reform efforts, Freire assists preconscious groups to become aware of who they are and what their social situation is. The people very rapidly conclude that their condition is an affront to human dignity. As they look about them with a critical spirit, they begin to understand that their lot in life is not dictated by gods, fate, or natural laws. On the contrary, it is the product of changeable human arrangements. During the process of discovering who they are, peasants, urban slum-dwellers, simple fishermen, artisans, and housewives reflect, often with a sense of awe, on their own "cultural" achievements. They are obviously able to make tools, however rudimentary, to tame nature and protect themselves from enemies. They can also fashion instruments with which to exercise mastery over living beings—slingshots or arrows for hunting purposes, nets for fishing, and agricultural tools to grow food. Eventually it "dawns upon them" that they themselves are cultural agents, that cultural tools can be used to domesticate animals, and that in society men can create certain kinds of "cultural instruments" enabling them to control other men.

Once this perception is gained, it is but a small step for them to discover that mastery over written language, technology, and administrative practices is also an instrument which some men can use to control other men. As they reflect on their own experience, which Freire illustrates with slides, film strips, and linguistic exercises, peasants discover that the hierarchical position of their superiors (in wealth, status, and power) is not a *natural or divine but merely a human phenomenon*. Therefore, it can be scrutinized without sacrilege, it can be criticized, perhaps even opposed. Their awakening consciousness to the universality of culture and to its human origins is the crucial point in the genesis of what Daniel Lerner has aptly called "psychic empathy." Before this point is reached, "underdeveloped" men are indeed aware of their poverty, of the misery it brings to their lives, and of its hopelessness. They may even be cognizant of the wealth of others, of the greater range of choices enjoyed by the privileged, of their lesser fragility in the face of disease, natural catastrophe, or even social struggle. But only after the poor acquire a new consciousness do they clearly see that:

(a) their own state is one of *under*development, situated *below* what ought to be and what can be;

(b) their condition relative to that of others can be changed; and

(c) they themselves can become agents of that change.

They now begin to experience their condition as unnecessary vulnerability in the face of death, disease, hunger, and the quest for dignity and freedom to control their own destinies. This growth in awareness is no exceptional phenomenon confined to a small number of localities where outside catalysts elicit new perceptions. On the contrary, it is experienced throughout the world, even where no one systematically provokes it.

The awareness of vulnerability on a worldwide scale has existed at least since the Bandung Declaration of April 1955. On that date the Third World presented itself as an entity distinct from the industrialized capitalist and socialist worlds. Underdeveloped leaders proclaimed their right to play a role in the making of history and declared their intention of intervening in the processes whereby technological mastery is acquired over the universe of things and of resisting the domination exercised by societies already developed.[7]

This Declaration must be interpreted in the light of its successors, however.[8] Among these, the two UNCTAD (United Nations Conference on Trade and Development) sessions, held in Geneva (1964) and New Delhi (1968), are especially important. Once again spokesmen for underdeveloped nations bore public witness to their nations' vulnerability. Underdevelopment is not merely poverty, unsatisfied wants, or minimal opportunities, but, above all, the powerlessness of societies in the face of destiny, of nature, of a machine age, of scientific technology, of advanced countries, of processes they cannot understand. Developed countries possess the knowledge, the wealth, and the experience needed to face the problems of nature with some degree of confidence, but "underdeveloped" societies feel exposed to forces they cannot control. To illustrate, Bolivia is "vulnerable" to fluctuations in tin prices on the "world market" because its foreign

[7] On the Bandung Conference, cf. George McTurnan Kahin, *The Asian-African Conference* (Cornell University Press, 1956), *passim*. The participant nations' perception of their vulnerability is evoked on p. 10 of this work.

[8] On this, cf. Henri Bazin, "De Bandoung à New Delhi, L'Evolution des Rapports entre les Pays du Tiers Monde," *Développement et Civilisations*, No. 33 (March 1968), pp. 13–26.

earnings are derived disproportionately from tin exports. That country's Andean peasants are also powerless to improve their level of living because they lack the knowledge and the power to do two things: (a) to wrest more food from their unprodigal lands and (b) to alter present distribution mechanisms whereby the "first fruits" of their labor go to others. This impotence is attributable to six convergent realities:

(1) no society is immune to disruptive demonstration effects whereby old values are challenged by an image of the good life which tampers with desire mechanisms and urges people to desire more goods;

(2) only advanced societies possess the knowledge and wealth "backward" ones need to satisfy their own new material aspirations;

(3) in the process of learning that these new aspirations can be met, non-developed societies also create or re-create for themselves a need for cultural identity;

(4) this search for collective identity and esteem is frustrated, however, by the structurally paternalistic relationships within which knowledge and wealth are "transferred" from developed to non-developed societies;

(5) therefore, the Third World's development efforts face a contradiction. The most rapid and efficient way to achieve material progress and technological organization is to accept these in effect as *gifts* from the rich world. To do so, however, is to sacrifice one's newly discovered social identity and independence. It is, in fact, to cooperate in the restoration, in a new mode, of the demeaning relationships that characterized colonialism. Were Third World leaders to accept financial and technical assistance without imposing their conditions and if they were to model their cultural patterns on dominant images uncritically borrowed from donors, they would thereby repeat the gestures of native upper classes in colonies. These classes either felt or simulated shame of their own culture. By aping the values of the colonizers, they gained entry into the "respectable" world of those having money, power, and "culture." All these were of course defined ethnocentrically according to the dominant attitudes, whims, and styles of the occupiers.

(6) At present, however, many authentic leaders in poor countries will not consent to having the rich world "domesticate" their own development efforts. To an almost paroxysmic degree this refusal is voiced in "revolutionary" societies like China or Cuba.

45

Mao Tse-tung preaches scorn for "Western democracy" and warns his people against the power of mystification contained in these words: "Those who demand freedom and democracy in the abstract regard democracy as an end and not a means. Democracy sometimes seems to be an end, but it is in fact only a means. Marxism teaches us that democracy is part of the superstructure and belongs to the category of politics. That is to say, in the last analysis, it serves the economic base. The same is true of freedom. Both democracy and freedom are relative, not absolute, and they come into being and develop under specific historical circumstances." [9]

Fidel Castro provides another example of the refusal by a fully conscious leader in an underdeveloped country to trade dignity for "development." He criticizes the tendency of some Cubans to rely on Socialist aid to rescue them whenever hostile countries apply pressure:

"Imagine that one day there would be a total blockade, through which no fuel, through which nothing could pass. I am sure, I have absolutely no doubt, that the people would be able to withstand such a situation . . . a situation where fuel would be reserved for the tanks, the lorries, for transporting the army and the armed services. And the population of the cities? We would all move to the country, and work by the side of the farmers, driving the oxen and digging with hoe, pick and shovel. And we would win through.

"This means that we have the right to hold our heads high, the right to speak our own opinions and ideas; the right to be an example to any of the small countries in the world, to any of the underdeveloped countries dominated by imperialism or colonialism in any part of the world. And this also means that we are committed to gain a place in world history." [10] The strident voluntarism of this—as, indeed, of every—revolutionary statement is born of the conviction that the structural vulnerability of the "underdeveloped" needs to be offset by resolute purpose. Castro knows Cuba is economically weak, but finds solace elsewhere: "They [i.e., the enemy] know their material strength, but we know our moral force, and that is our power." [11]

My point is not the obvious one that "revolutionary" countries are conscious of their vulnerability, but rather that many non-revolution-

[9] *Mao Tse-tung: An Anthology of His Writings,* edited by Anne Fremantle (Mentor Books, 1962), p. 268.
[10] Castro, *op. cit.,* pp. 18–19.
[11] *Idem.,* p. 22.

46

ary nations are coming to share that consciousness. Although such countries do not themselves engage in revolutionary action, their spokesmen nonetheless endorse the revolutionary analysis of their own state of fragility in the world. They too distrust the alleged benignity of political strings attached to "aid" programs emanating from the Rich World. Illustrations of this trend may be found in statements such as the following:

"We do not need paternalistic redemption. We need conditions so that those who are now abandoned may free themselves from their own underdevelopment with their own united force . . . the poor have no hope in those who still have economic power. And the poor are those who struggle for justice. If those who fight for justice are called subversive, then subversion is their hope." [12]

Kenya's leaders also formally insist on the "need to avoid making development in Kenya dependent on a satellite relationship with any group or groups of countries. Such a relationship is abhorrent and a violation of the political and economic independence so close to the hearts of the people." [13]

Although responsible Third World leaders want to achieve development by their own efforts, this may be impossible as long as rich nations decide which "ground rules" govern transfers of wealth and technology. The technologically advanced nations enjoy disproportionate bargaining strength and will not permit underdeveloped nations to develop in a manner which challenges their dominant position. However, it is not "development" which the rich world wants to keep to itself. On the contrary, it is quite eager to "share"—in an orderly way—the fruits of economic advancement. But it is unwilling to relinquish control over ideologies and effective world power. Low-income nations are therefore increasingly frustrated by their vulnerability in the face of disproportionately strong partners. This is why they demand power—as a precondition for dignity. Their quest for development may be symbolized by two objectives: Bread plus Dignity. Under present arrangements, however, they are often prevented from obtaining dignity in their search for bread.

A weak bargaining position is the basic component of vulnerability. Underdeveloped masses, if not elites, scarcely understand the forces

[12] "The Gospel and Social Justice," a speech delivered by Dom Antonio Batista Fragoso, Bishop of Crateus (Brazil), in Belo Horizonte, January 22, 1968, *mimeo.*
[13] Republic of Kenya, *African Socialism and Its Application to Planning in Kenya* (1965), p. 8.

47

that affect them. These forces have upset long-standing ecological balances and created new aspirations prior to the appearance of realistic possibilities of satisfying them. Vulnerable societies are obliged to accept the fundamentally competitive nature of the economic world. But competition among unequals is humiliating and can only lead to injustice.[14] Like individuals, rich societies "need" poorer ones which they can stigmatize in order to confer "merit" on their own obtention of wealth and, presumably, of success in a competitive setting.[15] Underdeveloped nations are weak in the face of industrialized countries, capitalist and socialist alike. The explicit recognition and rejection of this inferiority is the leitmotif of group statements prepared by Third World representatives at UNCTAD meetings. Thus, at the level of social reality as well as of personal existence, underdevelopment is perceived as vulnerability of three sorts: political, economic, and cultural.

Thanks to their *political vulnerability,* weaker nations can do little to escape the consequences of geopolitical strategies pursued by powerful antagonists in the Cold War. The degree of political leverage left to governments within underdeveloped countries is narrowed by the political interests of the Great Powers—and sometimes by the not-so-great Powers.[16] Native development efforts are sanctioned only if they do not threaten investments or ideological interests of rich countries which hold effective veto powers over internal policies in other lands. *Economic weakness* compounds political fragility in many countries. Whatever be its desires, for instance, Senegal depends so heavily upon French purchases of its peanut crop that it must sacrifice some measure of desired economic independence for the sake of economic development. Algeria is likewise obliged to make concessions to French technicians and educators and even allow military bases, in order to assure salary remittances by half a million Algerians employed in France. Even Cuba, for all its anti-Yankee rhetoric, can do little to evict the U.S. Navy from Guantánamo. China too has strong ideological and nationalistic motives for seizing Hong Kong and Macao, but

14 Karl Mannheim, *Freedom, Power and Democratic Planning* (London: Routledge & Kegan Paul, 1951), p. 194, writes: "it is fallacious to suggest that beneficial effects exist in present-day society governed by competition among unequals."

15 This point is analyzed by John Seeley, *The Americanization of the Unconscious* (Science House, 1968), p. 251.

16 Witness France's military interference in Gabon in 1964 to protect its interests there and restore President M'Ba to power after he had been overthrown by a military coup.

its foreign earning position is so fragile that it must "do business" with these vestiges of colonialism on Chinese soil. It is no doubt possible for a country to walk resolutely along the path of self-reliance (Tanzania) or refuse proffered "aid" (as did Sukarno while President of Indonesia) from the rich countries so as to pursue other goals. But these postures are difficult to maintain over long periods and exact a high cost. In a word, they are not always politically possible. Cuba was able to extricate itself from American economic influence only because its policy coincided with Soviet interests and capabilities at the time of dissociation. Yet Cuba has had to accept humiliation from the U.S.S.R. on numerous occasions and there is serious doubt whether other Latin American countries could rely on aid from the Soviet Union. Consequently, their alternative stances *vis-à-vis* the Colossus from the North are sharply curtailed.

Culturally, too, underdevelopment is experienced as vulnerability. The cultural values of many societies are being destroyed because judges often incompetent to decide declare these values to be incompatible with the "modern" values of productivity, efficiency, and impersonal relations. An interesting example of this global phenomenon is supplied by the U.S. educational system. White schoolteachers usually require black students within ghettos to assimilate white middle-class values and standards. Behind seemingly good objectives such as high standards of achievement, competent teaching, remedial programs for youngsters who are "behind," and enrichment programs for children who are "culturally deprived," a powerful campaign is waged, at times unconsciously by well-meaning benefactors, to destroy the pride of blacks in their own cultural achievements. Nevertheless, as a black educator once said, "A group without a past is a group without a future."

The general lesson is that every society must feel that its values are worthy of respect if it is to embark on an uncertain future with confidence in its own ability to control that future. The effort to make people "modern," "efficient," and "technologically cultured" runs the risk of being destructively ethnocentric by uncritically assuming that these are better qualities than those supplanted. Superstition or poor hygiene must not be preserved simply because they are picturesque, much less because they are ancient or "traditional." Any "folkloric" viewpoint on old values is worthless. On the other hand, Third World societies are now being subjected to the attacks of a technoculture which disdains their most cherished self-images as puerile and obso-

49

lete. The resulting vulnerability in the face of "contemporary" cultures becomes traumatic for leaders quite as much as for the unlettered populace. It induces in elites a deep schizophrenic tension between proud self-affirmation of their own values and rejections of those elements in the old culture which impede modernization. Even more pervasively than in the era of overt colonialism, when the metropole's educational ideals were held out as superior to native ones, today's culture media cast doubt on the worth of all values other than those exported *en masse* by the purveyors of progress. It is because some of the fruits of progress—lower death rates, better food and housing—are genuine benefits that the problem exists. The solution therefore is not to reject modernization, but to introduce discernment and creativity in impact strategies used to induce change. Change strategies now in vogue rarely consider the cultural trauma they cause, since culture is simply another realm in which underdevelopment is experienced by its subjects as vulnerability. The level at which vulnerability is felt is not merely local, as when induced change impinges on primary groups or individuals.

The total structures of international society, through the changes going on in their component parts and in the relations among them, are affected. In the words of the Brazilian sociologist Costa Pinto, "the profile of 'international stratification' established since then [i.e., the end of the Napoleonic wars] has changed many times but its basic structure remained—and this, according to different lines, is what is being changed today . . . the great and true issue consists, above all, in the fact that the people of the less-developed areas became less conformed to accept the existing economic and social cleavages and inequalities, so promising are the technological possibilities of a better life for all." [17]

Native efforts to develop are attempts to overcome that vulnerability. These efforts aim at strengthening the absolute and relative strength of a nation at several levels: technological, political, economic, cultural. One is impressed when reading Latin America's newspapers, watching its films, or listening to its campaign political oratory, with the prominence given to the theme of indigenous manufacture. When all the parts of a washing machine, radio, or motorcycle are manufactured in a country formerly regarded as "non-industrialized," short documentary films are made vaunting the

---

[17] L. A. Costa Pinto, "Modernization, Development and Dependence," paper delivered at Latin American Coloquium, Brandeis University, May 1967, p. 4.

national achievement, and newspapers and radios boast of the fact that the country has shown to the world what it is capable of doing by itself. There is, quite understandably, special cause for joy when a large prestigious undertaking, such as the building of a dam, succeeds without the help of foreign technicians.[18] On all fronts, therefore—economics, politics, psychology—choices made by underdeveloped countries become more comprehensible and "logical" if interpreted as attempts to minimize their vulnerable position *vis-à-vis* more powerful antagonists in the international arena of competition. Accordingly, policies which appear irrational may be explained by the need felt by societies to protect a fragile cultural or political identity still in its embryonic stage.

The Vulnerability of the Powerful

It must not be thought, however, that the concept of vulnerability applies only to underdeveloped countries. Developed nations as well, in their dealings with weaker partners, are vulnerable. They are in danger of not having their material, military, and technological superiority forgiven them unless they ratify their vulnerability. I am aware of the danger of applying to institutional relationships a concept derived from the operations of groups or of personal exchanges. Nevertheless, there exist valid grounds for extrapolation. Marcuse is correct: "The traditional borderlines between psychology on the one side and political and social philosophy on the other have been made obsolete by the condition of man in the present era: formerly autonomous and identifiable psychical processes are being absorbed by the function of the individual in the state—by his public existence. Psychological problems therefore turn into political problems." [19] Consequently, it is instructive to examine more closely how vulnerability functions in small group relations. It is not assumed that interpersonal phenomena are necessarily faithful mirrors of larger societal reality or that justice in the individual is a microcosm of justice in the state. Nevertheless, we cannot ignore the speed at which technology has increased human interdependence at every level. And heightened interdependence leads to greater proximity among groups

---

[18] Cf. Albert Hirschman's example of dam construction by Indian engineers in *Development Projects Observed* (The Brookings Institution, 1967), p. 134.
[19] Herbert Marcuse, *Eros and Civilization* (Vintage Books, 1955), p. xvii.

51

which heretofore experienced proximity only within very narrow circles. Moreover, it is not unusual for official representatives of complex societies to extrapolate the experience they have gained in their private or family lives into the realms of business, public debate, and negotiation with group adversaries. Once greater interdependence, proximity, and frequency of encounters are recognized as facts, the crucial question becomes: are encounters to be based on reciprocity or on domination? Weaker groups reject domination as a valid formula, and strong groups can no longer practice it in good conscience. Ultimately, reciprocity is necessary for esteem, an idea which has come of age. Indeed, the quest for esteem has taken a political form (independence), a cultural form (an identity consciously symbolized), a personal form (dissent against manipulation), and a therapeutic form (revolutionary violence as a cathartic act of self-affirmation). It is on grounds of realistic response to new levels of technological interdependence that the case for reciprocity is made, and from the conviction that reciprocity is the only standard which leads to non-manipulative relationships. But, as in personal life, so too in societal living, reciprocity faces serious obstacles.

Helper/helpee relationships are vitiated by a structural paternalism which impedes genuine growth for both partners. Every master is a slave and every exploiter himself an exploited man. Except where genuine reciprocity can be established in relationships, these lead to manipulation on the one hand, servility on the other. What should underlie relationships is what Lebret calls "active respect" [20] for others. Passive respect means simply not to interfere with the other's maturation, whereas active respect enjoins positive action to foster the self-actualization of others on their own terms. Only if the weaker partner in the relationship credibly perceives that active respect moves the other will his internal resistance to the "helper" be overcome and reciprocity become possible. And without reciprocity there is "aid," perhaps, but not cooperation or genuine development. If the fundamental emotion underlying underdevelopment is vulnerability, developed groups must revise their notion of how to encounter the underdeveloped.

The "developed" partner can never accurately observe underdevelopment in the detached mode of a spectator. Nor can he properly treat it as a mere problem, since he himself is part of the problem. The

[20] In *Manifeste pour une Civilisation Solidaire* (Economie et Humanisme, 1959), p. 18.

52

society in which he lives is responsible[21] for altering the aspirations of men in other societies. At times it is also the cause of the powerlessness of those other societies to meet these new aspirations. Part of that aspiration is to achieve dignity and become an agent of one's own development only if the stronger partner's technical or economic superiority is somehow neutralized. That very superiority (even relative) is the principal obstacle to the success of the endeavor dictated by the relationship. Thus, one's superiority has to be forgiven him by the weaker partner if a reciprocal relationship is to be established. Only after reciprocity is established can helpees cease being beggars and donors manipulators. Recipients are already vulnerable, but donors must in turn become vulnerable. Helpers must become like helpless because likeness is the precondition of reciprocity—and reciprocity must be rendered possible. In practice, of course, no one can make himself fully vulnerable: at best he exposes himself to the other's (relative) superiority and allows the other to make him vulnerable.

Concretely, the technical advisor or expert, the educator or administrator from a developed country, must somehow experience the other's underdevelopment as the source of his own vulnerability. He can do this in several ways. First, he can dispose himself to make the humiliating discovery that his own "superiority" is but a relative superiority designated as such only in virtue of the ethnocentrism dominant in his own society. Second, he can reflect that his knowledge and wealth remain powerless to answer basic value dilemmas posed by the development process. This should make him humble about his skills. Third, he can accede to the same kind of critical consciousness of his own values—usually latent in his program, policy, plan, or image of development—that the weaker partner gains of his own. Development and underdevelopment alike are but superficial manifestations of a universal crisis in basic human values. This crisis bears on the degree of freedom men can snatch away from the necessitating pressures generated by the larger ecological processes described in the introduction to this work. These broad processes are as poorly comprehended, in their totality, by the technologically sophisticated man as by illiterate members of "traditional" societies. This is true notwithstanding differences among them: technology's benefits come to them une-

---

[21] On the difference between "responsibility" and "guilt," cf. Pierre Antoine, "Qui Est Coupable?" in *Revue de l'Action Populaire*, No. 32 (November 1959), pp. 1055–1065.

qually, and the relative economic, political, and ideological positions of rich and poor are unbalanced. "Developed" countries have surrendered themselves to the dynamisms and determinisms of development much more totally—perhaps even irrevocably—than those who have just begun to seek development. Consequently, many of the values peculiar to pre-modern societies may hold the key to the solution of the post-technological problems faced by groups which long ago embarked on the processes of development.

Some voices from underdeveloped lands are now claiming that they know best how to run a leisure society. Others assert that "developed" people know how to make money but not how to spend it, that their systems of social security are fully impersonal and unsatisfactory.[22] It does no good, of course, to indulge in nostalgic romanticization of *Gemeinschaft* over *Gesellschaft* patterns. Yet there is cause to reflect on the profound meaning of the growing thirst, within mass-consumer societies such as the "developed" United States, for the restoration of relationships on a humanly manageable scale. Perhaps a major lesson to be learned from the failures of developed societies to abolish unhappiness is that the scale of operations posited by demands of productivity may possibly be incompatible with universal values of the good society. Until now it has been the uncritical tendency on the part of advocates of progress to assume that massive scale is essential to "external economies." The very incapacity of large-scale planning, pedagogical, or social-welfare enterprises to solve local problems of misery and exclusion from opportunity may be a hint that complacency is as little warranted in "developed" as it is in "underdeveloped" spokesmen. A realistic appraisal of experience in attempting to transfer technology must lead to humility before the scope of the problem and to considerable skepticism regarding the appropriateness of "existing" solutions. This is the sense in which even "developed" experts are vulnerable—that is, powerless to solve the most funda-

[22] On this, cf. H. Merrill Jackson, "Parallel Development of the Black and White Nations," Unpublished Memorandum #3, Center for Studies in Education and Development, Harvard University, dated May 30, 1968, p. 3. The author quotes a black leader who asserts that black people are better equipped to govern than white people in general because the U.S. is heading for a "post-work" society in which all kinds of labor have become obsolete. The claim is made that black people, who generally do not share the Protestant ethic about work, are better equipped to lead, plan, and govern in a post-work society. An analogous position is taken by a Latin American observer, Horacio H. Godoy, in "Latin American Culture and Its Transformation," in *Cultural Factors in Inter-American Relations,* ed. Samuel Shapiro (University of Notre Dame Press, 1968), pp. 166–174.

mental questions posed by underdevelopment. Once they resign themselves to being vulnerable, they are perhaps better able than before to
purge themselves of any superiority complex in their dealings with
underdeveloped counterparts. Indeed, they should be able to concede
that the domains wherein their own culture enjoys relative superiority
—technique, applied rationality—may be quite insignificant as compared with richer values embodied in the cultures they are facing. One
need not, for instance, glorify the supposed "spirituality" of India—
Koestler has eloquently laid bare the frailties of the lotus and the yogi
as well as those of the robot and the commissar! Nevertheless, there is
a deep truth, albeit only symbolic, in novelist Lawrence Durrell's belief that our "common actions in reality are simply the sackcloth cov-
ering which hides the cloth-of-gold—the meaning of the pattern." [23] If
this is so, it is puerile to judge societies in comparative terms, on the
basis of mere surface performance in economics, politics, or social
organization. The inner "meaning" of the patterns is far more significant.

There is no warrant for being patronizing when one's "underdeveloped" associates are perhaps more civilized than oneself. Nothing is more galling to a Chinese, for instance, than to have his nation
depicted as barbaric, primitive, or backward. Long before today's
technological masters acquired the deathly capacity to annihilate all
life on this planet, the Chinese had learned how *not to use* warlike
inventions to destroy human life. Gunpowder was used for firecrack-
ers on festival days—a blatantly uneconomic and unproductive use.
Available evidence does little to assure us that either *joie de vivre* or
wisdom in the face of death enjoys greater frequency among "developed" as compared with "underdeveloped" societies. If one grasps the
truly relative nature of economic progress, he will readily acknowledge his vulnerability in the presence of underdevelopment's deeper
questions. The man from a "developed" country must accordingly
neutralize the built-in ethnocentrism and structural paternalism in his
(relatively) superior position. This he can do by acknowledging his
own vulnerability. In so doing he will purge himself of the main obstacle to fruitful reciprocity in his dealings with "underdeveloped"
counterparts. This attitude is the only suitable one not only for individual experts, but for institutions as well. Moreover, it is valid within
the borders of a non-developed land: native "elites" likewise must
acknowledge that vulnerability is the prerequisite of reciprocity in

[23] In *Justine* (Cardinal Edition, 1957), p. 7.

55

their dealings with the non-elite. The occupational hazards of planners and policy-makers—to act as though they were all-knowing—cannot be exorcised except by offsetting the structural paternalism inherent in relationships among unequals. In this sense, vulnerability is the key to understanding development and to implementing it.

To place vulnerability at the heart of the development experience is to shift interest away from indicators usually employed in definitions of transitional societies. In a transitional society, legitimacy is based on some promise of future achievement necessarily requiring far-reaching changes. The means to be employed, however, in obtaining this change are not other-worldly—messianic or supernatural—but this-worldly. Consequently, as Ernest Gellner explains, "It is not poverty, nor even the partial presence of advanced technology and a population explosion as such, which turn a traditional society into a transitional one; nor is it the erosion of traditional institutions, which has not taken place everywhere. What does turn society into a transitional one is that the poverty and the other features are no longer considered tolerable, so much so that legitimacy comes to hinge on a credible promise that they will be abrogated. This is the essence of the social 'transition.' " [24]

The predicament of transitional societies, especially in the early stages of that transition, dramatizes their powerlessness. Basic institutions are under judgment and values which formerly guaranteed social cohesion now become problematic. Not surprisingly, therefore, strenuous efforts are made to imitate technologies, cultural forms, and political structures of societies perceived as being less vulnerable. Ashby, Curle, Vaizey, and others have testified to the almost compulsive tendency on the part of Africans, soon after independence, to endow themselves with universities rigidly patterned on the British or French system, however ill-adapted these were to their needs. Much the same mimesis takes place elsewhere: it is a symbol of the under-developed nations' drive toward the technical, economical, cultural, and political strength they think they need in order to eliminate their own vulnerability. Thus, even wasteful showcase projects are not always pure ostentation. On the contrary, they are usually deemed necessary to assure prestige without which a nation cannot take its proud place among peers. Accordingly, one of the most humiliating constraints suffered by poor countries is the need to sacrifice economic independence in the pursuit of economic development. Because

[24] Ernest Gellner, "Democracy and Industrialization," *European Journal of Sociology*, Vol. VIII, No. 1 (1967), p. 53.

they are so clearly at the mercy of others, richer and more powerful than they, they must often accept a subordinate role in their own economic affairs in order to improve their material levels of living or strengthen their productive infrastructure. At times they will take the opposite option: in order to assure more independence, they will sacrifice patent economic gains. The alternating frenzy and apathy sometimes manifested by Third World leaders in the pursuit of planned objectives can perhaps be explained by the structural vulnerability of their societies. The crest of frenzy represents a heroic voluntaristic effort to overcome impotence; the trough of apathy is the inevitable discouragement attendant upon the failure of such efforts. For this reason, an overt strategy aimed at reducing vulnerability provides sound practical guidelines for the pursuit of development.

The vulnerability concept has its greatest application in the manner in which representatives of "developed" countries or of powerful institutions must view their relations with underdeveloped persons and groups. The following illustration renders explicit what the implications of vulnerability are for development strategy.

An Illustrative Case: Itaparica[25]

Itaparica is a small island lying a few miles off the coast of Salvador, capital of Bahia state in Northeast Brazil. The interior of the island is inhabited by a community of some 900 people whose social identity is anchored to a conservative religious institution of ancestor-worship. These people are descendants of African slaves who have lived in Brazil for over ten generations. Occupants of the island's coastline include a few wealthy mainlanders who maintain summer homes there, as well as fishermen (not members of the cult) and a small number of landowners. For purposes of identification, we shall refer to the group of 900 as "the cult." Its men work as salaried farm workers on the island itself—since they own no land—or commute by ferry to Salvador, where they take sundry unskilled jobs (as street-cleaners, messenger boys, hod-carriers, and construction workers). The material level of living is extremely low.

The group is essentially theocratic and displays great zeal in its struggle to maintain cultural identity. Outside pressure for change, at least until 1966, has been repulsed as a threat to that identity. These

---

25 The case is described as of 1966, the date of the author's last visit to the island. It is presented solely to illustrate the principle of vulnerability.

PART I: The Development Experience

pressures come from well-meaning social agents or, more rarely, from government agencies interested in providing schools, dispensaries, and child-care centers. Except for these occasional overtures, however, the community is for the most part excluded from participation in the island's general social activities. It is, in a word, exploited by other groups on the island and the mainland. What sets the Itaparica community apart from other marginal groups is its great receptiveness to technological innovation notwithstanding its conservative beliefs and social mores. What is resisted is change imposed from outside and on the outsider's terms. Thus, the group welcomes change itself, but rejects the usual agents of change and their standard mode of presentation. This clearly suggests the importance of inquiring into the ability of such groups to help themselves if they are allowed to control their own institutions. Two factors make this inquiry particularly interesting: the precise nature of the group's problems, and the quality of its particular response. The group is dissatisfied with its present status, which it regards as unjust; it wants to change that status, but insists on setting its own terms for the change.

A woman psychiatrist from another country has been working to help the community see its problems realistically and master the structural constraints it faces. These efforts have led to the initiation of concrete action aimed at loosening constraints. The group has channeled its general openness to change into a concrete project, a farm cooperative. Pressure has been put on the state government to expropriate land, transfer ownership to the group itself, and provide technical advice, material (seed, fertilizer, equipment), and credit. The group has faith in its capacity to become "modern," but it sees its cultural identity as threatened unless it can move in its own fashion. For this reason it has thus far refused palliative assistance and rejected purely service-oriented projects for its improvement: a nursery, school, and health center. Since the government and other agencies interested have refused to expropriate land, the Itaparica cult has rejected all alternative changes proposed. This rejection has proved painful to the community, which recognizes the need to improve its material condition and achieve economic viability in order to free itself from the stigma attached to poverty. It is quite willing to live with the stigma attaching to its peculiar identity as an ancestor cult, however.

The community's resistance to a certain kind of change lays bare the contrary images of priority goals held by the group and by the outside agents of change. These agents are viewed with suspicion because they do not concede that the community should be the principal agent of its own development. In spite of the tensions born of this contradiction, however, the group has preserved its receptive attitude toward modern techniques. Its intense self-consciousness doubtless brings it at times into conflict with other groups. At the same time, its high sense of in-group integrity feeds the desire for visible economic improvement. Consequently, it aspires to deal with the larger community from a position of control over its own destiny. This explains its scant enthusiasm for health and educational facilities offered by the state, as well as its interest in having the state expropriate farmlands as a prerequisite for launching its own cooperative endeavor.

Itaparica is twice vulnerable: because it is "underdeveloped," and because it is culturally "different" from other "underdeveloped" groups around it. The group has understood that it can protect its cultural identity only by strengthening its economic position. Nevertheless, it will not accept economic improvement according to the normal patterns. On the contrary, these are seen as threats to its basic values. One can of course argue that Itaparica is an untypical marginal case unlike those generally encountered in situations of underdevelopment. Its degree of cultural homogeneity and self-consciousness are admittedly exceptional. Nevertheless, the principle at work is not limited to special groups like this one—namely, that underdevelopment is experienced as vulnerability.

The lesson of Itaparica is that vulnerability is relevant to institutional confrontations between developed and underdeveloped societies and groups. It is not a purely individual category providing insight only at the interpersonal psychological level and inapplicable to wider societal levels. On the contrary, official spokesmen of Third World nations have testified to the sense of vulnerability which prevails in their lands before the pressures of the world's strong military, trade, and cultural partners. Consequently, a sound strategy to induce developmental change ought to minimize, not reinforce, that vulnerability.

Such a strategy is outlined in Chapter 9 and is mentioned here solely to emphasize the practical importance of the vulnerability concept for development. Had government officials involved in the Itaparica case clearly understood the need to "make themselves" vulnerable, there is reason to believe that successful innovation could have been rapidly achieved. What they lacked was a correct vision of the relative importance of a society's goals. Accordingly, we shall now proceed to an examination, descriptive and prescriptive, of the goals of development.

CHAPTER THREE

Development Goals: Promise Versus Performance

Spokesmen for underdeveloped lands express their development goals in public manifestos, documents submitted to aid agencies, national plans, speeches to their own constituents, and private conversations. The latter source is perhaps the most revealing. Nevertheless, such declarations do not easily lend themselves to study. And although objectives listed in official plans do not necessarily mirror the true goals of a society, it is instructive to survey the values adduced by planners in their efforts to mobilize the energies of a populace. Yet documentary analysis has no overriding merits, and the failure to achieve formal planned goals is not the most significant index of failure. More will be said in Chapter Ten of the criteria for assessing the quality of development efforts.

The examination of documents is simply one accessible means of ascertaining stipulated goals. The task of the present chapter is, accordingly, to compare goals expressed in typical plans and aid documents with reports of actual performance. What emerges even from this comparison is a wide gap between promise and performance.

Plans

Development planning is, in most countries, an accepted instrument for defining priority targets, allocating resources, implementing and evaluating performance. Sound planning doubtless requires the existence of special institutions, personnel, procedures, and strategies, as well as minimum supportiveness from other institutions and procedures. Nevertheless, the mere acceptance by a country's leaders of the need for permanent planning implies their recognition that development efforts must be adjusted in the light of feedback derived from partial implementation. The improvement sought *in* development *by* planning has been variously described, "but in the lexicon of the typical economic planner the term connotes higher and rising real per-capita income, but with this perhaps modified by—or accompanied by—greater income stability, more equitable income distribution, and any one or more of a variety of other economic and non-economic considerations." [1]

According to Celso Furtado, author of several regional and national plans in Brazil, planning is "designed to anticipate the major structural changes required to sustain a certain pace of development and indicate the steps which should be taken so that the investments considered essential in order to bring about those changes be carried out at the proper time." [2] After the *coup* of 1964, Brazil's national planners began to place less emphasis than Furtado on structural change as the objective of national planning. Instead they sought the following objectives: an annual growth rate in real product of 6 to 7 percent; to reduce inflationary price increases of basic consumer goods to an annual level going progressively from 25 percent to 10 percent; to create a specified number of jobs per year.[3] During this period Brazil's Northeast regional planners declared their objectives to be: a growth rate of 7 percent per year; the incorporation of local communities into efforts made to develop them; an increase in the importance of private investment relative to public investment in development programs; and the decentralization of technical and admin-

---

[1] Walter Krause, *Economic Development* (Wadsworth, 1962), p. 201, n. 3.
[2] Celso Furtado, *The Experience of National and Regional Planning in Brazil* (mimeo, 1963), p. 3.
[3] Cf. *O Debate do Programa de Ação* (Rio de Janeiro: Conselho Consultivo do Planejamento, 1965), p. 18.

istrative decision-making institutions.[4]

Subsequent national plans added such objectives as:

—reduction of current social costs of development and better distribution of its benefits;

—lessening of regional economic disparities in the levels of living;[5]

—elimination of balance-of-payments deficits.[6]

Implied here are several value judgments about development itself. First, that economic growth is good. Second, that growth ought to be equitably distributed among regions and social classes. Third, that consumers should be defended against inflation. Fourth, that employment must be created, not necessarily for the neediest, but for those entering labor markets first.

Similar goals show up in other nations' plans. The one major exception is that some countries declare the edification of a Socialist state to be a major objective. Thus, for the Central Committee of the Chinese Communist Party, the basic task of China's first five-year plan is to "concentrate [the nation's economic] strength on the building of heavy industry so as to lay the foundations for the industrialization of the country and insure the steady growth of the socialist sector in the national economy." [7] According to Chia T'o-fu, then Vice-Chairman of the State Planning Commission, intensive growth in heavy industry can: (1) guarantee national defense, (2) safeguard the nation's complete economic independence, (3) pave the way for a full development of light industry, (4) create material and technical conditions for mechanized farming, and (5) facilitate the transition to a socialist economy. African nations have incorporated the realization of their own brand of "socialism" as a primary goal of development planning. Upon launching Ghana's Seven-Year Plan in 1964, N'Krumah assured his people that the Plan will enable "us to embark upon the socialist transformation of our economy through the rapid development of the State and co-operative sectors." The Foreword mentions other goals: "to establish in Ghana a strong and progressive society in

---

[4] In *III Plano Diretor de Desenvolvimento Econômico e Social do Nordeste* (Recife: SUDENE, 1965), preface, no page numbers given.

[5] In *Three-Year Plan for Economic and Social Development, 1963–65* (Rio de Janeiro: IBGE, 1962), pp. 7–14.

[6] Cf. *Programa de Ação Econômica do Governo, 1964–66* (Rio de Janeiro: EPEA, Document No. 1, 1964), p. 15.

[7] Ronald Hsia, *Economic Planning in Communist China* (Institute of Pacific Relations, 1955), p. 27. Cf. also Victor Ginsburgh, *La République Populaire de Chine, Cadres Institutionnels et Réalisations,* Vol. II: *La Planification et la Croissance Economique, 1949–1959* (Institut de Sociologie de l'Université Libre de Bruxelles, 1963), p. 95.

62

which no one will have any anxiety about the basic means of life, about work, food and shelter; where poverty and illiteracy no longer exist and disease is brought under control; and where our educational facilities provide all the children of Ghana with the best possible opportunities for the development of their potentialities . . . Apart from the welfare of the individual Ghanaian, we intend to use the resources which our participation in the productive economy yields to the State to promote the economic independence of Ghana and the unity of Africa." [8] Kenya's government, in turn, declares itself "dedicated to the creation in Kenya of a society based on the principles of African Socialism and to planning as a principal instrument for achieving that society." [9] Its plan calls for higher per-capita incomes, political equality, human dignity, equal opportunities, and social justice.

Japan limits its statement of goals to a single sentence: "The principal objectives of this plan are to provide for a steady increase in the standard of living and provide for full employment by accomplishing persistently the maximum rate of economic growth consistent with economic stability." [10] Malaysia's First Plan is confined to a vague statement about living standards and prosperity.[11] In contrast, Pakistan's twenty-year Perspective Plan explains that "massive improvement will still leave living standards far below the level of developed countries. It will, however, eliminate poverty and ensure that at least the basic minimum necessities of life are available to everyone." [12]

The people of Cyprus are informed that the "principal purpose of planning has been to provide for the most efficient use of all human, physical, and financial resources within a framework of individual freedom and democratic institutions. . . . The ultimate objective . . . is the maximization of the country's welfare function." [13] A rare example of explicit priorities among stated objectives comes, surprisingly, from Portugal. After listing acceleration of growth rate, more equitable distribution of income and revenue, and correction of

---

[8] *Ghana, Seven-Year Development Plan 1963/64 to 1969/70* (Office of the Planning Commission), pp. i–xvii.

[9] References are to *Republic of Kenya, Development Plan 1966–70*, containing an Introduction by President Jomo Kenyatta and a Preface by the Minister for Economic Planning and Development.

[10] *New Long-Range Economic Plan of Japan (FY 1958–FY 1962)* (Tokyo: Economic Planning Agency, Japanese Government, no date), p. 12.

[11] *First Malaysia Plan 1966–1970* (Kuala Lumpur, 1965), p. v.

[12] *Government of Pakistan, The Third Five Year Plan (1965–1970)* (May 1965), p. 18.

[13] *Republic of Cyprus, The Second Five-Year Plan (1967–1971)* (Nicosia: Planning Bureau, no date), pp. 1, 19, 28.

regional imbalances as their goals, planners explain that "this order is not arbitrary but reflects the order that in present circumstances we consider should be given to these aims, considered as the means of attaining higher aims. We believe that the first objective, the acceleration of the rate of growth of the national product, should have preference over the other two, since it decisively affects them." [14] The goal definitions found in typical Latin American development plans[15] are basically the same as those cited above from Brazilian documents. In general, objectives center on a better life, higher standards of living, greater equity, affirmation of national sufficiency and pride, building up a socialist system. Nevertheless, the discussion by African "socialist" countries of explicit values deserves further comment.

Max Millikan argues that planning ought to be "the presentation of certain key alternatives to the community in ways which will help shape the evolution of the community's value system." [16] It is a mistake, he adds, to assume that a society in transition has a clear view of its goals and a firm vision of its value objectives. Therefore, the planner's task cannot consist solely in showing the most efficient way to achieve these aims, since the actual path followed by a society in pursuing goals will be largely determined by the alternative futures portrayed by the planners. Millikan wants dialogue between planners and the community over a variety of critical value options whose costs must be weighed. Few countries, however, have proceeded in this fashion.[17] Plans almost always accept objectives uncritically; they do not generate debate over alternatives. After making initial assumptions as to desirable goals, they state targets. Consequently, we must inquire into the relative compatibility between assumed goals and the policy pursued, and ask whether targets themselves have been reached. Myrdal describes how India's Congress Party repeatedly employed the rhetoric and the slogans of socialism, but just as consist-

[14] Antonio Jorge da Motta Veiga, *Draft of the Third Development Plan for 1968–1973* (Lisbon: National Information Office), p. 21. This view was later confirmed officially in the formal text of the plan, *III Plano de Fomento Para 1968–1973* (Imprensa Nacional de Lisboa, 1968), I, 38.

[15] V.g., *Argentina, Plan Nacional de Desarrollo 1965–1969* (Buenos Aires, 1965), or *Colombia, Plan General de Desarrollo Económico y Social* (Departamento Administrativo de Planeación y Servicios Técnicos, 1962), Introducción, pp. 2–3.

[16] Max F. Millikan, "The Planning Process and Planning Objectives in Developing Countries," in *Organization, Planning and Programming for Economic Development*, U.S. Papers Prepared for the UN Conference on the Application of Science and Technology for the Benefit of the Less Developed Areas, Vol. VIII (U.S. Government Printing Office, 1962), p. 33.

[17] *Idem.*, pp. 35–37.

ently passed legislation favorable to capitalist entrepreneurs.[18] He cites numerous other Asian failures to meet targets.[19] The reason for such failure is suggested by Millikan's remarks: in the absence of a clear presentation of realistic alternatives, costs are not envisaged realistically.

For the most part, planning has been overly optimistic and declared targets have not been met.[20] Japan nonetheless constitutes a striking exception to the trend to overestimate future performance. "When the 1958–1962 plans were being prepared in 1957, nobody predicted the possibility of a 15% annual growth of GNP in real terms, an average which actually was reached during 1959, 1960, and 1961. When the Doubling National Income Plan of 1961–70 was being processed in early 1960, no economist ever expected the ratio of gross capital formation as compared to GNP to rise from the actual level of 30% for 1956–58 to a still higher level of 42.6% of GNP in 1961." [21] During those years, however, the Japanese plan was primarily an instrument for educating economic agents: it had no directive force, nor was it a necessary instrument without which economic growth could not be stimulated. Accordingly, Japan's performance does not disprove the general proposition that failure to meet assigned targets is the lot of most countries.

Since the needs of poor nations are almost limitless, it is impractical to assign targets solely on the basis of what is desirable. Careful attention must be given to estimating usable resources and tolerable social costs. Because most plans are not instruments of permanent debate between technocrats at the summit and the interested populace at the base, few planners can predict probable human costs accurately. In the hope of remedying this defect, some planners advocate a worldwide survey of all resources (including leadership capabilities and the willingness on the part of a population to "follow its leaders") and the conduct of planning as permanent dialogue among political leaders, technical elite, and populace over goals, targets, costs, and programs.[22]

[18] Gunnar Myrdal, *Asian Drama* (Pantheon, 1968), I, 297.
[19] *Idem.*, pp. 413–707.
[20] As shown in Albert Waterston, *Development Planning: Lessons of Experience* (Johns Hopkins Press, 1965), pp. 158–160.
[21] Reported in Saburo Okita and Isamu Miyazaki, "The Impact of Planning on Economic Growth in Japan" in *Development Plans and Programmes* (OECD, 1964), p. 42.
[22] A leading exponent of this view is L. J. Lebret, *Dynamique Concrète du Développement* (Les Editions Ouvrières, 1961), *passim.*

Aid Documents

The goals of development are often stated more explicitly in aid documents than in native plans. This appears paradoxical, but is easily explained. Many underdeveloped countries began to plan in response to conditions imposed by lending agencies. The United States, notoriously reluctant to plan its own domestic economy, required European countries after the Second World War to prepare an investment plan for reconstruction. It later imposed the same condition on Latin America when launching the Alliance for Progress. The intent, in both cases, was to avoid waste and maximize results by the selective allocation of resources to priority targets.

There is a second reason why aid documents state goals more explicitly than plans. Poor countries are so firmly convinced of their urgent need to improve conditions that a formal statement of what this improvement is for seems a luxury to be indulged in only after progress has begun. On the other hand, a rich country must convince itself that the assistance it gives to other nations is good for its security, its economy, its ideological preferences in the world, its own humanitarian conscience. Accordingly, aid documents often spell out the rationale for providing assistance in the form of statements about a fully developed world and a better life for all men.

Typical statements may be found in official documents of the United States Agency for International Development, the world's largest single donor of aid to underdeveloped countries.[23] The following excerpts are illustrative.

> The immediate goal of the U.S. economic assistance is to help countries reach the point at which their own increased human and capital resources, combined with their improved ability to attract and service foreign investment and credit, on commercial terms, are adequate to sustain satisfactory growth.[24]

* * *

[23] Cf. *The Flow of Financial Resources to Less-Developed Countries, 1961–1965* (OECD, 1967), p. 33. Between 1961 and 1965 the United States accounted for 57 to 59 percent of all total flows to less-developed countries, not including Soviet and Chinese aid.

[24] *Principles of Foreign Economic Assistance* (U.S. Government Printing Office, 1963), p. 5.

The major objective of the U.S. foreign assistance program is to assist other countries that seek to maintain their independence and develop into self-supporting nations.[25]

* * *

Three basic principles determine the countries to which development aid is offered and the amounts and kinds of aid which they receive: (1) the effectiveness with which the country can use available resources—both internal and external—to promote economic and social development; (2) the importance to the United States of sustaining or accelerating the economic growth of the country; (3) the availability to the country of other external resources in a suitable form. These principles derive from our basic objective of assisting selected countries to become self-reliant as soon as possible.[26]

* * *

We undertook to help, not because success was certain or imminent, but because help from outside offered the only hope of success either for those countries trying to withstand Communist pressure, or those trying to break the bonds of age-old poverty without resort to the harsh disciplines of Communist dictatorship.

* * *

The destiny of the hundreds of millions of people in the less-developed countries is of immediate concern to us. In helping them, we act in our own self-interest. But it is also true, as President Johnson has said, that "the pages of history can be searched in vain for another power whose pursuit of that self-interest was so infused with grandeur of spirit and morality of purpose!" [27]

* * *

Each nation must be permitted to develop in its own image.[28]

Still another major objective of U.S. aid policy is to create a climate of hospitality for the extraction of strategic materials required by U.S.

[25] *Idem.*, p. 1.
[26] *Idem.*, p. 2.
[27] *Proposed Mutual Defense and Development Programs FY 1966* (U.S. Government Printing Office, 1965), p. 1.
[28] *An Act for International Development* (U.S. Government Printing Office, 1961).

industry. In a chart entitled "Strategic Materials from Other Free Nations Are Essential to U.S. Industry" we learn from a government document[29] that the following percentages of total consumption by U.S. industry in 1959 were imported:

NICKEL	91%
COBALT	90%
BERYLLIUM	96%
MANGANESE	92%
INDUSTRIAL DIAMONDS	100%
CHROME	90%
TIN	100%
BAUXITE	84%
TUNGSTEN	61%
NATURAL RUBBER	100%
ANTIMONY	91%
PLATINUM	99%

Seven years later the relative dependence of the United States on the underdeveloped world's raw materials had not changed significantly. With a scant 6 percent of the world's population and but 7 percent of its land area, this country produces approximately 50 percent of world output and purchases 33 percent of the world's resources.[30] Nevertheless, one cannot adequately explain U.S. aid activities in terms of military purposes alone, or of concern with assuring markets. As Martin Needler writes, "much aid is extended by the United States to countries which are not formally military allies, for purposes which have no immediate bearing on military capabilities." [31]

Although the United States genuinely desires the development of the Third World, it seeks to "domesticate" the process so that U.S. strategic, ideological, and economic interests will not be threatened. This explains the ambivalence of language in U.S. aid pronouncements. When addressing the world, this nation supports development in other countries because this is a just and humane objective. But when it speaks to its own citizens and to its Congress, the government appeals to military security, economic advantage, and ideological guarantees. This plurality of motives leads to contradictions. Can poor

[29] *Ibidem.*, p. 166.
[30] Eugene Staley, "The Viewpoint of the United States," in Martin C. Needler, ed., *Dimensions of American Foreign Policy* (D. Van Nostrand Co., 1966), pp. 291–2.
[31] Introductory paragraph to Section IX, in *idem.*, p. 278.

nations be left to develop in their own image if they must also assure U.S. Cold War interests? Can they truly industrialize if they must continue to provide strategic raw materials on a massive scale to a dominant rich nation? Can they accept "aid" on their own terms if they must likewise provide a "safe climate" for American investment?

Soviet efforts in undeveloped countries have operated on similar premises. Constant appeals to "development" motives in order to rationalize its own nationalist interests differ little from United States practices.[32] The U.S.S.R. desires to foster a hospitable climate for Socialism as ardently as the U.S. longs to protect "free" enterprise. One major difference, of course, is the Soviet Union's relative lack of dependence on the rest of the world for strategic materials. Furthermore, its development philosophy leads it to support structural changes patterned on its own ideological model. Like the United States, however, the Soviet Union seeks to domesticate the development efforts of the Third World, even of Communist countries. The abrupt withdrawal of Soviet technicians from China in July 1960 is a dramatic illustration of this policy. Consequently, the expressed goals of development differ according as they are enunciated by spokesmen of the developed world or of the underdeveloped world. And to the question, "What are the objectives of development?" we must add, "As stated by whom?"

United Nations Documents

It is instructive, therefore, to examine a third source wherein development goals find expression—namely, United Nations documents.

The Universal Declaration of Human Rights (Article 25) states that "Everyone has the right to a standard of living adequate for the health and well-being of himself and of his family, including food, clothing, housing and medical care and necessary social services, and the right to security in the event of unemployment, sickness, disability, widowhood, old age or other lack of livelihood in circumstances

---

[32] Cf. Klaus Billerbeck, *Soviet Bloc Foreign Aid to the Underdeveloped Countries* (Hamburg: Archives of World Economy, 1960). Also John D. Montgomery, *Foreign Aid in International Politics* (Prentice-Hall, 1967), pp. 97–101; and Walter Krause, *Economic Development* (Wadsworth, 1962), pp. 470–495. For a view of Chinese assistance, cf. W. F. Choa, "China's Economic Aid to Developing Countries," *China Mainland Review*, Vol. I, No. 1 (June 1965), pp. 13–23.

beyond his control." Every person also enjoys rights to education (Art. 26), and to "participate freely in the cultural life of the community and to enjoy the arts and to share in scientific advancement and its benefits" (Art. 27). Finally, "Everyone is entitled to a social and international order in which the rights and freedoms set forth in this Declaration can be fully realized" (Art. 28). United Nations Progress Reports on social development in the world reveal that although most underdeveloped member countries give lip service to these broad objectives, their budget allocations and performance prove that purely economic development is in fact their real goal. They pursue aggregate economic goals, wealth, and productive installations above "social progress, better standards of life and larger freedom."

The U.N. *1967 Report on the World Social Situation*[33] illustrates the point: "In Asia as elsewhere, there is unanimous agreement that substantial economic growth is essential to the steady improvement of levels of living; this assumption is a central 'plank' in the underlying philosophy of all national development plans in the region [p. 10]."

The document regrets (pp. 19–21) that human-resource policies have not greatly contributed to greater social mobility, equality of opportunity, or making available remunerative employment. Notwithstanding the formal statement of social aims, only marginal attention is given to social development. In practice, planners and investors treat economic growth—usually conceived in distorted macroeconomic terms—as the end and social development as the instrumental means. Meanwhile (p. 23) "social programmes continue to show particular vulnerability in times of unusual financial stringency; the record of budgetary reductions and transfers made in the course of plan implementation indicates that these programmes are normally the first to suffer."

More broadly still: "The subordination of social to strictly economic policy considerations is nowhere more evident than in the powerful centripetal tendency exhibited by Asian development strategy in general. Broadly speaking, this strategy has tended to favor industry over agriculture, urban over rural areas, the modern over the traditional sector, metropolitan over outlying regions, and large capital-intensive projects over smaller but more labour-intensive undertakings. *The apparent outcome has been an over-all increase of welfare disparities* in many Asian countries—between rural and urban areas, and between high and low income groups generally and in cities par-

[33] *Document E/CN.5/417* and *Addenda* dated 12 December 1967.

70

ticularly. It scarcely needs to be pointed out that this *trend represents a contradiction of the basic intent of development planning,* at least in so far as that intent is overtly expressed." (P. 32, italics mine.)

The U.N. report highlights even more strongly the distance separating promise and reality in its discussion of objectives and performance in Latin America. Greater stress is placed in Latin America than in Asia on the need to reform land-tenure structures and fiscal, administrative, and educational systems. Greater progress has been realized toward facing problems regionally than in Asia. Nevertheless, even the accomplishments resulting from regional efforts have been meager. There is general recognition of the need to redistribute income more equitably and to enlist the participation of the whole population in the development effort. Yet development progress in Latin America is insecure and uneven. Unemployment and agrarian reform are proving intractable problems. Income disparities continue to widen, access to social services remains the privilege of a few, and national planning entities have largely failed to influence the national decision-making process as it affects relationships among internal regions, urban and rural areas, and diverse social classes. More alarming is the new form taken by political upheavals. These upheavals do not bring profound revolutionary changes to existing structures. They are taking on rather a cyclical character: "the inability of the 'normal' political process to meet the rising demands on it and satisfy contending interest-groups has repeatedly brought in the armed forces, whether as guarantors of the status quo, arbiters, or proponents of specific solutions to developmental crises, but with military regimes eventually withdrawing or forced out by the previous political contenders" (p. 43). Because of turmoil within national boundaries, it has often been impossible to mobilize effective political support for official regional development objectives and policies.

The documents just cited testify to incompatibilities among declared goals themselves and to a wide gap between stated objectives and actual performance. The U.N. Report concludes its review of Latin American efforts (pp. 40–98) pessimistically: current development theories and planning techniques have bred generalized frustration, and neither plans nor policies have had any significant impact on several broad problem areas. These are: (a) rapid and over-concentrated urbanization; (b) rural crises flowing from a combination of stagnant income and production allied to the disintegration of previous systems of power relationships; (c) the incapacity of econ-

71

omies to provide sufficient employment to a rapidly expanding labor force whose qualifications are few; (d) the proliferation of new kinds and large numbers of "marginal" populations with little or no commitment to national institutions, economic, cultural, or political (p. 52). The only case in which the trend toward excessive urban "polarization" has been reversed is Cuba, where a deliberate policy of incentives has created a two-way flow and granted priority to creating industrialized agriculture over urban industry (p. 54). Special circumstances leading to a mass exodus of urban middle classes from the country highlight the uniqueness of the example.

Frustration over the gap between the promises of development and the performance is the common experience of Latin America, Asia, Africa (U.N. Report, pp. 98–145), and the Middle East (pp. 145–181).

Besides plans and aid documents, group statements issued by Third World representatives also specify the objectives of development. These manifestos are especially concerned with making world trade more equitable. They challenge the prevailing international division of labor whereby poor countries serve mainly as suppliers of raw materials and markets for expensive manufactured goods. The world system of development financing is also condemned. More importantly, less-developed countries urge rich countries to modify their *domestic economic life* if international justice is to become possible. In the "Charter of Algiers" we read that developed countries must change "their production patterns so as to eliminate the possibility of resorting to restrictive trade policies or escape clause actions on ground [sic] of market disruption in relation to products of export interest to developing countries in order to establish a new international division of labour that would be more equitable." [34] The Group of 77 further insists that "No developed countries should decrease the existing level of their aid to developing countries, especially those forms of aid granted through negotiations." [35] These measures are declared to be necessary if the goals of world development are to be met. The goals themselves are defined as follows: "The international community has an obligation to rectify these unfavourable trends and to create conditions under which all nations can enjoy economic and

[34] *Trends and Problems in World Trade and Development, Charter of Algiers,* U.N. Conference on Trade and Development, Document TO/38, November 3, 1967, p. 11.
[35] *Idem.,* p. 15.

social well-being, and have the means to develop their respective resources to enable their peoples to lead a life free from want and
fear." [36] Although acknowledging that primary responsibility for their
development rests on them, and that poor countries must help each
other, the signatories at Algiers argue that effective mobilization of
their own resources is possible "only with concomitant and effective
international action" (p. 5). Neither traditional corrective approaches
nor isolated measures and limited concessions can suffice. "The grav-
ity of the problem calls for the urgent adoption of a global strategy for
development requiring convergent measures on the part of both developed and developing countries" (*Idem*). In sum, for the Group of 77,
the goals of development are: economic and social well-being; effective opportunities for poor countries to develop all their potential resources; and the provision to their citizens of a life free from want and
fear. They consider these goals unattainable unless rules governing
exchanges between rich and poor nations are modified and rich countries alter their internal production patterns. Considerable progress
has been made in the interval between the two UNCTAD conferences
(1964–1968) in the analysis of problems and the formulation of possible solutions. It is generally acknowledged, however—although not
universally regretted!—that no significant gains have been made in the
implementation of policy recommendations. The pattern is similar to
that observed in domestic planning: considerable refinements in the
statement of goals and the identification of means suited to obtain
them are accompanied by extremely modest gains in practice. How
does one explain this gap between the promise and the reality?

Why the Gap?

The facile explanation of the gap is that development is difficult
and that poor countries nourish unrealistic hopes. Indeed, as they
survey their poverty, illiteracy, and bad housing, poor countries frequently set development targets on the basis of need, without first
making a realistic assessment of possible resources available. Nevertheless, there are exceptions: a considerable number of countries set
planning goals on the basis of abilities rather than of needs.[37] The
trouble with this strategy, however, is that "it is likely to yield a rate

[36] *Idem.*, p. 5.
[37] Cf. Waterston, *op. cit.*, pp. 156–160.

of growth which is lower than most governments are now prepared to accept." [38] Malaya's Second Five-Year Plan, for instance, fixed its targets on the basis of the country's resources and capabilities. But the rate of increase achieved during the period of the Plan was a paltry 0.8 percent yearly. For this evident reason, most planning efforts combine elements of the needs approach with elements of the resources approach. The key variable thus becomes the willingness of a society to pay the costs of its development effort.

Little is explained, however, merely by asserting that many societies refuse to pay the price required to reach declared goals. We must first ask why expectations are unrealistic and why costs are rejected. To reply adequately, we must analyze how demonstration effects occur, at what speed, through which agents, with what degree of prior preparation, with what effects? The tentative answers which follow help explain bloated expectations and the refusal to envisage social costs realistically.

The equilibrium between acquisitive desires and effective access to resources has been ruptured in most societies. This balance is expressed facetiously as follows: "One shouldn't want what he can't get." The psychology of needs in "traditional" societies has always been based on this principle. It was frankly recognized that all men have acquisitive desires for things and for benefits associated with persons. In many such societies, men "owned" wives in much the same way that they owned houses, goats, or jewelry. Most pre-technological societies lived in ecological conditions wherein material abundance for all was impossible. The prevailing state of productive arts was rudimentary, and effective access to resources, free from harassment by enemies or from natural catastrophes—storms, floods, droughts, endemic diseases—was limited. If group survival was to be assured, and if disruptive conflict among members of the group was to be managed, it became necessary—*and therefore morally good!*—for individuals to curb their acquisitive instincts. This did not mean, of course, that all acquisitive instincts were declared illegitimate or that no individuals could gain privileged freedom to acquire for themselves more than a *pro rata* share of total available goods. The contrary proved true. Social values legitimized a man's need for minimum food, shelter, sexual satisfaction, and some access to arable land (fishing or hunting areas) or whatever economic resources existed. Moreover, most societies also allowed greater material rewards, prestige,

[38] *Idem.*, p. 157.

and influence to certain individuals or classes enjoying some hierarchical, functional, or charismatic superiority to others in the society. Consequently, it was right for some men to accumulate wealth while others were taught to regard it as normal to have only those goods barely sufficient for survival. Notwithstanding privilege, the poor had a sense of vicarious identification with the wealth, display, power, and prestige of their society's privileged members. In such social structures, the crucial element is not the permissivity accorded to a few to expand their acquisitive instincts, but rather the general constraints on acquisitiveness imposed on the majority. The rationale for constraint was that under no conceivable circumstances could enough resources become available to allow all men both to want more and to obtain significantly more. Consequently, social norms and symbols had to control the instincts of acquisitiveness and accumulation. In some cases those with greater strength, eloquence, or shrewdness simply "conned" the rest of society into legitimizing what was in effect an exploitative structure working to their advantage. Frequently, however, there gradually emerged from the very dynamics of interaction within the society guidelines conferring "privilege" on some, either on a functional basis (worship, magic, defense against enemies, dispensation of wisdom, etc.) or because they were deemed to represent the will of some deity or supreme principle (prophets, oracles, kings, and the like). Members of such societies lived their history across multiple generations in obedience to an unwritten rule: it is bad for one to want more than he already has or can obtain in the "natural" course of events. Curbing desire was good because to do otherwise would unleash forces of greed which could only cause disruptive competition for limited goods. The problem changes, however, when demonstration effects from outside begin to challenge the fundamental assumptions of this society's symbolic and normative systems. For the first time, the majority of men begin to think unthinkable thoughts: (a) maybe there is enough wealth for all to have as much as they want; and (b) maybe it is not bad for me to want more than I have been wanting.

It is true that demonstration effects exercise a beneficial influence in stimulating entrepreneurship among innovative individuals. They are also a powerful incentive propelling governments to make necessary developmental investments. Even among the mass of potential workers, they stimulate new efforts. Notwithstanding their positive influence, however, demonstration effects cause great difficulties in the early phases of the development process.

Regardless of their source or precise mode of impact, demonstration effects remove the curbs on desire *before providing men with the means to expand resource availability.* They remove curbs on desire by revealing to men that it is possible for other men (and, by extension, it could become possible for them) to give free rein to desires for satisfactions (requiring goods) without necessarily destroying society and, more importantly, without violating the "will of the gods" or the "rules of fate." The very fact that other men have built societies where "wanting more than one is born with" is condoned testifies to the powerlessness of the gods, the falsity of the rules of fate, and the arbitrariness of their own systems of restricted privilege. Inasmuch as subsistence living excludes a wide range of enjoyable activities, it is no surprise that men in every culture harbor unexpressed wishes to have more in order to be more. Once it becomes evident to them that it is possible to desire more, they will, by and large, begin to want more. Even while they remove the brakes from their own desire mechanisms, however, they remain ignorant of the technological requisites for multiplying available resources. Although they may be informed of the need to expand the range of wealth-producing functions, they lack the effective ability to generate additional wealth for themselves. It is easy for them to grasp that it is "good for a man to be able to want more." But it is not easy for them to understand the complex requirements for being able to satisfy those wants. Thus men's desires are tampered with before they can realistically satisfy these desires. *This, I hold, is the main reason why development objectives are so frequently unrealistic.* There is an inevitable time lag between the initial awakening to new possibilities and the first practical grasp of the distance which must be traversed to make that possibility real. Moreover, elites in underdeveloped countries have long suffered from illusions harbored by their counterparts in advanced countries. Specifically, they hope, or think, that development can take place if only the right measures are taken or the right formula is found. Yet "developed" experts no less than "underdeveloped" leaders have underestimated the difficulties inherent in the process of development. Realism is difficult to achieve: (a) because of the very nature of the delicate prior balance between desire mechanisms and norms governing access to resources, and (b) because it is only by trial and error that even "experts" have learned how profoundly development is a matter of values, incentives, and intangible human responses as well

76

as a problem of resources, skills, and rationalization of procedures. Although we now witness a general recognition of the unrealism and efforts to correct it, leaders in underdeveloped countries continue to use language which raises false hopes. Spokesmen for rich countries do likewise. Both have become slaves to the rhetoric of optimism. This is not a case of a deliberate "political lie," but rather an unconscious repugnance on the part of scholars and policy-makers to face up to the frighteningly high costs of development. Consequently, optimism serves as a defense mechanism, a kind of voluntarism to wish away the difficulties of the endeavor. Deep down in their psyches, however, both developed and underdeveloped thinkers catch a glimpse of the high price they will have to pay to achieve for themselves or for others the better life which they so compulsively dangle before their own eyes.

Other factors as well impede good performance. One useful way to identify performance is to examine budget allocations. At times these contradict the goals proclaimed in development plans. Several Latin American countries, for instance, incur defense expenditures incompatible with meeting the priorities professed in their plans: education for all, the rapid creation of jobs, and the provision of adequate low-cost housing. Moreover, government budgets are usually top-heavy, with disproportionate sums spent on recurring salaries or maintenance at the expense of investments which increase the stock of goods and services provided. Even construction budgets for new schools, potable water systems, or hospitals tell us little about the representativity of their beneficiaries. The declared goals of reducing regional disparities and favoring dispossessed classes are largely ignored by budgets. They mask what Myrdal has aptly called the circular causation which brings benefits to those who already enjoy them and worsens the lot of those who begin life in dire straits. "Put your money where your mouth is"—this idiomatic expression is eminently applicable here. In effect, it says to the leaders of a country: "If you spend funds on your development goals, you are serious about those goals."

One examines with equal dismay the Rich World's "aid" to less-developed nations. The outflow is small,[39] both in absolute and in rela-

[39] On this, cf. *The Flow of Financial Resources to Less-Developed Countries, 1961–1965* (OECD, 1967), p. 27: "The small increase of 2.5 percent in the dollar value of net official disbursements by OECD/DAC Members compares with an increase of 40 percent in the combined gross national product and of 35 percent in the combined net national product at factor cost (national income) during the same period." For a more general view, cf. Goran Ohlin,

tive terms. Yet United States officials point with pride to the schools their money has built in Latin America. Only a few voices[40] remind us that the original schooling targets of the Alliance for Progress have had to be repeatedly downgraded and that massive building has in many cases created financial burdens for recipient governments (for maintenance, supplies, teacher salaries) without substantially improving the quality of teaching. The grandeur of expressed goals is belied by the modesty of accomplishments. I do not minimize the difficulties of implementation or the persistence of obstacles faced. American public opinion of late has grown even more unsympathetic than before to foreign aid. Given this mood, Congress sees its duty as cutting, not expanding, aid budgets. Notwithstanding this mood, inquiry must be made into the reasons for the chasm between promise and reality. One need not show surprise at the paltriness of appropriations made by rich nations on behalf of the Third World. Rich nations also find it easier to spend on defense or consumer wastefulness than on their own depressed areas, blighted school districts, or jobless marginals. Ironically, technical experts from advanced countries freely urge counterparts in backward countries to carry out needed development measures with courage and realism. Courage and realism are conspicuously absent, however, from their own domestic affairs. The truth is that no nation, developed or underdeveloped, has been very successful in meeting the goals universally professed in such facile terms: a better life for all; the abolition of regional, sectorial, and class disparities; the use of resources to meet priority needs; the imposition of national sacrifices equitably so as to improve the quality of life and the quantity of goods for the entire nation.

I shall not here conduct a detailed study of budgets, a task best left to economists. My aim is merely to identify budget analysis as a fruitful avenue for discovering whether goals have been met: budget performance has only to be contrasted with the promises contained in development plans.

One reaches similar conclusions by reading United Nations progress reports on economic and social development. Some economic gains and some progress in distributive equity have been made. But trends in housing, income distribution, and urbanization fill one with

---

Foreign Aid Policies Reconsidered (OECD, 1966), *passim*. Also, John Pincus, *Trade, Aid and Development* (McGraw-Hill, 1967).

[40] Cf., v.g., Ivan Illich, "The Futility of Schooling in Latin America," *Saturday Review*, April 20, 1968, pp. 57ff.

pessimism. One U.N. survey describes efforts made by governments and aid agencies to alleviate slum conditions in urban and rural areas of South Asia. Yet achievement has fallen steadily behind rising needs and "the general housing situation seems bound to become even worse than it is at present." [41] Although investment in residential construction, the survey adds, amounts to between 15 and 25 percent of gross investment, it mainly represents private buildings in the cities, often of a luxury nature. This finding is duplicated in Latin America, the Middle East, and Africa.

Still another declared goal of development plans is income redistribution among poorer wage-earners. The U.N. document just cited reports, however, that rural per-capita income has fallen in Pakistan.[42] And Myrdal sees an over-all trend toward widening income disparity in Asia: "It is generally believed that in the early stages of industrialization in Western Europe the income distribution became more unequal and that only later, with the diffusion of spread effects and rising production, and later as an effect of social legislation, this tendency was reversed. From this point of view, increasing inequality may be thought to be symptomatic of economic growth and dynamism. But we have already noted the lack of vigorous development in South Asia, except perhaps to some extent for the Philippines and latterly for Thailand. Thus if inequality is in fact increasing in most of the South Asian economies, this provides another example of the irrelevance of past developments in the West for the present situation in South Asia. As with urbanization and the relative growth of tertiary industries, the apparent increase in inequality has not accompanied rapid growth. Indeed, as with urbanization, it may be the failure to develop rapidly." [43]

[41] U.N. ECAFE, "Review of the Social Situation in the ECAFE Region," *Economic Bulletin for Asia and the Far East,* Vol. XVI, No. 1 (June 1965), p. 37. Cited in Myrdal, *op. cit.,* I, 555.

[42] 1967 *Report on the World Social Situation,* U.N. Document E/CN. 5/417, December 12, 1967, p. 12, where we also read: "A good deal of wage and salary legislation (including legislation protecting the rights of trade unions) has also been introduced in a number of Asian countries, largely with a view to promoting more equitable distribution of income. As in the case of direct taxation, however, it is usually only a minority of income earners who are affected; the measures (where they have been enforced) have benefited mainly the relatively small number of workers in large-scale organized industry—individuals who are already in a comparatively privileged position."

[43] Myrdal, *Asian Drama,* I, 571. In note 3 Myrdal cites *Indonesian Economic Studies* as follows: "In spite of official reiteration of the goal of a just and prosperous society, the impression of many observers has been that along with a decline in per capita income, the contrast between rich and poor has actually

The wage policies of most Latin American governments in periods of inflation have likewise generated hardship on lower-income groups. Even during periods of national "austerity" it is not uncommon for governments to vote salary increases—sometimes as high as 40 percent—to the military forces. Once again the promise of development is wiped out by the performance. One meets these contradictions at every level of analysis. These cases illustrate the general proposition that professed development goals are largely unrealistic. An exhaustive study, clearly beyond the scope of this work, would add testimony drawn from policy-makers, aid-donors, and recipients. No less valuable is the witness to their own condition borne by the citizens of the "republic of poverty."

A single example illustrates the point. In 1957 I lived in the workers' *barrio* of Zofio in Madrid. Upon revisiting the neighborhood eleven years later, I questioned old residents about living conditions, jobs, and relative satisfaction. Many had remained in Zofio, although a few could now afford to move elsewhere. Random interrogation showed that people considered themselves to be better off materially, but more frustrated psychologically. While striving to satisfy old needs they had acquired new ones. They had become conscious for the first time of the competitive element in their lives, at work and in consumption. Consequently, they could no longer rest content with the simple joys in life, but they were not free to withdraw from the "rat race." No valid conclusions can be inferred from this fragmentary bit of evidence. Zofio's inhabitants had improved the quality of their diets, housing, heating, clothing, and recreation. Notwithstanding these gains, a considerable number did not declare themselves to be happier or "better off" than before. Why is this so in many cases besides that of Zofio?

The answer may lie in part in the need felt by officials to provide emotional satisfaction to their constituents by identifying themselves with their aspirations. They adopt the popular language of hope and dreams—in Sorel's term, of "myth." "Duplicity" need not be conscious: leaders may truly believe that their expressed goals will ensue from plans and policies. Myth-making finds legitimate expression in development plans, which are powerful tools for accelerating the "emotional integration" of societies in transition. One disadvantage of

---

sharpened. Real wages have fallen heavily. Yet the scale of conspicuous consumption in Djakarta seems to have grown."

myths, however, is that they remain silent as to the price to be paid for development.

Plans would be depressing documents to read if they spelled out the cost of achieving their aims. Even if costs were known, sound tactical reasons might dictate presenting them only in small doses. For it is no trifling thing to alter the world-view of societies, and one sympathizes with the reluctance of planners to spell out the difficulties.

Students of development are beginning to understand the dynamisms which underlie value change in the early moments of the development process. A value is "a conception, explicit or implicit, distinctive of an individual or characteristic of a group, of the desirable which influences the selection from available modes, means, and ends of action." [44] A value may reside either in an object outside the perceiving subject or in an internal image. Although social scientists[45] have proposed many definitions of value, all include such notions as "preferable" and "worthwhile." Most simply, however, a value is any object or representation which can be repeatedly perceived as worthy of desire. Many kinds of values exist, but for the present purposes it suffices to distinguish between *normative* and *significative* values. Normative values point to behavior which ought or ought not to take place. Significative values refer to the meaning of reality. Not all values dealing with desirable action are authentic norms: some values do not effectively govern specific behavior choices, they merely propose actions "worthy of acting upon." A given subject may consider himself excused from conforming on grounds that his circumstances do not permit him to do so or that he has a higher preference at the moment. A genuine norm, on the contrary, is perceived by a subject, not only as "worthy of acting upon," but as laying an effective claim beyond mere "normative homage" on his choice of action. Significative values, in turn, are concerned not with good and bad actions but with the deep meaning of life and death, suffering, destiny, and nature.

This is not the place to undertake a detailed investigation of the

[44] This definition is given by Clyde Kluckhohn and others in "Values and Value-Orientations in the Theory of Action," *Toward a General Theory of Action,* ed. Talcott Parsons and Edward A. Shils (Harper Torchbooks, 1962), p. 395.
[45] E.g., Franz Adler, Ethel M. Albert, Cyril Belshaw, Clarence Case, Raymond Firth, Clifford Geertz, Arnold Rose, and others. It seems reasonable to adopt Kluckhohn's definition in order to avoid multiplying definitions needlessly. On multiple definitions, cf. Philip E. Jacob and James J. Flink, "Toward an Operational Definition for Use in Public Affairs Research," *The American Behavioral Scientist,* Vol. V Supplement (May 1962), No. 9.

societal, individual, dominant, and variant dimensions of value. What is pertinent is to call attention to an important difference between developed and underdeveloped societies in the structure of links existing among their different values. My contention is that one can understand why change is resisted and why the human cost of accepting change is so high only if he adverts to this difference. The following propositions summarize my view.

(1) In pre-developed societies, a close nexus exists between normative and significative values. "What ought to be done" in any domain—family relations, work, commercial exchange, dealings with leaders—is intimately related to the symbols society uses to explain the meaning of life and death.[46]

(2) In developed societies, on the other hand, this nexus does not exist and no unifying interpretation of total reality is shared by society's members. On the contrary, a variety of significative values are tolerated. Accordingly, a Mormon businessman can behave professionally in quite the same way as an atheistic businessman. Their norms may be the same, but not the significance of those norms for each of them.

In underdeveloped societies, differing value categories are highly integrated, but their economies are fragmented. The opposite condition prevails in "developed" areas: symbols are not directly linked to norms, but economic activity is so highly integrated that autarchy is practically impossible, even at levels of bare subsistence.

The importance of the nexus between norms and meaning lies in this: in traditional societies work is a cosmic act, in developed societies it is a specialized function.

(3) Traditional societies receive change stimuli which challenge their prevailing *normative values*. These stimuli propose different ways of doing things: planting crops, educating children, or practicing hygiene. More fundamentally, they introduce new objectives to human effort: to improve one's level of living, to obtain a "better" house or more food, to gain greater mobility.

(4) By challenging extant norms, these stimuli either create or reveal crisis. A new problem unfolds: should the members of society continue to act as before or change their norms and act as they are

---

[46] One case of a close nexus between a *Weltanschauung* and the guidelines of behavior has been studied by Jacques Austruy in *L'Islam Face au Développement Economique* (Economie et Humanisme, 1961), esp. pp. 29ff. Much the same case is made in Edward C. Banfield, *The Moral Basis of a Backward Society* (The Free Press, 1967).

being stimulated to do? [47]

(5) This challenge is not limited, however, to a society's norms. Because norms are intimately bound to significative values, these stimuli also threaten that society's entire structure of meaning. Traditional norms of behavior are derived from a given universe of explanations. When norms are challenged, that belief-system itself is by the very fact also attacked. I have witnessed, for example, the profound deterioration of a Bedouin father's authority over his sons during the Algerian war of independence because scarcity of food obliged his sons to take a salaried job on a French road-construction gang in the northern Sahara. His degree of control over his wives was also lessened because the French government, so as to counteract propaganda efforts by the FLN (Algerian National Liberation Front), organized a referendum (in September 1958) to induce natives to keep the French government in power. Relentless efforts were made to pressure Moslem women to vote in this referendum. Even in the small desert town where I lived with two semi-nomadic tribes (the Ouled Sidi-Aissa and the Ouled Sidi-Cheikh), the referendum campaign conducted by the French had overwhelming impact on the entire Islamic life-view of the community. Any development agent has had similar experiences. There can be no doubt that stimuli to modify important behavioral norms also attack the symbolic system of pre-developed societies. As a result, the nexus between normative and significative values is shattered.

(6) Once the nexus is shattered, affected societies are left with two options, both very unpleasant.

(7) The first option is to hold fast to significative values even if these become incompatible with norms of behavior which increasingly determine day-to-day activity. Such fragmentation is psychologically harmful for men who have always been accustomed to see "meaning" on a cosmic, if not on a mystical, scale even in simple actions carried out in the home, in the field, or on the pathways. Not only is a serious social identity problem posed, but the motives which can be presented in order to induce new behavior tend to be rejected totally or, in the opposite case, uncritically assumed, often with damaging side-effects. Western development writers are fond of praising "achievement orientation" and the spirit of initiative. Nevertheless, in many societies

---

[47] Kluckhohn, *op. cit.,* pp. 405–408, has shown that crisis and conflict situations throw values into relief for a group. Thus, periods of conflict and crisis are good moments to study values.

(among villagers in India, gypsies of the Middle East, Indians of the Amazon) such achievement orientation is viewed as a moral aberration just as reprehensible as theft or criminal neglect in other societies. This is not to argue that change should not be proposed, but that one must perceive what price is exacted in proposing it. Advocates of development have usually shown insufficient regard for the speed and intensity at which innovation ought to be proposed so as to optimize receptivity to desired change and to protect societal values necessary for dignity and self-esteem. In a later chapter I shall outline a new strategy of induced change based on the concept of "existence rationality." At present it is sufficient to assert that one of the options made available to incipient "transitional" societies is to live in a state of painful cultural fragmentation.

(8) The other choice theoretically available to them is to fashion a new nexus between values which give meaning and those which provide rules for action. From the very nature of the case, however, this synthesis is impossible to them. How can groups undergoing their first experience with modern technology develop a synthesis of meaning when advanced countries themselves, after almost two centuries of familiarity with technical practices, have proved incapable of devising a wisdom to match their sciences? Critics in the West correctly denounce the failure of their societies to provide an intellectually valid framework of broad goals and criteria against which to evaluate the partial accomplishments of science or technique. As Danilo Dolci writes, "We have become experts when it comes to machinery, but we are still novices in dealing with organisms." [48] Pre-developed societies lack familiarity with specialized science and quasi-autonomous technologies which would enable them to make a new nexus or synthesis. Therefore they have no realistic hope of maintaining unity in their "world of values" on the basis of assimilation of new techniques. They are doomed to social disruption.

New methods of studying transitional societies and of inducing change within them can provide valuable safeguards against such disruption *before human societies are prepared to cope with them.* The problem is not that technology is a villain or that "achievement" reward systems are bad, but that purveyors of these values have not been sufficiently critical of their impact on certain kinds of environments. They have often introduced them irresponsibly, under the false

[48] Danilo Dolci, "Mafia-Client Politics," *Saturday Review*, July 6, 1968, p. 51.

assumption that they are disseminating progress. This is obviously a poor way to proceed until a more critical view is taken of the image of progress underlying these innovations and of the merit of existing value systems in non-developed lands in terms of human goals viewed as consummatory ends, not as mere instruments for economic improvement or social modernization.

In short, the gap between the promise and the reality of development plans and aid documents is explained in large part by the insensitivity of change agents to the dynamisms of value change. Hopefully, such failings may begin to be rectified by a reconsideration of the ethical dimensions of social change in the light of broader human goals and appropriate normative strategies. At the very least, it is necessary—though clearly not sufficient—to inquire critically into the goals of development.

A Critique of Goals[49]

Few terms and few experiences are as ambiguous as development. At times it refers to a process, whereas in other contexts it suggests certain goals. Whenever development is treated as a particular kind of social change process, *quantitative* indicators are stressed—income, productivity, output, literacy rates, occupational structure. On the other hand, when it is discussed as a goal, development evokes an image of life deemed *qualitatively* better than its opposite, underdevelopment. Planners and policy-makers frequently take goals for granted, and such uncritical acceptance breeds confusion. There may be considerable merit, after all, in asking whether higher living standards, self-sustained economic growth, and modern institutions are good in themselves or necessarily constitute the highest priorities.

After characterizing development as an irreversible process, Professor Robert Browne asks: "What is our moral license to alter peoples' lives irreversibly in so fundamental a fashion? What evidence do we have that what we conceive of as development is an absolute good, or even an improvement over what those we 'develop' now have? In view of population projections and the attendant ills anticipated from this explosion, ills not restricted to our ability or inability to feed the

---

[49] In this section I have made use of my two earlier essays, "Development for What?", *Comparative Political Studies*, July 1968, pp. 295–312; and "On the Goals of Development," *Cross Currents*, Fall 1968, pp. 387–485.

increased numbers but ills having to do with the very quality of life as the pressure of even greater numbers presses upon a fixed land area, can we be certain that even massive saving of life is justified?" [50] One needs to ask: given a certain conception of life, of human worth, and of the ideal society, how close does economic development come to the ideal? Many students of the problem uncritically assume that existing values, or even values in gestation, ought to be treated instrumentally—i.e., as mere impediments or aids to development. It is wiser, on the contrary, to ask whether development itself is an impediment or an aid to the good life and the good society as conceived in a variety of value systems. The same question can be asked in practical terms by inquiring into the goals of a society regardless of its degree of development. No *a priori* claim is made that universal goals exist. Yet, as anthropologist David Bidney notes, "All absolutes are not necessarily ethnocentric, and all cultural ideologies are not of equal value. Belief in trans-cultural absolutes, in rational norms and ideals which men may approximate in time but never quite realize perfectly, is quite compatible with a humane policy of tolerance of cultural differences." [51] In fact, all advocates of development, however they define it, pursue some common objectives. What is more important is that societies which oppose development can be shown, upon examination, to pursue these same goals.

As stated earlier, development goals, although expressed in quantitative terms, relate to qualitative improvement in human life. Within subsistence economies, life is short, disease rampant, poverty general, and opportunity limited: all these conditions easily appear "less human" than those which prevail after higher levels of living are achieved. Paradoxically, however, the form of interpersonal relationships one finds in subsistence groups may appear more humanly satisfying, less impersonal, and more closely attuned to some important registers of human need. Notwithstanding their perplexity in the presence of terms like a "more human" or a "less human" existence, most men are instinctively repelled by the "inhuman" quality of mass misery, whether it be found in the streets of Calcutta or among the

---

[50] Professor Robert S. Browne, then at Fairleigh Dickinson University, in a personal communication to the author dated August 11, 1968.

[51] David Bidney, "The Concept of Value in Modern Anthropology," *Anthropology Today*, ed. A. L. Kroeber (University of Chicago Press, 1965), p. 697. Bidney distinguishes "cultural universals" from "cultural absolutes" and supports Malinowski's view that "There are cultural universals because there are universal human needs."

fellahin of Egypt. The term "less human" manifestly assumes that different qualities in human life can be observed and that some visible signs point to what "human" ought to be. But any judgment about the greater or lesser quality of life is impossible except with reference to what constitutes human happiness and, more fundamentally, to man's image of himself. Any culture or sub-culture may have "culturally absolute" values, but the real problem is to learn whether there exist any "cultural universals," in Bidney's term. Are there certain goods which development purports to provide and which are desired by all societies, developed and non-developed alike, regardless of their concept of man or society? Such goods need not enjoy identical relative importance in all societies, it is simply required that they be present in all. I shall not here undertake to examine all possible conceptions of development itself, or even of the good life.[52] It suffices to ask whether we can identify any common values which all societies desire and which development claims to foster. In my view, three such values can be recognized as goals sought by all individuals and societies. These are properly universalizable goals inasmuch as their forms and modalities can vary in different times and places. Nevertheless, these goals relate to fundamental human needs capable of finding expression in all cultural matrices at all times.

The first of these values is *life-sustenance*. The nurture of life is everywhere treasured by sane men. Even where human sacrifices were offered in propitiation to deities or where female infanticide was practiced by parents desiring sons, the rationale for such violation of life was its putative contribution to over-all vitality in the community or the family. All objects that satisfy men's basic requirements for food, shelter, healing, or survival can be called life-sustaining "goods." There is compelling truth in Mumford's assertion that "real values do not derive from either rarity or crude manpower. It is not rarity that gives the air its power to sustain life, nor is it the human work done that gives milk or bananas their nourishment. In comparison with the effects of chemical action and the sun's rays, the human contribution is a small one. Genuine value lies in the power to sustain or enrich life . . . the value lies directly in the life-function; not in its origin, its rarity, or in the work done by human agents." [53] One of the strong-

[52] On this cf. D. Goulet, "Le Développement dans un Monde Pluraliste," *Développement et Civilisations*, No. 7 (September 1961), pp. 35–47.
[53] Lewis Mumford, *Technics and Civilization* (Harcourt, Brace and Company, 1934), p. 76.

87

est arguments invoked by "conservative" peasants in resisting proposed innovations (fertilizer, new seed, modern tilling practices) is precisely that life-sustenance is too important and too precarious to warrant "risk-taking" on their part. The modernizer in turn invokes his own allegedly superior power to assure life and maintenance. Thus, underlying opposite prescriptions regarding such a vital activity as food-growing we discover a common adherence to life-sustenance as a value. Mumford's lines were written in 1934. Since that time, technological advances have rendered obsolete his declaration that the human contribution is a small one as compared to that of chemistry or of the sun's rays. Indeed, it is the reversal of that equation which constitutes a major difference between those who take "traditional" and those who adopt a "developed" outlook on survival. The former still regard nature as the basic provider, whereas the latter rely increasingly on human knowledge and artistry. For both, however, at the lowest threshold of value, life-sustenance is of decisive importance.

For this reason, little dispute arises over the importance of life-sustaining goods. It is generally acknowledged by developed and underdeveloped alike that death control, a by-product of better nutrition and medicine, renders life more human by the simple fact that it allows more life to exist. Death control is endorsed without hesitation even by societies which resist birth control. Accordingly, wherever there is a dearth of life-sustaining goods—food, medicine, adequate shelter and protection—we may state that absolute underdevelopment exists. Quite clearly, one of development's most important goals is to prolong men's lives and render those men less "stunted" by disease, extreme exposure to nature's elements, and defenselessness against enemies. Nevertheless, prolonged life can appear *desirable* to men only after they become aware of its *possibility*. As long as men remain convinced that it is the will of the gods that their children die in infancy or that to combat certain diseases is sacrilege, they will adjust to hard, brutish reality and, if they are wise, they will gain equanimity. The shocking feature of stunted or shortened human life is that it is so grossly unnecessary. The carriers of modern medicine's demonstration effects—missionaries, government health agents, volunteers—have now reached the most remote areas of the world and brought to their inhabitants visible proof that life can be prolonged. Indeed, the average life-expectancy of a people is usually taken to be one of the general indices of development. This practice reflects the prominence of life-sustenance as a goal of development.

88

A second universal component of the good life is *esteem*—what Everett Hagen calls every man's sense that he is a being of worth, that he is respected, that others are not using him as a tool to attain their purposes without regard for his own purposes.[54] All men and all societies seek esteem, although they may call it identity, dignity, respect, honor, or recognition. Under present world conditions, poor societies with a profound sense of internal self-esteem suffer in their contacts with economically and technologically advanced societies because material prosperity has now become a widely accepted touchstone of worthiness. The self-esteem of the Itaparica community described in an earlier chapter was damaged by the shabby treatment received from out-groups, to whom members of the cult were simply specimens of "underdeveloped" folk: poor, shabbily dressed, unskilled, "uninteresting" folk. Because of the importance attached to material values in "developed" countries, esteem is nowadays increasingly conferred only on those who possess material wealth and technological power— in a word, "development." The pervasive human need for esteem goes far to explain both the frenetic desire of some societies to achieve development and the resistance by others to development's innovations. The first want to achieve development in order to receive some of the esteem so prodigally dispensed to those nations already developed. At the same time the second resist development because they feel deeply wounded in their own sense of worth, independently of levels of material living. Galbraith comments with humor on the difference between poverty in England two centuries ago and poverty in the United States today. After quoting Pitt's remark that "poverty is no disgrace but it is damned annoying," Galbraith concludes that in contemporary United States, however, "it is not annoying but it is a disgrace." [55] The relevant point is that underdevelopment is the lot of the majority of the world's populations. As long as esteem or respect was dispensed on grounds other than material achievement, it was possible to resign oneself to poverty without feeling disdained. Conversely, once the prevailing image of the better life includes material welfare as one of its essential ingredients, it becomes difficult for the materially "underdeveloped" to feel respected or esteemed. One may lament the materialistic bias present in prevalent standards of respect attribution. Nevertheless, it remains true that the poor need to climb

[54] Everett E. Hagen, "Are Some Things Valued by All Men?" *Cross Currents,* Vol. XVIII, No. 4 (Fall 1968), p. 411.
[55] John Kenneth Galbraith, *The Affluent Society* (London: Hamish Hamilton, 1958), p. 259.

out of their wretched condition in order to gain the esteem of others which is so crucial to the preservation of their own internal sense of worth. This is the deep significance of the protestations of the American black who parades the streets bearing the inscription I AM A MAN, or of the Mexican who takes conscious pride in his "Indian," not his Hispanic, cultural achievements. We find the same lament expressed in song by French Gypsy poet-minstrel Lick le Sinto, who pleads with the *Gadjé* (non-Gypsies) to stop judging his people according to legends or stereotypes and to recognize in them human beings like themselves. Just as nineteenth-century Japan embarked on the path of industrialization to avoid humiliation by technologically and militarily superior "barbarian" powers, so nowadays the Third World seeks development in order to gain the esteem which is denied to societies living in a state of disgraceful "underdevelopment." Therefore, the conviction is gaining strength throughout the world that mass poverty cuts societies off from due recognition or esteem. Once deprivation of esteem reaches an intolerable point, people are quite ready to begin desiring material "development." There is no doubt that wealth can be desired for motives other than esteem. Nevertheless, when esteem is not associated, by a populace or its reference groups, with material abundance, that populace is apt to remain indifferent to "development" and to its alleged material benefits.

According to the dominant world-view held in many traditional societies, the fullness of *good* (some ideal image of the good society or the worthwhile human life) is distinct from, when not opposed to, the abundance of *goods*. Although it need not romanticize misery, this view profoundly mistrusts acquisitiveness and challenges the merits of the systematic pursuit of wealth by an entire population. Therefore, under the pressure to improve their capacity to sustain life and prodded by the need to gain respect in a world where technology and abundance enjoy enormous prestige, traditional societies begin their quest for abundance. Development is legitimized as a goal because it is an important, perhaps even an indispensable, way of gaining esteem. In certain cases, however, the need for esteem is an important reason why development is resisted. If the impact strategy consciously or unconsciously employed by change agents humiliates a community, its need for self-respect must lead it to resist change. This is the sense in which esteem and life-sustenance can be called universal goals of societies: whether development is accepted or rejected, these values lie behind the choices.

A third trans-cultural component of the good life, valued by developed and non-developed societies alike, is *freedom*. Countless meanings attach to this troublesome word.[56] At the very least it signifies an expanded range of choices for societies and their members, together with the minimization of constraints (external, though not necessarily internal) in the pursuit of some perceived good. To regard freedom as a general goal of development and non-development alike is not, however, to assume that all men desire freedom to govern themselves or determine their own destinies. Nor is it to suppose that they will all tolerate the insecurities attendant upon freedom. There is compelling evidence, as Fromm has observed, that most men even in "developed" societies seek to "escape from freedom." This escape from freedom's responsibility is often associated with a strong desire for security. At the societal level, however, security can properly be viewed as freedom *from* unforeseen or uncontrollable dangers, although it is admittedly not freedom *for* self-actualization or exploration of some possibly exhilarating unknown. Most members of societies wish to have only that degree of freedom they need to engage in spheres of activity for which they feel competent and wherein the use of their skills and judgment is, if not stimulating, at least satisfying. For most people these spheres comprise a very circumscribed orbit indeed. To step outside that orbit may be to flirt with unmanageable anxiety. Whatever holds true at this psychological level, it can nevertheless be claimed that development is perceived as one way to emancipate oneself from the social servitudes of ignorance, misery, perhaps even exploitation of others. To this extent at least, it is a search for a *freedom from* even if not a *freedom for* actualization of one's self and group. Nevertheless, the proposition that freedom is enhanced by development appears outrageous to some observers. Hannah Arendt believes that under no circumstances can economic growth "lead into freedom or constitute a proof for its existence." [57] She alludes unmistakably to the new constraints which must be imposed if development is to be successfully launched. Yet it appears naïve to isolate this dimension of freedom from two others no less crucial, viz.: (a) the prior degree of freedom (economic, psychological, as well as political) extant before the commitment to development is made, and (b) the realistic alternatives open to one in the worldwide context of competing forces.

Regarding the first, Brazilian economist Celso Furtado draws our attention to the high price paid for remaining underdeveloped: unnec-

---

[56] Cf. the essay by Donald P. Warwick, "Human Freedom and Human Development," *Cross Currents,* Vol. XVIII, No. 4 (Fall 1968), pp. 495–517.
[57] Hannah Arendt, *On Revolution* (Viking Press, 1963), p. 218.

essary deaths, perpetuated exploitation of masses by privileged classes, very low occupational and symbolic mobility for most people. As a result, "the masses in the underdeveloped countries have not generally put the same high valuation on individual liberty that we do. Since they have not had access to the better things of life, they obviously cannot grasp the full meaning of the supposed dilemma between liberty and quick development . . . the liberty enjoyed by the minority in our society is paid for by a delay in general economic development, hence is at the expense of the welfare of the great majority . . . Very few of us have sufficient awareness of these deeply inhuman characteristics of underdevelopment. When we do become fully aware, we understand why the masses are prepared for any sacrifice in order to overcome it. If the price of liberty for the few had to be the poverty of the many, we can be quite certain that the probability of preserving freedom would be practically nil." [58] A perpetual battle rages between those who base their definition of freedom on external political forms and those who grant primacy to emancipation from alienating material conditions of life or psychological constraints. Notwithstanding Arendt's case against freedom, it is difficult to disagree with W. Arthur Lewis' conclusion that the "advantage of economic growth is not that wealth increases happiness, but that it increases the range of human choice." [59] Wealth can make it possible for men to gain greater control over their environment than if they remained poor, to choose greater leisure, to have more goods and services. Without doubt, development also imposes new disciplines and in the long run may even place men at the service of technological dynamisms over which they have little or no control. Of greater import, however, is the range of effective alternatives. For practical purposes, societies have little choice but to come to terms with development: they simply are not free to reject it outright. In Lewis' terms: "The leaven of economic change is already working in every society— even in Tibet—thanks to the linkage of the world which has been achieved in the past eighty years by steamships, by imperialism, by airplanes, by wireless, by migration, by Hollywood, and by the printed word." [60] Aided by these and other agencies, aspirations have grown

[58] Celso Furtado, "Brazil: What Kind of Revolution?" in *Economic Development, Evolution or Revolution,* ed. Laura Randall (D. C. Heath and Company, 1964), pp. 36–37.
[59] W. Arthur Lewis, "Is Economic Growth Desirable?" in *Studies in Economic Development,* ed. Bernard Okun and Richard W. Richardson (Holt, Rinehart and Winston, 1962), p. 478.
[60] *Idem,* p. 490.

faster than production, and death rates have fallen more rapidly than birth rates. These two developments suffice to introduce in non-developed societies elements of imbalance making it impossible for them to postpone decisions regarding the kind and speed of contemplated development. It may well be esthetically satisfying to keep a portion of the world "pure" and free of modernity: a kind of game preserve for human beings similar to our sanctuaries for wildfowl. But in real life no group can long remain beyond the reach of disruptive influences.

I personally recall the vivid impact made by the first radio ever brought to the tiny hamlet of Sertão da Quina in São Paulo State, Brazil. Although situated only fifty miles from highly industrialized São Paulo city, this locality had lived in total autarchy, buried in the Serra do Mar mountains. After 1961 a new road was built and life has taken a different hue. But early in 1961 a nineteen-year-old boy, returning home on furlough from military service, brought with him the first radio ever seen by his fellow villagers. Very rapidly this simple demonstration effect began to dramatize their own estrangement from the world of "development" lying just outside their immediate confines. A similar phenomenon takes place when a plane crashes in a tiny mountain village in Turkey and a rescue operation for the pilot places government personnel in touch with natives for the first time, or when research anthropologists unexpectedly appear to disturb the placid life of a forest community in Guatemala. Throughout the world, isolated communities are being denied the effective alternative of ignoring development. The real issue then becomes: what margin of freedom can they gain to fulfill even their minimal purposes, such as survival and the protection of cultural identity? Whether they choose to pursue development, to resist it, or simply to postpone it, at least in part they do so in order to protect or enhance some perceived freedom to be and to do. The most pertinent question, therefore, is the relationship between freedom and economic well-being.

Although it is widely assumed in modern societies that freedom increases as men possess more goods, this view flatly contradicts numerous traditions wherein wisdom consists in minimizing one's desires. Sahara Bedouins, for instance, look with scorn upon men who "need" a multitude of encumbering objects; they believe a man's freedom is inversely proportional to the quantity of goods he must have. Marginal Gypsies in southern Spain pass similar judgment on men who are not "free" to roam at will because they are "tied down" *to* their possessions, and ultimately *by* them. One need not here debate whether greater freedom results from having fewer or more goods. Much depends on what level of freedom is being discussed. What is germane to our investigation, however, is that some sense of freedom is treasured both by those who pursue development and by those who disdain it. This is why freedom must be included, along with life-sustenance and esteem, as a universalizable component of the good life.

Development is a particular constellation of means for obtaining a better life. Irrespective of possible other purposes, development has for all groups at least the following objectives:

—to provide more and better life-sustaining goods to members of societies;

—to create or improve material conditions of life related in some way to a perceived need for esteem; and

—to free men from servitudes (to nature, to ignorance, to other men, to institutions, to beliefs) considered oppressive. The aim here may be to release men from the bondage of these servitudes and/or to heighten their opportunities for self-actualization, however conceived.[61]

All other goals of development may be subsumed, without doing violence to their peculiar characteristics, under one or another of these more general objectives. The construction of a new "Socialist man," for instance, is simply one form of actualization, not of the individual self but of collective man. Furthermore, the ultimate *rationale* for emancipating collective man is to create social conditions wherein personal actualization of all men becomes possible without alienating any of them.

It need hardly be added that the precise content of self-actualization may vary widely both for individuals and for entire societies. Moreover, diverse options as to goals have enormous consequences on patterns of decision-making and the choice of institutions in a given social system. The form of government, the educational structure, and the constellation of economic incentives are but a few of the institutions directly affected.

From this brief reflection on development goals it follows that a wide range of judgments is possible as to the degree to which "development" or some feature of it—let us say, rationalization of work procedures to raise productivity, or merit systems of status conferral, or large-scale urbanization—does in fact lead to a "better" life or not.

[61] On self-actualization, cf. Christian Bay, *The Structure of Freedom* (Atheneum, 1965), pp. 83-101.

As it is generally described and practiced in the world, development implies one particular image of the good life. There is no guarantee that this is a more appropriate or more satisfying image than other images—*all things considered.*[62] This qualifying phrase acknowledges that men in developed societies can control disease, prolong life, and provide themselves with defense against the ravages of the weather and natural catastrophes. Yet, there is no evidence that "developed" men are either happier or more "human" than underdeveloped men. It is only because of their greater ability to influence events that developed countries have been able to impose a disjointed economy characterized by domination and structural vulnerability on societies which, although poor and perhaps even economically stagnant, formerly enjoyed considerable social cohesion and some form of harmony with nature's cosmic forces. Similarly, it is because of their greater power that the First and Second Worlds can present "development" itself to the Third World as necessary, if not as desirable. The old cohesion and harmony just evoked cannot long survive the onslaught of forces which have been unleashed by the "developed" agents and which impinge on societies already wounded by those agents. This is why the ancient goals of protecting life, nurturing esteem, and freeing oneself as much as one could in order to be oneself must now become the yardsticks against which development itself is to be judged. It is not those goals which must be judged by development.

Much of the confusion over goals arises because development spokesmen persist in *assuming* that development will enhance life-values, respect, and freedom. If my analysis of the larger processes at work in the world today is correct, however, the fragility of this claim is laid bare. These processes place the Third World in a vulnerable posture wherein their own conceptions of respect and freedom are attacked. Even if they perceive development's "benefits" as enhancing their capacity to sustain life, they understandably fear that it may destroy their esteem in a highly competitive world and free them from certain constraints only to plunge them into others. After investigating in explicit terms the goals of development, it is also necessary to examine the nature of the process. It is these goals and an understanding of the developmental process as dialectical which preside over all normative strategies adopted in the pursuit of development.

[62] For a sharply delineated example of a different image, an example of monumental scope and importance, cf. Feliciano V. Carino, "The Revolutionary Consciousness of Asia and the Rise of China," in *Report of a North American Working Party on the Rise of China* (Geneva: World Student Christian Federation, January 1968), II, 315–344.

CHAPTER FOUR

Development as Dialectical Process

During the "passage" from underdevelopment to development, several interrelated processes go on simultaneously. Although these processes are conceptually distinct, they have no separate existence: it is only methodological convenience which isolates economic from political or social development. Development, moreover, is simply one particular form of social change, modernization is a special case of development, and industrialization is a single facet of development.[1] Generally, these processes are described not dynamically but in terms of the social characteristics they leave behind and those toward which they move. F. X. Sutton lists the following traits of a "modern" society in typical fashion:

(1) the predominance of universalistic, specific, and achievement norms;

(2) a high degree of social mobility, in a general though not necessarily in a "vertical" sense;

(3) a well-developed occupational system, insulated from other social structures;

(4) the existence of an "egalitarian" class system based on gener-

[1] These statements are based on David E. Apter, *The Politics of Modernization* (University of Chicago Press, 1967), p. x.

alized patterns of occupational achievement;

(5) the prevalence of functionally specific, non-ascriptive structures in a pattern of "associations." [2]

Although change occurs in all societies, even those regarded as static, most analysts treat modernization as a unique and thoroughgoing transformation of society, involving changes in all sub-systems: political, cultural, economic, religious, and psychological.[3] Decisive alterations in large part take the form of responses to applications of technology which increase social interdependence and accelerate urbanization, literacy, and social mobility. These alterations render obsolete many functions of social integration formerly performed by old social units—tribes, castes, extended families, and villages. One can study modernization in a variety of ways: as an economic phenomenon linked to industrialization and the achievement by an economy of the capacity to sustain growth in productivity and levels of per-capita product; as a socio-psychological reality modifying attitudes, behavior, and symbols; as a network of political changes by which allegiances are transferred from lesser units to a nation-state and political participation acquires new scope and new forms. The basis for describing social change processes in this manner is the cumulative knowledge gained from empirical study of facts in the light of disciplined theoretical formulations. Something essential is missing, however, in this factual and "objective" grasp of development processes, or even of broader social change processes.

The missing element is "dialectics," or what Marcuse calls "the power of negative thinking." [4] This power is a tool for analyzing facts in terms of their internal inadequacy. To speak of inadequacy is to make an overt value judgment in which the alleged distinction between values and facts is denied. Instead, all facts are considered as stages in a single process wherein subject and object are so intimately joined that truth can be determined only within the subject-object totality. In some bewilderingly complex sense, "objects" contain "subjects" in their very structure. Dialectical thinking, therefore, becomes a necessary mode of approach to dialectical reality, wherein man's

---

[2] F. X. Sutton, "Social Theory and Comparative Politics," in H. Eckstein and David E. Apter, eds., *Comparative Politics: A Reader* (Free Press of Glencoe, 1963), p. 71, cited by Apter, *op. cit.*, p. 44.

[3] On this, cf. Claude E. Welch, Jr., *Political Modernization* (Wadsworth, 1967), p. 5.

[4] Herbert Marcuse, *Reason and Revolution* (Beacon Press, 1964), p. viii. The following paragraphs are based in part on Marcuse's essay "A Note on Dialectic," inserted as Preface to this work.

experience of the world is unfree despite his aspiration to freedom. Institutionalized realities are always to some degree false, because they are never what they should be in order for man to be fully man. History at times reveals reason as the legitimizer of unreason, freedom as the pretext for tyranny, progress as a mere veil for alienation. When this happens, "all thinking that does not testify to an awareness of the radical falsity of the established forms of life is faulty thinking." [5] Technology, however, has bound object to subject so pervasively that to abstract from their union is to deceive oneself and lose objectivity. For this reason, therefore, an essential part of the meaning of any contemporary process is the consciousness of that process displayed by those undergoing it.

Contemporary societies have been rendered collectively self-conscious to an unprecedented degree. There are three realities the world has grown particularly *conscious of:*

(1) that change is part of the very essence of nature;

(2) that conflict and competition of interests are inherent to social dynamics; and

(3) that latent realities exercise decisive influence even upon manifest phenomena.

This enumeration evokes the names of Darwin, Marx, and Freud, historical midwives of this triple consciousness. Although awareness originated in the "Western" cultural orbit, it has now spread throughout the world, thanks to mass communications and transportation. Among the salient images thus propagated is that of "development": the vision of a better material life for all. Granted that dialectical understanding of the broad historical processes of change is necessary, the more specific and immediate task is to determine in what precise sense development constitutes a dialectical process. Before replying, it may help to review briefly the meaning of the term in the history of thought.

The Meaning of "Dialectical"

The term "dialectical" has a long history. For Plato, dialectics was a movement of the mind, a search, through dialogue and discussion, for the clarification of a concept. It also meant the ascent of the mind from the lower understanding of concrete forms—of beauty, justice,

[5] *Ibidem,* p. xiii.

or harmony—to the contemplation of universal essences said to exist in a realm of Pure Ideas.[6] With Aristotle the term changed meaning: dialectic was an attempted demonstration which, on principle, could not be apodictic because it was based solely on probable, not on conclusive, evidence. Medieval scholastics adopted this usage and perpetuated it for many centuries in Europe, notwithstanding the attacks by fideistic theologians, who insisted that "not through dialectics can man gain salvation." The implication, of course, was that free inquiry interferes with simple and loving faith in a supernatural order of reality. For Kant "dialectics" came to mean whatever exists only in the realm of illusion—that is, any reasoning which moves beyond the stable domain of the critical understanding. Only with Fichte, Hegel, and Marx, however, do we approximate current usage. Contrary to a widespread impression, Hegel himself rejected the notion that dialectics is a dynamic movement in which a *thesis* or position necessarily generates its opposite, the *antithesis,* both of which are then reconciled or subsumed in a new reality, the *synthesis.* According to Kaufmann, Hegel's dialectic never adopted this ritualistic three-step.[7] Before Hegel, it was Fichte who had introduced into German philosophy the terminology: thesis-antithesis-synthesis. This three-way dialectic "takes the form of a progressive determination of the meanings of the initial propositions. And the contradictions which arise are resolved in the sense that they are shown to be only apparent." [8] Nevertheless, in practice Fichte did not view dialectics merely as the progressive clarification of a meaning which is initially given. He admitted the introduction, at later stages, of new ideas or limits conditioning the original datum. Hegel explicitly rejected Fichte's terminology and preferred to speak of affirmation, negation, and negation of negation. Nevertheless, he called attention to the ironic reversals throughout history in master/servant relationships and to the role of error in elucidating truth itself. He claimed that any position, if sufficiently developed, would uncover or manifest contradictions that would lead it to a new interpretation of itself. *In his vision of the world and of man, development comes through conflict.* Human passions have great moving power and sudden reversals are ironically frequent. Thus,

---

6 This historical review borrows from Wilfred Desan, *The Marxism of Jean-Paul Sartre* (A Doubleday Anchor Book, 1965), pp. 37ff.

7 Walter Kaufmann, *Hegel: A Reinterpretation* (A Doubleday Anchor Book, 1966), p. 158.

8 Frederick Copleston, *A History of Philosophy* (Image Books, 1965), Vol. VII, Part 1, p. 67.

Hegel defends a dialectical world-view, but he steadfastly refused to employ his dialectic to predict the future or even to admit that prediction was possible.

Marx, more forcefully than his predecessors, emphasized the view of history as dialectical. History's propelling force, he declared, lies not in ideas but in matter: economics commands the historical process, and relations of production determine man's freedom or servitude. Ideas are useful only insofar as they contribute to changing reality in some desired direction. Labor itself is the raw material on which the dialectic exercises itself. Whenever work is done, it negates what it works with. Thus, agricultural labor negates the land, and the landowner's usufruct negates the labor. The fundamental process in human affairs is historical materialism which "will go its dialectical way until freedom for all and everyone is obtained. This will of course mean the end of all alienations, as well as the end of all dialectic. This end, and the new beginning, are not yet in sight. In the meantime, action is necessary, even violent and 'illegal' action, for that, too, is part of the *negation* within the dialectical process." [9] At the empirical level of action, of course, the most dramatic expression of this dialectic is class warfare.

Sartre has struggled heroically to lay bare, in contemporary language, the critical dimension of dialectic, in the belief that to unmask is to modify reality. He accords such overwhelming primacy to the conscious subject that he is sometimes accused of minimizing the importance of societal reality, of symbols, of culture, even of other subjects. Notwithstanding this objection, however, Sartre's dialectic does strive to reconcile subject with object, with the clear stipulation that man, isolated in his liberty, is lord of nature. Unlike Marx, he rejects a dialectic of nature, although he insists on a dialectic of human thought and of human choice. For Sartre, "nature without man would be a deaf mute." [10]

One important trait is common to all these positions: the rejection of an equilibrium model of change based on homeostatic accommodation or unilinear movement. Basic processes are said to involve if not contradiction, at least opposition, sudden reversals of fortune or position, a degree of unpredictability which escapes purely rational understanding, an element of discontinuity at the very heart of continuity, of new beginnings out of old deaths. We are now ready to ask: in what precise sense then, if any, is development a dialectical process?

[9] Desan, *op. cit.,* p. 40.
[10] *Ibidem,* p. 41.

The Dialectics of Development

Behind any dialectical view of history is belief in "the opposition of forces in a state of mobile equilibrium." [11] What we call history is a procession of events governed by confrontations among diversely stratified [12] classes, nations, and trans-national interests. Although a comprehensive dialectical view of development may appear superfluous to the empirical social scientist, Furtado insists that at present levels of economic knowledge, history cannot be reconstituted from a mere analysis of the multiple phenomena which comprise it. Some unifying intuitive vision of the whole is necessary, to explain both the past development of advanced economies and the dynamisms operative in contemporary transitional societies.[13] As a conceptual aid, dialectics helps explain in what sense capitalism was necessary at an early phase of capital accumulation and why it necessarily gave rise to new forms of social conflict. More importantly, it draws attention to the dualisms present each time technological innovation seriously challenges prevailing modes of material production. Above all, a dialectical explanation leads one to conclude that development is not some unilinear evolutionary movement which obeys intrinsic natural laws. Rather the development process inevitably releases opposing forces competing in identical arenas or "fields" of influence. Action, reaction, and interaction among these forces produce advances and regressions, or perhaps stalemates. Deliberate changes are always inextricably embroiled in quite unintentional changes.[14] To call development a dialectical process also signifies that its effects are ambiguous and unpredictable. Even well-planned change does not produce only benefits; nor can a plan anticipate all the consequences of the measures it advocates. Once set in motion, identical forces may generate too much development (in a purely material sense) in one area or

[11] Celso Furtado, *Dialética do Desenvolvimento* (Rio de Janeiro: Editora Fundo de Cultura, 1964), p. 13.
[12] It is worth noting the subtitle of Irving Louis Horowitz's work, *Three Worlds of Development* (Oxford University Press, 1966): "The Theory and Practice of International Stratification."
[13] Furtado, *op. cit.*, pp. 14–15. This argument has been expounded at length in other works by Furtado, especially *Desenvolvimento e Subdesenvolvimento* (Fundo de Cultura, 1961) and *Teoria e Política do Desenvolvimento Econômico* (São Paulo: Companhia Editora Nacional, 1967); *Obstacles to Development in Latin America* (Anchor Books, 1970).
[14] A good illustration is provided by an Indonesian scholar, Selosoemardjan, in *Social Changes in Jogjakarta* (Cornell University Press, 1962), pp. 379ff.

sector and too little in another. It is in the Hegelian rather than the Marxian sense that development processes are dialectical. *For Hegel, dialectics is a tool of analysis and interpretation—even of pedagogy and mobilization—but not of rigorous prediction.* We need not think that future development *has to* proceed with the frequent and serious ruptures characterizing past development (e.g., the creation of internal proletariats, imperial expansion and domination to secure raw materials and markets, cultural monopolies over technological research). Nevertheless, the confrontation between developed and underdeveloped nations, as between domestic classes, is an interplay of opposing forces in which each is transformed by its contact with the other. From this clash of opposites emerges a third set of forces which supplant or subsume, for a time at least, the original ones. With time, such third forces acquire legitimacy until they are themselves challenged by new forces which carry the process of confrontation still further.

Not all periods of developmental history are characterized by acute conflict, although upheavals have occurred often enough to give plausibility to a cyclical theory of conflict. Moreover, a diagnosis of present cultural, economical, and political forces engaged in development suggests a highly competitive struggle in which no basic consensus exists regarding the terms of the competition. Democratic practice, in contrast to theory, indicates that democratic competition (wherein both parties to conflict abide by common rules) can succeed only if fundamental values are not at stake.[15] There is, however, a fundamental competitiveness about the revolution of rising expectations. False imagery pictures a respected father in a patriarchal family dividing the huge cake of prosperity among his contented children, who confidently expect him to exercise distributive justice and equity. A more appropriate image is the biblical banquet of Dives, the rich man, and Lazarus, the beggar. Lazarus barely manages to gather a few crumbs left over from the sumptuous feast enjoyed by the plutocrat and his friends. The Third World is an assertive Lazarus, however, resolved to get more than mere crumbs. The Lazarus nations and the Dives nations alike know full well that the present division of spoils on a famine/feast basis cannot endure. If pressed too far or permanently thwarted, the Third World will no longer confine its claims to simply winning its share of the spoils. As Fanon explains: "The well-known

---

[15] On this, cf. Ernest Gellner, "Democracy and Industrialisation," *European Journal of Sociology,* Vol. VIII, No. 1 (1967), pp. 47–70.

principle that all men are equal will be illustrated in the colonies from the moment that *the native claims that he is the equal of the settler.* One step more and he is ready to *fight to be more than the settler.* In fact, he has already decided to eject him and *to take his place.*" [16]

Thus is the stage set for a dialectical reversal of roles between master and slave. Yet violent eruption is not inevitable, since relatively moderate adjustments may still be possible. Moreover, some claimants may be domesticated, co-opted, or simply isolated. Nevertheless, the basic relationship which is discernible can only be described as dialectical. The structural vulnerability of the Third World, allied to its high degree of consciousness, suffices to account for aggressivity and tension in the confrontation. Beyond the realm of consciousness, however, development is also a dialectical process on historical grounds.

The moving forces which launched development in England, Europe, and the United States were at first contested, not only by reckless Luddites who physically destroyed machinery, but by moral and esthetic norm-setters as well. Moralists decried the "immorality" and "brutality," at times even the sacrilegiously presumptuous nature of economic innovations.[17] Science, technology, and productive innovations were vigorously contested by the societies in which they were introduced. As societies progressively conferred legitimacy on practices formerly condemned, the condemnation itself became obsolete. Class relationships between suppliers of capital and labor have never been static: the ground rules governing relationships between them have been constantly revised according as either group obtained, by violence or chicanery, greater bargaining power. Much the same situation has prevailed between developed and underdeveloped societies. Interestingly enough, dialectics takes a strange twist inside developed countries: the prevailing mentality is so receptive to "innovation" that a favorable bias toward what is new exists even before old values can defend themselves against the challenge posed by the new. Concur-

---

[16] Frantz Fanon, *The Wretched of the Earth* (Grove Press, 1966), p. 36. Italics mine.

[17] For example, cf. Robert L. Heilbroner, *The Worldly Philosophers* (Simon and Schuster, 1966), p. 18: "In England a revolutionary patent for a stocking frame is not only denied in 1623, but the Privy Council orders the dangerous contraption abolished. In France the importation of printed calicoes is threatening to undermine the clothing industry. It is met with measures which cost the lives of sixteen hundred people! In Valence alone on one occasion 77 persons are sentenced to be hanged, 58 broken on the wheel, 631 sent to the galleys, and one lone and lucky individual set free for the crime of dealing in forbidden calico wares."

rently, however, developed societies display a persistent inability to transform their educational, political, and social institutions in ways compatible with their own professed social goals and with the internal requirements of technological innovation itself. Consequently, blatant dialectical tensions exist within developed societies. These societies have not yet learned whether or not there is a contradiction between mass-consumer affluence and freedom to seek the good life. One theorist of the industrial society, Raymond Aron, suggests that the thorniest questions posed by the Third World's drive toward development are generated by the possible contradiction that comes from "wanting both material development and a good society." [18] On the other hand, a dialectical situation exists in underdeveloped countries because the traditional social equilibrium is being radically challenged. It is in the relations between developed and underdeveloped nations, however, that one most visibly detects opposition, sudden reversals, unpredictable structural mutations, or, in Hegel's terms, affirmation, negation, and negation of the negation. Worldwide development is surely a dialectical process.

Development results in great gains for some and serious losses for others, at the very moment that it increases the wants of the latter. Investors are strongly attracted toward existing centers of power and profitability, not toward areas of priority need. Development poles are self-reinforcing magnets of progress. Left to themselves, the dynamisms of development operate in cyclical causation patterns whose results contradict the hopes raised by development's mobilizing symbols and promises. Even centrally planned development faces insoluble problems, for it must maximize goals which, at the very least, appear to the populace at large to be opposed to ideals of egalitarianism and release from exploitation which hold such a salient place in the rationale for central planning. As for foreign aid, no donor countries have taken the Third World's development as normative of its assistance; instead they have subordinated the granting of aid to their own strategic and ideological interests. At a time when few nations enjoyed political independence and fewer still actively sought development as a priority goal, incoherent policies could remain unchallenged. Now, however, challenge is a central ingredient of the development process.

The "widening gap" between levels of living in developed and

[18] Raymond Aron, ed., *World Technology and Human Destiny* (University of Michigan Press, 1963), p. 19.

underdeveloped countries creates still another dimension of dialectics in the transitional process. New desires grow faster in poor countries than the capacity to satisfy them. Moreover, explicit consciousness makes men impatient with inequality, not merely with absolute want or insufficiency. Yet the gap will widen unless the fundamental priorities within the developed world itself are reversed. What is needed is a change in values and behavior of such scope as to constitute a veritable cultural revolution. There are not many "Philippe Egalités" in the world, privileged individuals, classes, or nations who will freely abdicate their favored position out of idealism or deference to the priority needs of others. Consequently, a reversal of present modes of development cannot be anticipated unless the Third World acquires greater bargaining power with which to pressure the rich. Notwithstanding gains in the clarification of issues and in declarations of principle at the two UNCTAD conferences, progress realized by the Third World is small. Fear may possibly accelerate the advent of wisdom in the world's affluent societies, inasmuch as some poor countries will soon possess atomic weapons. Perhaps it will then be recognized that a Third World kept poor is a Third World rendered dangerous. Furthermore, new forms of mass alienation and social anomie inside rich countries themselves may lead them to abandon their pursuit of "misplaced abundance." They may discover, in Fromm's terms, that "affluent alienation" is as dehumanizing as "impoverished alienation." [19] The next step toward wisdom lies in the discovery that an essential connection exists between the misplaced abundance of the few and the impoverished alienation of the many.[20] Misplaced abundance is a major contributor to the widening gap. Productive priorities which allow a small number of wealthy nations to waste prodigally while others lack essential goods are structurally evil. Heilbroner rightly castigates the United States because it throws "on the junk heap vehicles which would furnish invaluable transportation to a world which still totes much of its burdens on its backs; we discard outmoded wardrobes which would clothe men and women who have never known what it was like to have an unused garment; we spend in night clubs a sum which would cover the national budgets of a dozen pinched nations. Not to use this abundance for the betterment of

[19] Introduction to *Socialist Humanism: An International Symposium,* ed. Erich Fromm (Anchor Books, 1966), p. ix.
[20] Cf. Denis A. Goulet, "Voluntary Austerity: The Necessary Art," in *The Christian Century,* June 8, 1966, pp. 748–752.

105

mankind would be evidence of a moral decay as destructive of the West as any number of external revolutions." [21]

A dialectical reversal is necessary, a complete reorganization of productive priorities in the world. The Third World knows this and urges developed countries to undertake "measures for anticipatory structural readjustments and other measures for bringing about such changes in their production patterns as to eliminate the possibility of resorting to restrictive trade policies. . . . The developed countries should not promote the development in their territories of industries of particular interest to the developing countries." [22]

Not equality, but satisfaction of minimal needs as a first priority, is the goal. Opposing views prevail between the developed and the undeveloped regarding the dynamics of wealth distribution. Those having wealth maintain that they have a right to keep what they have and to continue getting more. Those without wealth, on the contrary, insist on their prior right to obtain enough *now*. The rich reply that the poor will get more (and, presumably, enough) just as speedily as productivity rises. To this the poor retort that productivity rises in accord with patterns which are advantageous to those who already have much and detrimental to the most needy. Perspicacious observers among the poor acknowledge, of course, that mere redistribution of existing wealth is no acceptable solution. There is an element of self-protective realism behind this attitude, for they grasp full well that the rich would fight to resist radical redistribution. And the rich would surely win! What the poor ought to advocate, therefore, is a universal policy of austerity for themselves and for those already in abundance. If it is to succeed, a rational austerity policy requires of developed societies that they alter their image of the good life and develop a coherent theory of the hierarchy of needs in which all men's necessities enter into consideration.

To summarize, development processes inevitably breed profound conflicts. Marx had no patience with responses to the problem of human existence "which try to present solutions by negating or camouflaging the dichotomies inherent in man's existence." [23] There is scant reason to hope that beneficiaries of extant privileged social sys-

[21] Robert L. Heilbroner, *The Great Ascent* (Harper Torchbooks, 1963), p. 146.
[22] *Trends and Problems in World Trade and Development, Charter of Algiers*, U.N. Document MM 77/1/20, dated 30 October 1967, p. 11.
[23] Cf. Erich Fromm, *Marx's Concept of Man* (Frederick Ungar Publishing Co., 1966), p. v.

tems will meet the demands of poorer claimants in time to obviate serious conflict. Available evidence suggests, on the contrary, that power elites will adamantly refuse to alter the rules of the game, except insofar as they can "domesticate" change to their advantage. Their attitude need not surprise us, for, as Barrington Moore[24] has shown, violence has been exercised for centuries within the framework of law and order and the Western mind has yet to admit the legitimacy of counter-violence, on the grounds that it is not lawful or orderly. With a dialectical perspective, however, it becomes reasonable to suppose, along with Fals Borda,[25] that violence is not only normal in the development process, but also an effective problem-solving instrument, a mobilizing tool, an affirmation of fragile cultural or class identity, an institution-building mechanism. Even short of mass violence, however, grave conflicts of interests will abound simply because privilege structures can no longer enjoy universal psychic legitimacy. And instead of disappearing, as they should, these structures continue to influence decision-making.

There is still another dimension to development's dialectical nature: the total unpredictability of its outcome. The great ascent may fail. Similarly, the take-off into self-sustained growth may never come or prove lasting. One errs if he imagines development to be a necessary progressive movement. Some countries may experience just enough development to destroy their traditional values irrevocably, but not enough to become modern except in a socially pathological manner. Others may lose their impetus before they achieve autonomous development, either because of excessive demographic pressure, their inability to generate enough foreign exchange to service burdensome debts and finance needed capital imports, or because the tension between national integration and economic gains is never resolved. There is considerable likelihood that the entire world could become, like the United States, a global affluent society within which a number of depressed areas or pockets of underdevelopment would subsist. Distorted development, in a word, can be the outcome. Another possibility is what Stephen Rose calls the Apocalypse, the cataclysmic disruption of the world's technological edifice.[26] Colonialism harbored

24 Barrington Moore, Jr., *Social Origins of Dictatorship and Democracy* (Beacon Press, 1966), pp. 20, 29.

25 Orlando Fals Borda, *Subversion and Social Change in Colombia* (Columbia University Press, 1969).

26 Stephen C. Rose, ed., *The Development Apocalypse*, Geneva: *Risk*, Vol. III, Nos. 1 and 2 (1967).

within itself a principle which doomed it to extinction in the face of certain challenges. During World War II natives were made to fight the colonizers' wars on grounds of nationalism; it was of course impossible for "nationalism" not to contaminate the natives themselves. The case with development may be similar; some of the distortions inherent in present modes of development may make it impossible for these modes to endure. It is not implausible to anticipate massive destruction or great stagnation for huge portions of the world. Stagnation might conceivably coexist along with a depersonalized, tyrannical, technologically sophisticated and developed "fortress world." The only certainty is that development for the world at large is uncertain, notwithstanding pronouncements which seem to assume that it is inevitable. In my opinion, development can succeed only if the world realizes that it can fail.

For all these reasons, development is a dialectical process, a risky venture fraught with contradictions and irrationalities which cannot be analyzed in purely rational terms. Vulnerability, arbitrariness, and domination all enter into the development equation. Furthermore, even intended change for development's sake produces unintended consequences. One errs if he supposes that the task of the planner is to sketch out fully the consequences of a projected policy. Even the most severely reasoned strategy is filled with unforeseeable consequences. Ultimately, development is, to borrow Austruy's[27] terms, a scandal, a shockingly ambiguous admixture of goods and evils, a veritable dialectical process.

[27] Jacques Austruy, *Le Scandale du Développement* (Paris: Marcel Rivière, 1965).

PART II

Ethical Strategies for Development

CHAPTER FIVE

General Requirements

Decisive responsibility for achieving internal development rests with underdeveloped societies themselves. Political will diffused throughout a population, judicious goal-setting and resource allocation, vigorous implementation and perpetual correction are the measures required for development. For some time to come, however, it is unlikely that development can be pursued except within a framework of nationalism. Whether this likelihood is deemed regrettable or not, low-income countries are engaged in self-conscious nation-building and consolidation of national identity. Although they have nominally enjoyed political independence for a century and a half, Latin American countries are now redefining for themselves what it means to be an autonomous unit of political, economic, and cultural life. New nations in Africa and Asia are explicitly scrutinizing their destinies now that colonizers can no longer treat them as zones of European or American influence. The definition of nationalism proposed by Kalman Silvert casts special light on the development problem. Silvert acknowledges four traditional modes of viewing nationalism: as formal juridical concept, symbolic concept, ideology, and social value. He reduces these four to unity around a succinct definition: *"Nationalism is the acceptance of the state as the impersonal and ultimate arbiter of human affairs."* [1] Although he recognizes the danger of oversimplifi-

[1] K. H. Silvert, ed., *Expectant Peoples, Nationalism and Development* (Vintage Books, 1963), p. 19. Silvert defends his definition against a variety of

cation and the overtones of totalitarianism in his formulation, Silvert claims that his definition goes to the heart of nationalism: the establishment of a fully secular area of life regulated by a social institution before which all men are, at least in certain public senses, equal. The state comes to be viewed as the only institution legally authorized to use force in settling disputes. Citizens consent and give allegiance to an explicit community to which they concede greater rights than to family, tribe, village, religion, or other claimants to their loyalty. Accordingly, movement toward self-conscious nationhood is the very essence of political development.

This definition is cited here for purely illustrative reasons. My point is that development efforts are deployed within a framework of nationalism—sought, defended, or consolidated. Myrdal sees India's early national effort as an attempt to establish effective central governmental control over the entire population after independence and, more importantly, to achieve "emotional integration" of vast masses into the "nation." [2] Even staunch internationalist developers agree that the most important single locus of decision-making in development is the national government. This is true for the determination of domestic policy as well as for the dealings of underdeveloped countries with neighbors in the world at large. Although not conceptually synonymous, the terms "economic development" and "economic independence" merge powerfully in their psychological appeal. Many leaders and peoples believe their nation cannot be economically free until it becomes economically developed. Conversely, it cannot develop satisfactorily unless it gains relative economic autonomy, if not self-sufficiency. This ambition raises grave questions, one of which is the proper scope of nationalism itself. Within transitional societies, resistance is frequently offered by village, tribal, religious, and other allegiances to the claims of the secular state. In a deep psychic sense, no fully conscious person and no mature religion can totally endorse the proposition that the state is the ultimate and impersonal arbiter of *all* human affairs. Neither persons nor religious institutions, however, can challenge, within the limits of temporal and historical existence, the greater power of the state to play this role. Furthermore, only a secular state or one which practices religious tolerance inspired by secular models can govern a citizenry on a wider basis than the partic-

---

objectors in K. H. Silvert, ed., *Discussion at Bellagio* (American Universities Field Staff, Inc., 1964), pp. 16–27.

[2] Gunnar Myrdal, *Asian Drama* (Pantheon, 1968), I, 257–303.

ularistic bonds to which persons and religious groups give deeper allegiance. Consequently, national governments, which usually act as the most vigorous advocates of developmental change, are rarely trusted by the populations they profess to serve. This explains in part why Third World nations surround their nationalism with the aura of symbol and myth. States are not inclined to surrender or attenuate national sovereignty at the precise moment when they must strengthen it in order to unify their populace and assert themselves in the face of more powerful countries. A serious problem arises because international structures which interfere with the autonomous development of poor countries can be neutralized only by restraining national sovereignty. But it is neither possible nor desirable to restrain nationalism in non-developed countries. In developed countries, on the contrary, such restraint is necessary.

Why this apparent double standard? For the same reason that double tariff structures are defensible on grounds of equity. It is now acknowledged that nascent industrialization in poor countries must be nurtured by protective tariffs whereas rates must be lowered in highly industrialized nations. The demands of equity postulate, therefore, what seems to be, on the surface of things, a double standard. In reality, it is no double standard at all. Nevertheless, many Western thinkers find it difficult to concede that justice does not take universal forms, or that the advocacy of "universal" models can serve particularistic interests—in this case, their own. And so it is with nationalism: strong nations must be the first to limit their sovereignty if a viable world order is to ensue. Yet strong nations are prone to condemn "excessive nationalism" in weaker partners, thereby justifying the maintenance of their own sovereignty until "all countries make the same concessions." As in tariffs, however, equity dictates that initial concessions be made by those countries whose present development helps keep others in a position of structural vulnerability.

Nationalism is but one example of issues which must be settled in the light of normative development strategies based on the principles described in the following chapter. These principles are: that all men must have enough in order to be human, that universal solidarity must be created, and that the populace must have the greatest possible voice in decisions affecting its destiny. From these ethical principles precise strategies must be forged to achieve development's goals—life-sustenance, esteem, and freedom for all men. Change agents must invent appropriate strategies suited to their own specific arenas of decision. Thus, underdeveloped countries will need to devise an ethical strategy to regulate their domestic efforts as well as their dealings with other nations of several types: neighboring underdeveloped nations, distant trading or cultural partners, and others. Developed countries, in turn, must articulate a different practical ethic to cope with under-development within their own borders, to orient their investment, aid, and geopolitical relations with different categories of countries. International organizations, regional and worldwide, must likewise discover coherent normative positions as to their goals, their choice of means, their judgment as to which costs are tolerable in the pursuit of objectives, and their criteria for evaluating performance. One must conclude that no single over-arching ethics of development supplies practical instructions valid for all agents of development operating in all sectors of development activity. Nonetheless, decisions must be reached by all concerned on several fundamental issues: the role of technology, the limits of manipulation in mobilizing people, and the degree of "outside" interference to be tolerated or practiced. Each major actor in the developmental drama must define—in the light of his own values, brought to the surface of critical self-awareness—his role in improving the quality of human life. In order to be meaningful, ethics must meet specific development problems; consequently, normative strategies cannot be defined conceptually and in ideal terms suited to all situations. The exigencies of justice and esteem for the victims of present structures impose what appears to be, in conceptual terms, a double standard. But in reality there is no double standard at all, merely a universal principle which recognizes a certain priority order of needs for life-sustenance, dignity, and freedom for all. Realism no less than justice declares that those in greatest need have prior claims on world resources and on the imaginative energies of men.

Several important questions will need to be answered by permanent research and experimentation with tentative ethical strategies.

It is through mobilization, institutionalization, and legitimization that policies are implemented. Development ethics must, accordingly, define the priority tasks of each of these three instruments and evaluate the tasks which are carried out. Painful options must also be made regarding which values must be changed in a transitional society. How fast, by whom, under what incentives, and in what way will these values be altered? Granted that *some* old values foster privilege, social parasitism, and inhumanly low productivity, no presumption need be made, however, that *all* traditional values must be subordinated to maximizing productivity or generalizing achievement standards in society. Should a merit system in the distribution of economic rewards be adopted in a given society? Should men be forced to enter "necessary" professions against their will? What are the moral limits of manipulating incentive structures in order to induce behavior compatible with "modernity"? There are no clear answers to such questions. They can be answered only if development, like all historical enterprises, is seen as a relative, not an absolute, value. Certain forms of development are not worth the price they exact, and the manner in which development is obtained has a decisive bearing on the kind of man who will be around, at the end of the long march to development, to enjoy its alleged "benefits."

Concern over possible new determinism is no argument for apathy or inaction. It is ethically irresponsible to perpetuate hunger, disease, and premature death. As Furtado reminds us, "underdeveloped peoples are quite prepared to pay a price, even a very heavy one, for their development. . . . the masses are prepared for any sacrifice." [3] Whether or not masses are prepared for any sacrifice, it is unethical to demand unnecessary sacrifices of them. It should be clear, moreover, that a concern for the irresponsible destruction of human value in the name of development must not lead us to romanticize underdevelopment. Men are wasted when they are thwarted from being what they could be, or when they are reduced to being mere instruments of production and consumption. One major task of ethical strategy is to abolish the waste of human potentialities.

No single strategy is suited to all countries, or even to clusters of countries with similar problems. Normative strategies are not autonomous "ethical plans" superimposed on over-all development policies. They are, on the contrary, criteria which remind decision-makers, each time they weigh the merits of alternative policies, that these must not only be efficacious, but must also widen the range of ethical life for all men. There is clearly no ethical life without enhanced freedom and responsibility for men. Since all options create new determinisms, the crucial issue is to make options with a view to gaining optimum control over their finalities. This is why no normative strategy can be fully articulated until specific developmental means are chosen; it is these very means which must be grasped in their relativity and trans-

[3] Celso Furtado, "Brazil: What Kind of Revolution?" in *Economic Development, Evolution or Revolution?* ed. Laura Randall (D. C. Heath and Co., 1964), pp. 36–37.

figured into humanizing forces. Viewed in this light, China's campaign to make intellectuals work in factories and fields is no arbitrary manipulation of a class. On the contrary, it is an effort to instill in professional men populist values which they might otherwise disdain: respect for manual labor, direct contact with primary materials, symbiosis with physical tools. Such mobilization builds up inter-class solidarity and thereby constitutes a profoundly ethical strategy of human resource development.

Great sensitivity and wisdom are required to endow development policies with ethical worth. Ethics must become a "means of the means": a transfiguration of means into something more than purely technical, social, or political instruments. Circumstances alone can reveal whether any given strategy is progressive, regressive, or ambivalent. What, for instance, is the ethical merit of such measures as nationalization, the imposition of stringent monetary controls, the freezing of wages under inflationary conditions? We can never answer the question: is this moral or immoral? Each of these measures can be moral or immoral, depending on total circumstances. Property rights are not absolute and can be superseded. Moralists have always taught that a victim of exploitation may legitimately practice "occult compensation"—that is, he may seize clandestinely and on his own authority some object legally belonging to the exploiter. Urban squatting and rural land invasions are twentieth-century examples of compensation which are no longer "occult." A government may at times seize private property without compensation in payment for past injustices, if that nation lacks the resources to indemnify and if it urgently needs to correct a gravely unjust structure. This does not necessarily mean, of course, that every seizure is moral. However paradoxical it may appear, such an act is moral when it is both necessary and free. "Necessary" here means that it is a prerequisite of release from the stranglehold of dominant economic forces. The act can nonetheless be free if seizure provides the government with additional leverage to foster basic values pursued in development. Such an act is also free if performed without guilt, not merely because its agent possesses greater power than his victim. Freedom is thus seen to be a breakthrough out of resignation in the face of a structurally unjust situation: it is a first step toward self-affirmation.

Neither justice, liberty, nor any historical value can be absolute, however, because values which are not self-limiting beget tyranny or idolatry. Development itself is a limited value. Leaders in

116

underdeveloped countries may be tempted to subordinate their citizens' personal wishes to the cause of nation-building. Yet, in a profoundly Taoist sense, personal wisdom generalized in a society's population is a higher value than a hundred prosperous cities. Pascal long ago argued the superiority of pure love over pure accomplishment. Usually, however, public officials and social theorists are inclined to confer primacy on societal goals and to treat them, for practical purposes, as absolutes. Given this strong tendency, any normative strategy for development must set limits. In real life, of course, and independently of ideologies, nations accept limits. Mao regards the erection of authentic Chinese Communism to be more important than economic development. And Castro deems the quality of Cuban social relations to be more important than crop diversification or heavy industrialization. Long ago Salazar decided that stability and cultural pride brought greater benefits to Portugal than mere economic "progress" or political modernization.

Relatively few national leaders have formulated explicit normative strategies to guide their pursuit of development. Theoretically, if not in fact, industrial build-up in Socialist countries is subordinated to the creation of a "new man." Although it lies beyond the scope of the present work, an appraisal of China's performance would prove instructive in this regard. China's official policy rejects with equal vigor both the bourgeois vision of comfort and passive acceptance of mass poverty. While resisting the world's technological power centers, China strives to achieve breakthroughs in technology itself: atomic prowess, steel production, rational fertilizer campaigns. Its aim is to reshape the objective world in accord with its own self-image, itself in perpetual evolution. China's normative strategy aims at producing large numbers of heroic revolutionaries who will resist the twin blandishments of mass consumption and the international status which comes from being a "responsible" nation. If alienating mass consumption is to be averted, technology must be assiduously cultivated, although subordinated to ideology and politics. If pressures to accept "respectable" international standards are to be neutralized, accommodation with other political systems has to be denounced as a betrayal of basic Chinese cultural values. Only after outsiders begin to respect these values can the posture be modified. So goes the Chinese argument. Far from being mysterious or enigmatic, this strategy, once understood, allows one to "make sense" of China's foreign policy, her internal manpower decisions, even her tolerance of vestigial "capitalists" in key industries

117

and of residual "colonialism": Hong Kong, Macao, and, in China's eyes, Taiwan. In China more than in any other country the long march toward development is expressed in explicit ethical terms concerning the basic quality of life and the central values of a civilization.

Nevertheless, every development policy contains an implicit ethical strategy. This strategy may dictate that industrialization is to be gained at all costs, or that all values must be sacrificed to greater wealth, prestige, and power, conceived in nationalistic terms. Or the latent strategy may condone maximum consumer comforts for minority groups while simultaneously initiating, cautiously and controllably, marginalized groups into economic and social circuits where rewards and mobility are greater than before. These are all very imperfect strategies; indeed, no perfect strategy can ever be devised. Perhaps all that is now possible is to warn against the harm caused by unchallenged strategies and to evaluate the small number of explicit strategies presently observable. It is not enough even for indigenous leaders and elite to entertain noble ideals concerning desired values. What is needed is widespread endorsement of the ethical values which lie at the heart of development: life-sustenance for all, optimum esteem, and freedom. Development policy becomes an ethically valid strategy if its inner dynamic leads it to optimize life-sustenance and material improvement for all; to institute reciprocal esteem for all individuals, classes, groups, interests, nations; and to open a new gamut of possibilities for all categories of freedom. Until they are translated into rights and duties enforced upon all members of a social system, however, norms remain meaningless. A minimal list of essential rights and duties would include the following:

1. Every society is entitled to have access to the resources it needs in order to provide minimum quantities of life-sustaining goods to all its members.

2. Poor nations have prior claims on the resources contained within their boundaries, independently of the sufficiency of capital they may have available to exploit those resources.

3. Nations with high levels of living and abundant resources are under obligation to needier nations to grant them some access to a part of their own resources.

4. The precise form to be taken by this access, and the time span over which it must extend, are not predetermined. Realistic policymakers must invent practical answers to these questions.

5. The rights just mentioned are also operative, *mutatis mutandis,*

118

among diversely endowed social classes, interest groups, and individuals within nations. These rights can be effectively exercised only if reciprocal obligations are acknowledged and enforced. Although life-sustenance is a minimum need for all men, it does not follow that no other needs can be satisfied until misery is universally abolished. Even poor men spend portions of their scanty resources on such "gratuitous" activities as festivity, celebration, and emotional release from the constraints of penury. However irrational such manifestations appear in terms of pure economic calculus, they are an essential part of men's quest for esteem. Therefore,

6. Recognition or esteem must not be accorded primarily on the basis of wealth possessed or functional excellence. Logically, this means that societies must not be based on the integral application of an achievement reward system which thwarts the promotion of the esteem-needs of society's total membership. The failure of many change agents to accept this constitutes a leading cause of "resistance to modernization" by underdeveloped communities.

Underdeveloped nations are also entitled to receive political esteem in the arena of international affairs. Normative strategies must therefore devise ways of rewarding reciprocity and respect instead of domination and self-glorification. Since interdependence is inevitable, it is idle for the ethician to speak only of rights within poor nations and only of duties in rich countries. The first emphasis may mask structures of domination and legitimize palliative solutions. The second emphasis implies that development depends primarily on "converting" rich nations to a posture of good will, a false and unrealistic assumption. *Development ethics must contest the established order, which is the order of underdevelopment for the majority of men in the world.* As a minimum, ethics advocates the following changes:

a. the organization of production and distribution of wealth so as to assure minimum satisfaction of basic physiological, psychological, and esthetic needs to all members of the human race;

b. the elimination of flagrant economic and social inequalities among and within societies;

c. the suppression of domination by powerful groups (nations, elites, social classes, privileged individuals, parasitical coteries) over weaker groups;

d. a challenge to the legitimacy of all institutions which contribute to the maintenance of these disorders;

e. the rejection of all accommodation strategies which enable those presently enjoying positions of privilege to "domesticate" development efforts of others in such wise as to leave these privileges intact.

These deficient structures must be replaced by:

a. A network of reciprocal obligations between wealthy and poor based on priority needs of all men.

b. Machinery for decision-making at all levels in which paternalism is minimized.

c. Optimization of "potential freedom": the ability of each man and each cultural group effectively to resist manipulation by others.

d. The introduction of interpersonal and intersocietal solidarities based on a community of existence, of ecology, and of destiny. These solidarities limit untrammeled individualism and total collectivization with equal force. Solidarities are not assumed to exist: they must be created to meet the twin demands of self-interest and of communality.

e. The provision of sufficient educational opportunities to all men throughout their lifetimes so that they may share in the collective knowledge of the human race and become capable of exercising authentic options regarding the values to which they will give allegiance.

None of these goals can be reached immediately. Therefore, strategies must be designed to help societies with divergent interests and capabilities to take steps to "free the present from the past."

Moreover, all progress is fundamentally ambiguous. Practical choices are necessary regarding the price paid to obtain successive, though not necessarily progressive, approximations toward a more equitable and freer life, expressed in a variety of cultural and societal modes. The development process, like Pandora's box, contains many surprises. No one knows whether development, once achieved, can make men happier or reduce conflict among them. But development can eliminate certain well-known forms of human misery. Perhaps generalized development can do no more than satisfy what Maslow calls men's pre-potent needs. Once these are satisfied, men may be healthy enough to pursue more consciously and deliberately than before their lifelong needs for self-fulfillment, however these be defined. Even for orthodox Marxists the advent of the classless society does not eliminate all problems. As Pierre Hervé wrote in 1946, "Communist society will be one where men will still have to struggle, where problems will still exist, where contradictions will still be present. Were it to be otherwise, we should have a dead society, in a sense it would be the end of humanity." [4]

[4] Cited in Henri Chambre, *De Karl Marx à Mao Tse-tung* (Paris: Editions Spes, 1959), p. 289.

Inasmuch as satisfactory normative strategies cannot be fully drawn up until precise choices present themselves, underdeveloped nations ought to pursue three over-all goals. The first is to acquire and consolidate some measure of national autonomy. The components of autonomy are relative control over the workings of the national economy; political identity as a national polity in command of its own domestic decisions; the possession of a discernibly separate voice in international affairs; and a cultural identity solid enough to assure internal cohesion and differentiation from other cultural units. Chauvinistic nationalism or absolute sovereignty cannot be ethically good. Nationalism is good only to the extent that it fosters a society's quest for dignity, freedom, and mastery over wants, and prepares that society for the abdication, at some ulterior period, of nationalism itself in favor of political association with other states, whether under a global federation, confederation, unitary state, or other form. A second general aim is to optimize the participation of a populace in significant decision-making and to provide checks against manipulation by elites. Authority must abolish privilege and create new ground rules for rendering social, political, and cultural mobility universal. Unresolved tensions between the demands of democracy and those of efficiency abide. Yet, in the long term, efficiency itself requires diffused responsibility. Conversely, general participation is meaningless unless accompanied by diffused knowledge and operative skills, without which realistic options in response to complex problems cannot be made. We ignore how far subjective will can substitute for objective conditions in the process of modernization. Subjective conditions can substitute to some degree for objective conditions in the conduct of revolution. But how far substitution is possible in over-all development strategy remains unknown.

The scale of an enterprise and the human density it involves are germane to the quest for answers. Thus, computers can process all the information required by immense numbers of men, but how can computers be programmed in non-elitist fashion? Assuming this is possible, how protect society against moral errors approved by the majority? The problem grows more serious as the numbers of men on the planet increase.

A third goal is to educate men to a value system in which austerity, imposed at first but becoming voluntary with the passage of time, replaces unbridled material desires. Heraclitus wisely believed that "it is not good for men to get all they wish to get. It is the opposite which is good for us." No social body can remain vital unless some balance exists between its desire mechanisms and the real access to resources it provides to its members. In many "underdeveloped" settings, social wisdom curbs acquisitive desires because the unfettered wishes of all cannot be gratified without producing social catastrophe. Among development advocates the myth prevails that the technical capacity to create infinite wealth justifies removing all curbs from desire mechanisms. This is to assume that everyone can reach the good life through the abundance of goods. Several fallacies lie hidden in this naïve equation, however:

1. consumption in the Third World cannot be substantially improved until productive capacity is greatly expanded:

2. new aspirations usually center on consumer goods having lower priority than urgently needed vital goods;

3. unbridled consumer aspirations interfere with the growth of solidarity among differentiated classes, whose self-consciousness is newly emerging;

4. the absence of limits on desire reinforces the tendency inherent in technological processes to become absolute goals instead of simple means; and

5. desires themselves are, on evidence, unsatiable. To foster the illusion that they can be satiated prepares the way for generalized social anomie, frustration, and *acedia*.

These, in summary, are the general requirements of normative strategies. I shall now inquire into the normative principles which ought to regulate development.

CHAPTER SIX

Three Strategic Principles

The strategic principles of development are normative judgments as to how goals ought to be pursued. They provide standards for devising solutions to specific problems and for appraising performance.

The first of these principles states that the good life is not defined by the abundance of goods, although men must surely "have" enough goods if they are "to be" good men. The second principle asserts the need for global solidarity in development. It views development as the integral ascent of all men and all societies: the quintessence of cultural, spiritual, and esthetic maturation, as well as of economic and social improvement. But development's benefits must extend to all societies and to every person in society; solidarity is meaningless if it is restricted. A third principle postulates optimum participation in decision-making as desirable. Development must be pursued in such a way that all men are allowed to become agents of their own social destiny.

Before discussing these principles in detail, I wish to answer two preliminary questions: (1) What is the order of priority among goals themselves? (2) Can the goals be considered terminal states?

No inert imagery can adequately portray the relationships among the several goals of development: it is futile to list them in static fashion as first, second, or third. Life is clearly not worth sustaining unless it can be lived with some measure of dignity. And genuine freedom is impossible if esteem is totally lacking or if one's livelihood is too precarious. It is no tautology to say that life exists so that men can give meaning to life; life is both a precondition for the realization of all human values and itself the term of those values. To live *well* is the ultimate reason for living at all. Hence, all other values are instrumental to the good life. Freedom from ignorance and disease is subordinated to freedom for actualization. Whether one thinks of human fulfillment in terms of existential philosophy, Zen wisdom, Marxian socialism, or cosmic hominization as outlined by Teilhard de Chardin, any significant statement as to the relative importance of goals implies some view of the final purposes of human existence.

Divergent philosophies of life nonetheless concur in certain broad social goals: all regard life as worth protecting, esteem as valuable, and freedom from needless constraints as desirable. Conflicting definitions of man abound, on the other hand. For some, man is the fragile possibility of freedom hurled into an absurd metaphysical space known as existence; others postulate a fixed essence to which man must be true; for still others, man is a feebly emerging rationality who is part of a vast evolutionary movement toward ever more complex and diversified forms of life. All these notions assume a final direction which confers meaning on human effort. Implicitly at least, personal perfection and group perfection are presented as models which suggest, if they do not embody, an ideal. Realistic social philosophers know that Utopianism is inapplicable to earthly conditions. This is why they propose the "ideal" as a pattern toward which societies can only strive by successive approximations. The ideal will never be attained, but is a standard against which partial achievements are evaluated.

The conclusion to be drawn is that development is not a self-validating goal. Under certain aspects it is sought for its own sake, but at a deeper level development is subordinated to the good life. Harbison and Myers assure us that "there need be no conflict between the economists and the humanists. . . . The development of man for himself may still be considered the ultimate end, but economic progress can also be one of the principal means of attaining it." [1]

It matters greatly what significance is attached to development. At a gathering of scholars in Rheinfelden, Switzerland, in 1960, Raymond Aron argued that even if material scarcity could be universally abolished, societies would place different interpretations on their ma-

[1] Frederick Harbison and Charles A. Myers, *Education, Manpower, and Economic Growth* (McGraw-Hill, 1964), p. 13.

terial prosperity.[2] George Kennan thought that developed societies can do little more than provide members with a "reasonable stake of choices" with which to occupy their leisure time. But Jeanne Hersch objected that human life goes deeper than the range of choices available for achieving cultural fulfillment. According to her, human life includes mysterious tragic elements, and no degree of "development" can truly solve problems of identity and meaning. She feared that exaggerated material development could make men powerless to make profound value choices because they will have become "distracted" (in the Pascalian sense) by the abundance of goods and activities from properly human considerations.[3]

Development, therefore, quite as much as underdevelopment, poses value problems. We are thus reminded of the relativity present in any concept of human fulfillment. If development's goals are life-sustenance, esteem, and freedom, no priority among these goals can be established except as a function of some precise image of desired realization. Even this formulation remains ambiguous because, in the view of many, the exercise of freedom is itself the highest form of actualization, independently of stipulated goals or moral content. The interplay among the goals of development is dialectical; life-sustenance, esteem, and freedom interact in ever shifting patterns of mutual reinforcement or conflictual tension. A high degree of freedom from wants and of self-esteem is compatible with a society having low life-sustenance or low out-group esteem, provided disruptive effects from outside are weak. If it is sheltered from other images of life and its wants remain few and simple, a society can subsist with a high degree of social cohesion and member satisfaction. "Remote" cultures are doubtless finding it ever more difficult to isolate themselves from modernity.[4] Nevertheless, basic options as to goals affect any society's major institutions: its form of government, educational system, and economic incentives. Conversely, economic abundance and high prestige are compatible with low levels of genuine want-satisfaction, low self-esteem, and low freedom. A "developed" society's wants may increase so quickly as to be insatiable. The combination of expanding

---

[2] In Raymond Aron, ed., *Colloques de Rheinfelden* (Paris: Calmann-Levy, 1960), p. 89. The English translation is *World Technology and Human Destiny* (University of Michigan Press, 1963).

[3] *Ibidem*, p. 256.

[4] For a striking example, cf. the study of Australian primitives by John Greenway, "We Are All Aborigines in a New World," *The New York Times Magazine*, November 10, 1968, pp. 30 ff.

wants, industrial power, and technological modernity can bring prestige to such a society while leaving its members profoundly dissatisfied and insecure as to their identity. Numerous combinations of the three factors are possible. What is important is to recognize the qualitative difference between freedom *from* wants and freedom *for* wants. The first exists when genuine human needs are adequately met, the latter when men control the dynamisms by which their wants are multiplied. The essential point is not how many wants can be met, but the degree of mastery men exercise over the forces by which their wants are generated. If entry into mass-consumer economic patterns is achieved in alienating fashion, it creates a society wherein a contradiction exists between happiness and freedom.

The strategic principles of development refer the goals of development to humane ways of obtaining these goals. Without imposing precise operating norms, they suggest limits within which policies may be conducted.

The reply to the first question formulated above, therefore, is as follows:

The priority goal is freedom for the actualization or fulfillment, variously defined, of persons living in community. Nevertheless, all three goals must coexist in a state of creative tension if any single one is to survive. Thus, freedom for actualization is impossible without some degree of life-sustenance and esteem, themselves conditioned by varying historical forces and images. Similarly, esteem and life-sustenance cannot flourish unless accompanied by some measure of freedom.

It lies outside the scope of this work to determine whether any models of self-actualization enjoy validity across cultural lines. Worthy of note, nonetheless, is Maslow's[5] view that autonomy in the face of environmental stimuli is the defining characteristic of full individuality and true freedom in individuals. If this be so, many persons in "underdeveloped" societies may be more "developed," psychologically speaking, than members of affluent technological civilizations who are enslaved to external stimuli, not the least of which is compulsive advertising. This raises the unsettling possibility that progress in freedom *from* constraints may entail regression in freedom *for* internal self-actualization. It need not be so, however, if we attend to *how*

[5] Abraham Maslow, *Toward a Psychology of Being* (D. Van Nostrand Co., 1962), p. 33. On this point Maslow's views coincide with those of Christian Bay, *The Structure of Freedom* (Atheneum, 1965), pp. 83ff.

126

freedom from constraints is obtained. A high level of material emancipation need not exclude a high degree of autonomy from external stimuli. Celso Furtado judges it "probable that in the future material abundance will coexist with forms of socio-political organization which permit the full realization of authentic human values." [6] If this is to be achieved, however, a wisdom which is conspicuously lacking in today's "developed" societies will be needed. "Underdeveloped" lands suffer from the opposite deficiency: they have no "science to match their own wisdoms." For both kinds of societies, therefore, the development process raises universal value questions.

I shall refrain from asking whether actualization resides ultimately in the personal selfhood of each man or in his societal being (however defined). This dichotomy is a false one, and many solutions are admissible. Nor shall I repeat here what I have written elsewhere on different actualization values lying within or outside historical experience.[7] What needs to be stressed is the self-validating quality of ultimate ends and the correlative proposition that development is an instrumental end. This is an inversion of the usual treatment by theorists who discuss development as though it were a terminal goal and view other values as impediments or aids to development. This procedure is legitimate, provided it is recognized as a methodical fiction serving the purely utilitarian purposes of setting program priorities. At a more critical level, however, the terms of the development equation must be inverted and values must be treated non-instrumentally. Otherwise, human rationality will prove unable to assert itself in the face of the tendency displayed by efficiency and productivity to absolutize themselves, independently of alternative human goals.

The answer to the second question, therefore, is that only in a relative sense are the goals of development terminal states. Like history itself, development is an open-ended, ambiguous adventure whose ultimate meaning is created by man. Provided technological and ecological standardization do not gain full sway, men can create different meanings for themselves, whether in great poverty or in great wealth. When compared with "developed" societies, all "traditional" societies seem to share certain attributes—ascriptive standards, non-differentiated social functions, and so on. Among themselves, on the other

[6] Celso Furtado, "Brazil: What Kind of Revolution?" in Laura Randall, ed., *Economic Development, Evolution or Revolution?* (D. C. Heath, 1964), p. 38.
[7] Denis A. Goulet, "Secular History and Teleology," *World Justice*, Vol. III, No. 1 (September 1966), pp. 5–19.

hand, their self-images and symbols are highly varied. By analogy, industrial societies could give rise to diverse life-styles and ultimate explanations of life, death, suffering, and love. Not that all societies will become mass-consumer societies, or that all which set out to do so will succeed. The point is that "development" signifies the end of human freedom if it results in full homogenization of values and culture. Admittedly, one cannot rule this possibility out on *a priori* grounds. But if development processes breed iron determinism, it is futile to plan social change in the belief that to do so is more rational than to submit passively to unplanned change. To Bertrand Russell's question "Has man a future?" we must reply that it depends in equal measure on the goals he sets himself and the means he chooses for reaching them. Were man to lose the possibility of choice in his selection of means, his future would be imposed by the very mechanisms of the processes he underwent. Such a future is not a *human* future. Russell judges that modern man is suffering from undigested science; he therefore pleads for an educational system which would allow this undigested mass to be assimilated.[8]

The folly Russell fears most is nuclear extermination. But the alternate folly of losing control over processes which lead to abundance is no less alarming. This is why men must be alerted to the ethical costs of their development. We are not certain of being able to control the world simply by understanding it. Of one thing, however, we are sure; we cannot control it if we do not understand it. It matters little how much information we possess about development if we have not grasped its inner meaning. The search for meaning has led us to render explicit the goals of development and to conclude that all goals must coexist simultaneously. Authentic growth, which is a continuous process ever thrusting individuals and societies beyond goals already achieved, is never definitive. What then are its governing principles?

First Principle: To "Have Enough" in Order to "Be More"

The fullness of good and the abundance of goods are not synonymous: a man may *have* much and *be* mediocre or *have* little and *be* rich. Nevertheless, men need to have a certain quantity of goods in order to be fully human. The corollary is that some goods enhance

[8] Bertrand Russell, *Has Man a Future?* (Penguin Books, 1967), pp. 126–127.

128

man's being more than others. These statements cannot be understood unless we first inquire into the reasons why men need to "have" goods at all.

All organisms must go outside themselves to be perfected. A limited being could perfect itself by drawing on its internal resources only if its needs were coextensive with its limitations. A perfect being, on the other hand, would have no desires at all; or if it had them, it could draw upon its own existential wealth to gain satisfaction. Man's needs express the particular dynamism of his conditioned existence in time and space. Biological needs dictate the assimilation of outside elements: air, food, water. The ontological significance of needs resides in this: that if man were fully perfect, he would not need to need. If on the other hand he were totally imperfect, he would be incapable of needing certain goods. An illustration is found in comparing a withered hand, incapable of feeling a burn, to a healthy one which senses the painful stimulus caused by fire and reacts to protect itself. Men have needs because their existence is rich enough to be capable of development, but too poor to realize all potentialities at one time or with their own resources. Men draw other beings into their orbit to sustain their own precarious act of existence. And although man has managed to escape from nothingness, he will revert to nothingness unless his existence is nurtured.

Beyond survival, man seeks goods capable of enriching his existence. By action, passion, desire, choice, and realization he adds new qualities to his naked act of being. Even his need for non-essential things is a summons to be more. Thus, when man "has" things, he "is" more than he was before. "To have" helps him "to be." So true is this that unless man "has" minimum goods, he ceases to "be" altogether. Even when he has enough to be, he feels stunted in his being until he has more.

"To have," in the ontological sense, is not to own in economic or juridical terms, but to assimilate for vital inner purposes. Juridical and economic notions of property are derivative. One understands this by reflecting on the futility of having property rights or title to such vital goods as air or food. It does a man no good to "own" these goods in any legal sense unless he can use and absorb them. Conversely, it makes no difference who "owns" these goods provided the man in question has access to them. Economic possession or legal property becomes relevant to the extent that scarce objects cannot be interiorized by a living being unless they are first "possessed." This is a relational term, because an object is possessed only with reference to someone who is excluded from use. Clearly, this has nothing to do with possessing internal riches such as knowledge, talent, wisdom, or health. Internal riches are distinct from external goods, the kind now under discussion. At any given time man *is* less than he can *become,* and what he can become depends largely on what he can have. In order to become more, men must have "enough." The central questions are: How much is enough? And does the term "enough" have objective meaning?

"Enough" is relative when applied to some quantity of goods presumed necessary to human fulfillment. No one can say how much is enough without first stating what man's capacities are and how important it is for man to develop these capacities. Notwithstanding relativities brought to light by anthropologists and psychologists, we can make sense out of this seemingly unmanageable question. General agreement exists that "excessive" poverty stunts human lives. Gandhi saw misery as a special kind of hell, and whoever lives with destitute groups knows first-hand that disease, apathy, and escapism diminish humanity. As a minimum, to have "enough" must mean that men's basic biological needs are met sufficiently so that they can devote part of their energies to affairs beyond subsistence.

Life is considerably more than survival, a full stomach, or a warm body. If the goals of development are life-sustenance, esteem, and freedom, men need those goods without which they cannot gain esteem and freedom. A wide range of goods may be psychologically and socially necessary for the "good life." Although we here swim in the high seas of relativity, most men, once they awaken to modern possibilities, aspire to some share in the world's knowledge, mastery over nature, and sense of discovery. Accordingly, educational and opportunity needs and the desire for association with the collective efforts of men to explore knowledge and technology acquire new importance even for humble farmers, fishermen, housewives, and artisans. As a result, such people may genuinely "need" newspapers, books, radios, and bicycles.

One may object that this fluid concept of "enough" sets no operational limits to the amount and kinds of goods which ought to be supplied. The objection is met by making judgments about the suitability of different goods to satisfy human needs. An object or service is desirable only in virtue of a real or presumed compatibility between that thing and man's being. Minimal correspondence rests on the fact

130

that both exist. "Good" is what is perceived as apt to satisfy a need; this proportionality between a needy being and an object judged fit to satisfy need is a second level of correspondence. Within this perspective, "to have enough" is to have those goods without which men cannot "be" or "be well." One reason why the term "enough" appears completely relative to many observers is that they have grown unaccustomed to assess putative needs in the light of the value systems, overt or covert, which underlie them. If, on the other hand, the values latent in systems of need-satisfaction are rendered explicit, some light appears as to what constitutes "enough." The decisive question is: enough of what for what? And the reply is rooted in historical relations among men and societies. Consequently, we must observe how little some men have in the light of how much others have. This is so because "enough" is determined by men's conscious perceptions at different times, not by minimum standards set by experts in objective terms.

Needy men lack "enough" not only relative to what affluent neighbors possess, but in absolute terms as well. Millions of human beings lack enough to live lives suited to the human condition, regardless of what others have. Whatever be the theoretical difficulties of logically defining "enough," who can deny that millions of paupers in India do not have "enough" to live human lives? Who can seriously affirm that there is no difference between the struggle for survival waged by an Egyptian fellah, a Bolivian sharecropper, or a "coloured" South African mining worker and the placid need-satisfaction of prosperous businessmen or professionals? After surveying the living conditions of Manchester's poor workmen a century ago, Engels concluded that "workers' dwellings of Manchester are dirty, miserable and wholly lacking in comforts. *In such houses only inhuman, degraded and unhealthy creatures would feel at home.*" [9]

Not moral passion but knowledge of factual conditions leads men to view extreme poverty as an "inhuman" state of affairs. Myrdal, Josue de Castro, Lebret, and other development writers have evoked the anomalies of world economic structures which allow millions of men to live in squalor while others tax their ingenuity to find new ways of wasting goods. While millions suffer deficiency diseases caused by malnutrition, a few favored men fall prey to hitherto un-

[9] Friedrich Engels, "The Condition of the Working Class in England in 1844," *Engels: Selected Writings,* ed. W. O. Henderson (Penguin Books, 1967), p. 51.

known degenerative diseases induced by excessive food and drink. Under such circumstances, it is trivial to claim that the notion of "enough goods" is a relative one not amenable to analytical or operational precision. The stark illogical fact is that millions of men do not have enough food, medicine, clothing, and shelter to live human lives. Their quest for full humanity is thwarted by an insufficiency of goods. The man driven by chronic hunger is either obsessed with food or grows apathetic. When one has no defense against sickness or death, he clings to life with brutal ferocity or he vegetates in resigned expectation of fate. In both cases, he becomes something less than a man. Even destitute men at times display remarkable wisdom, lucidity, fortitude, creativity, or compassion, but such exceptional victories testify to the indomitable strength of man's spirit, not to the adequacy of his social conditions. Notwithstanding these exceptions, the physical conditions of "underdevelopment" deprive men of goods normally required for them to "be fully human."

This absolute dearth of necessities is aggravated by a growing awareness among the poor of shocking inequalities and of technology's power to abolish misery. They instinctively conclude that there are enough goods in the world to meet the needs of all, but not enough to satisfy the greed of each one. The problem now assumes a surprising new dimension and the question becomes: can rich men or affluent societies live worthy lives in a world where masses lack essential goods?

No facile answer will do, for Veblen and others have convincingly traced the role of prosperity and leisure in producing culture. Great collective works of art and the seven wonders of the world have all been borne in travail on the backs of toiling slaves or exploited servants. Besides, as Galbraith once quipped, "wealth is not without its advantages and the case for the contrary, although it has often been made, has never proved widely persuasive." [10] Accordingly, one hesitates to speak of some absolute ceiling of wealth beyond which each additional possession would diminish the moral quality of its owner. For centuries Western tradition has taught that "superfluous" wealth is morally acceptable if put to a noble use or enjoyed in a noble spirit. Nevertheless, great wealth easily leads men to rationalize their insensitivity to the pressing needs of others. We need to know whether any essential difference exists between "superfluity" in the past and in the

[10] John Kenneth Galbraith, *The Affluent Society* (London: Hamish Hamilton, 1958), p. 1.

present. Contemporary global consciousness adverts to two facts: (a) the mass of men lack "enough" basic goods; and (b) technological means for eliminating misery exist. These means have not yet been harnessed to social institutions capable of achieving this goal. Given these circumstances, can the existence of "superfluous" wealth in the hands of a few individuals, classes, and nations be justified?

Two opposite traditions regarding the legitimacy of "superfluous" goods have existed within Christianity. One expresses "truth" in static terms, the other dynamically. According to the static tradition, every man has a "station in life" within which a given level of expenditure is morally acceptable. If he is king or prince, he may spend as king or prince. But if he is a modest yeoman, his style of life should be that of his peers. Anyone possessing wealth beyond that required to "maintain" himself at his proper level is morally bound to give part of his superfluous wealth to needier individuals or groups. As time passed, authorized interpreters of this principle introduced upward mobility into the concept of "station in life." A further refinement of the doctrine judged a rich man's moral worth by his over-all commitment to society rather than by any specific allocation of wealth to the poor. The more dynamic ethic of superfluous wealth was formulated by early Fathers of the Church, notably Basil the Great and John Chrysostom. Its cardinal principle is that all wealth, natural and manmade, is destined by God to serve the needs of all men. Consequently, men are permitted to "appropriate" wealth only to serve the common needs of humanity. This is the well-known "steward-responsible-to-God" theory. Basil and Chrysostom minced no words, accusing the wealthy of having "stolen" whatever goods they possessed over and above their own needs.[11] Centuries later Gandhi also declared that pervasive poverty has a terrifying effect on those who enjoy wealth. "Whenever I live in a situation where others are in need," he said, "whether or not I am responsible for it, I have become a thief."[12] By giving alms to the poor, therefore, wealthy men simply restitute what rightfully belongs to the poor. These and similar arguments were usually based on Scripture texts. They assumed that all men believed in a

[11] These paragraphs are based on such works as: *A Pobreza na Igreja* (São Paulo: Livraria Duas Cidades, no date), an anthology of writings on wealth by church figures; Robert Theobald, ed., *Dialogue on Poverty* (Bobbs-Merrill, 1967); *Maitriser l'Opulence* (Economie et Humanisme, 1964); P. R. Regamey, *Pauvreté Chrétienne et Construction du Monde* (Aubier: Editions Montaigne, 1967).

[12] Quoted in *Dialogue on Poverty*, p. 60.

Creator who is the final judge of men's "stewardship." Although a review of these positions is not without historical interest, it is more pertinent here to explore the issue of "superfluity" in the context of a secular world wherein numerous views of the origin and destiny of the universe compete. What is needed, in a word, is an inquiry into the basis for a *rational ethic* of the relations between abundance and mass destitution.

That absolute want exists alongside relative superfluity is an incontestable fact. More than half of the human race lives in chronic deprivation while a small percentage of men wastes prodigally. The relative excess of goods enjoyed by the minority contrasts sharply with absolute want in the majority. But does relative surfeit lessen the quality of human existence, or, in Fromm's terms, does alienation flow from misplaced abundance as surely as it does from destitution?

Viewed collectively, the perpetuation of relative superfluity alongside absolute insufficiency for most men necessarily entails a stunting of the human race. Because contacts are unavoidable, the desires of the poor are constantly aroused by demonstration effects.

Predictably, men will not tolerate huge disparity if they suffer absolute want. If those in abundance continue regarding their own affluence as justified, they will perforce become insensitive to others' pressing needs. Now that the poor articulate their demands, one cannot in good faith close his eyes to their misery. The privileged and the needy share a common faith in the power of technology to abolish misery. As Myrdal explains, however, the poor "put part of the blame for their poverty on the rest of the world and, in particular, on the countries which are better off—or, rather they attribute the inequalities to the world economic system which keeps them so poor while other nations are so rich and becoming richer." [13] Not only do a majority of people in the world lack the bare minimum, but the gap between rich and poor is widening. And Lebret warns that "increasing literacy will make a non-privileged people become more aggressive toward the privileged members of their own race and also toward those other countries which are better off." [14]

Insensitive men, quite as much as those who are undernourished, are stunted men. "Human quality" consists in perceiving reality as it truly is and in having compassion for fellow humans. One conse-

[13] Gunnar Myrdal, *Economic Theory and Under-developed Regions* (London: Duckworth, 1963), p. 7.
[14] L. J. Lebret, *The Last Revolution* (Sheed and Ward, 1965), p. 88.

quence of the rebellion by the wretched of the earth is to show mankind's privileged members that they can no longer, under pain of dehumanization, adopt attitudes of equanimity and self-justification in the face of disparities which formerly seemed acceptable. The rich are now "responsible" for abolishing absolute want in others even if they have not been "guilty" of producing it in the past. The distinction between responsibility and guilt is crucial. Responsiblity concerns the present and the future; it presupposes freedom—that is, the possibility of responding to an exigency which is perceived and accepted. Responsibility is founded on the belief that human agents are not always subject to absolute determinisms, but rather that they can respond to the solicitation of goals perceived by them as humanly worthy. Precisely because they are human, men are "responsible" for creating conditions which optimize the humanization of life. Guilt, on the contrary, is the negative burden of past fault or injustice. Guilt is passive and recriminating, not active and creative. In an illuminating essay on "collective responsibility," P. Antoine explains that "individuals, groups and nations which, even by ethical means, have secured for themselves an advantageous, strong and prosperous position in the world, and by so doing have impeded (even if it is only indirectly because goods available on this planet are limited) the economic development or the social promotion of other individuals or other peoples, are responsible to the latter for the deprivation and they ought to remedy it, by making use of the very possibilities which their better position confers on them . . . an obligation rooted in justice can exist, as a consequence of our acts, even when no fault of injustice has been committed." [15]

Thus, the "responsibility" of rich classes and nations for creating justice does not rest on a scapegoat theory of history which would brand them "guilty" of the unequal distribution of riches. Recent experiences between black communities and white communities in the United States demonstrate that the desire of well-meaning whites to redeem "guilt" feelings is the worst basis on which to base cooperative action with blacks. There is, moreover, a qualitative difference between neurotic guilt and what Maslow calls "real" or "humanistic" guilt.[16] The rich are responsible for abolishing the absolute poverty of their fellow human beings. Therefore, they can refuse to do so only at

[15] Pierre Antoine, "Qui Est Coupable?" in *Revue de l'Action Populaire*, No. 32 (November 1959), pp. 1055–65.
[16] Maslow, *op. cit.*, p. 114.

the price of stunting their own humanity. For this reason, the maintenance of superfluity alongside massive absolute want is dehumanizing both for those who have and for those who have not.

The dynamics of social conflict which permits a few men to increase surplus wealth also works dialectically to pressure them to share that wealth. Countervailing energies released by untrammeled accumulation generate powerful demands for economic compensation. As privileges mount, so does the rebellious spirit of victims. Exploitation and conspicuous consumption can be pushed only so far before marginalized men assert their claims by rebelling. If pushed too far, desperate men will tear down the old order even if they have no hope of building a new order. This dialectic interplay between the insensitive accumulation of superfluous wealth and perpetuated misery is neither fatalistic destiny nor nature's moral vengeance on men's hardness of heart. Rather it is the natural outcome of dynamisms operative in society ever since the first technological revolution maximized, concurrently with the accumulation possibilities of the few, the hope of emancipation from need in the many. To conclude that such a suicidal and destructive climax to the pursuit of wealth destroys human value is also to assert that the attitude of privilege which exacerbates this condition is dehumanizing.

There is a further reason why superfluous wealth can prove socially destructive. Economic goods surreptitiously tend to substitute themselves for human good. To be a good man easily comes to mean, in a society where the pursuit of economic goods is dominant, to own more goods. The spread of conspicuous consumption in advanced countries has already revolutionized the image of the good life in the world. Men's notions of "being more" increasingly come to mean "having more." As long as men desired more goods from a low plateau, "having more" represented genuine progress toward "being more." And it would be rash to postulate any "absolute" threshold of superfluity above which man is automatically dehumanized. Nevertheless, unbridled surrender to processes aimed at generating more goods poses special value problems. By nature, economic goods are utility goods. Thanks to the wily imperialism of consumption, however, useful goods tend to become absolute or self-validating goods. This monumental inversion of values—well under way in "developed" countries—augurs a disturbing future. It obscures the difference among priorities in needs. Worse still, it sows unrealistic hopes in underdeveloped populaces and prevents advanced countries from

136

making structural changes in world market mechanisms and their productive systems demanded by worldwide development. "Developed" countries refuse to redirect their own economic progress or revise their over-all economic effort in terms of priority needs.

Economically speaking, it matters little whether men spend wisely or wastefully. Insofar as he is a responsible social critic, however, even the economist must feel troubled over waste and compulsive consumption. Although he warns his readers not to be deluded by Socialist utopias of wealth-redistribution, Alfred Marshall nonetheless refuses to acquiesce in wealth inequalities. "The drift of economic science during many generations has been with increasing force toward the belief that there is no real necessity, and therefore no moral justification for extreme poverty side by side with great wealth." [17] Marshall thinks it may be desirable to lower the wealth level of those at the highest rung if this helps raise that of those at the lowest rung. Later in this work I advocate world-wide "austerity" and explain the difference between imposed and voluntary austerity. But austerity cannot be imposed on the world's poor nations unless developed societies also accept a measure of voluntary austerity. To be sure, judiciously selective austerity must contribute to the transformation of world structures with a view to the development of all men. Critical examination must be made of the extent to which different levels of material abundance affect freedom and man's capacity for growth. A major ethical crisis may be in the making because, in Lebret's words, "The rich are covetous, desiring more than they need; and this covetousness is rapidly spreading to poorer peoples. A greedy world can only be a divided world, ethically sordid, heading toward barbarism." [18]

The dynamisms of acquisition are useful in stimulating men to start acquiring things they genuinely need, but may leave men unfit to exercise freedom in the pursuit of other goods. A theory of priority needs is mandatory; in a later chapter such a theory is outlined. What is asserted here is the importance of reappraising the notions of "superfluous" and "enough" in a developmental setting.

My conclusions can be summarized as follows:

(a) all men need certain goods to realize themselves as men;

(b) an objective basis exists for deciding what is "enough";

---

[17] Alfred Marshall, "Principles of Economics," in *Classics of Economic Theory*, ed. George W. Wilson (Indiana University Press, 1964), p. 632.

[18] *Op. cit.*, p. 4.

(c) both the absolute insufficiency of goods and relative excess de-humanize the quality of life;

(d) an explicit theory of priority needs must be elaborated.

The first principle of any development strategy, therefore, is that underdeveloped men "need more in order to be more."

Second Principle: Universal Solidarity

Pervasive communications now render isolation impossible. As Mumford has written: "the joint stock of knowledge and technical skill transcends the boundaries of individual or national egos: and to forget that fact is not merely to enthrone superstition but to under-mine the essential planetary basis of technology itself." [19] And Per-roux adds that "technical conditions for the establishment of a plane-tary economy now exist." [20] No country can erect walls around itself without thereby destroying the international foundations of tech-nology.[21] Technological production (research and organization) and consumption of its fruits have unified the globe. Men's dreams and life-styles have everywhere felt the standardizing impact of technology, and homogenization of behavior is well under way. Businessmen in Japan, Turkey, India, or the United States have more in common with one another than with their own countrymen. The same is true of professionals and technicians.

More important than identical patterns of consumption are the gen-eral *images*[22] gaining ascendancy throughout the world. One finds everywhere the same confidence in man's ability to master nature, a sense of the importance of earthly life, the notion that all men should be judged according to their performance. These ingredients of "mod-ernization" are fast becoming generalized values. The environment within which information is processed as well as the "receptors" of information become more homogeneous. Beyond technology's unify-ing effect, however, lie deeper bases for human solidarity.

Men are one by their common humanity. Although thinkers differ

[19] Lewis Mumford, *Technics and Civilization* (Harcourt, Brace and Com-pany, 1934), p. 142.

[20] François Perroux, *La Coexistence Pacifique* (Presses Universitaires de France, 1958), III, 409.

[21] Mumford, *op. cit.*, p. 232.

[22] Cf. Kenneth E. Boulding, *The Image* (University of Michigan Press, 1963).

over the meaning of "human," each makes universal claims. All agree that beyond differences of race, nationality, culture, or social organization a common "human-ness" is present. Factual unity is the first ontological basis for solidarity among men.

A second foundation is the common occupation of the planet by all men. Throughout its physical extension the earth is governed by identical laws and is subject to the same indeterminisms. Despite variations in climate, relief, and geography, this planet has a specific identity distinct from other cosmic bodies. All men dwell on *one* planet.[23] The symbiosis between men and "nature" presupposes an intimate link between the two. Each man is part of nature and the world of objects. Were it otherwise, he could not be treated as a mere "object" by other men. Moreover, physical occupation of this planet is the lot of all men, not only of some. Even if men do not interact directly with other men, they are related at least *indirectly,* thanks to their common links to the same planetary system. The prospects opened up by recent space exploration in no way modify the organic relations tying every man to this planet as to his cosmic home so long as men are born on this earth and dwell here. Were permanent emigration to other planets to take place in the future, human solidarity would acquire an expanded basis—namely, the unity of cosmic planetary systems instead of a single planet. In either case, men are interdependent because of identical ties to one system, planetary or cosmic.

Along with men's common humanity and their ties to one cosmic environment, a third basis of solidarity exists: men's unity of destiny. Whatever be their personal sources of occupational fulfillment—as farmers, fishermen, politicians, artists, machinists, housewives, or salesmen—all men must fulfill themselves in a human mode. All systems of thought postulate, at least implicitly, a common destiny for men: the fate of one is the fate of all. The universality of human destiny represents no sectarian point of view, therefore, but the common patrimony of human thought.

Men rarely translate their existential solidarity into cooperative behavior. They consistently act as though they were not bound together in webs of solidarity. Partial claims assert themselves as though they were of supreme importance. Classes and nations seek to dominate other classes and nations. Although lip service is given to the "common good of humanity," world development problems continue

[23] This remark leaves open the possibility that other planets may support living beings similar to earthly men.

to be defined through the prisms of parochial, mercantile, strategic, and ideological interests. Even within international organizations, solidarity is often sacrificed to narrow political interests. Men have not yet learned how to respond to the exigencies of solidarity. Nevertheless, only with universal solidarity can development be achieved for all. It is unrealistic to expect problems to be solved by some hidden hand which arbitrates competing interests. Ironically, genuine solidarity can be won only after much conflict, because worldwide community can be established only if the rules presently governing exchange and access to power are totally revised. The same holds true for competing interest groups within nations. The implantation of world solidarity, therefore, faces great obstacles.

One source of trouble is the discontinuity of development enjoyed by countries and social classes. Countries once colonized or now dominated need to assert their nationalism virulently in order to wage war against underdevelopment. Developed nations, on the other hand, need to limit their sovereignty if harmful structural domination effects are to be neutralized. Identical norms cannot be applied to all types of nations. It is likewise with tariffs: non-industrial countries need high tariffs to nurture fragile incipient industry, whereas industrialized countries must lower tariffs to admit Third World goods to buyers' markets. Until all countries accept global solidarity and complementarity on the basis of acknowledged need-priorities, double standards in politics or trade will appear irrational or unjust to some. Given men's present dispositions, authentic solidarity cannot be gained without serious conflict. Consequently, the manner in which conflict is envisaged has decisive importance.

Within consensus models, social harmony is presumed to be normal and conflict is viewed as subversive. Such models assume that existing institutions are just. Where underdevelopment prevails, however, existing structures are often unjust and devoid of legitimacy, despite a façade of legality. When this is the case, conflict may be necessary to challenge established disorder. The history of revolutionary movements attests to their institution-building role. Camilo Torres has described the transformations wrought in Colombia's rural society in the wake of guerrilla activity.[24] Not every conflict arises from armed revolution, however; it may emerge from a campaign to politicize peasant

[24] *Camilo Torres, por el Padre Camilo Torres Restrepo 1956–1966* (Cuernavaca: Centro Intercultural de Documentación, 1966), Sondeos Series, No. 5, p. 174.

masses, organize urban workers into a labor union, or launch a coop-erative. Resulting conflicts generate more developmental energies than placid social harmony. Conflict enables peasants to "integrate" them-selves to urban society, thereby expanding their networks of solidar-ity. The general lesson is that where the domination of the strong relies for its maintenance on the apathy of the weak, conflict is a breeding ground for the growth of *solidarity* among those who hitherto formed an inactive mass. True solidarity implies powers of self-disposition in those who practice it. Consequently, disharmony is often a necessary prelude to the solidarity required for development. Many black leaders within the United States diagnose their own situa-tion in these terms. They want no alliances with white groups until they obtain power to determine their own affairs. During their struggle for power, however, they enter into conflict with those whose concept of social justice postulates the maintenance of blacks in subordina-tion. As they organize, blacks develop internal solidarity and prepare the social terrain for authentic solidarity with non-blacks at a future date.

Recent events in underdeveloped and developed nations alike have rendered social scientists increasingly skeptical of consensus theories. Horowitz asserts that "dissensus, while dysfunctional with respect to the ruling powers, is quite functional for the newly emergent na-tions." [25] Consensus based on mass apathy or the manipulation of a populace by an elite is sham consensus. And solidarity founded on threats to those who "rock the boat" of social equilibrium is fragile. "Any serious theory of agreements and decisions must at the same time be a theory of disagreements and the conditions under which decisions cannot be reached." [26] Because it expresses social needs and aspirations, conflict is a prerequisite for solidarity. Even radical Marxism views class warfare as the instrument of heightened solidar-ity within the proletariat and as the political vehicle of non-conflictual solidarity within the entire society after the communist revolution is over. What is thus stated in the language of one ideological system is true of all: whether conflict is judged to be disruptive or constructive, it is always viewed as disruptive or constructive of some terminal con-dition of solidarity.

The practical question is: how much solidarity is feasible at any

[25] Irving Louis Horowitz, *Three Worlds of Development* (Oxford University Press, 1966), p. 365.
[26] *Idem.*, p. 376.

given time? Where little solidarity has existed in the past, or where it has been based on the power monopoly of rulers strong enough to "paper over" dissent, the creation of genuine solidarity requires disruption of old rules of "cooperation." To succeed in this disruption, however, dissenters need to forge bonds of in-group solidarity far deeper than those imposed from above by superordinate rulers. Limitless sacrifices are required of genuine "subversives," who must subject personal ambitions to a larger cause and view the exploitation of others as an attack upon their own humanity. Even enemies must be "re-educated," not destroyed or suppressed. The internal solidarity nurtured among partisans exemplifies the terminal solidarity of society as a whole after revolution triumphs. The dynamism of conflict turns out to be a luminous principle of development.

I have asserted that worldwide development cannot succeed unless solidarity is optimized. What precisely does this mean? Concretely, this means that world development cannot ensue if present rules governing differential power and influence remain in force. These rules favor those societies which already "domesticate" others who struggle against the vulnerability which characterizes underdevelopment. At present levels of consciousness, underdeveloped classes and nations reject "solidarity" with a system which victimizes them or with "donors" of aid whose own interests are further advanced by that very aid. Galbraith aptly remarks of the United States that "We are led, as a nation, by our present preoccupations, to adopt numerous of the least elegant postures of wealth. Though we have much, and much of the remainder of the world is poor, we are single-mindedly devoted to getting more. . . . We do, each year, provide some aid for others. But first we have a prayerful discussion of whether or not we can afford the sacrifice. . . . The nineteenth-century plutocrat who devoted his energies to expanding his already considerable income, who wanted by his competitive position in the plutocracy to live on a suitably ostentatious scale, who found, as a result, that his income was never entirely adequate, who came to the aid of the poor only after a careful consideration of their worth, his ability to spare from his needs and the realistic likelihood of revolt and disorder if he abstained, and who believed withal that God inspired his enterprise and generosity and often said so, was not in all respects an attractive figure. So with nations." [27]

Only by building solidarity among themselves can underdeveloped

[27] Galbraith, *The Affluent Society*, p. 140.

nations effectively challenge their unenviable lot, thereby hastening the advent of global solidarity.

Partial solidarities, however, cannot promote universal development. Technology's unifying effects will ultimately prove disastrous unless men allocate resources, access to information, and decision-making power in terms of world equity and not on the basis of prior occupancy or greater political influence. Technology divides more than it unites men unless it operates in conditions where self-development of societies can flourish. As stated above, the "ontological roots" of solidarity are common humanity, mutual occupancy of one planet, and identical destiny. Disaster will ensue if these roots are not translated into rules effectively obeyed. Men may prove unable to express universal solidarity except by digging a common grave for themselves as a monument to their failure of will. On grounds of efficiency and economy, planned use of resources is the only rational policy of world development. Clearly, it is irrational to pretend that national sovereignty is a beneficent myth. At best, nationalism provides limited sanctuary to vulnerable societies. Tagore believes that only what is compatible with the universal has permanent survival value and anything less is doomed to perish.[28] He may be right, since technological production cannot keep pace with expanding acquisitive instincts. The appropriation of goods on any basis other than universal human solidarity in the face of needs is not a viable ethic now that development is universally desired. Mankind may be obliged to choose the moral course under pain of collective death. Henry Miller has written that "it is not our religious convictions but the very conditions of our life on earth which will make angels of us." [29] The requirements of human survival, quite as much as those of justice, dictate universal solidarity. Such solidarity is incompatible with competition among grossly unequal competitors and presupposes the abolition of domination structures.

Neither individualism nor collectivism is a sound principle of development. The first renders justice, the second integral human growth, impossible. Some optimal blend of innovation and risk, allied to projective identification with group interests by social creators, is required if the development process is to construct solidarity.

[28] *Vers l'Homme Universel* (Gallimard), p. 210, cited in Lebret, *Développement = Révolution Solidaire* (Les Editions Ouvrières, 1967), p. 52.
[29] Claude Sarraute, "Un Entretien avec Henry Miller," in *Le Monde*, April 20, 1960, p. 8.

Third Principle: Broad Popular Participation in Decisions

Secular debate between proponents of elitism and populism has not revealed a practical way to avoid the former or to make the latter work. Whenever a certain scale and structural complexity are reached, decisions must be made by a few men more competent than others. Populists of varying shades have tried to mitigate the elitism of political systems by requiring that electors be consulted periodically to confirm or to remove representatives. Sporadic appeal to an electorate rarely entails, however, a popular role in the elaboration and execution of policy. Within modern economic units, elitist claims are even more compelling: central decisions must be made by qualified managers and technicians. This is true of large units like steel mills or hydroelectric plants, doubly so of national economies, in which planners, fiscal experts, and macro-economists are the decision-making elite. This apparent requisite for efficiency is disapproved, however, by the populace. The prospect of living in a world wherein technocrats are the dispensers and people at large the beneficiaries of development is distasteful. Such distaste is nonetheless offset by the reluctance of most men to assume responsibilities beyond their competence.

Everett Hagen has described the workings of this complex sentiment in a perceptive essay.[30] Most individuals, he observes, find it satisfying to take part in decisions only within the narrow sphere of activity in which they have had experience or feel competent. Outside these realms, the need to make decisions generates anxiety. In many societies this anxiety can be avoided by transferring responsibility to officials higher up in a hierarchy. When this happens inside a structure of institutional legitimacy, a decision taken by a leader is right, not by any operational test, but simply because the leader has made it. The chances of achieving political "democracy," according to Hagen, are as follows:

"If within any society, say five percent of the adults of the society find it stimulating and satisfying to exercise their judgment concerning the broader economic, social, and political affairs of the country, then there will be individuals scattered throughout the villages, towns, and

[30] Everett E. Hagen, "Are Some Things Valued by All Men?" in *Cross Currents,* Fall 1968, Vol. XVIII, No. 4, pp. 406–414.

cities of the country who like to be leaders. They express viewpoints, other voters turn to them, and democracy will work well, and be satisfying even though facing decisions in broad areas makes nineteen persons out of twenty anxious. But if the number of persons who feel stimulus and satisfaction in facing the use of their judgment in broader areas is only, say, one-fourth of one percent rather than five percent, then an authoritarian hierarchical social order will seem preferable and right." [31]

Available evidence suggests that no large majorities in any society desire an active role in decision-making, even when they are informed of possible options. By the very nature of his condition, the underdeveloped man is powerless to affect his own lot. But new desires are generated once consciousness is taken of the reversibility of that lot. Third World elites speak for their majorities, not only for the privileged few, when they repeat with Senghor: "we do not wish to be mere consumers of civilization." How does one reconcile these antinomies —most people fear decision-making while simultaneously aspiring to greater control over their destinies? On what ground should optimum participation be a regulating principle of development? Where does this optimum lie? I shall attempt to answer by commenting on the defects found in prevailing elitist solutions and on the different social matrices out of which elites emerge.

(A) *The Participation of All Is Impossible*

Hagen is right—most people do not want to exercise great responsibilities. Communitarian movements have repeatedly foundered because they have not come to terms with the real motives which impel men to sacrifice. Only the naïve will suppose that large numbers of men can long sustain a commitment to such values as solidarity, community, austerity, and the common good. Generally, only a small number of "militants" can do so. And over long periods of time even militants are tempted by the less altruistic values which move the masses: private advancement, greater ease, and recognition. This phenomenon recurs in many cultures. In one large cooperative housing project in Paris, for instance, "idealistic" members are no longer willing, as they were ten years ago, to work at collective tasks like landscaping or the construction of meeting rooms. Throughout the movement's eight projects, the forward thrust has been lost.[32] A similar

[31] *Idem.,* p. 408.
[32] Example supplied orally on September 29, 1968, by the director of these

situation prevails in the *kibbutzim* of Israel; the old flame is gone and no longer are members "scandalized" by the hiring of salaried workers to till collective lands. Self-management farms in Algeria have suffered the same lot since independence: economic performance has been poor, largely because individuals do not respond creatively to group responsibilities for very long. Patterns of factory work in several popular democracies of Eastern Europe attest to the same phenomenon. Thus, in Poland, Hungary, Czechoslovakia, and Yugoslavia, monumental waste is practiced by workers, much of it deliberate and systematic. After they finish their "state" jobs, workers earn extra income by performing tasks abolished by Socialist decrees: small plumbing jobs, auto repairs, and the like. After a time, workers begin to perform the "second" (and illegal) job on work time supposedly reserved to the state. They frequently "steal" parts from the state in order to perform their moonlighting tasks.[33]

I cite these cases to draw attention to the difficulty of finding an alternative to elitism for performing tasks which benefit an entire society. All these examples are drawn from environments where intense pedagogy had been carried on with a view to convincing the populace that "elitism" is bad and that the best substitute is to hand over full responsibility to the "people." Nevertheless, in each instance populism broke down and functional elitism developed spontaneously. One is led to ask, therefore, whether large-scale development can be conducted except in an elitist mode, irrespective of the demands for participation which spring up when consciousness is awakened in the masses. Stated differently, is "optimum" popular participation in decision-making any different from that dictated by efficiency in the division of labor?

An efficiency optimum may differ from the optimum for promotion of the populace to a more humane level of conscious existence. But even in terms of efficiency, over what time span is the optimum to be determined? Common experience shows that foreign technicians can often "get the job done" more quickly than native personnel if these lack required skills. Does this mean that the optimum procedure is not to train those who will be responsible for the long-term success or

---

projects. I have myself surveyed several of the eight community housing projects in Paris.

[33] Information obtained orally from a Socialist political organizer who had studied work conditions in the countries named. His request for anonymity has been respected.

failure of the enterprise? Likewise with elite questions: trains no doubt run more efficiently and there is less waste of time—even in purely economic terms—under conditions of wartime mobilization. Nevertheless, societies shrink from perpetuating such discipline because values more precious than efficiency are thereby sacrificed. The adoption of elitism and populism in some kind of mix is inseparable from the larger question: what kind of man does a society want to create? Even if we grant the need for a big push toward development, we still do not know how to set an optimum which avoids technocratic elitism on the one hand and unproductive popular participation on the other. All we know is something of the unpleasantness of elitism in technological and pre-technological societies alike. We also know of the existence of broad popular support for the cause of participation. Yet the situation is fluid and no lessons can be dictated *a priori; praxis* must be our teacher.

We do well to recall that, contrary to the belief that populism is impossible in large-scale enterprises, the world's most populous nation, China, has formally rejected the elitist model of mobilization. Quickly and dramatically China has abolished starvation in its midst, and is on the way to eliminating illiteracy, social privilege, and endemic diseases as well. These enormous developmental accomplishments have greater significance than gains in GNP or rates of capital investment.

Another experimental Socialist country, Cuba, has likewise realized spectacular gains in realms where solutions have seemingly eluded other Latin American nations. Illiteracy and real-estate speculation have been practically eliminated in Cuba. More importantly, Cuba has reversed the unhealthy flow of population between countryside and city. As reported by the United Nations, "A two-way flow of population between city and countryside is systematically encouraged, particularly through urban study by rural youth and rural harvest-work and social activities by urban youth, while development policy —after some vicissitudes—has favored large-scale 'industrialized' agriculture over urban industry. In these as in many other respects Cuba is moving toward a social organization that represents a deliberate rejection of the trends in the rest of Latin America." [34]

A recent comparison of industrial efficiency in Israel of six managerially controlled enterprises and six cooperatively administered en-

[34] United Nations, 1967 *Report on the World Social Situation,* Document E/CN. 5/417 dated 12 December 1967, p. 54.

terprises is equally suggestive. The author of the study, Seymour Melman, Professor of Industrial Engineering at Columbia University, concludes that in a variety of conditions cooperative decision-making is equal or superior in efficiency to managerial, elitist decision-making in industrial enterprises.[35]

These examples warn us not to conclude that elitism is inevitable in the quest for development, or that alternative strategies are doomed to fail. The principle of optimum participation in decision-making as defended in these pages asserts normatively:

(a) that development pedagogy ought to portray development in terms of progressivity of the economy rather than economic progress;

(b) that all men are entitled to become agents, and not mere beneficiaries, of their own development;

(c) that only experimentation can provide specific answers as to the optimum blend of specialized competence with popular sharing in decisions.[36]

I include optimum participation among development's strategic principles because unless efforts are made to widen participation, development will interfere with men's quest for esteem and freedom from manipulation. The United Nations document just cited warns against the dangers of uncritical surrender to elitism. "Various social scientists find reason to fear that the Latin American *elites* participating in the previous systems of compromise, unable to face the dangers unavoidable in the transition to a social order in which popular participation might be effective as well as economically viable, are becoming increasingly inclined to seek shelter behind regimes of armed force." [37]

Elites nonetheless must have the power to make effective options. It is essential, therefore, to create conditions under which popular elites may emerge.

(B) *A Popular Elite*

The term "elite" is widely used to designate a small privileged group holding a monopoly over influence or access to political rule.

[35] Seymour Melman, "Managerial vs. Cooperative Decision-Making in Israel," *Studies in Comparative International Development*, Vol. VI (1970–1971), No. 065.

[36] A look into possible futures of the U.S. under different models of elitism/populism is provided by Rexford G. Tugwell in "U.S.A. 2000 A.D.," in *The Center Magazine*, Vol. I, No. 7 (November 1968), pp. 23–34.

[37] United Nations, *op. cit.*, p. 50.

Regardless of a society's system of government or values, leading minorities make effective choices for the whole society. Etymologically, the term "elite" means "worthy of choice." Consequently, it refers to the quality of leadership quite as much as to the degree to which leaders represent their electors. We "need to distinguish between *de facto* power and rightful power," writes Sartori, "between those who lead (the actual political class) and those who are capable of leading (the potential political elites). And for this purpose we must be able to speak of elites without guilt complexes." [38] Sartori alludes to hoary debates of political scientists over the relative merits of elite analysis and class analysis. Yet one need not argue that class analysis is irrelevant or that policy-makers should ignore the masses to grant that influential minorities exist in every society. As two recent authors have said, "one of the requisites for development is a competent elite, motivated to modernize their society." [39] The decisive questions are whence do elites come, by what selective processes are they chosen, how do they exercise their power, and whose values do they defend?

My purpose here is not to analyze class origins of political or economic elites, or to examine the manner in which power is exercised. I merely seek to clarify what is meant by "popular elite" in the light of the stated principle that development ought to optimize participation in decision-making. This position implies that the populace at large is the breeding ground whence elites are to emerge. They are not to be "recruited," a term which suggests external rules or agents charged with finding the elite within a population. Any populace can "secrete" its elite if properly challenged by agents of change in a manner respectful of its cultural identity. Observers throughout the world have testified that most groups contain in their midst individuals with the capacity to grasp the problems affecting their community and to lead their peers in group response to that challenge. These "natural" elites are often distinct from formal, hierarchical leaders—chieftains or their sons, elders, or members of respected classes. "Natural" elites are individuals who can perceive, with an understanding of the forces at work and a sense of synthesis, the deep *meaning* of changes proposed. They are not necessarily technical, political, or entrepreneurial elites, but people who know how to discern what is acceptable in new values offered, what elements in old values enhance their society's

[38] Giovanni Sartori, *Democratic Theory* (Praeger, 1965), p. 112.
[39] Seymour Martin Lipset and Aldo Solari, eds., *Elites in Latin America* (Oxford University Press, 1967), Preface, p. viii.

quest for better life-sustenance, esteem, and freedom, and what practical margins of decision are open to the group. In terms of the theory of "existence rationality" presented in a later chapter, such leaders are innovators at the outer boundaries of their group's existence rationality while remaining faithful, at least in essentials, to the inner limits of that strategy. So as to situate such elites relative to the usual typologies, we may borrow terms used by Lasswell and Kaplan to describe types of rule. They speak of *demosocracy,* a system wherein popular trust and affection are vested in leaders, and of *ethocracy,* related to the moral competence recognized by people in their leaders.[40] These terms must be understood analogously: they refer, not to a system of rule, but to influence over the responses of a populace outside the framework of formal authority.

Leaders who emerge in this fashion personify the aspirations, values, and interests of their fellows. To a remarkable degree, the group trusts them, identifies with them, and looks to them as pedagogues of the change experience. A strategy for induced change must facilitate the kinds of encounter with the population best suited to generating the emergence of such leaders. No assumption is made that these are always present; nevertheless, the chances of allowing them to "surface" must be optimized. Certain structures are required if these chances are to exist. A particular image of the relationships between summit planners, regional and sectorial agencies, and local groups is necessary. All such models attach great importance to a practice which the French call "animation," a pedagogical device designed to identify leaders and assist them to emerge. Such leaders can guide their community on its own terms toward a degree and rate of change which have been critically examined. If "animation" is to succeed, suitable administrative structures must be implanted at every level: national, regional, local.[41] Unless these structures exist, it is impossible to transmit meaningful information and influence to small groups, through larger units, all the way up to the national society. Rural "stimulus agents" should be trained in a milieu resembling their native habitat. Experience shows that even a few weeks spent in modern settings can seriously weaken the psychic capacity of poten-

[40] Harold D. Lasswell and Abraham Kaplan, *Power and Society* (Yale University Press, 1965), p. 210.

[41] On this, cf. L. J. Lebret, *Dynamique Concrète du Développement* (Les Éditions Ouvrières, 1961), pp. 389–421. Cf. also, e.g., Roland Colin, "L'Animation, Clef de Voûte du Développement," *Développement & Civilisations,* No. 21 (March 1965), pp. 5–10.

tial village leaders to work in their original sites with enthusiasm. What must be safeguarded is the allegiance of an upward mobile elite to the values of the popular groups from which they emerge, so that they do not identify themselves with privileged-class interests after they become influential. This is impossible to achieve except through an overt pedagogy based on communitarian conceptions of responsibility. One of the most striking features of China's utilization of political, educational, scientific, managerial, and technical elites is the degree to which these are held accountable to the populations for whose benefit they presumably enjoy their elite position. Although Westerners frequently lack valid information regarding this gigantic effort, and notwithstanding their general lack of sympathy with the ideological *content* of the Chinese mobilization strategy, one begins to suspect that its *mode* of procedure, if we discount elements of psychic manipulation, is well attuned to certain authentic requirements of participation.

Democratic theory is ambiguous as to the relationship between the quantitative criterion employed to choose elites and the qualitative content of their performance once chosen. The voice of the majority has no meaning apart from the end toward which choice is ordered—namely, the quality of leadership exercised by those chosen.[42] In the situations just described, the mode of selection may be less important than the degree to which elites, after emerging, incarnate popular wishes (even unconscious, unstated wishes). Malcolm X, for instance, appears to have represented in authentic fashion a large constituency even of those who disagreed with his prescriptions for action, this in virtue of the remarkable lucidity with which he diagnosed the black man's condition in the United States.

Although, as stated above, elites who emerge "naturally" need not enjoy ruling positions, it is desirable that such positions be made accessible to them. This is one of the basic functions of optimum participation in decision-making. Another important application of the same principle lies in the realm of international affairs. Many demands made by the signatories of the Charter of Algiers are defensible among nations as interacting units in a worldwide system on the same grounds as those just described at a micro-community level. No global solution to the world's development problem can be achieved until Third World countries—of diverging types and interests—gain a substantial voice in the formulation of new ground rules by which world

[42] Cf. Sartori, *op. cit.*, p. 104.

markets, world transfers of technology and research, and world development financing function. The present system of differential power, wealth, and ideological influence must give way to a less rigidly stratified world distribution of elites in planetary decisions. More will now be said, therefore, on world planning and resource use.

CHAPTER SEVEN

Development Planning as Dialogue

The drafting of plans is merely one part of planning, which, in ideal terms, ought to be a permanent activity since projected targets must be constantly corrected, revised, and updated. Planning, moreover, occurs at several levels: it deals with macro- and micro-economic structures, with the entire nation and with regions, and, finally, with various sectors of activity. In most non-developed countries, however, the harmonization of diverse planning operations has not been the object of rational effort. As a result, national plans are poorly coordinated with a country's regional plans; and sectorial plans are often prepared with little regard for their impact on other sectors. Yet incoherent planning is irrational. Besides, certain important elements of social change are not amenable even to good planning.

Several functions are common to all forms of planning—identifying objectives, translating these into quantified targets, allocating resources in optimum fashion so as to reach targets in specified time spans, implementing, supervising efforts made to implement plans, and evaluating performance and its consequences. Serious problems arise from the treatment of inputs which are not readily subject to quantification and from the impossibility of anticipating all consequences even of choices made on "rational" grounds.

The following pages outline a strategy for integrating heterogeneous plans around dialogue with a populace, an effort intended to minimize the difficulties just cited and to harmonize planning with the goals and regulative principles of development. Fragmented planning has several drawbacks. (1) It multiplies priorities without providing criteria for choosing among competing claims. (2) It tends to assign social costs of development on the basis of centralized decision, thereby violating the principle of diffused popular participation. (3) It is wasteful. (4) It increases political frustration because central authorities do not endorse the priorities of local and regional governments. Conversely, local priorities are construed by national planners as "diversions" of scarce national resources away from important global objectives. These four deficiencies flow largely from the "occupational hazards" inherent in the very conduct of planning.

The Planner's Occupational Hazards

Latin languages translate the term "occupational hazard" as "professional deformation," a phrase which evokes the tendency to create distortions which is inherent in the very exercise of a profession. One major occupational hazard of planners is the illusion of omniscience. Development experts may imperceptibly come to regard themselves as wiser than other mortals regarding society's true needs. Even when they are personally unpretentious, planners are often forced to work *as if* they possessed infallible answers about their country's priorities. Deadlines imposed upon them are often so tight that unless they resist the temptation to doubt their own certitudes they become impotent. This is one reason why development plans are so imperfect. Many planners would agree with these words uttered by Brazil's former Planning Minister, Roberto Campos: "Our planning in this first period—we must confess—has been a sort of 'creative introspection' conducted in a desperate race against time. It now should be transformed into 'democratic dialogue.' A second failing is faulty coordination of the federal plan with state and regional initiatives. A third defect is the dearth of concrete and mature investment projects capable of giving substance to over-all growth targets. What we have at hand is much more a catalogue of wishes than a stock of projects. . . . We must convince ourselves that projects of factories are not enough. What we need is a 'factory of projects.' " [1]

[1] Roberto de Oliveira Campos, *Política Econômica E Mitos Políticos* (Rio de Janeiro: APEC Editora, 1965), p. 31.

These three defects are interrelated. There is no remedy for poor coordination between national and regional planning without some measure of democratic dialogue. Similarly, coordination can be obtained only by procedures which generate good projects as well.

A second occupational hazard of centralized planners is their inclination to impose goals instead of multiplying agents of human promotion. Community planners no doubt seek human promotion as their primary goal, but their working procedures are rarely imitated by macro-economic or macro-regional planners. Nevertheless, the qualities of good community planning should be allied to the best in summit planning of global problems. More specifically, local, regional, and sectoral planning must be redefined as the conquest, by representatives of localities, regions, and sectors, of an increasingly active role in drafting and implementing general development plans. Consequently, summit planning must be redesigned so that "inputs" from other levels effectively determine its own "output." At stake is not only a guarantee of good "results," but, above all, an adequate way of conducting the planning operation itself. At issue is the distinction between human promotion and imposed goals. What precisely is "human promotion"?

Development is not a cluster of benefits "given" to people in need, but rather a process by which a populace acquires greater mastery over its own destiny. Even in purely economic terms, a vital difference separates economic progress from a progressive economy. The first is measured by gains in production, increased revenue, or volume of trade. Thus, economic progress takes place when local production is doubled, thanks to the installation of a new factory, even if technicians and skilled workers must be brought from other regions to staff it, or even if the factory monopolizes markets or eliminates local handicrafts. It is tempting but nonetheless false to think of economic progress primarily in terms of investment, technical aid, or increased production. What is more important is to multiply the number and improve the quality of the agents of progress. Certain modes of investment confirm underdeveloped men in their passive attitude of awaiting favors from government, industrialists, landowners, or employers. Investments made in paternalistic fashion can perhaps generate economic progress in material terms, but they do not make the economy progressive. An economy becomes progressive when men who had hitherto been passive now conjugate their efforts to eliminate ignorance, disease, hunger, mendicity, servility, and exploitation. A progressive economy likewise signifies that economic progress itself

155

ceases to depend primarily on the good will of government, the charity of the wealthy, or the favors of heaven. Progress becomes the fruit of men's own will and work. The "beneficiaries" of development are also its agents. If human promotion is development's chief result, wide participation of local and regional communities is clearly necessary in defining as well as in executing plans. Plans ought not be formulated exclusively at the summit, but should arise from dynamic interflow between aspirations at the base and expertise at the summit. New intermediate technical, administrative, and informational channels must be created. Partly at least, the imposition of goals from the top down gives way to the formulation of goals from the bottom up.

At times innovations can be stimulated only by central planners since they alone can assess the probable impact of specific measures on macro-economic and macro-social performance or supply statistics needed to make sound public-investment decisions. Central planners can likewise influence the instruments of large-scale mobilization—mass media, government policy, and incentive structures. Especially in distant or sparsely settled regions, central authorities may be required to supply investment, managerial, and administrative personnel which are unavailable locally. Hence the formulation of goals from the bottom up can be only a partial, never an absolute, ideal.

Underdeveloped communities, at least through their more critically conscious spokesmen, seek a voice in their own destiny as much as they crave bread, electric power, or drinking water. Dignity is achieved only when economic progress itself flows from the progressivity of the economy. This is why Perroux' description of progress merges into that of progressivity: "If progress is considered to be a process of propagation of innovation for the benefit of all in the briefest delays, it then follows that given an identical increase in real median revenue within a relatively short period, there will or will not be progress according as the conditions just enumerated are or are not met." [2]

A third occupational hazard of centralized planning is the danger of over-abstraction. To the professional eye of the economist, statistician, or planner, human misery reads as a column of statistics. Numbers of course tell an objectively tragic tale: a life expectancy of 38 years, let us say, an infant mortality rate of 125 per thousand, an

[2] François Perroux, "Les Mésures du Progrès Economique et l'Idée d'Economie Progressive," *Cahiers de l'I.S.E.A.*, Series I, No. 47 (December 1956), p. 15.

illiteracy index of 65 percent, an average daily caloric intake far below 2,400. Abstract idiom, however, easily leads its practitioners to mistake statistics for reality. But in real life, underdevelopment is no mere statistic: it is the subjective experience of a man helplessly observing his son's belly bloated with worms. Or reaching home when the last bowl of rice has been eaten to find his wife, pregnant once again, chasing away the flies which ply on the face of their year-old infant and announcing: "There is no work in the fields till next planting season and I'm out of money." Sentimentality is no cure for underdevelopment, but the cold abstract logic of statistics crushes men unless it is tempered by "intelligent love." This quality leads developers to use, without cynicism, all the wiles of technique and politics in the service of compassion as well as of efficiency. Successful development calls for men who are both hard-headed and tender-hearted. Tragedy comes when one polar quality is missing or when they are inverted, leaving us with men having hard hearts and flabby thought. Individuals and groups must of course be treated as statistics by development planners. What is essential is that they not be treated solely as statistics.

The fourth and most harmful occupational hazard faced by planners is the temptation to treat human values as mere instruments of development. In truth, however, development benefits are relative goods which must themselves be judged in the light of evolving value systems. Unless summit planners listen attentively to the putative "beneficiaries" of development and consent at times to doff their counselor's role, they cannot gain the acceptance they need to implant in recalcitrant populations the new vision of life demanded by sound development. Why is it that in numerous African countries herds of cattle are raised, not to supply meat, but as prestige symbols for their owners? Meanwhile children die of protein deficiency! Several years ago I watched agronomists assigned to state-owned experimental farms in Northeast Brazil's arid *"sertão"* tediously plant greens and vegetables to provide an example for imitation by neighboring peasants whose diet needed improvement. All in vain, however, because peasants declared that they "are not rabbits and won't eat grass." In 1960 I visited several mountain villages in Lebanon where eggs were hoarded as jewels while youngsters famished. Any developer can multiply such anecdotes. They tell of starving peasants who continue to plant downhill, thereby accelerating soil erosion, or who waste fertilizer because it "dirties" the land, or practice harmful absenteeism

157

from work, all because they reject the world-view which underlies the quest for efficiency. After entire societies have grown accustomed for generations, if not for centuries, to limit their acquisitive desires to modest real possibilities, it is difficult for them to welcome the strange logic of achievement orientation. And unless they begin to sympathize with a new philosophy, they cannot adopt a system which urges both the expansion of wants and the manipulation of nature and society alike in pursuit of economic success.

The only way to overcome inertia without damaging psyches is to take goal-setting out of the hands of planners alone. As long as communities suspect that government is alien to their authentic needs, plans hatched in a national, regional, or local planning office are likely to provoke overt resistance or indifference. On the other hand, it is paradoxically cruel but true that men who live in misery often ignore what their own needs are. They must be assisted to choose whether or not they wish to move toward a new life-pattern wherein:

—innovations are rewarded, not punished;

—workers appropriate the fruits of their own efforts;

—today's sacrifices pave the way for the enjoyment of advantages tomorrow;

—there are reasons for things in a world of rationality; and

—men live in a universe of open explanations, not of fixed answers.

The central question is: can planners realistically expect a populace in misery to reject its obsolete outlook on life unless planning itself ceases to be the esoteric art of an elite whose values are incomprehensible when not hostile, to that populace? Certain viewpoints are mandatory if a society is to function as a modern developed unit. Tinbergen explains that "among the qualities that are required of quite a high proportion of the population of a developed society are an interest in material well-being, an interest in techniques and in innovation, an ability to look ahead and a willingness to take risks, perseverance, and an ability to collaborate with other people and to observe certain rules." [3] So long as planners assume that "underdeveloped" populations lack these qualities, they will communicate to them paternalistically from above.

Therefore, if they are to deal with value changes adequately, planners require a coherent strategy of harmonized planning. Deficient handling of value questions raises broad questions regarding plan-

[3] Jan Tinbergen, *Development Planning* (McGraw-Hill, 1967), p. 26.

ning's capacity to manage non-quantifiable development variables. Planning is by nature designed to treat elements amenable to numerical measurement. Yet such intangibles as motivational systems, the psychic abilities of people to accept change, and the degree to which national leaders can "inspire" sacrifice in a nation are crucial for development. Because qualitative elements are difficult to identify, evaluate, and control, they are usually left to the discretionary political judgment or to the intuitive sense of policy-makers and advisors. Unfortunately, however, such reliance on subjective political judgment promotes arbitrariness in the exercise of power. When political judgment is not informed by accurate empirical knowledge, it becomes unrealistic and renders leaders disdainful of the limits of possibility. Thus, decision-makers can fail to understand that nationalization of certain industries may be incompatible with a land-reform program for the simple reason that funds are insufficient to effectuate both simultaneously. As for the intuition of macro-economic planners, it is perhaps the best we can hope for until improvements in planning methods are made. The crucial problem is not that such intuition is unreliable but rather that it is incommunicable. I am reminded of a planning team headed by a brilliant generalist who could swiftly and accurately fuse disparate sectoral and regional studies into a coherent synthesis of the major causal factors in underdevelopment. Relying on his intuitive judgment, he would then prescribe measures to solve both essential and ancillary problems. Although his colleagues had been initiated to his methodology and shared his general outlook, they were obliged to call upon him repeatedly as an itinerant "fireman" to bring unity out of myriad problems. I cite this example not to impugn the man's genius, but to illustrate the essential weakness of making global decisions on a non-transferable basis. Therefore, one important element of the planning strategy I recommend is a new pedagogy aimed at improving the capacities of planners to conduct synthesis and, more particularly, to develop a critical sense of the relevance of non-quantifiable elements in the planning endeavor. Quantitative planning has exercised what amounts to methodological imperialism largely because no useful ways existed for incorporating other elements into decisions about goals or the allocation of resources. Until suitable methods are discovered, therefore, it is wise to posit counterweights to quantified planning by subjecting it to the criticism of numerous non-expert voices, representing interests and value preferences not usually heard in planning councils. Much as economists use shadow prices to simulate the anticipated behavior of future economies in econometric models, so it may help to employ "shadow plans" or tentative formulations of a perspective plan and medium-term targets submitted to the population's scrutiny for criticism, revision, and possible rejection. Social scientists conduct "pre-tests" before embarking on large-scale surveys; developers could likewise give plans a trial run. Were this practice adopted, it might counteract the facile assumption many governments make—namely, that a populace should be mobilized only to *execute* a plan, not to *draft* it.

This suggestion raises a fundamental question as to who ought to be heard in the planning procedure. Tinbergen intends to be generous when urging that people be consulted "according to the functions that they fulfill in the production process." [4] He cannot be taken literally, however, since elsewhere he advocates including representatives of consumer groups. The principle that consultation on planning priorities enjoys autonomous status apart from consultation on broader value issues is open to challenge.[5] Value consultations must be related to the central activities of planning itself. I have criticized the "instrumental" treatment of values which prevails in planning. The nature of "instrumental" treatment is illustrated in the following episode. During an informal seminar attended by a dozen French development planners some years ago, the question arose: what kind of housing and residential environment would be "humane" if a large glass factory were to be installed in a given valley? After much discussion on the need to take human factors into account, it suddenly dawned on one participant that "the cart had been placed before the horse." One does not assume that to erect a factory is a good thing and then proceed to inquire how to make its implantation beneficial to the inhabitants of a place. One must start with the people of that place: their attachments, emotions, aspirations, and need for jobs. After consulting with them, developers may or may not conclude that a glass factory is the best answer to the employment problem if these men are to have a satisfying life *on their terms*.

This is not to imply that economics has no voice in the matter, or that large-scale productive enterprises should never be cogitated by planners. But general consultations are advisable. And consumers are not necessarily those best qualified to say what production is ulti-

[4] *Idem.*, p. 179.
[5] On this, cf. Appendix III, "Research on Value Change."

mately for. One may also wish to interrogate men attuned to symbolic values—poets, artists, writers, and mystics. Furthermore, it is a mistake to assume that ordinary people are, by the mere fact of lacking expertise, devoid of valid notions as to what production is for and what ought to be the content of plans. On the contrary, consultation on values must not be dissociated from the choice of specific programs in an over-all development effort. For the benefit of skeptics who would hastily affirm that such consultation is unfeasible, a brief description of successful action conducted in this spirit is presented.

An Alternative: The Caillot Formula

French developer Robert Caillot has experimented during twenty years on modes of involving communities in decisions affecting their own destinies. Of particular interest is a special form of "participation-survey" he has devised. In standard research methodology, an observer is at times required to participate in a society's life for purposes of study. Caillot, however, stimulates the observed populace itself to participate directly in the elaboration of rules governing the research being made on its own needs. More importantly, the population serves as the principal judge of which development actions ought to be taken in its region. The entire operation is conceived so as to reduce elitism in survey and in mobilization. For Caillot it is axiomatic:

(1) that problems which are concretely experienced are not reducible to any intellectual or ideological perception anyone has of them;

(2) that the possession of knowledge confers on no man, including planners and technical experts, the right to decide on behalf of less-knowledgeable men; and

(3) that every man, no matter who he is, can possess only a partial view of reality.

The study of development must lead to action. Accordingly, Caillot's survey takes on the character of an instrument for providing culture; it does not rest content with studying or measuring. The people studied probe their individual and group problems in broad contexts of national and regional development. They are likewise initiated into the scope and character of their civic relationships to other men across the web of their multiple affiliations with them. Finally, they learn how to assume increasing responsibility for themselves by implementing solutions proposed. "Experts," of course, gain from associating their special competence to the expressed needs of interested parties in a non-paternalistic mode.

The five phases of this participation process are:

(1) definition and qualitative description of the structures which comprise development;

(2) geographic localization of these diverse structures;

(3) analysis of these structures, to a large extent by those who live within them;

(4) synthesis of all these elements. This effort is made in the presence of all participants;

(5) an operational phase which consists in transforming study groups into action teams.[6]

Several features of this method deserve special mention. First, this enterprise combines study and action. The topic of study is the whole gamut of development actions which ought to be undertaken in a village, region, or nation. Those affected by decisions are widely consulted and participate in drafting the specific measures to be taken. They are provided with the macro-data on demography, economic structures, employment, and investment without which their local aspirations would remain unenlightened and parochial. Although advanced statistical methods are employed at later stages, in the beginning of the process the populace is required to analyze and classify the data by hand. This constraint is imposed deliberately, on the grounds that mechanical or electronic treatment leads to undue abstraction. Another interesting feature is Caillot's stress on the dialectical relationship between formation and information. Information is not sought for its own sake; conversely, no action is recommended unless it is organically linked to studies which justify it. An attempt is made to wed the experience of those who experience problems to the analytical skill of those who conceptualize them. The expert's role consists in supplying broad information, posing problems, eliciting critical reflection and accurate observation, and coordinating the work of numerous multi-disciplinary teams. Quite apart from stimulating cooperation between experts and people, the method encourages the collaboration of different sub-groups among the people themselves. Its

[6] Cf. Robert Caillot, "L'Enquête-Participation à Economie et Humanisme," first appearing in 1963 and reprinted in *Cahiers de l'Institut Canadien d'Education des Adultes,* No. 3 (February 1967), pp. 121–144. Also Caillot, "Une Connaissance Engagée: L'Enquête-Participation" in *Options Humanistes* (Paris: Les Editions Ouvrières, 1968), pp. 55–80.

originality consists in transforming study and discussion groups into action groups. Nevertheless, action groups themselves are prodded into existence only under the stimulus of a collective study conducted by permanent heterogeneous teams. The larger goal is to create what Caillot calls "organic cells of authentic democracy." The precise action contemplated is regional development in the spheres of economic, cultural, physical, and political life. Summit decisions are organically related to lower echelons of administrators, pedagogues, entrepreneurs, and "little people" who would otherwise be relegated to the function of being mere "beneficiaries" of development. The ideal is a rich mosaic of dovetailing actions aiming at constant synthesis each time a new sector or a new problem is reached. Its author considers this form of participant-observation as a "laboratory *in vivo* for the elaboration and especially for the control of the principles of a humane economy, as well as the privileged instrument of the implementation of those same principles." [7] Nevertheless, the first two phases of the operation are conducted by development experts together with leaders and influential men in the region. Only at the third phase does the general populace enter the process. Were they to become involved earlier, says Caillot, mass participation would lack direction and be unmanageable.

Caillot explains that the method was born "from the need to render coherent the goal he [Caillot] was pursuing (to elaborate a human economy and to test its realism), and from his project on man (how to promote all human values in every man?). It is this desire for coherence and, therefore, for efficiency which leads us unremittingly to seek to apprehend better the totality of the real world and to associate men ever more progressively in this search. . . . In a certain sense, there is no longer any distinction between surveyors and the surveyed; there are only instigators and actors. The former help to clarify the dimensions of problems, the latter exercise choices and make decisions, each one at his own level in professional or administrative life." [8]

Caillot's strategy is concerned throughout with problem-solving, although he uses methods usually associated with pure research. His procedure is to focus on the fears, hopes, and frustrations of the groups surveyed so as to relate the subjective data thus obtained to specific development programs proposed to these groups. The survey

---

[7] Caillot, "Une Connaissance Engagée," *op. cit.*, p. 56.
[8] *Idem.*, p. 79.

is seen primarily as a mechanism whereby the populace becomes its own leading problem-solver. Stated differently, the survey is transformed into a suitable instrument by which the "surveyed" study their own problems and devise their own solutions. During the process the survey is metamorphosed into a vehicle of general mobilization on behalf of the entire development effort. Caillot's method for constructing the survey is noteworthy. He initiates preliminary discussion about projects through a public debate on the structural characteristics of the specific problems to be dealt with—e.g., agrarian reform, new farm practices, and so on. His primary objective is that the people undergoing induced change should become involved in projecting their future possibilities. Although structural topics are discussed early, items vary from one situation to another. Nevertheless, they always include basic demographic, ecological, and macro-economic information. People are then invited to respond to the presentation in terms of the general question of what can be done to improve their present conditions. Only afterward are they asked to help conduct a survey whose purpose is to discover, in detail and in quantifiable form, their problems and possible solutions. The populace is thus gradually made sensitive to the issues, constraints, and costs involved in its development problem. The survey's final goal, obviously, is to transform a populace in the very process of studying it. This is done on its own terms, however, and the team never begins its work unless it is invited by wide cross-sections of the population. This idea is not in itself new; behavioral scientists have long known that any attempt to examine a population has effects on it.[9] The originality lies in that this fact is formally incorporated into the survey process and used as a strategy for implementing social change in a participatory mode.

Development Poles

Although his experiments have been carried out largely at local or regional levels, Caillot believes there is no reason on principle why they cannot apply to national mobilization. The use of "shadow plans" recommended above is suited to all geographical levels and in all sectors. Optimum consultation stands as a valid goal both because it is anti-elitist and because the masses' knowledge, sensitivity, and

[9] Cf., v.g., William L. Kolb, "The Impingement of Moral Values on Sociology," *Social Problems*, Vol. II (1954), pp. 66–70.

dreams are indispensable inputs to the development equations which planners cannot ignore. Efforts in this direction will succeed, however, only if macro-planners adopt a coherent regional strategy of poles and zones of influence.

The most articulate spokesman of development-pole theory is François Perroux. Several points must be clarified, however, before one can grasp the import of Perroux' notion of development poles. The first is that economic growth is distinct from development *tout court,* even from economic development. As explained above, progressivity and progress are not identical terms. More specifically, economic *"development* is the combination of mental and social changes of a population which render it apt to cause its real global product to increase, in a cumulative and durable fashion." [10] This means that global product can increase in aggregate or even in per-capita terms without a population and its economy being placed in "conditions of development." For Perroux it is the "construction of men by men" [11] which lies at the core of development as a process. Yet growth and the transformation of mentalities and societies must start at some given point. It is at this point (or points) that innovation is concentrated and from which progressivity spreads. A development pole is the geographical point at which developmental innovation is centered in such wise that it can transmit effects which accelerate progressive change and remove impediments to the "construction of men by men." This is not the place to analyze how poles function.[12] What is important here is that the normative principles implicit in development-pole theory be noted. Needless to say, the theory is incomplete without a minute examination of the zones of influence affected by each pole and the networks by which isolated poles are linked to each other in optimum fashion. At the heart of this approach lies a desire to rationalize the structural imbalances resulting from innovation in such a way as to capitalize on the creative tensions thereby produced.

Because it supplies an analytical rationale for the localization of investment, according to criteria of diffusion and of harnessing creative imbalances, pole theory is most valuable to planners. The reason of course is that any plan needs to be translated into specific projects

10 François Perroux, *L'Economie du XXième Siècle* (Presses Universitaires de France, 1964), p. 155.

11 *Idem.,* p. 157.

12 Benjamin Higgins has done this in an unpublished essay communicated to the author in 1965 and entitled " 'Pôles de Croissance,' Regional Interactions, and National Development."

located in precise places. Furthermore, explicit criteria must exist for determining the types and scale of links which ought to exist among diverse elements of a development plan. If applied not mechanistically, but in a broadly consultative manner, the pole approach provides a healthy blend of economic, demographic, administrative, spatial, and political criteria of localization. Although the two are not indissociable, this approach to integrated planning is fully compatible with the regulative principles of development outlined in this book. Pole theory recognizes overtly the need to *concentrate innovations* in optimum centers, in order to foster the *propagation* of benefits and decisions throughout zones of influence, and to unify disparate zones and poles through a network of interrelated systems of exchange (of knowledge, of people, of goods) within which all innovations disseminated acquire new *signification*. Indeed, it is signification itself quite as much as innovation which is created and disseminated.[13]

Although the pole approach is well suited to solving problems of regional disparity and sectorial disequilibrium, it is not founded on a static vision of "balanced growth." On the contrary, it deliberately seeks to create assorted kinds of dynamic imbalances without, however, overlooking such long-term objectives as heightened solidarity and the establishment of reciprocal interdependence. In short, it supplies the elements needed for integrating geographical with economic variables contained in a plan. As such, it is a necessary complement to the strategy of diffused consultation described above, which is designed primarily to meet the psychological, pedagogical, and political needs of sound planning. The spatial approach links project-making with intangible "humane" goals. Only solid expertise can decide such matters as the number and quality of poles chosen in a given planning region (how many primary poles, secondary or tertiary poles), how the "vocations of regions" or homogeneous zones are to be determined, how zones of influence are to be measured, whether they can be created by a deliberate act of will, and the like.[14]

13 For a more complete exposition of the general theory of development based on the triad "innovation," "propagation," and "signification," the reader is referred to Perroux, *Cahiers de l'I.S.E.A.* (Institut de Sciences Economiques Appliquées), Nos. 1, 2, 3 (Series I, 1957) and No. 12 (Series F, 1959); to "La Méthode de l'Economie Généralisée et l'Economie de l'Homme" in *Economie et Civilisation*, Tome 2 (Les Editions Ouvrières, 1958); and to *La Coexistence Pacifique*, 3 vols. (Presses Universitaires de France, 1958).

14 For this, cf. L. J. Lebret, *Dynamique Concrète du Développement* (Les Editions Ouvrières, 1961), pp. 257ff.

The Diffusion of Responsibility

Finally, the integration of partial planning at all levels is inseparable from decisions concerning the distribution of responsibility for integration. This raises hard questions as to optimal planning organization, both internally or within the central government structure, and externally or throughout an area and a population. Given the purely seminal nature of these summary reflections on strategy, it lies outside the bounds of this work to settle outstanding disputes.[15] The crucial principle is that all procedures aimed at integration be tested against their greater or lesser contribution to the values expressed in the three regulative principles of development elaborated earlier. Tinbergen correctly asserts that little serious thought has been given to an optimum procedure. By this he means "the procedure leading, with the minimum expense and trouble, to a plan that will satisfy certain requirements of realism and consistency. . . . Only very abstract statements can be made about the method by which it is possible to find the optimum procedure." [16]

Lebret, for his part, has summarized his own principles for solving the problem as follows: *"The overall administrative scheme,* in this perspective, is extremely simple. Authorities in lesser geographical units ought to include a political official who is directly responsible to the Ministry of the Interior, as well as an official responsible for development and who depends directly on the Ministry for Development. The development officer is to remain subordinate to the political officer with whom he should work in continuous liaison. But the political officer in turn must abide by economic directives formulated by the Ministry of Development. Technical personnel within the administrative bureaucracies of large and small regions nonetheless are to remain dependent on the implementing ministries, although such personnel must insert their action within the regional plan. Evidently the political modalities to be envisaged are extremely varied according

---

[15] On this, cf., e.g., Graeme C. Moodie, ed., *Government Organization and Economic Development* (Development Centre [OECD], 1964); also *Organization, Planning and Programming for Economic Development,* Vol. VIII of U.S. Papers Prepared for the United Nations Conference on the Application of Science and Technology for the Benefit of the Less Developed Areas (U.S. Government Printing Office, 1962), esp. pp. 1–15 and 130–137.

[16] Tinbergen, *op. cit.,* pp. 177–178.

to the political institutions which pre-exist in each country, and according to particular needs and possibilities." [17]

Lebret is confident of the validity of his prescriptions because his over-all methodology of development is organic and embraces all stages: preliminary studies, coordination of research, training, institution-building, planning, and mobilization. He has insisted particularly on the need for flexible multi-disciplinary action teams working regionally and sectorially so as to join vertical (administrative) directives to horizontal (regional and sectorial) decision-making. However one judges the technical merits of his approach, it is imbued with the kind of normative sensitivity I advocate. If, as I maintain, the goals of development are optimum life-sustenance, esteem, and freedom; if, furthermore, all normative strategies ought to obey the principles of subordinating quantitative gains to qualitative progress, create expanded webs of solidarity, and optimize participation, it makes good sense to integrate planning along the lines sketched out by Perroux and Lebret. If, on the other hand, these goals and principles are rejected, one can rest content with procedures designed merely to increase efficiency, viewed as a self-validating end and measured in macro-economic indices. Needless to say, ethical considerations cannot prescind from questions of available manpower or from real possibilities existing in given time spans. Without such realism, ethics is clearly a futile exercise.

A serious challenge to my position is embodied in Hagen's view, cited earlier, that most people do not seek responsibility for their own destiny and are quite happy to escape from freedom.[18] To a considerable degree, Hagen argues, the reason for their attitude is that they fall prey to anxieties if they enter arenas of decision-making in which they feel little or no competence. My reply is simply that one's self-image of his competence need not remain static. In any case, if a population, after having been respectfully informed and consulted about changes affecting its vital future, chooses to delegate its responsibilities to its own hierarchical leaders, so be it!

People will not have had something imposed on them by leaders not of their choosing or, at least, tacitly accepted by them. The case for non-elitist participation in the planning procedure does not, in a word, rest on the presumed universality of a desire for free and re-

[17] Lebret, *op. cit.,* pp. 418–419.
[18] Everett E. Hagen, "Are Some Things Valued by All Men?" *Cross Currents,* Fall 1968, Vol. XVIII, No. 4, pp. 406–414.

sponsible self-management. All it requires is a value judgment about the desirability of respecting the preferences of a populace, whatever these may be. It should be obvious that what I present is no detailed blueprint for strategies to be employed in planning, but merely a perspective within which the means selected for achieving stipulated ends become amenable to ethical appraisal.

CHAPTER EIGHT

Technical Cooperation in a
New Key

The transfer of knowledge and skills from one category of people to another with a view to fostering development is known as "technical assistance." Although the term usually applies to advisors working in a country other than their own, technical assistance problems are also met within nations, in transfers from one region, sector, or stratum of society to another. Disappointment with results has led to considerable soul-searching of late concerning the proper aims, modalities, and extent of technical assistance. Recurring criticism centers on the very term "assistance," which smacks of charity, paternalism, or some other attitude demeaning to the recipient. This being so, it is preferable to speak of technical "cooperation," which implies a twofold exchange, not the unilateral conferral of knowledge upon inert receivers.

This chapter examines briefly the nature of cooperation, the major flaws in technical assistance as now conducted, and the structural reasons for these deficiencies. Finally, an ethical strategy for remedying these deficiencies is proposed. As here employed, "technical assistance" designates transfers of expertise via personal services *as presently conducted.* "Technical cooperation" refers to the same procedures *as they ought to be.* Accordingly, technical "assistance" carried out in the right mode, with the proper attitudes, and within a healthy structural setting, is "cooperation." Each context suggests which nuance is being stressed, since no unbridgeable chasm separates the two notions. Practical concessions are made to the fact that development documents repeatedly speak of technical "assistance."

The Nature of Technical Transfers

Technical transfers are linked to the social conditions extant in donor and recipient societies alike. Whenever techniques invented in particular social matrices are exported to vastly different settings, there is a risk that great psychological and value changes may occur. This is particularly true when the techniques in question are derived from the application of the social sciences. Most technical transfers made for development purposes do in fact rely on social sciences: transfers in education, manpower strategy, administration, research, community organization, and so on.[1]

Transfers of technique for development purposes made by persons of one society or subdivision thereof to those of another have special effects on the culture and politics of recipients. *The transfer itself is not merely a technique, but a value-laden political act with far-reaching implications.* Therefore, it can be variously defined and visualized according to one's general perceptions in politics, psychology, or sociology. This explains why one may speak of technical aid in terms of "charity," "exploitation," or "investment."[2] One may also speak of it as "reciprocity," in which case justice, not charity, exploitation, or investment, is its basis. One's general philosophy of development necessarily conditions his perception of what "aid" ought to be. Much also depends on whether the speaker is a donor or recipient of "aid." My own underlying assumptions are as follows:

—the role of "technical assistance" is accessory, not central to development;

—it can at times be a useful complement to internal efforts;

[1] This paragraph draws from Celso Furtado, "Les Conditions d'Efficacité du Transfert des Techniques," *Développement et Civilisations,* No. 26 (June 1966), p. 21.

[2] These three views are outlined by Neil H. Jacoby in *The Progress of Peoples,* Occasional Paper, Vol. II, No. 4 (June 1969), Center for the Study of Democratic Institutions, p. 10.

171

—*how* assistance is given is as important for development as *what* is provided;

—recipients are entitled to a major voice in defining the modalities of transfers;

—since different kinds of aid exist (bilateral, multilateral, international; grants, loans, "tied aid," etc.), no guidelines are equally applicable to all types;

—my own ethical norms governing aid are derived from the goals and regulative principles of development I have outlined earlier;

—technical assistance poses special problems at each of its different levels: local, regional, national, trans-national, global.

Some notion of the scale on which technical assistance is carried out in the world is obtained by recalling that in 1966 approximately 103,500 people were engaged in bilateral technical assistance (including teachers and volunteers) from member countries of the Organization for Economic Cooperation and Development alone. Concurrently, some 68,000 students and trainees were being subsidized.[3] These figures do not include personnel supplied by the United Nations, the Soviet Union, or China, but they suffice to suggest the scope of the activities under consideration.

Senegal's President Senghor declares that "culture is the beginning and the end of development."[4] Similarly, the central thesis of this book affirms that development deals with the quality of life and the values of civilization. Culture is not simply a setting from which and into which "techniques" are transferred, but a value universe affecting the total vision of society's life. It is this totality which is at stake in transfers, although not always dramatically. The major task of the recipient of technical assistance is not to assimilate techniques for mastering nature, but rather to gain full control over his own cultural evolution. Such mastery more than anything else depends on what one African writer has called the donor's "aptitude for understanding and a manner of loving."[5]

Understanding and loving are necessary because helper/helpee relationships are marred by structural paternalism. It is humiliating to

[3] From *Development Assistance Efforts and Policies, 1967 Review* (Paris: OECD, 1967), p. 46. On the United Nations, cf. *15 Years and 150,000 Skills* (New York: United Nations, 1965). Cf. also *Technical Assistance and the Needs of Developing Countries* (Paris: OECD, 1968), p. 19.

[4] Cited in Alassane N'Daw, "Pensée Africaine et Développement," *Développement et Civilisations,* No. 26 (June 1966), p. 13.

[5] *Idem,* p. 12.

have to beg, and annoying to communicate one's "superior" knowledge to one who makes claims on it. The giver easily concludes that the receiver is a parasite, whereas the recipient suspects that donors give simply in order to keep him in a state of servitude. As long as these judgments prevail, consciously or unconsciously, technical assistance cannot occur in the proper spirit. Donors need to be purged of superiority sentiments and recipients of inferiority feelings. This can happen only if the values of societies out of which technical knowledge is transferred are critically examined, and if the structure of these transfers is analyzed independently of the motives governing them.

To criticize this matrix, one must advert to the relative worth of what is communicated and the reason why transfers take place at all. What is the worth of technological expertise as compared to other values? Ellul urges us—correctly, I believe—to de-mystify technique: we must ruthlessly destroy the "myth" of technique, "the whole ideological construction and the tendency to consider technology [as] something possessing sacred character." [6] Technique is simply a particularly efficient way of solving problems. Although it has enabled men in "developed" societies to satisfy material needs, this has not been done except at great cost: wasted natural resources, expansion into other lands, and the creation of new social determinisms. The corollary to high specialization in technical achievement is the neglect of excellence in other domains: esthetic, recreational, spiritual, and emotional. Not surprisingly, many "underdeveloped" societies are the repositories of human values unmatched in "developed" societies. On balance, "technical" superiority is simply a relative good. By considering himself "superior," however, a technical "expert" reveals that he is humanly inferior and has not yet learned the primordial Socratic, Confucian, and Buddhistic lesson of humility in the face of mystery and respect for interlocutors. This structural paternalism can be offset only by a form of reciprocity which defines the purpose of transfers as follows: the creation of new value syntheses by partners from diverse cultures and technical levels. The transfer of motivations is an unavoidable element in technical cooperation. But, as Colin writes, "each man must be the proper master of the evolution of his own motivations. . . . And if someone embraces the motivations of another when these do not correspond to his own genuine human needs, he

6 Jacques Ellul, in *The Technological Order* (Wayne State University Press, 1963), p. 26.

has become the object of a certain kind of colonialism." [7] Domination effects must be explicitly recognized if effective counterpoises are to be established. The main objective of technical assistance is to help men plan their own development, not to plan it for them. This is why good technicians seek to become superfluous as rapidly as possible. Is technical assistance presently conducted in this mode, however?

Deficiencies of the Present System

Technical cooperation is inherently difficult and, by definition, a country in need of technical assistance is ill-prepared to make optimum use of proffered help.

For years donors labored under the illusion that development was relatively easy and that technical assistance was a simple operation. Now that these simplistic hopes have been dashed, there is greater pessimism, and greater realism, than before. Even flawless technical assistance, however, cannot succeed unless it is matched by sound over-all development policies within a country, and a favorable conjuncture in the world at large. For this reason it is difficult to identify with precision the deficiencies in technical assistance as it is now practiced. The difficulty is compounded by the fact that technical aid-giving follows many patterns and operates under diverse auspices, on different time scales, and for different purposes. The deficiencies listed below summarize complaints frequently voiced about transfer procedures.

Elitism exists as a general problem. The view of development presented in this book emphasizes popular participation in development decisions. Quite logically, therefore, it judges any formula of technical assistance which buttresses elitist patterns of transfer to be unacceptable. A general impression of elitism is created when the life-style of technicians, native or foreign, differs greatly from that of the populace and when foreign cooperators in particular adopt consumption patterns closely modeled on those of privileged groups within the undeveloped society. A populace must unmistakably see the dedication of a technician to its welfare if he is to enjoy high chances of success.

[7] Roland Colin, "L'Assistance Technique un Instrument au Service de l'Anthropologie du Développement," *Développement et Civilisations*, No. 26 (June 1966), p. 26.

A further obstacle arises from the fact that technical assistance in-escapably serves the national and global interests of donor nations. These interests are at times incompatible with the requirements of development inside the host country. To illustrate, the Alliance for Progress[8] is still poorly understood in the United States, notwith-standing monumental publicity. Nor has it fired the imaginations of Latin American development enthusiasts, for it remains essentially a bilateral program posing as a multilateral one, subordinated to the United States' hemispheric strategy. The hopes voiced at Punta del Este in 1961 harbor a contradiction. The Charter urged long-term planning and tax, administrative, and land reforms, excellent objec-tives all. Nevertheless, any Latin American who seriously espouses these goals is, within the political and ideological spectrum of his own country, a "leftist." Yet U.S. policy-makers dislike leftists and prefer native groups willing to create a "safe" climate for foreign investment and subscribe to the U.S. spheres-of-influence doctrine in the Cold War struggle. Obviously, these groups cannot be, in their own coun-tries, "leftists." Consequently, American policy toward reform gov-ernments is plagued with inconsistencies. Understandably, a wide-spread belief exists in Latin America that the Alliance for Progress is an instrument used by the United States to domesticate Latins' devel-opment efforts and keep them tamely within bounds considered "palat-able" to U.S. policy-makers. This country's unwillingness to alter the trade and tariff regulations it imposes on underdeveloped nations rein-forces Latin suspicions. And Latins wonder why the U.S. so strongly urges reforms upon them while itself remaining so reluctant to reform structures inside the United States. They also object to hearing ser-mons on wasteful arms expenditures preached by a country whose own defense budget is astronomical.

Even a sensitive and enlightened U.S. technical assistant labors un-der severe handicaps in such circumstances. Latin Americans may welcome his contribution if they recognize their need for technical skills, but they can hardly display enthusiasm for a program which subordinates their drive for development to the exigencies of a strategy aimed at maintaining U.S. hegemony. What is true of the Alliance for Progress is likewise true, in greater or lesser degree, of all bilateral programs. Multilateral and international assistance are somewhat freer of this debility. Nevertheless, the artificiality which governs the

[8] On this cf. Denis A. Goulet, "A Missing Revolution," *America*, April 2, 1966, pp. 438–440.

composition of "international" aid teams along national criteria is a symptom of the problem. The fundamental issue is that national and global interests served by technical-assistance missions are frequently hostile to development objectives in the host country.

A third major defect is the chaotic disorganization of technical assistance. Priorities are rarely formulated explicitly. As a result, host countries are often ill-prepared to use assistance fruitfully. Not enough attention has been paid to optimum sequence in the provision of advice, or to procedures for following up experts' recommendations. And general ignorance prevails among donors and recipients alike as to the absorptive capacity of any given country for different kinds of technical advice. It is difficult to gauge this capacity accurately except negatively by observing the wasteful use of expertise.

The locus of another serious organizational drawback resides in recipient countries themselves, which rarely solicit technical advice in accord with a sound order of priority needs. Equally rare is a sound sequential scheme for assistance, although certain kinds of information may be less *important* but more *urgent* than others because they constitute impediments to the fruitful use of other expertise. Project and program planning are wasteful unless preceded by a broad review of over-all needs and potential (as well as possible) resources.[9] Only in the light of needs (i.e., the distance between a normative view of the desired state of affairs and the existing situation) can objectives be delineated, at least tentatively. The coordinated series of these objectives, expressed in a definite timetable, is equivalent to a long-range perspective plan.[10] Several pre-conditions exist for non-wasteful technical assistance both within countries and on the worldwide scale. Domestic assistance cannot be well utilized unless the outlines of a general plan exist. Lacking such a plan, as Gert Brand warns, societies will continue to be "characterized by an enormous waste of mental and spiritual energy, by a waste of our most precious commodity, human beings, because we lack fundamental insights and thus cannot avoid dangerously false orientations." [11] Ideally, a three-way dialogue among technicians, politicians, and citizens is required. But without a

[9] For the distinction between potential and possible resources, cf. L. J. Lebret, *Dynamique Concrète du Développement* (Les Éditions Ouvrières, 1961), p. 195.
[10] On this cf. Denis A. Goulet, "Desenvolvimento de Comunidades," *Comissão Organizadora do Encontro do Nordeste, Anais* (Recife, 1965), pp. 187ff.
[11] Gert Brand, in *Development Plans and Programmes* (Paris: OECD, 1964), p. 19.

long-term perspective plan, even a meaningful two-way dialogue between technicians and politicians is precluded.

Assuming valid priorities, demands for diverse categories of technical cooperators must be coordinated and a sequence in these demands observed. An important difference exists between high-level advisors and specialized technicians such as agronomists, educators, extension workers, engineers, and surveyors not directly concerned with policy formulation.[12] Criteria for determining needs in each of these categories vary, as do the length of time each must serve and the working arrangements with native "counterparts." Many difficulties met in these domains are due to low absorptive capacity in recipient nations. Irrationalities are also found in the recruiting procedures of experts by agencies supplying technical assistants. Technical cooperation has not yet gained recognition as a distinct profession with specific career opportunities and responsibility. Consequently, recruiting is often done haphazardly; it obeys the capricious law of the availability of men who also happen to be professors, industrial engineers, or public bureaucrats. There rarely seems to be any objective reason for "sending them in the field" at a given time. We may without exaggeration assert that the recruitment criteria of foreign cooperators is only incidentally related to the objective needs of the host nation.

Another serious defect is the absence of suitable follow-up after missions. Like plans which get interred in archives, the recommendations of advisors are often consigned to oblivion after they depart. At times the reason is that the suggestions are unrealistic—technically sound, but oblivious of political or psychological feasibility. At other times the advice is bitter medicine which is simply ignored. Most often, however, recommendations are buried because no systematic mechanism exists for processing, evaluating, and incorporating them into ongoing national decision-making.

Not that all technical programs are inefficient, since many enjoy at least partial success. Yet, it is almost impossible to assess technical efforts supplied by governments or international agencies, since these are but a part of the total development effort. Furthermore, outsiders sometimes perform well only to have their efforts neutralized by poor domestic performance. The defects just listed, however, are symptoms of a general malaise surrounding the provision of technical assistance.

[12] Cf. Angus Maddison, Alexander Stavrianopoulos, and Benjamin Higgins, *Foreign Skills and Technical Assistance in Greek Development* (Paris: OECD, 1966), p. 13.

Until role expectations change, a truly cooperative reciprocal spirit cannot prevail.

Too frequently the inviting government, the host institution (e.g., a specific ministry, university, or particular agency), the donor government, and the individual technician all entertain conflicting notions of what the mission's purpose is. Experienced advisors cite instances of rural cooperative experts being made to work in large cities, of community developers required to teach their own language in middle-class schools. Upon further probing, it is readily apparent that A's reasons for "sending" are quite different from B's reasons for "receiving." Forthright discussion and agreement on precise roles is hard to achieve unless a great degree of confidence prevails at preliminary meetings. So long as donors imagine they are doing a "favor" by sending advisors or technicians, reciprocity is unattainable. Recipients in turn often solicit aid under misleading pretexts and try to make experts serve purposes incompatible with those stipulated in agreements. Until competent technical cooperators of integrity gain formal recognition as genuine professionals, these suspicions will remain pervasive. Perhaps a world pool of development technicians and advisors needs to be formed, whose members will constitute a professional order having clearly specified responsibilities. The precise initial steps taken toward its establishment are not of decisive importance provided the final objective is kept in view: the creation of a corps of competent, sensitive, dedicated "developers" committed to the development of all men.

World Developers

Development is a universal task, a "grand design" of immense proportions. Success calls for men with professional competence and unstinting allegiance to a common good transcending lesser loyalties to nations or ideologies. Perroux calls such men "witnesses of the human species, disengaged from their nations." Pressures will be brought to bear on these men to give their primary allegiance to merely national goals. Perroux writes: "Mandatories of states cannot, in a conference or a meeting among states, speak otherwise than as partisans and representatives of their states. Properly national leaders deprive themselves of all *immediate* influence if they consent to speak in the name of an experience or ideal higher than that of a single nation. Such vicious circles threaten the destiny of all mankind, however, and already foreshadow the death of innumerable masses or of the entire species. These [vicious] circles can only be shattered by the tacit, active allegiance of scientific elites throughout the entire world who are capable of refusal and of bearing 'heretical' witness." [13] Boulding rightly adds that what is needed is not some "professional priesthood who will symbolize the idea, propagate it, organize it, and so shepherd mankind into the post-civilized fold." [14] Rather it is a new brotherhood of developers whose function must be rendered statutory. Without doubt, mandatories of states, as of international agencies which recruit candidates as citizens of given states, cannot speak "heretically" on behalf of universal human interests. Nevertheless, conflicts of interest inherent in the transfer of technique by men loyal to particular nations cannot be dissolved unless their allegiances are expanded.

"Recipients" of technical aid must be protected. They must have the guarantee of receiving experts of proven competence who meet professional standards, men who are not at the service of other nations or business firms but formally committed to universal development objectives. It will be reassuring for these people to know that the "experts" sent them have been educated to believe in the relativity of their own technical superiority. After some years it is a consummation devoutly to be wished that all technical "assistance" be effectively transformed into genuine "cooperation."

The benefits to be gained by those who suffer most from bad technical transfers justify internationalizing and professionalizing the art of technical transfers. Nonetheless, it is necessary at this juncture to lay to rest the fears of those who assert that an internationalized technician might become not a "citizen of the world" but a veritable psychic expatriate, a man without the health-giving cultural roots which allegiance to a country ordinarily supplies. But the dangers faced by a "man without a country" can be overcome if we heed a recommendation made long ago by Mannheim. Men truly emancipated from the demon of national allegiance place scant value on their place of residence or birth. We usually call this process uprooting, and Mannheim explains that "the pejorative sense of the term is justified insofar as with most people loss of identification with a definite locale and nonparticipation in community life leads to disintegration of character.

13 François Perroux, *La Coexistence Pacifique* (Paris: Presses Universitaires de France, 1958), III, 623.
14 Kenneth Boulding, *The Meaning of the Twentieth Century* (Harper & Row, 1964), p. 198. For an interesting viewpoint on the "priesthood" of technocrats, according to Saint-Simon and Rathenau, cf. Georges Duveau, *Sociologie de l'Utopie* (Presses Universitaires de France, 1961), pp. 62–64.

This detachment from a locale of one's own leaves a feeling of belonging somewhere either undeveloped or unfulfilled. It makes for mental insecurity and unattached emotional states, leaving people easy prey to propaganda." [15] Nevertheless, it is a mistake to overlook the positive aspects of uprooting for "personality formation and the construction of a world community. Uprooting, viewed positively, might be called emancipation. Hardly anybody will doubt that the establishment of larger communities—possibly a world-wide community—is possible only if people overcome the state of unconditional subservience to the power demon of national sovereignty and aggressive nationalism. Partial uprooting, emancipation, is therefore necessary and is indeed achieved by progressive man." [16]

Professionalization on a fully international basis is a major step toward achieving better technical cooperation. After commenting on the technical incompetence of many visiting experts and warning "that anything short of a good performance can be disastrous," Indian economist Jagdish Bhagwati concludes that "the whole procedure of recruitment should be institutionalized." [17] Moreover, as I have written elsewhere, "Development specialists have long worried about the unprofessional manner in which many advisors are recruited for service in Third World countries. A few psychologists have even hinted privately at the existence of a special 'foreign technician' syndrome. A number of complaints have been voiced about the lack of standards for overseas service in such categories as length of service, chain of command in the country of service, the obligation of the foreign advisor or technician to train native replacements, different pay-scales operating as counter-incentives to qualified native personnel, rules concerning the communication to host countries of information gathered during a mission. Lebret has urged the international adoption of a code of ethical standards that would assure host countries that they are receiving only qualified reliable professionals. Yet there is a general reluctance to discuss this publicly. I therefore propose that the idea of such a code be brought into the open and seriously considered." [18] Professionalization, in short, ought to take place. A profession meets three criteria: it embraces practical skills, implies knowl-

[15] Karl Mannheim, *Freedom, Power and Democratic Planning* (London: Routledge & Kegan Paul, 1951), p. 62.
[16] *Idem.*
[17] Jagdish Bhagwati, *The Economics of Underdeveloped Countries* (McGraw-Hill, 1966), p. 227.
[18] Denis A. Goulet, "That Third World," *The Center Magazine,* September 1968, p. 54.

edge of a body of abstract knowledge, and includes specific moral commitment to virtue in the exercise of those skills. Quite obviously, no plan to institutionalize technical cooperation suitably can be implemented instantaneously; it is feasible only in conjunction with the preparation of a world development plan. Nevertheless, initial steps can be taken to legitimize and upgrade the arts of technical cooperation. There already exists an embryonic consciousness among large numbers of development cooperators belonging to a larger brotherhood—what Boulding calls the "invisible college" [19] of men dedicated to broad human goals. Although professionalization is no cure for all present deficiencies, it could play an invaluable *pedagogical* role by educating technicians to the trans-national, trans-cultural, and trans-ideological dimensions of development. However modestly, it would summon men endowed with the knowledge and skills most urgently needed for development to place their talents at the service of the human race's priority needs. In 1950 Stringfellow Barr wrote a short book entitled *Let's Join the Human Race*. Developers might well take the lead in doing just that!

This recommendation is but one step toward a generalized ethic of technical cooperation. The Hippocratic Oath might conceivably be transposed to fit the situation of technical cooperators. Doctors swear: "Whatsoever house I enter, there will I go for the benefit of the sick, refraining from all wrongdoing or corruption . . . and the regimen I adopt shall be for the benefit of my patients according to my ability and judgment, and not for their hurt or for any wrong." Developers might swear: "Whatever community I visit, there will I work on behalf of those in greatest need, with them and on their terms, not as a dispenser of superior wisdom but as a cooperator in the common task of creating wisdom to match our sciences. I will refrain from all condescension, paternalism, exploitation and manipulation . . . and the regimen I adopt shall be for the benefit of men's universal needs, not for any particular interests." Such an oath would confirm the lofty goals of the Universal Declaration of Human Rights proclaimed by the United Nations in 1948 regarding the right of each individual to share in the cultural and scientific progress of mankind and to live within an international order suited to his own freedoms and aspirations (Articles 27 and 28).

It is not necessary, or perhaps even useful, to draft a detailed professional "code." Circumstances of underdevelopment are so fluid and varied that no "code" can adequately express the kind of commitment

[19] Boulding, *op. cit.*, pp. 191–199.

visualized. I do not propose to frame a detailed ethic of technical cooperation,[20] but merely to urge that its provisions optimize the values embodied in the regulative principles of development. The aim of such an ethic is to dramatize the nobility of a high "calling," to introduce greater rationality in recruitment and career-promotion processes, and to assist skilled men to make their contributions where needs are greatest. It seems reasonable to hope that creative research and experimentation in this vein would lead to new solutions to the brain-drain problem. If successful, this scheme could eliminate much ill-will over sharply differential salary scales paid to foreign and to indigenous developers. Moreover, disciplinary rules touching on length of service, vacations, retooling education for experts, and the like would be imposed. Admittedly, problems of salary differentials and retooling are not solved merely by creating an international guild of developers for foreign technicians, educators, and developers. Native counterparts working within their own countries must also be given access to membership in the same guild. And both categories of developers would contribute on an equal basis to the progress of all peoples. The suggestion is not startling to those who take seriously Robert Buron's recommendation to "create a doctrine and an ethic which are capable of mobilizing energies at the service of international solidarity." [21] The major tragedy of underdevelopment is that enormous potential human energies are allowed to lie dormant for lack of a rational plan of attack on problems of global magnitude. According to one African observer, foreign assistance and aid "breed *the waste of goods.* Dispensed according to the criteria we know and subordinated to conditions which are determined unilaterally, they are rarely adapted to the demands of harmonious development. Aid constitutes in certain cases a vain sacrifice for the donor, whereas its recipient profits very little from it." [22] Lebret further laments the "*considerable waste* of rare specialists." [23] Above all, we must do away with the stereotype that citizens of one country are always on the

[20] This ethic must set standards for such diverse questions as the kind of work suited to different categories of technical cooperation, length of service in varying circumstances, salary policies, guidelines for vacations, security, tenure, pensions, and so on. Major attention must also be given to the de-politization of technical cooperation, issues of cultural adaptation, conflicts of interest, sanctions, life-styles.

[21] Robert Buron, *Développement et Civilisations,* No. 1 (1960), p. 19.

[22] Michel Dembele, "Les Nouvelles Voies de la Coopération Internationale," *Développement et Civilisations,* No. 26 (June 1966), p. 5.

[23] L. J. Lebret, "La Coopération Technique Devant les Perspectives du Développement Authentique," in *ibid.,* p. 50.

"giving" end and others on the "receiving" end of technical expertise. A tentative outline of the professional obligations which ought to be assumed by world developers has come from the pen of Lebret. He lists twelve principles[24] to be observed if optimal use is to be made of technical assistance. They are:

(1) Indivisibility. Development is a complex operation whose parts are interconnected. It requires interventions which relate to the whole and to each phase;

(2) Proper sequence in the conduct of preliminary studies and subsequent operations (cartography and statistics first, survey of needs and resources next, etc.);

(3) Honesty in the face of bad projects: an advisor can sometimes render his best service by denouncing an error before it becomes a morass of irreversible catastrophes;

(4) Appeal to competent specialists. Experts are required not to promise what they cannot deliver and to work in teams with colleagues possessing complementary skills. Due to unforeseen difficulties, it is sometimes necessary to appeal to a high-level expert for short periods. Technicians responsible for the success of an operation must not, out of pride, refuse to make this appeal;

(5) Sufficient time. Circumstances vary, but in general it is sheer irresponsibility to undertake tasks within periods of time which are too short;

(6) Authentic teamwork. Objectivity demands complementarity among members, the habitual capacity to work together constructively, the sharing of a basic viewpoint on development, the common practice of a precise method tested through numerous experiences, and unanimous earnestness in the search for solutions to urgent problems.

(7) Collaboration with technicians and research personnel of the host country. Continuous interaction is required between foreign and native personnel. The latter must enjoy roles of responsibility in the

---

[24] L. J. Lebret, "Alerte à l'Assistance Technique," *Développement et Civilisations*, No. 2 (June 1960), pp. 15–26. For more details on Lebret's view of the professional ethic, the sequence of studies, and the proper administrative structures, cf. his "Ensemble des Opérations d'Analyse Préalables à Tout Développement Ordonné," *Développement et Civilisations*, No. 3 (September 1960), pp. 35–49; "La Coopération Technique Devant les Perspectives du Développement Authentique: Quelques Aspects de l'Evolution Nécessaire," *Développement et Civilisations*, No. 26 (June 1966), pp. 46–56; and "Analyse des Compétences Nécessaires à l'Etablissement d'un Programme de Développement et à Son Execution," *Développement et Civilisations*, No. 9 (January/March 1962), pp. 49–62.

"foreign" team itself, and outsiders are morally bound to prepare counterparts to dispense with their own services. Finally, leadership must be conferred on local personnel at the earliest opportune moment;

(8) Assistance at middle and grass-roots levels. Expertise at the summit alone is not adequate;

(9) Governmental and administrative organizations most favorable to development. Lebret urges policy advisors to insist that host governments adopt governmental and administrative structures well adapted to the requirements of development;

(10) Follow-up. "Follow-up is so important that each team ought to leave behind at the disposal of the host country temporary or permanent counselors, chosen among the best-qualified members of the team, to assist in implementing recommendations and continuing operations. This is a way of attenuating that kind of anguish which takes hold of a developer when he leaves a country for which he has worked with genuine love. He understands that the report he delivers to local authorities expresses but a tiny fraction of what the team has learned. Moreover, the practice now advocated would reduce the impression gathered by the one to whom the report is destined that he has been left with the bare skeleton of a plan in his hands";

(11) Integral assistance. Lebret believes that the sums already spent on technical assistance by 1960 would have sufficed, had they been well spent, to gather sufficient data for establishing a worldwide development plan. Efforts must henceforth tend in this direction. An operation of such magnitude can succeed only if carried out in a spirit of total disinterestedness. "A greater degree of cooperation must be established among multilateral, bilateral and private assistance, as well as with recipient countries. Its purpose would be to avoid futile duplication of effort, reduce the cost of studies undertaken, and establish plans for national entities and for large economic spaces capable of being coordinated one with the other";

(12) Guaranteed quality of experts and technical assistants. Lebret explains that: "Given the constellation of technical and moral qualities which assistance requires, each expert or assistant ought to be the bearer of a document which attests to his titles and mentions all the specialities he has acquired and all the field work he has done.

"It is even worth asking whether it is not appropriate to establish an 'Order' of experts, analogous to the professional Order of lawyers and medical doctors. To diagnose the general and detailed problems of a country requires no less competence, nor less professional honor, than to examine a case in justice or an individual patient who is ill. Since it is difficult to imagine such an Order on an international basis, it might perhaps be better to start with individual countries or groupings of countries, in such manner that the quality of each member is guaranteed within a framework of mutual controls which engage the responsibility of the whole Corps of experts.

"Even if we do not go this far, it would no doubt be possible to find ways of assuring countries which request assistance as to the qualifications of expert and technical personnel, and draw up rules making it mandatory that genuine teams be constituted, characterized by suitable competence, conscientiousness, complementarity and cohesion.

"As for conscience, a kind of 'code of honor' might be drafted. Acceptance of this code would be a condition '*sine qua non*' for admission into a development team."

After drafting these principles, Lebret declares that "the profession of expert is one of the noblest and most demanding possible. The ethics of the expert, of the assistant, and of the advisor has not yet been elaborated. It would be urgent to begin working on it if we do not wish to risk losing prestige and lowering morale to such an extent that international cooperation in a domain where ethics ought to rule would be rendered difficult."

One major question to be clarified is that of professional qualifications. Who is included in the "profession" and what credentials must he have? Something more than mere "paper" qualifications are needed, because the capacity to handle cross-cultural problems is one of the prime qualities sought. So are the ability to recognize the limits of one's knowledge, and the refusal to pretend to possess abilities one does not in fact have. Competence may need to be defined in explicit terms at different levels, ranging from qualities required of a UN "junior expert," a volunteer worker, through the range of middle-level technician, to that of top-level policy advisors.

Serious provision needs to be made for re-educating cooperators periodically in accord with a coherent and global inter-disciplinary view of development.[25] By "interdisciplinary training" in development is meant something other than the mere juxtaposition of diverse fragmentary bodies of knowledge or the breakdown of problems into their

[25] An appraisal of ten years' experimentation in the pedagogy of development is found in "L'IRFÉD, d'Hier et Demain," *Développement et Civilisations*, No. 34 (June 1968), entire issue.

analytical components. At the very least, interdisciplinary training for developers has these three requirements:

(1) broad examination into the ideological settings of existing major cultures and civilizations and into their responses to technology and mass communications;

(2) mutual initiation of all "developers" to the basic theoretical assumptions and methodological procedures of all important disciplines concerned with development (e.g., economics, demography, planning, human geography, etc.); and

(3) common responsibility for a development operation in its entirety or, at least, for portions of that operation having a certain autonomy. Full responsibility must be assumed by members of all disciplines working as a team. As these members exchange views and dialogue with the populace destined to become the co-agent of its own development, they must speak in three distinct, interrelated capacities:

—as specialists;

—as generalists attempting to produce a synthesis of the whole of reality; and

—as bearers of values, biases, and preferences.

All three kinds of discourse will generate knowledge which is to be debated and criticized by all. Moreover, specialized training and upgrading programs for developers are to be designed on principles consonant with the requirements just outlined. Fully developed standards for technical cooperation, however, must necessarily await direct experimentation in multiple settings. The purpose of these pages has been to suggest principles and possible modalities of initial action. They are submitted as one example of what a normative strategy for technical cooperation might be.

CHAPTER NINE

*Existence Rationality and the
Dynamics of Value Change*

The ability to change their external environment in ways suited to the satisfaction of perceived need is one hallmark of developed societies. But men also have an inner environment comprising the world of their aspirations and motives. Not surprisingly, therefore, psychic empathy is an important index of their capacity for change. Psychic empathy is the quality possessed by people who can project themselves in roles other than their own and introject the attributes of others within their own self-image. It is, in the words of Daniel Lerner, the "inner mechanism which enables newly mobile persons to operate efficiently in a changing world." [1] Men become capable of desiring development when they perceive that their internal and external environments alike are subject to change. Whether or not "traditional" societies are shackled with attitudes hostile to change is, therefore, an important question.

One common assumption holds that underdeveloped societies are mired in the incapacity to manipulate natural forces rationally in the service of economic ends. Impotence in the face of nature is said to breed a passivity uncongenial to precisely those changes which are

[1] Daniel Lerner, *The Passing of Traditional Society* (The Free Press, 1964), p. 49.

most needed if technology is to be harnessed to the satisfaction of wants. Change agents often blame resistance to development on such passivity. This view distorts reality, however, and this chapter proposes an alternative explanation of receptivity and resistance to change. Its focus is the question: how can a strategy for *inducing* value change best be devised? Elements of a strategy for conducting *research* on value change are outlined in Appendix III.

Existence Rationality

Societies are conventionally designated by writers on development as traditional, transitional, or modern, although in truth a small number of societies are now entering the post-modern stage. My central thesis is that the acceptance or rejection of developmental change depends primarily on the manner in which change is proposed, not on any basic hostility to change inherent in traditional societies. The key to understanding why receptivity varies is "existence rationality," defined as the *process* by which a society devises a conscious strategy for obtaining its goals, given its ability to process information and the constraints weighing upon it. All societies treat survival as a minimum goal. Moreover, all men depend on society for the satisfaction of certain needs related to esteem and freedom. By definition, underdeveloped societies are unable to maximize material satisfactions as well as a wide range of psychological satisfactions whose enjoyment presupposes an abundance of goods. On the other hand, they can optimize choices aimed at meeting minimum demands for survival, identity, solidarity, and esteem. Any sound strategy of induced change must, therefore, restructure the outer boundaries of a society's existence rationality, not eliminate its core. Initially at least, the image of rationality implicit in modernization appears "alien" to minds not already conditioned by it. It is erroneous to conclude, however, that irrationality prevails in the instruments used by pre-modern societies for meeting the demands of survival and other basic needs. This is true even when economic activity appears stagnant. For this reason, whenever one image of existence rationality challenges another, several conditions must be met if the entrenched image is to be displaced by the intruder image. Because existence rationality concerns survival and need-satisfaction under present capacities of processing information and under total constraints, suitable means must be found enabling

188

men to process a greater amount and variety of information than previously. In addition, whether they are rooted in the paucity of resources or in rigidities of the allocation system, old constraints must in some way be rendered unacceptable and unnecessary. Inasmuch as the core values of all existence rationalities are designed to nurture survival, basic esteem, and freedom, these values should not be challenged frontally. Such an attack risks being arbitrary and unduly threatening to basic identity. If change is to be welcomed, three conditions must be met: (a) new capacities for handling information must be generated; (b) vital resources hitherto not available must become exploitable; and (c) the alien rationality implicit in "modernization" must be re-interpreted in terms of traditional existence rationalities. Innovation must be rendered compatible with the demands of both present existence and what we may call "expanded" existence. This means in practice that impact on the attitudes of depressed populations can be made only at the margins of their existence rationality.

Two distinct problems arise, however, in the encounter between existence rationalities drawn from a "modern" and a pre-modern society. One difficulty relates to the quality of modernization realized in the former. Is the pattern of development being proposed for acceptance a sound one? Or does it embody a distortion of what authentic development is? The second difficulty bears on the *manner* in which innovation is presented. It will be evident to the reader that I regard much of what is called "development" to be spurious— in truth, to be anti-development. The problem is *how* authentic development can be communicated to men living in societies whose existence rationality is based on values totally different from those operative in supposedly "developed" societies. Even if we assume the soundness of what is culturally exchanged, receptivity is a major problem. As stated above, the core of pre-modern existence rationality must be respected and innovative efforts, by insiders as well as by outsiders, must concentrate on the outer margins of that strategy for survival and meaning.

Even narrow existence rationalities offer considerable scope for new achievements, provided these reinforce the dominant strategy adopted by society to assure life-sustenance, the search for esteem (especially in-group esteem), freedom from unwanted constraints, and some form of actualization of its own choosing. In the absence of the ability to plan a different future for themselves or gain occupational and social mobility, depressed people frequently portray freedom to themselves in spatial or symbolic terms. This is why mobilization strategies must protect the inner limits of old existence rationalities while expanding their outer boundaries. Such safeguards can be achieved by providing tangible rewards to those in the underdeveloped group who remain faithful to the core of their existence rationality while contributing to its expansion. Similarly, rewards must be denied to those who "betray" the existence rationality of the group by accepting development uncritically. Native as well as foreign agents of "progress" are usually uncritical carriers of values which lie hidden behind the screen of visible benefits. Since change agents' critical abilities are so meager, development's putative beneficiaries need to develop a critical capacity *before* their destiny is decided in accord with unexamined norms. Inertia is so great that most transfers will be made uncritically unless an explicit strategy is fashioned to counteract present tendencies. To conclude from largely unchallenged evidence that development is incompatible with "traditional" value systems is not only inhuman but also foolish, even on grounds of pure efficiency. One practical consequence of this error is that few planners tailor development's potentially attractive benefits to the dimensions of traditional existence rationalities. Perceptive students of development have long known, of course, that certain traditional values are consonant with innovation. Hirschman has analyzed with great acuity the difference between an ego-focused and a group-focused image of change.

He rightly states that "the feeling that change and progress is possible and desirable is bound to represent a highly dynamic force in a hitherto stationary society. But if this feeling is due primarily to outside demonstration rather than to one's own experience, it may lead to a variety of misconceptions about the process of change that inhibit the achievements of the new goal until a modicum of learning has been achieved." [2] Some non-developed societies nourish predominantly group-focused, others ego-focused, images of change. An overly group-focused image is unsatisfactory because many sound development projects are incompatible with the view that any progress must produce gain for everyone in the community. Such a view grew out of a situation in which total product was stationary and in which all individual advancement was seen as damaging the welfare of others and group cohesiveness. Because good policy dictates priorities and the creation of economic opportunities which some will seize

[2] Albert O. Hirschman, *The Strategy of Economic Development* (Yale University Press, 1965), p. 11.

upon and others will let pass, this image proves congenial only to certain kinds of change such as anti-malaria campaigns or general welfare programs, which in fact do benefit everyone simultaneously. Yet it interferes with projects whose benefits are not equally distributed. An unduly ego-focused image of change, in turn, is harmful because it encourages personal initiative via short-cuts which "diminish the flow of energies into activities that will stimulate economic development." [3] The ability to elicit agreement among cooperators, to delegate authority, to direct a staff—in brief, to manage in the modern mode—is hostile to the ego-focused image of change. For these reasons, only a proper mix of ego- and group-focused images of change leads to optimum development. Cooperation as well as creativity is needed. Leaders in underdeveloped countries, however, find it difficult to harmonize these two exigencies. As a result, they tend to oscillate between extreme ego- and group-focused approaches to development.

This analysis sheds light on the difference between the "inner limits" and "outer boundaries" of existence rationality. Inner limits may be viewed as the indispensable core values and aspirations without which a society lacks cohesiveness and individuals lose minimum cultural identification with the group. Outer boundaries, in turn, are broad zones of attitude and behavior in which departures from normal social demands are possible. At times innovation accentuates creativity and takes the form of highly individualistic entrepreneurship. But it is also possible for innovation to generate new forms of collaboration. Most frequently, even in societies whose product appears stationary to economists, latent psychic empathy allows some members to "imagine" with relative ease hypothetical conditions wherein total product would not be stationary. Consequently, great latitude may exist in the degree to which even personally advantageous innovation can be tolerated. Such innovation need not be viewed as injurious, either to society's other members or to the group's core values. Stated differently, most "traditional" societies display no congenital hostility to innovation. Much depends on how innovation is proposed to them. If change is "clothed" in garments which do not threaten the inner limits of existence rationality, it can elicit flexible responses in the arena of existence rationality's outer boundaries. Existence rationality, it will be recalled, is a strategy for survival, for obtaining esteem and freedom from needless determinisms. Within this perspective, the psychic mobility present in "traditional" societies may be consider-

[3] *Idem,* p. 16.

able, although less apparent than change dynamisms easily discernible in "transitional" or "modern" societies. If this is so, traditional value structures do not of themselves create obstacles to change. On the contrary, it is insensitive, narrow impact strategies for inducing change which snuff out traditional societies' latent potential for change. This latent capacity often lies hidden beneath deceptive appearances of immobility. If properly stimulated, however, such potential can be kineticized and allow innovation to be grafted onto present existence rationality.

Before commenting on the policy implications of this perspective on change, I shall describe, for illustrative purposes, the "existence rationality" of one marginal underdeveloped group: Gypsies in southern Spain. Admittedly, Gypsies differ from the majority of the world's underdeveloped populations. I must therefore explain how findings obtained from marginals are applicable to typical underdeveloped populations.

The Representativity of Marginals

Any population not integrated into modern economic, social, and political circuits is in this sense marginal. Marginality is the lot of the majority in underdeveloped areas where the bulk of the population is rural or has recently moved to the city physically while remaining psychically distant from the urban world-view.[4] For the sake of convenience, we may call underdeveloped people M_1 marginals, since they are effectively excluded from circuits of modernity and of transition toward modernity. The term M_1 marginals also evokes their numerical importance; these people constitute the majority of an underdeveloped region or nation. Peasants in India, *fellahin* in Egypt, and fishermen in the Greek islands, for example, all qualify as M_1 marginals.

Smaller groups can be found who, in addition to being underdeveloped, have some distinct ethnic, religious, or cultural trait. Montagnards in central Vietnam, primitive Indians in the Amazon, and Harratin ex-slaves in the Sahara fit into this second category, which we may call M_2 marginals. Their marginality has two layers: exclu-

---

[4] The situation of recent arrivals in large cities from farm areas is analyzed by Richard W. Patch, "La Parada, Lima's Market," *American Universities Field Staff Reports*, Vol. XIV, No. 1, 2, 3, all dated 1967.

sion from society's modern sectors, and differentiation from majority "underdeveloped" groups around them. Certain borderline cases can doubtless be found. On the other hand, so-called "pariah" groups (Lebanese in Africa, overseas Chinese in South Asia, Indians in East Africa) are not fully marginal to the developed sectors of the societies in which they live. They are often engaged in entrepreneurial activities like trade, banking, and small industry. The basic question, however, is not what constitutes a marginal man but rather: do findings about M_2 groups constitute a valid source of information regarding M_1 marginals?

Without doubt, M_1 marginals are of primary interest to researchers seeking to understand the causes of underdevelopment. They constitute the hard-core problem, the people for whom development is the crucial issue. Scholars encounter great difficulty, however, in studying adequately large groups of peasants, unskilled city workers, or small artisans. Where these groups comprise large majorities of total population, reliable statistics are often lacking. Consequently, many research instruments employed successfully by social scientists in other contexts cannot be used. A good sample, for example, presupposes the existence of valid statistics from which random units to be studied can be selected. When such information is grossly defective in quality, one cannot proceed with security. Moreover, certain characteristics of typical underdeveloped populations make them exorbitantly expensive to study, in virtue of the need to repeat visits in order to find respondents at home or to induce them to answer questionnaires. Certain methods which have produced good results in the anthropological study of social change are useful. But even these risk treating reality in static fashion, whereas many dynamisms of change are not amenable to study by these methods. Accordingly, efforts at identifying common traits in both kinds of marginal groups can facilitate the task of generalizing about all underdeveloped groups. This is why the Gypsy case study described below is relevant to the study of value change in the broader development universe. There are, in summary, four reasons why illustrative materials drawn from a small group of M_2 marginals throw light on receptivity to change among M_1 marginals, the underdeveloped masses of the Third World.

(a) By definition, M_2 marginals are more homogeneous than M_1 marginals. Since development efforts within national boundaries are usually conducted, at least nominally, in the interest of the masses of M_1 marginals, the transition from underdevelopment to modernity is perceived by M_2's as posing a greater threat to group existence than by M_1 marginals. The reason is that development programs must be publicized as being beneficial to "underprivileged masses," not to small, twice-marginalized groups. A government's commitment to development, therefore, creates a special crisis for small M_2 marginals. And it is well known that periods of crisis create the most favorable conditions for studying values.[5]

(b) It is easier to isolate value changes in M_2 marginal groups because their values are more explicit than those of M_1 marginals. The "inner limits" and the "outer boundaries" (different kinds of values) are easier to identify in small atypical groups than in highly differentiated and large underdeveloped populations. The notion of "existence rationality" is hypothetical; accordingly, its explanatory force must be tested by further research, perhaps also by experimentation. Yet research and experimentation are easier to conduct in small groups than in large underdeveloped populations, some of whose characteristics render ordinary methodologies inapplicable or too expensive.

(c) The major problem in extrapolating from studies of untypical to typical marginals is representativity. Hence, it becomes important to identify similarities no less than differences between M_1 and M_2 marginals. Equally important in both cases is to determine the locus of conflict with innovating agents, whether change is resisted or greeted with indifference. Comparative information drawn from both types of societies provides a useful starting point for analyzing the challenge of development faced by large M_1 marginal populations. Moreover, the relative importance of distinctive traits found in M_2 groups in determining their response to developmental innovations may offer interesting hypotheses for study and action on behalf of M_1 groups.

(d) A final reason concerns diversity in social development. René Dubos[6] argues persuasively that ecological and cultural diversity must be promoted if the human species is not to be stunted biologically and culturally. It is therefore important for development policymakers to learn how small M_2 groups have preserved their identity in the face of secular pressures. Equally important is the discovery of

[5] As shown by Clyde Kluckhohn and others, "Values and Value Orientations in the Theory of Action," in *Toward a General Theory of Action*, ed. Talcott Parsons and Edward A. Shils (Harper Torchbooks, 1962), p. 408.
[6] René Dubos, *Man Adapting* (Yale University Press, 1965), *passim*.

how they preserve (or lose) identity in the midst of contemporary pressures to modernize. Careful scrutiny of small marginal groups may suggest which psychological, sociological, or mythical forces support a society in its resistance to assimilative or integrative pressures. The nurture and consolidation of such forces can itself become a suitable objective of development policy.

Gypsies

These general remarks concerning existence rationality are concretely illustrated in the specific conditions faced by an unusual group of M_2 marginals, the Gypsies of southern Spain. Gypsies are economically underdeveloped and form a cultural minority distinct from larger underdeveloped populations around them. A neglected ethnic group which has preserved its identity in the face of secular discrimination, Gypsies form a ghetto culture. Although they were originally nomadic, they are now largely sedentarized and withdraw behind barriers of tradition in the face of external threat or curiosity. Their general condition is nevertheless dependent: they are not self-determining in relation to other sectors of societies among which they live. In this respect they resemble M_1 marginals in underdeveloped lands everywhere. Interesting parallels can be drawn between Gypsies and peasant populations in many continents. Similarities with urban populations throughout the Third World are even more striking. Quite apart from similar profiles of development indicators (viz., per-capita income, literacy rates, employment structure, standard of living, and limited participation in monetary circuits), Gypsies and "typical" underdeveloped populations both contact the modern sectors of life largely through formal institutions which operate on them coercively (compulsory military service, mandatory school attendance, police controls over movements and documents, and tax impositions). There are weightier reasons, however, why the study of Gypsies helps developers understand the general problems of receptivity and resistance to change.

First, the resistance to acculturation fiercely maintained by Gypsies shows signs of breaking down. This is due to the difficulty they now experience in earning their livelihood by traditional occupations, in part also to an incipient rise in aspirations. A second relevant consideration is that Gypsies are a true ghetto society. All ghetto peoples have common traits. They are geographically isolated and conscious of being visibly different from those living in the larger out-group society; they also maintain in-group patterns of solidarity designed to protect them against the depredations—actual or potential—of majority out-groups, and they lack self-determination in their relations with other sectors of society. Almost always they must submit in humiliating fashion to rules drawn up by outsiders. Jews are a large ghetto populace which has survived for centuries. Two important differences, however, distinguish Jewish from Gypsy ghetto cultures. Jews possess a strong historical sense and a messianic consciousness, neither of which is discernible among Gypsies. Gypsies have no history: their collective memory of the past embraces only what the oldest living survivor personally remembers and can report on his own authority. Their historical memory covers three or four generations at most. They also lack any sense of mission, whether based on a special mandate from heaven or on destiny.

The Gypsies' special condition is pertinent to an understanding of development, in part because the structural constraints common to any ghetto society suggest that it may be easier to mobilize them than other marginals around a cause recognized as acceptable. More particularly, the absence of history implies that Gypsies might show great receptivity to innovation, since traditions are neither sacred nor permanent. On the other hand, low historical sense can also mean that there is very little common tradition to which all Gypsies may relate. The absence of messianism may likewise make it difficult for Gypsies to "identify" with any nation-building or developmental effort.

Most "developed" peoples harbor stereotyped images of "backward" societies. Gypsies in particular have been the object of unflattering out-group stereotypes. They are widely rumored to be thieves, to be lazy and poor workers, to be untrustworthy, to practice magic, and to lie unabashedly. False or misleading stereotypes encourage isolation and suspicion, sometimes open conflict. Stereotypes founded on fact, on the other hand, contribute to self-fulfilling behavior. If the stereotypic traits commonly depicted are unfavorable to development, self-fulfilling behavior becomes by that very fact an obstacle to desired change. Consequently, it is useful to learn what a stereotyped group itself thinks about the traits attributed to it.[7] An equally ger-

[7] On this, cf. Robert A. LeVine, "Outsiders' Judgment: An Ethnographic Approach to Group Differences in Personality," *Southwestern Journal of Anthropology*, Vol. XXII, No. 2 (1966), pp. 101–115.

mane consideration is the function of "pariah entrepreneurs." Their alienation from out-groups is psychological and cultural, rarely economic or juridical. Consequently, it is relatively easy for them to develop incentives for engaging in productive entrepreneurial activity: handicrafts, shopkeeping, or banking. Gypsies, on the contrary, suffer economic and legal discrimination as well as psychological and cultural rejection. The last to be hired and the first to be fired, they are also deprived of educational opportunities which would enable them to compete even with "underdeveloped" peers. After tolerating discrimination for centuries, Spanish Gypsies are now beginning to make demands.

The conduct of interviews among Gypsies in southern Spain (October and November 1967) has confirmed experiences in other settings and led me to postulate the "existence rationality" concept outlined above. The belief that a closed, suspicious, and traditional society would resist change has proved inapplicable in this case, as in others. Instead, great innovation potential and psychic empathy become apparent once the distinction between "inner limits" and "outer boundaries" is admitted. No claim is made that these hypothetical constructs have been definitively established, even for Gypsies themselves. I do suggest, however, that they point the way to new strategies for inducing social change in a manner which minimizes the violence done to existing value systems. It lies beyond the scope of this work to supply a detailed description of the probe conducted among Gypsies in Málaga, Granada, Almería, and Guadix.[8] Related to present purposes are tentative conclusions reached concerning the implications of research in three domains: education, planning, and the future of Gypsies as a separate cultural entity. Notwithstanding problems of representativity, these conclusions suggest policies of far-reaching consequences in general development efforts.

It should be explained that several modes of interrogation (closed and open questionnaires, projective questions) were employed. Themes discussed revolved around seven polarities:

(1) Fatalism: planning future performance versus passive acceptance.

(2) Privileges: achievement versus ascription in granting privileges within the family and the larger society.

---

[8] Cf. Denis A. Goulet and Marco Walshok, "Values Among Underdeveloped Marginals: Illustrative Notes on Spanish Gypsies," unpublished monograph, Indiana University, June 1968, 82 pp. A summary of this report is to appear in *Comparative Studies in Society and History,* Vol. XIII, No. 4 (Oct. 1971).

197

(3) Death: one's attitude toward death affects the way one lives or has no significance on behavior.

(4) God: does one think more about God when things go well or badly, or does one think of God equally at all times?

(5) Technology: one stresses positive effects of technology versus bad effects of technology.

(6) Decision-making: reliance on group opinion versus individual decision-making.

(7) Tradition: a preference for traditional ways of doing things versus a willingness to choose whatever is quickest, cheapest, or most efficient.

Projective questions dealt with (1) the most important thing in life; (2) the happiest moment in one's life; (3) the desirability of establishing a Gypsy nation; and (4) what makes today better than yesterday?

The picture derived from these studies is that of a typical depressed and excluded minority, as indicated by a high response rate on passive acceptance and cognate items. This result is somewhat surprising because certain items to which passive acceptance is linked seem to have a positive effect on the group's outlook toward its condition. Thus, a favorable view of technology, attaching no behavioral significance to belief in afterlife, and a preference for individual decision-making all appear to be elements of a viewpoint supposedly correlated with development. Nevertheless, although Gypsies understand that progress generates benefits, they do not perceive these benefits as relevant to their daily existence. Responses to the question "What makes today better than the past?" indicate a recognition that modernity brings certain gains. But the overriding passive acceptance of their present lot undercuts these positive appraisals of development. What emerges in profile is a structurally powerless group conforming to the typical apathetic pattern of marginals. While they know that the larger social system exists and perpetuates the injustices from which they suffer, Gypsies feel nothing can be done about it. This explains their resignation notwithstanding their perception of benefits to be gained by taking certain initiatives.

Amid these negative traits, however, one detects a highly refined existence rationality: that is, the ability to create strategies to attain goals of survival and cultural preservation as well as to choose between different ends within the limits of existing conditions. Gypsies are no different in this regard from other rational societies which adapt their practical thinking to the constraints imposed by their existential condition.[9] Relatively low rationality in the development of higher processes of logical manipulation is conditioned by circumstances affecting the lives of marginals. These circumstances embrace not only the structural constraints of poverty, but the psychological deprivation and the impoverishment resulting from extremely imperfect knowledge as well.[10]

Within the constraints of chronic poverty, however, this rationality keeps Gypsies alive and allows them to preserve a cultural identity. Food, health, and work are understandably the main concerns of all those interviewed. This rationality also accounts for individuals who plan, who accept the use of achievement standards in the larger society, and who display individuality in their decision-making, although they continue to verbalize passive acceptance of life's chances. Although individuals who develop these qualities are better equipped than others to satisfy survival needs, they are not yet ready to cross the threshold which would make them view positive change as imminent to their condition.

Moreover, their "existence rationality" is not a purely instrumental activity. Numerous secondary processes support the use of this rationality and help make it an attractive alternative. This is done so as to allow Gypsies to react with confirmed self-esteem to the injustice and contempt they experience. Inasmuch as rationality *per se* can only satisfy cognitive problems, there must also exist affective and symbolic supports for using it. Gypsies need to feel that their particular way of solving problems satisfies not only the logical demands of survival, but also the psychological and moral exigencies of a sense of well-being. The image of Gypsies as expressive and flamboyant, which to a great extent they like to perpetuate, is a manifestation of generalized support given to the "Gypsy way of life."

The modest probe conducted in southern Spain did not "prove" anything of course; its aim was to explore, not to test any rigorously formulated hypothesis. Nevertheless, it opens the way to important conclusions, albeit tentative, regarding the future of Gypsies, research on marginals, and development planning in general.

[9] On this, cf. Harold Garfinkel, *Studies in Ethnomethodology* (Prentice-Hall, 1967), Ch. 1 and 2.

[10] This assertion does not prejudge the correctness of the views on the relative influence of genetics and environment expressed by Arthur R. Jensen, "How Much Can We Boost IQ and Scholastic Achievement?" in *Harvard Educational Review*, Vol. XXXIX, No. 1 (Winter 1969), pp. 1–123.

(A) *The Future of Spanish Gypsies*

Gypsies in southern Spain have created a realistic strategy for coming to terms with their impoverished and precarious state. In struggling to derive maximum advantage from a seemingly hopeless situation, they have made excellent use of their ethnicity by devising esoteric forms which maintain in-group solidarity and protect them from outside intrusion. This strategy blends flexible innovation for purposes of survival with a fatalistic acceptance of the impossibility of altering their subsistence horizons. It enables the group to resist disruption in the face of chronic poverty, discrimination, and isolation. It also provides a secure haven in which a vulnerable "philosophy of life" can be sheltered from the threat posed by exogenous values more powerful than itself. Yet the strategy has its drawbacks: it tends to reinforce escapism and channel innovative energies into narrow conduits which impede far-reaching structural changes. Besides, it rests on the assumption that Gypsies can survive as a marginal sub-system, a fragile assumption, at best, inasmuch as traditional Gypsy occupations are disappearing quickly in the face of the modern organization of retail trade and services in urban centers, and the mechanization of agriculture. Paradoxically, Gypsies may have a better chance of surviving if Andalusia remains poor. Were the region to develop successfully, Gypsies would be left with no marketable skills—even as field workers. The interviews also brought other problems to the surface.

Most Gypsies bemoan the neglect of their language (Caló) in homes; in fact, most Gypsy youngsters cannot speak Caló. Numerous respondents favor teaching Caló in schools. Furthermore, all Gypsies regard flamenco singing and music as central ingredients of their "way of life." But musical directors explain that pure flamenco is degenerating because of commercialization in tourist caves and because Gypsy youngsters are fascinated with modern music. Since they are bereft of historical sense, heroes, holidays, and a sense of collective mission, Gypsies understandably attach great significance to their musical values. But their music, like their dialect, is threatened with extinction or degradation. Therefore, unless conscious efforts are made to teach these cultural values in the schools, group identity may be dissolved as "transitional" Gypsies move out of ghettos and are swallowed up by the larger society. Several Gypsies perceived this danger and expressed alarm over present trends.

Respondents, especially those having steady jobs and large families, repeatedly invoked the pejorative traits most frequently met in stereotypes—namely, that Gypsies are lazy and refuse to work. They added, however, that any man would be reluctant to work if the only jobs available to him were menial. Injurious stereotypes have made deep inroads in the group's consciousness and seem to have caused the very behavior it pejoratively depicts. Here is a clear case of self-fulfilling prophecy. If this effect is to be reversed and if Spanish society at large is to provide suitable opportunities for Gypsies, an active campaign must be waged to eliminate stereotypes in the out-group. Various agencies engaged in "promoting" Gypsies concur in believing that the re-education of fellow Spaniards is a priority task if efforts on behalf of Gypsies are to succeed.

Gypsies are willing to sacrifice material gains to keep members of their family close to them, or themselves remain with friends. This attitude is consonant with their indifference to material goods once modest subsistence is assured. No sacrifice is too great to stay alive or meet basic needs. Beyond this point, however, many values take precedence over improved economic condition. Interestingly, most respondents revealed a strong group orientation when replying to projective questions as to what they would do if they had lots of money. One would build a factory to provide jobs for other Gypsies, a second would buy a farm and hire others to work it, a third would build a house for poor neighbors. Only one man imagined himself spending money "having a wild time with women" and he had worked as an "extra" for an American movie company in Almería. When interpreted in conjunction with their strong family orientation, typical responses suggest that Gypsies have a predominantly "group-focused image of change." Hence it is plausible to believe that Gypsies could modernize within a pattern of austerity which limits their demands for consumer goods without causing great psychological deprivation among them. On grounds of improvidence, on the other hand, one can reach quite opposite conclusions. It is pertinent to add that Gypsies on the whole are favorable to granting differential rewards to individual effort or talent. This combination of traits leads us to conclude that Gypsies possess a healthy balance of ego-focused and group-focused images of change. In practical terms, therefore, sound development could perhaps result quite easily if their latent capacity for change were properly harnessed.

Notwithstanding apparently negative responses obtained on the question of the Gypsy homeland, a fruitful lesson in political mobilization lies beneath the evidence. Gypsies tended to react negatively to the idea at first, raising countless objections about probable in-group fighting, chaos, disorganization, and pilfering. But further discussion often led to a kind of fascination with the idea and the admission that perhaps, with some help, it might work. This response in two stages seems to have been anticipated by the founders of the movement, Lionel Votaru and Vando Rouda.[11] This suggests that mobilization around the "Gypsy homeland" theme might conceivably produce significant results, whether such a homeland is finally created or not. Why do I say this? Because Gypsies express the opinion that such a plan would work, provided they were re-educated and assisted in developing new attitudes toward work. Therefore, a convincing presentation of the homeland as the great Gypsy "myth" (the substitute of "nation-building" for Africans or "economic emancipation" for Latin Americans) might conceivably serve two purposes: supply the Gypsies with a symbol around which to rally while the traditional supports of their collective identity are being challenged, and legitimize the adoption of new attitudes toward work in ways conducive to modernization and development. Given the high value Gypsies place on freedom, however, it should be stressed from the outset that each person would remain free to migrate to the new homeland or not. The degree of interest shown by Gypsies in the homeland idea, after initially rejecting it, renders this view quite plausible.

Vocational re-education is crucial to the future of Gypsies. Traditional occupations—crafts, commerce in horses or mules, occasional jobs as tinkers or ambulatory repairmen—are quickly disappearing. To the extent that Andalusian farms modernize, demand for unskilled field hands decreases. Many Gypsies express alarm over present trends which are quickly rendering their skills superfluous. Acculturated Gypsies feel that nomadism is no longer a viable way of life because it creates legal difficulties over documents, schooling of children, and stability of employment. These are the main reasons why the access to good jobs and to opportunities for economic and social promotion through their own work is central to the future of Gypsies. For identical reasons, judicious vocational training and the provision of broader job incentives are indicated as a "must" policy if Gypsies are to develop successfully.

[11] On the Gypsy homeland, cf. J. Castella-Gassol, *El Problema Gitano* (Madrid: Editorial ZYX, 1967), pp. 37–40.

Implications for Research

The group profile derived from the interviews is that of "generic marginality." This suggests that it may be legitimate to extrapolate from Gypsies, a particular case of M_2 marginals, to the larger universe of marginals *tout court*. In one sense, this is a major "finding" of the study; to the extent that they are underdeveloped, Gypsies are similar to other marginals excluded from modernity. On the other hand, to the degree that they constitute a peculiar ghetto culture, they differ from M_1 marginals whose marginality consists solely in being "underdeveloped." Gypsies have a special brand of social consciousness, a-historical and non-teleological, which centers on such values as symbolic identification with nomadism as a way of life personifying spatial and temporal freedom, an innate and generalized talent for highly creative and expressive music and dancing, and a code of honor in which female virginity, unquestioning obedience to parents, and unconditional kin-solidarity are honored. One begins to suspect that traits proper to M_1 marginality better explain the existence of underdevelopment, whereas traits linked to M_2 marginality can be viewed as conditions which heighten or lessen chances of successful mobilization for development.

Moreover, the "existence rationality" ascribed to Gypsies is not totally different from patterns discernible in other "underdeveloped" populations. Banfield found "amoral familism" to be the prevailing ethos of the inhabitants of a small village in Sicily. This ethos in effect rested on a double normative principle: solidarity and moral accountability within the confines of kin relationships, indifference or hostility beyond the pale. In my terms, "amoral familism" is the "existence rationality" of Banfield's Italian village. Andalusian Gypsies, on the contrary, notwithstanding a few superficial resemblances, reject the "amoral familism" ethos because they hold themselves bound to practice solidarity with others outside their kin group, even outside their ethnic group. One respondent declared that the chief difference between Gypsies and "Payos" [12] is that the latter will not help a Gypsy in need, whereas a Gypsy will always share what he has, even with a Payo. Another Gypsy stated that he could not be loyal to his family if the latter made "unjust" claims. Several others responded to projec-

[12] The Gypsy name for non-Gypsies.

tive questions by declaring that certain deeds must never be done even to survive or assure the well-being of one's family, because justice or "right" is higher than "interest." In sum, the study of Gypsies tends to support the hypothesis that M_2 marginals are sufficiently like other "underdeveloped" populations to warrant some generalizations, whereas their unique aspects give rise to group characteristics which make them easier to study than M_1's as one seeks generalizations. Similar probes among other marginals, both M_1 and M_2 marginals, might well reveal that, as with Gypsies, the perception of the positive virtue of technology accompanies apparent fatalism, ascription standards within the family, and "secular" unconcern with the afterlife. Similarly, individualism in decision-making may coexist with a planning orientation and achievement standards in the larger society and with the passive acceptance of one's state of being. We are thus led to suppose that the crucial issue in appraising the potential change of marginals is the level of information and understanding to which they can gain access.

Several other tentative conclusions are also implied in the results:

(1) Heterogeneous marginals (those living in mixed environments or surrounded by people who differ from them) are less likely to be escapists than homogeneous marginals, given identical conditions of material and psychical hardship. The basis for this statement is the observation that all respondents from Almería, where Gypsies lived side by side with "Payos," seemed less bitter than those living in "pure" Gypsy ghettos over the discriminatory treatment dispensed to them by "Payos." Where no ghetto or psychological "haven" exists, individuals are forced to become more realistic. But Gypsies have not lost their pervasive sense of ethnic solidarity even outside the ghetto. This lends plausibility to the hope that ethnicity or some other constituent of M_2 marginality may make it easier for family solidarity (and even kinship solidarity) to survive among M_2's than among M_1 marginals in the face of the depersonalization of relationships brought about by "modernization." To illustrate, the most "modern" Gypsy interviewed attached great importance to the fact that he was recognized by any Gypsy as "one of his own." Wherever he traveled anywhere in Spain, he immediately felt himself to be in the presence of an "uncle" or "cousin."

(2) The resistance to change allegedly characteristic of marginals may operate only below certain thresholds. *It is not change as such which is perceived as unacceptable, but the threat change poses to*

survival, to identity, or to group solidarity. Once minimum security in these three "values" is assured, there may be, on the contrary, little or no resistance to change. When replying to projective questions wherein they suppose themselves to be rich, respondents favor the use of "tractors," "machines," "factories," and other modern technological instruments. Only when they picture themselves as poor (as they truly are) do these things seem dangerous to them. Further exploration seems to reveal that if retraining and temporary credit were given to them, technology would be a good thing even if it temporarily put some men out of work. Many respondents were strongly impressed by the argument that countries with more "machines"—namely, France and Germany—were also countries capable of providing more "jobs" than Spain. So true is this that many Spaniards, including marginals, emigrated to these countries because they could find work there. Somehow this example conveyed to Gypsies the message that technology helps rather than hurts even its apparent short-term victims. There is no reason to think that responses on this point are attributable to any peculiarly Gypsy trait; it is more plausible to attribute them to the marginality they hold in common with M_1 and other M_2 marginals.

Responses suggest that both "traditionals" and "transitionals" cling to the distinctive traits of their M_2 marginality, while simultaneously aspiring to gain esteem from out-groups including M_1 marginals. M_2 marginals complain, for instance, that they are the last to be hired and the first to be fired. They also resent being singled out by the police as special targets of law enforcement. In abstract terms, M_2's cling to their second layer of marginality and judge, at least implicitly, that the esteem of out-groups should be granted or denied to them on the basis of M_1 marginality. More simply, M_2 marginals do not object to being treated as "inferiors" to the extent that they are in fact ignorant, poor, or dirty. What they resent is being disdained in virtue of their peculiarly M_2 marginal traits. Discrimination against them *qua* M_2 marginals doubtless creates additional obstacles barring them from overcoming poverty, filth, and ignorance. Yet their implicit assumption seems to be that M_2 marginalization ought not (as a normative matter of human "right") constitute fair grounds for deprivation of social recognition. If one pursues this reasoning further, he is led to suppose that M_1 marginals assimilate "modern" sectors of life with greater psychological facility than M_2 marginals. These, on the other hand, may be easier to mobilize for specific developmental tasks. It may be a mistake, therefore, to assume that mobilization presupposes assimilation; the very opposite probably comes closer to the truth.

Implications for Planning

Four implications for development planning emerge from the probe:

(1) Improvidence is inevitable in subsistence situations. It may appear logical to think that very poor people would be less poor if they were more provident and paid greater attention to their own future. Yet all respondents affirm that it is impossible for a man to make plans, or allocate time, attention, and energy to the future, unless he already possesses enough money or goods to assure his survival in the present and the immediate future. Psychologically speaking, a person who lives at a subsistence level cannot entertain realistic expectations that any conceivable increment to his available wealth will not immediately be swallowed up by the satisfaction of urgent "basic needs." If this is so, the desire to defer gratification is impossible until that person has begun to improve his material position. Therefore, immediate tangible increases in consumer satisfactions may be required before "underdeveloped" people can begin to adopt those attitudes toward consumption (critical deferral of satisfactions, substitution over different time spans, savings) deemed favorable to long-term development. To attack the "improvidence" of underdeveloped marginals is to misunderstand the experiential realities of underdevelopment. At subsistence levels, providence is not realistically possible, whatever one's desires or wishes. What exists is not *im*providence, but *pre*-providence. When replying to projective questions in which they were presumed to be rich, Gypsy respondents readily visualized many criteria according to which they could set priorities among alternative allocations of resources. Perhaps this implies that any plan which tries to build up productive infrastructure too rapidly is doomed to fail: it will either provoke violent demands for ever more consumer goods or fail to "mobilize" people on behalf of "someone else's" modernization. On the other hand, major emphasis on consumer goods may lead a poor country to bankruptcy and delay the obtention of gains in real productive wealth. It is extremely difficult to strike a proper balance between planning for consumer and for productive priorities. What is noteworthy is that this result was obtained from Gypsies, who are

notoriously frugal in their demands for material things. The argument, therefore, applies with even greater force to other groups.

(2) The interviews suggest that M_2 marginals have a predominantly group-focused image of change, along with elements of the ego-focused image. Given their internal solidarity and the "brakes on desire" placed by their "existence rationality," it seems unlikely that "innovators" with a strong "ego-focused" image of change can serve as acceptable agents of diffused change in the group. Such individuals are likely to be ostracized, and the fruits of their innovation may undergo collective expropriation. Even highly individualistic and critical respondents expressed a reluctance to be repudiated by their fellow marginals for the sake of purely personal gain. The tentative policy conclusion to be drawn is that plans ought to maximize "group innovations." Cooperative ventures, even as pilot projects, may possibly enjoy the greatest chance of succeeding among M_2 marginals. The case is perhaps different with M_1's, among whom one expects to find greater latent "achievement-orientation." It is also worth noting that the approval given by M_2's to group decisions harmonizes with their need to combine reliance on competent "experts" in decision-making with confirmation by the majority. Otherwise stated, decision-making among M_2's is potentially very democratic.

(3) Providing education to "traditionals" may lead to results quite different from their transformation into "transitionals"—i.e., converts to the virtues of modernity. Quite the opposite may ensue. Education can leave the "existence rationality" of an individual or group unchanged and simply increase his (its) frustration at not being treated in accord with achievement standards, by life in general and by out-groups in particular. Such frustration weakens rather than strengthens the hesitant commitment such a man feels to achievement norms. If any conclusion from these remarks seems even tentatively valid, it is this: development pedagogy must postulate initial assumptions consonant with the prevailing "existence rationality" and not challenge it directly. Whatever be the inadequacies of this rationality, it constitutes the soundest basis a marginal society has for surviving, maintaining its integrity and identity, and guaranteeing whatever freedom it can snatch from existence and the agencies over which it lacks control. Viewed in this light, many development pedagogies and educational strategies are seen to be inefficient simply because they accentuate the frustrations. They thereby strengthen ascription standards within the marginal group because these standards protect any poten-

tial "transitional" against the failure of the wider society to grant him recognition in "achievement" terms. A striking illustration of this phenomenon is supplied by the probe: the only apparent difference between educated Gypsies and others is that the educated ones are more pessimistic and cynical regarding their chances of breaking out of the determinisms surrounding them.

(4) As mentioned earlier, significant impact on depressed populations can best be made "at the margins" of their existence rationality. Development strategy must aim, therefore, at protecting the inner limits of existence rationality while expanding its outer boundaries by providing rewards to innovators who remain faithful to core values while contributing to the expansion of existence rationality. It is both inhuman and inefficient to assume that "development" is incompatible with "traditional" values. This mistake is caused by the ethnocentric conception of change held by many modernizers, and their resulting biased judgment that "traditionalism" is static. The reality is otherwise: the psychic and symbolic mobility at work within existing limits of "traditionalist strategy" may turn out to be far greater than the more conspicuous dynamisms present in "modernizing" change. Thus, the problem is not that "underdevelopment" is an obstacle to change, but rather that insensitive impact strategies for inducing modernization prevent the potential for change hidden behind the apparent immobility of traditionalism from bearing fruit and "grafting" progress onto itself. The implications for development planning are enormous: it means that the major task may be to teach planners to appreciate old values instead of educating underdeveloped men to the merits of new plans.

How does the proposed strategy differ from earlier practices? No simple reply is possible because many partial strategies have been tried in order to induce developmental changes. Ideological mobilization has played an important role in Socialist countries, although no single line of action has been followed. China's policies have oscillated from "better Red than expert" to crash programs to make everyone expert.[13] Generally speaking, the utilization of Marxist class analysis has made it relatively easy for governments in Socialist countries to denounce enemies of development as worthy targets of popular

[13] On this, cf. Immanual C. Y. Hsü, "The Impact of Industrialization on Higher Education in Communist China," in Frederick Harbison and Charles A. Myers, *Manpower and Education: Country Studies in Economic Development* (McGraw-Hill, 1965), pp. 202–232.

wrath. Conversely, productive efforts can be mobilized in favor of "nation-building," the construction of Socialism, the elimination of vestigial colonialism, or waging the war against imperialism. Entry into the technological era is frequently described as a "Socialist" victory. Even in non-Socialist countries industrial triumphs are often publicized as a "national" demonstration of a people's unique capacity to conquer nature or to innovate brilliantly in the modern mode.

Western suppliers of technical and financial assistance have usually sought to maximize entrepreneurship. Underlying their strategy of induced change is the principle, often unstated, that emerging middle classes are primary motors of developmental progress. Closely allied to this view, though not limited to it, given the strong Socialist preference for heavy infrastructure, is the belief that spectacular large projects (e.g., steel mills, dams, petro-chemical plants) produce astounding multiplier effects on development. This view tends to place great emphasis on material factors of economic production. Its main assumption seems to be that men will be swept along toward new attitudes and new levels of performance, thanks to the symbolic and real appeal of prestigious installations. The hope is that large projects can galvanize a nation's energies and elicit general efforts on behalf of the great "myth." This assumption may be valid, however, only if large projects are clothed by their sponsors in an imagery compatible with core values of social identity and pride. Somewhat more modestly, there is a widespread belief among planners that financial incentives are a powerful instrument for inducing desired behavior. Without denying the potent influence exercised by the appetite for gain, one must nonetheless point out that excessive reliance on these incentives simply skirts the issues raised by Hirschman's analysis of the relative merits of different images of change. There is something unrealistic about assuming the gain motive to be the primary catalyst to action for people long conditioned to condemn deliberate profit-seeking. Development experts have sometimes been startled by the seemingly bizarre response of new industrial workers to salary increases: they simply practiced greater absenteeism. If properly coordinated with other means, financial incentives are a useful auxiliary device for inducing desired value and behavioral change. They are no substitute, however, for an over-all strategy which is both pedagogical and motivational. Much depends on the relative importance attached by any total inducement scheme to monetary incentives alone. As Hirschman suggests, encouraging ego-focused achievement may maximize the creative aspects of innovation at the expense of the spirit of cooperation.

Still another approach to eliciting change has relied heavily on the demonstration effect of consumer goods. This instrument avoids the crucial question of the hierarchy of needs, however, and assumes that people do in fact prefer what is best for them. There is something naïve about this assumption in the face of the liberty granted to entrepreneurs to tamper with people's desire mechanisms before they have learned how to resist the manipulative blandishments of need-creation. This is not to say that consumer goods are bad or unimportant. But it does imply that, apart from a general policy of value priorities, spontaneous responses to solicitations for new kinds of consumer goods will obey the law of maximum profitability and easiest psychic manipulation, not of genuine need-satisfaction. The trouble with relying on the demonstration effects of consumer goods is that such a tactic overlooks the psychic vulnerability of populations exposed for the first time in their personal or societal experience to consumer demonstrations. They are stimulated to consume before they have learned how to produce.

Pilot projects are another instrument often relied upon to generate new attitudes. Here the assumption seems to be that the major obstacle to greater productivity or sound technical practice is lack of knowledge. Accordingly, a pilot experience will show people that something is possible or illustrate how it is done. The real problem, however, is not to show that something is possible or to illustrate how it is done. Rather, it is to succeed under conditions identical to those faced by the large numbers of farmers, fishermen, or artisans in whose benefit the pilot demonstration is conducted. If a pilot project receives more money, better supervision, greater technical help, and more favorable conditions than those possible elsewhere, how can it be imitated by those lacking these favorable conditions? Numerous pilot projects have been immensely successful from a technical viewpoint but failed to be disseminated because they cost more than the sponsoring agency could give as credit to others outside the project or because "the cards were stacked in favor of the pilot" in a manner not replicable elsewhere except at exorbitant cost. As in other cases, there is no substitute here for a sound over-all strategy of induced change.

The great ascent toward development now enjoys legitimacy throughout the world, thanks in part to the unconditional endorsement of this lofty objective given by the United Nations and other prestigious world bodies. Furthermore, rich countries have repeatedly emphasized in the last two decades the importance of development for the Third World. Within non-developed countries themselves, planners and political leaders have enthusiastically preached the merits of development. All this has no doubt released social forces whose role in preparing people to desire and undertake development is considerable. A general approach has been lacking, however, for eliciting internalized support for the basic values inherent in development goals. Consequently, much induced change has been obtained at unnecessarily high costs in human suffering. Opportunities have been lost because planners have failed to utilize the potential for innovation latent in the existence rationalities of traditional groups. When a development campaign respects native values (e.g., Nyerere's policy of self-reliance and personalistic communitarianism in Tanzania), a satisfactory balance is achieved between the requirements of economic, social, and cultural development and society's self-conscious quest for greater dignity. If the demands of the Third World can be symbolized by the formula Bread + Dignity, it matters greatly to dignity *how* bread is obtained.

Existence rationality is not a new notion. It merely formulates systematically what has happened when development proved successful and relatively painless because it was grafted onto pre-existing old values which, viewed superficially, appeared uncongenial to change. Serendipitous policy, not always fully conscious, has occasionally brought about desired innovation. The Meiji Restoration in Japan (1867) inaugurated a period of rapid development, thanks to a happy blend of consonance with traditionalism and creative modernism which channeled national energies constructively.[14] David Apter argues that the type of traditionalism determines receptivity to change. My own view is that the case he presents, Buganda, is better explained by emphasizing the strategy employed to propose change, rather than the type of traditionalism from which one starts.[15] One striking example of a sound application of the existence-rationality strategy is provided by China, in dealing with traditional and modern medicine. A systematic effort has been made to integrate modern and traditional medical practices. Western-trained doctors are urged to ac-

[14] On this, Everett E. Hagen, *On the Theory of Social Change* (Dorsey Press, 1962), pp. 310, 313, 348.

[15] David E. Apter, "The Role of Traditionalism in the Political Modernization of Ghana and Uganda," in Claude E. Welch, Jr., ed., *Political Modernization* (Wadsworth Publishing Co., 1967), pp. 64–88.

quire knowledge of traditional practices on grounds "that since traditional methods unquestionably cure patients, there must be something good in them and therefore they merit study." [16]

This chapter advocates a deliberate strategy for inducing desired change and outlines a broad framework for setting policy with a view to maximizing the chances of getting developmental changes accepted by "traditional" populations. The goal of such strategy is to impose the least possible violence upon core value structures pre-developed groups themselves deem central to their identity, dignity, survival, and eventual progress. The strategy of existence rationality here recommended need not supplant partial strategies heretofore employed with greater or lesser success. It may, however, provide a broader framework for solving the problem of resistance or receptivity to change by dealing with their causes.

[16] In Felix Greene, *China* (Ballantine Books, 1963), p. 323.

PART III

What Kind of Development?

Anti-Development and the Constraints upon Development

Upon critical examination, much apparent development proves to be "anti-development." Conversely, seemingly modest accomplishments often constitute genuine progress. No assessment of the quality of performance can be realistic if it ignores the constraints faced by societies in their efforts to develop. The aim of the present chapter is to trace some of the limits within which development performance and policies may properly be evaluated. A brief profile is first given, however, of "anti-development."

One corollary of the view of development's goals, guiding principles, and dialectical nature presented in this work is that development is not always genuine. In the final analysis, economic, political, and cultural development are means for obtaining the good life. It follows, therefore, that material standards may improve and institutions become modern in the absence of qualitative improvement in society. This conclusion rests on what Erich Fromm calls "normative humanism." [1] One need not postulate the existence of a fixed human essence

[1] Erich Fromm, *The Sane Society* (Fawcett Publications, 1967), p. 21.

to engage in normative thinking; he has only to grant that societies may foster social health, personal integration, and realization or, conversely, promote pathological states, disintegration, and the waste of human energies. To determine what is good and what is bad development implies some qualitative view of life and society. Yet, unless one wishes to judge a society solely by the number of radios or miles of highway it has, he must appeal to qualitative indicators. As Marx aptly remarked, the truly wealthy man is the man who *is* much, not the one who *has* much.[2] This applies to nations as well: the truly "developed" land is one where men are rich even if they do not have riches.

Anti-Development

Developed societies are, by definition, in an excellent position to assure life-sustenance for their citizens. Their score on behalf of esteem and freedom, however, may prove less satisfactory. Social criticism within the United States bears witness to a widespread "alienation of abundance," as destructive perhaps as "alienation in misery."[3] Ecologists see a high correlation between the internal health of a society and its relationship to environment. In the words of L.K. Caldwell, "A civilization reveals the nature of its internalized goals and values in the environmental conditions that it creates. . . . Environmental deterioration has frequently preceded social decline, and this sequence appears to follow more from a failure of perception and an incompleteness of value structure than from inadequacy of alleviating or corrective technologies."[4]

The distinction between quantitative and qualitative indicators of development has been experienced personally by thousands of Peace Corps volunteers. Many have learned for the first time, while sharing the lives of "underdeveloped" Africans, Filipinos, Latin Americans, or Indians, of the existence of rich human values.[5] The reason why

[2] Karl Marx, *Die Fruhschriften* (Stuttgart, 1953), p. 243. Cited by Fromm, *op. cit.*, p. 223.

[3] Terms suggested by the Introduction to *Socialist Humanism,* ed. Erich Fromm (Anchor Books, 1966), p. ix.

[4] Lynton K. Caldwell, "Shaping the Environment of Civilized Societies," paper delivered at Vassar College, April 9, 1968, p. 1.

[5] This is the theme of a book by a former Peace Corps country representative. Cf. Lawrence Fuchs, *Those Peculiar Americans* (Meredith Press, 1967), esp. last chapter.

216

economic development can be a lesser good has been analyzed by Walter Weisskopf: an industrial economy tends to lose its proper status as a means and to eliminate every sphere of non-economic value from life.[6] Modern institutions, economic growth, and efficiency easily become ends in themselves.

A prosperous society whose members are manipulated by an impersonal system is not developed, but distorted. A society has "anti-development" if its "development" breeds new oppressions and structural servitudes. Class and power analysis in the United States suggests that the unholy alliance among what C. Wright Mills[7] calls "the big three"—government, industry, and the military establishment —has spawned a new privilege system no less anti-democratic than that which characterizes "underdeveloped" societies.

One can object by alleging that the qualitative defects of a "developed" society do not justify one in terming its performance "anti-development." This objection assumes, however, that "development" is a purely descriptive label reflecting quantitative conditions expressed in certain levels of economic performance and social efficiency, or in the prevalence of specific attitudes toward time, work, achievement, and secularity. But this is to overlook the ambivalence of the term "development," which, in its deepest sense, evokes ideas of maturation, progress toward perfection, justice, greater consciousness, perhaps even greater happiness. Uncritical use of the term leads many to mistake means for ends.

There is, after all, much truth in Everett Hagen's view that the only ethically justifiable goal of development is to make people happier. It is also the only ethically justifiable goal for not developing, he adds. In any case, economic development will make some people happier, others less happy. Those who benefit may do so at the expense of others, and it is highly questionable whether more goods make people happier.[8]

Development processes, as presently conducted, reinforce a tend-

---

[6] Walter A. Weisskopf in *Looking Forward: The Abundant Society,* Occasional Paper, Center for the Study of Democratic Institutions, December 1966, pp. 3–12.

[7] C. Wright Mills, "The Structure of Power in American Society," in *C. Wright Mills, Power, Politics and People,* ed. Irving Louis Horowitz (Ballantine Books, 1963), p. 27. The point is reinforced in Galbraith's *The New Industrial State, passim.*

[8] From transcript of remarks made by Professor Hagen at a seminar sponsored by the Center for the Study of Development and Social Change. The seminar was held on May 3–5, 1968, at Waltham, Massachusetts.

ency already rampant within technologically advanced societies toward the absolutization of means. And notwithstanding their private denunciation of the folly of treating development in economic terms alone, many development economists recommend policies which in effect give primacy to mass consumption as a goal. One serious consequence of this practice is that policy-makers often relegate precious values to oblivion prematurely because they judge them to be incompatible with development. I refer to such values as personal communion in friendship because it is time-consuming, contemplation of nature because it is useless, communal celebration because it is inefficient. Le Corbusier long ago complained that "skyscrapers are greater than their architects." [9] Have the architects of economic prosperity, while building towering edifices, repeated this error? If so, the fault lies not in their ambition, since economic well-being is eminently good. But a high standard of living, like the Sabbath, was made for man, not man for the Sabbath. [10]

If we are to assess the effects of development on social values correctly, we must distinguish two forms of materialism. The first is healthy and guards men against escapism, which treats material wants as unimportant and views misery as the result of fate, the will of gods, or some necessary phase in a trans-migratory cycle. All such outlooks hold material things in disdain. Healthy materialism, on the contrary, gives due emphasis to life's physical conditions. It gives ethical approval to reasonable acquisitive desires and frankly acknowledges that human virtue cannot consist in closing one's eyes to human suffering. There also exists, however, a second form of materialism which transforms man into a manipulator or the object of manipulation. Man's being is reduced to what he possesses: worth, measured in monetary terms, is substituted for value. At once innocent and deadly, this brand of materialism feeds on a mindless and insensitive system which allows the quest for abundance to depersonalize life. By its uncritical complacency toward material wealth, it blinds men to the presence of authentic human values within cultures of poverty and affluence alike. Things dominate persons, and man becomes, in August Heckscher's phrase, "islanded in an encroaching sea of things." [11]

[9] Le Corbusier, *Quand les Cathédrales Etaient Blanches* (Paris: Librairie Plon, 1937), p. 308.
[10] This point is expanded in Denis A. Goulet, "Ethical Issues in Development," *Review of Social Economy,* Vol. XXVI, No. 2 (September 1968), pp. 97–118.
[11] August Heckscher, *The Public Happiness* (Atheneum, 1962), p. 61.

But the "immensity of desires paralyzes man" if "unlimited desires are dictated by a law of civilization." [12] Authentic development, on the other hand, must free people from the thralldom of misery and satisfy their needs at a pace which allows them to control the dynamisms of their desire.

The French eighteenth-century writer L. S. Mercier[13] conceived of luxury as "the executioner of the rich" because exaggerated ease in gaining access to pleasures makes one lose the capacity to enjoy these very pleasures. Accordingly, if development simply makes it possible for all men to have the same executioner as the rich two centuries ago, it is regressive. Of the rich, Mercier adds: "luxury is to them as much an affliction as poverty is to the poor." Whether a society is non-developed, underdeveloped, partially developed, or highly developed, its members repeatedly make conscious or unconscious choices of the values and vital qualities they seek. The systematic pursuit of economic improvement, social modernization, and cumulative science represents an option in favor of a certain notion of human progress and social maturation. One needs to go further, however, and examine the instruments chosen to obtain these goals. As important as the goals themselves are the means and their consequences on human life. Maslow's warning in this regard is pertinent: "Americans have learned that political democracy and economic prosperity don't in themselves solve any of the basic value problems." [14] This is why anti-development results whenever some basic element of the good life as normatively defined by the interested population itself—its view of life-sustenance, esteem, freedom, and actualization (self and collective)—is diminished instead of enhanced. The danger of losing core values is not imaginary. On the contrary: harmful images of the good life are disseminated throughout the world by ideological and commercial propaganda, unexamined demonstration effects, and cultural transfers of all types. Norms borrowed from "developed" societies have sometimes proved to be trivial or dehumanizing. In its contacts with Africa, for instance, the West has acted as a one-eyed giant. To cite poet Lauren Van der Post, "The one-eyed giant had science without wisdom, and he broke in upon ancient civilizations which (like the

---

[12] These evocative phrases are drawn from George Perenc's *Les Choses* (Paris: Editions Julliard, 1962), pp. 21, 42.

[13] Author of *Tableau de Paris* (1783). Cited in Werner Sombart, *Luxury and Capitalism* (University of Michigan Press, 1967), p. 62.

[14] Abraham H. Maslow, *Toward a Psychology of Being* (D. Van Nostrand Co., 1962), p. 10.

medieval West) had wisdom without science: wisdom which transcends and unites, wisdom which dwells in body and soul together and which, more by means of myth, of rite, of contemplation, than by scientific experiment, opens the door to a life in which the individual is not lost in the cosmos and in society but found in them." [15]

The patterns of modernity taken by today's "developed" societies represent a mixed blessing which must not be fully imitated. Developers must invent alternatives both to traditional static wisdom, which is powerless to satisfy many needs, and to the modern "pathology of normalcy" [16] which lacks a wisdom to integrate its sciences.

As I have written elsewhere, "it is a serious mistake to portray high living standards and efficiency as unequivocal goods and to condemn their opposites as unmitigated evils. Progress in one sphere usually entails regression in some other domain. Nations achieve success in such realms as specialization of knowledge, efficiency at work, and high levels of individual performance only because they sacrifice other values such as synthesis in knowledge, tolerance of conversation, music and play during work periods, and maintenance of extended family solidarity to provide emotionally satisfying roles to old people." [17] The basic task is to discover new modes of social accounting enabling men to estimate probable costs and benefits of different patterns of development. Alternatives lying open to underdeveloped societies must not be reduced to the simplistic dyad: either remain stagnant or embrace all the ills of current patterns of modernity. Douglas Steere[18] asserts that it could become possible to obtain industry without ugly cities, greater food production without demoralizing speculation, and education without cultural alienation. So long as men continue to treat development in predominantly quantitative terms, however, they cannot devise new forms of social cost-accounting. This is the case within the United States, where great practical difficulties are encountered by advocates of a social State of the Union message.[19] One major role such a document could play is to help experts evaluate

[15] Laurens Van der Post, in *The Dark Eye in Africa.* Cited by Thomas Merton in the Introduction to *Gandhi on Non-Violence* (A New Directions Paperback, 1964), p. 1.

[16] A term used by Fromm, *The Sane Society,* p. 15.

[17] Denis A. Goulet, "Development for What?" in *Comparative Political Studies,* Vol. I, No. 2 (July 1968), p. 302.

[18] Douglas V. Steere, in *Development for What?* ed. John H. Hallowell (Duke University Press, 1964), pp. 213–235.

[19] Cf. Bertram M. Gross, "The Social State of the Union," *Trans-Action,* November/December 1965, pp. 14–17.

differential performances as greater or lesser development on the basis of ethical standards.

One writer[20] has gone so far as to suggest that payments should be made by governments to men whose psychic security is shattered by a macro-social development in which they are unsuited to share. Underlying this recommendation is the principle that compensation for mental damages is due to those who are unhappy because their desire mechanisms have been damaged by a general process over which they lack control and from whose benefits they are excluded. The idea does not appear economically feasible; it nonetheless dramatizes issues too often ignored when development's cost is appraised. The true costs paid to obtain development are terrifyingly high. What is easily overlooked, on the other hand, is the cost of *remaining developed and maintaining efficiency after development is reached.* Reflecting on his country's long history, Lin Yutang evokes the high tribute exacted by efficiency. "It is evident anyway," he writes, "that the Chinese as a nation are more philosophic than efficient, and that if it were otherwise, no nation could have survived the high blood pressure of an efficient life for four thousand years. Four thousand years of efficient living would ruin any nation." [21] At present levels of technological development, however, tribute is paid long before four thousand years have elapsed. Certain "developed" nations may well experience early ruin because they pay too high a price to maintain what is in fact "anti-development." Ecologists, biologists, and psychologists warn emphatically of the dangers of narrowly maximizing purely economic goals. This is why development performance must be judged, not by purely quantitative indicators, but in the light of qualities which relate to intangible values. "Anti-development" can coexist alongside excellent nutrition, high income, general literacy, bureaucratic efficiency, and expanding investment capacities. Since these are all relative goods, much depends on what is sacrificed to obtain or preserve them. Like Esau of biblical lore, societies will be tempted to sell their cultural birthright for developmental pottage!

The strong deterministic forces at work in development processes must be recognized. Inasmuch as enhanced freedom is one of development's major goals, it is extremely difficult to assess what makes for

[20]Jules Klanfer in *Le Sous-Développement Humain* (Les Editions Ouvrières, 1967), p. 176.
[21] Lin Yutang, *The Importance of Living* (New York: John Day Company, 1937), p. 3.

sound development. Prosperity and happiness for all may be attainable in a technological society only at the price of freedom. New structural constraints are imposed on the world by the development processes themselves. Beneficiaries and those left behind are differently affected by these determinisms. An over-arching deterministic system exists wherein nations are diversely positioned in their struggle to conquer freedom. Whereas certain possibilities are sealed off from vulnerable nations, others are denied to developed and underdeveloped alike. Because development is situated in a broad ecological and symbolic context, massively though not fully deterministic, central decisions bear on basic values. It is no less irresponsible to launch societies on irreversible paths in the name of development than it was a century ago to destroy forests, animal species, and farmlands on the naïve assumption that resources would prove inexhaustible.

Another qualitative indicator of development, closely related to a society's degree of civilization, is the capacity of its members to face death. One recent author affirms that "the nature of a society, it could be argued, is decided by the relationship which obtains in that society between the living and the dead. In a modern progressive society or in a modern revolutionary society the relationship will be fairly negative, will consist, in fact, in the independence of the living from the dead, but it will be nonetheless decisive, for it will be this relationship of independence which the living have toward the dead that will make the society progressive or revolutionary." [22]

If we use this criterion to judge which societies are least alienated from reality—including death (which in "developed" countries has become a major taboo)—the ranking of nations is profoundly altered. Camus noted with irony in *The Plague* that one learns all that is truly important about a city if he knows how its inhabitants work, love, and die. Freud held a similar opinion in his later years, believing that genuine human development in individuals and societies is expressed in the capacity to love and to work creatively. The point here is not that improved food, housing, and banking services are not good, but that the norms ordinarily used to measure success have been too narrowly material. Many have falsely assumed that men's most significant needs are their material needs. Yet Marx himself recognized late in life that he had exaggerated the material aspects of human need to the detriment of others.[23]

[22] John S. Dunne, *The City of the Gods: A Study in Myth and Mortality* (Macmillan Company, 1965), p. 16. Cf. also pp. 184–217.
[23] As reported by Fromm in *The Sane Society*, pp. 233 ff.

The healing relativism of standards disposes us to heed the reminder of Lévi-Strauss that "A primitive people is not a backward or retarded people: indeed it may possess a genius for invention that leaves the achievements of civilized people far behind." [24] Accordingly, for members of "developed" societies, wisdom may consist in humility amid affluence. Paul Goodman suggests that the Empty Society is but "the obverse face of the Affluent Society. When Adam Smith spoke of the Wealth of Nations, he did not mean anything like this." [25]

My argument is, in short, that development as presently conducted in the world may have led to economic growth, improved living standards for some, and even to a healthy diminution of fatalism and feudal exploitation. But these benefits have not reached the masses of the world's poor, nor have they been obtained in a manner consonant with certain values required for the total ascent of mankind as a whole. Although development goals are proclaimed in lofty moral terms, its agents, both native and foreign, have tampered irreversibly with people's desires before endowing economic systems with the ability to satisfy new demands. Men in pre-modern societies have been given the power to exercise death control before gaining control over their lives.

Sources of Anti-Development

The influence of more-developed on less-developed societies has caused harm in three distinct spheres. The first is the notion of development disseminated in the world. The dominant imagery equates, at least implicitly, the abundance of goods with the fullness of good. Quite logically, men come to be valued in monetary terms, and all other values are, in practice, subordinated to money. "Developed" societies have escaped the full damage which this image can cause, thanks to the fragmentation of their knowledge and the specialization of their vital activities. Men learn to conduct their business life as though money were the supreme value, while continuing to abide by other values in their private lives. Such normative schizophrenia creates great personal stress, it is true. But it has at least protected modern societies from bearing the full consequences of the values to which they subscribe in the realm of productive activity. *Non-modern*

[24] Cited in "Man's New Dialogue with Man," *Time,* June 30, 1967, p. 34.
[25] Paul Goodman, *The Moral Ambiguity of America* (Canadian Broadcasting Corporation Publications, 1966), p. 12.

societies, on the other hand, are not psychologically prepared to dissociate economic values from more intimate value spheres. If economic achievement is portrayed to them as important enough to warrant casting off all other concerns—including their most treasured family and religious practices—then why should their quest for more goods be moderated by considerations of the rights of others, prior claims of needier men, or the need for austerity in consumption so as to build up a solid production base in the nation? One need not postulate impenetrable psychic traits in Asians, Latin Americans, or Africans to understand why ostentation, waste, corruption, and conspicuous consumption are predictable consequences of the image they nourish of "developmental" success. There is, in short, a profoundly materializing force at work in the Western myth of the abundant life. When this myth is taken seriously by modernizing elites in the Third World, it easily generates anti-development. In *False Start for Africa,* René Dumont has graphically portrayed the aberrations to be expected in this domain. Yet it is hypocritical to condemn leaders in poor nations for practicing corruption, graft, and nepotism when these very practices are honored in wealthy countries, albeit in subtler forms.

A second source of anti-development is the mode in which much technical assistance and financial aid has been provided by donor nations. Assistance has been accompanied, for the most part, by disdain for the "beggar" and a haughty sense of donor superiority injurious to the dignity of the recipient. A complacent sense of cultural superiority has generally prevailed on the part of those possessing the technical skills needed in poorer lands. Even sensitive scholars and development experts have not always known how to purge themselves of superior feelings toward technologically backward societies. Although gains in one realm of life are always made by sacrificing progress in other realms, ethnocentrism has blinded wealthy nations to their own grave cultural defects and allowed their citizens, with good conscience, to regard other societies as inferior simply because of their low productivity. Not surprisingly, transfers made in this spirit foster self-righteousness in the giver and impede the nurture of dignity in recipients.

Finally, existing patterns of development are bad because they have bred in many Third World leaders an exaggerated fondness for the *ersatz* values of advanced countries. Many elites have become alienated from their own values and their own society, frequently growing

224

ashamed of their own identity; they aspire, sometimes unconsciously, to be African Europeans or Latin imitations of North Americans.

Certain norms do exist, however, for evaluating over-all development programs and partial accomplishments. Programs and projects alike can be judged in the light of their contribution to meeting the vital needs of all men, increasing respect and esteem for all men and communities, and providing access to different levels of freedom, particularly that which expands cultural and psychological breathing space for self-actualization. Realism demands, of course, that present societies not be compared with non-existent ideal societies. No just assessment can prescind from an examination of the constraints operative in a society, of the range of options effectively open to it, of past options taken, of human costs it has consented to pay to obtain its "development," and of the consequences of prior policies. Each is now discussed briefly.

The Constraints

The nation-state is acknowledged to be the basic unit of development even by those who deplore the fact. But no country develops adequately if only a few of its regions progress. And since development is a relative term which necessarily presupposes trans-national comparisons, it is important to judge how well a country has fared in the light of constraints it faces. Time is, of course, a pervasive constraint. No matter how equitable a development policy may be, it can realize gains only over time. Although planners may wish to achieve progress throughout all regions and sectors, it is clearly impossible to invest scarce resources in all of them at once. If one sacrifices region or sector A by concentrating efforts in B, he hopes thereby to create conditions wherein new resources will be generated to meet the needs of A at some future time. This is the reasoning adopted in 1955–1960 by Brazilian President Juscelino Kubitschek, whose policy favored industry with massive governmental subsidies, direct and indirect, to the almost complete neglect of agriculture. His argument was that industry could thrive thanks to a big boost and thereafter produce a surplus which could be applied to the modernization of agriculture. Not surprisingly, many spokesmen for his country's agricultural regions found the argument somewhat less than persuasive. Certain countries are small and have few resources, others are immense and dispose of

225

abundant minerals, arable lands, forests, and water. Some nations enjoy favorable geographic or climatic conditions, others not. The proximity of a country to more developed lands is another pertinent consideration. Population density and the degree of entrenchment of a particular privileged class (as of *"marabouts"* in several African nations) also seriously affect a society's chances of developing successfully.

For purposes of illustration, we may advert to Cuba's former dependence on U.S. investment and markets, its limited area and population, its past history as a Spanish colony and as an economic dependency of the United States. Granted these constraints, Cuba has performed quite well. Although sugar production has not been spectacular, the island has begun diversifying agriculture and industrializing the countryside. Notwithstanding the departure of large numbers of middle-level technicians and professionals for political reasons, peasants and workers have quickly become literate and learned new skills, thereby solving many serious manpower problems. Castro also appears to have gained mass adherence to his policies. Considering its proximity to the United States, the fact that it was once invaded and subsequently threatened with nuclear annihilation, and the further fact that Cuba is practically obliged to spend huge sums of money on military expenditures, it has remained relatively free of Soviet political tutelage, notwithstanding massive financial and technical aid from the U.S.S.R. Remoteness from Moscow has, of course, helped Cuba to stake out some degree of autonomy.

Senegal provides the example of an African nation whose development effort has centered largely on eliminating external control over domestic agricultural circuits at the price of tolerating considerable foreign influence in industrial sectors. Among the constraints Senegal cannot ignore is its pressing need to sell its large peanut crop to France. Hence the country is tied to France through the franc zone. Moreover, at the time of independence Senegal inherited a pitifully small resource base in minerals (except for phosphates), industrial raw materials, and electric power. Notwithstanding the sincerity of its leaders in professing socialism as a preferred development model, Senegal needed large numbers of teachers, French-speaking technicians, and a secure outlet for its peanut exports. It could not afford to offend France without suffering grave economic hardship and becoming even more vulnerable than before to political domination by outside powers. As with Cuba, therefore, Senegal's development efforts

226

must be judged, not against some ideal standard of achievement, but against the range of choices effectively open to it, given the constraints it faced.

Many constraints are maintained by the advanced nations engaged in the Cold War. The Soviet Union, for instance, has imposed a structurally exploitative division of labor on associated states in Eastern Europe. The United States has established, somewhat more subtly, quite similar relations with a number of Latin American states. The presence or absence of constraints obviously exercises its principal influence on the range of policy options available to any developing country.

(A) *Effective Options*

The most decisive option is that taken by a government to pursue development systematically. It matters greatly, of course, what policymakers understand by development. Is it imitating consumer patterns followed in countries already developed, or constructing a few showplace cities with luxury hotels, a modern airport, and a Western cinema, or building industrial plants while neglecting to modernize agriculture or to educate the masses? Initial options made by governments are meaningless unless they reflect choices of long-term goals, given the present state of existing needs and resource availabilities. A decision must be reached as to one's desired position at a target date fifteen to twenty-five years hence. Such an option provides general direction to precise quantified goals to be incorporated into medium-term plans and short-term programs.

Besides decisions on national goals, specific options need to be made regarding the economic and social "vocations" of zones and regions. Competing claims put forth by social classes and interest groups need to be arbitrated. Yet states are not neutral arbiters. But whom should they favor? Should agricultural credit be extended to medium- and large-sized farmers growing export crops, or to peasant farmers raising food for urban markets? Are wage policies to favor government bureaucrats or unionized textile workers? What is the relative importance and urgency of conflicting needs? [26] Should attention

---

[26] Priorities of urgency and of importance must be distinguished. An action can be more urgent (i.e., demand immediate solution), although it is less important (i.e., of lesser consequence), than others. It may be more *urgent* to arrange short-term rescheduling of a foreign debt, but more important to *rationalize* export/import monetary controls so as to eliminate future dependence on foreign hard-currency loans.

to housing or nutritional needs be deferred so as to provide health education? And will investment be made in fertilizers or in electric plants? Such questions demand answers consonant with clearly set goals.

It is no less necessary to know whether available resources are sufficient to meet priority needs. Distinctions must be made between possible and potential resources,[27] as well as between resources which are internally and those which are externally mobilizable. Experience in many countries reveals that planners are usually too sanguine in their estimates of the possible. Perhaps they unconsciously overstate objectives in order to obtain greater financial aid from lending sources and to elicit the enthusiastic support of their own population in carrying out plans. Whatever the reason, valid ethical judgments about performance can never be made except with a view to the constraints faced by planners: the rate of population growth, physical conditions of production, investment capacity, anticipated changes in productivity, regional differences, and the costs of arbitrating social class conflicts. Preliminary options, as well as the more technical decisions which follow them, are clearly impossible without prior systematic study of needs and resources.[28] Above all, however, an ethical appraisal of options made in any particular case appeals to two norms: the proper sequence to be observed and a realistic view of how free a nation is to observe this sequence.

Technical options include choices affecting the relative importance to be attached to consumption and investment, localization of infrastructure and equipment, number and location of poles of develop-

[27] A possible resource is one whose existence is known and which can be exploited given the present state of technological knowledge. To illustrate: potash is a possible resource in Saskatchewan, Canada. It is known to exist and no technological breakthrough is needed to extract it economically. A potential resource, on the other hand, is one which might be discovered later, which cannot be utilized in the present state of knowledge, or one whose extraction is prohibitively expensive. The precious timbers of the Amazon region in Brazil are a potential resource because they presently cost more to extract than their selling price on the market. Likewise, food substances (other than fish) in the ocean are potential resources, because man has not yet learned how to use them on a large scale in an economical manner. Systematic prospection, or at times fortuitous discovery, can transform a potential into a possible resource. This was the case with oil in Libya a few years ago. On this, cf. the different assessment of Libya's chances for development in the first and second editions (dated 1958 and 1968 respectively) of Benjamin Higgins, *Economic Development, Principles, Problems, and Policies* (W. W. Norton & Company).

[28] For a summary of how these studies are to be conducted, cf. L. J. Lebret, *Dynamique Concrète du Développement* (Les Editions Ouvrières, 1961), pp. 317–379.

ment, production for internal use or export, structures of national product and national budget. Other decisions bear on political and social measures to be taken for achieving development goals. Greater or lesser degrees of centralization are theoretically possible, as are varying degrees of association of a grass-roots populace with summit decision-makers. Optimum governmental and administrative structures must be determined—the particular foreign-policy stance, the degree of dependence on ideology (which ideology? how flexibly interpreted?) in mobilizing support for development objectives, and the manner in which social tensions will be arbitrated.

Options mean little if taken in isolation because they are fragments in a total pattern which alone gives sense to a country's development strategy. Some underdeveloped nations underestimate the importance of over-all norms for making options. Worse still, many advanced nations engage in multiple activities, ranging from studies of all kinds to the dispensation of financial and technical assistance, while displaying scant regard for the wastefulness caused by doing things out of sequence. Developers have at times been insensitive to their obligation to avoid waste in providing advice and services. They may also have contributed, perhaps unwittingly, to reinforcing in the minds of leaders in the Third World a neglect of a long-term perspective on the consequences of development options.

Within developing countries themselves, ideological rigidities frequently generate a double standard which allows decisions to be couched in the language of a particular ideological doctrine although they are in fact implemented (by specific legislation or executive action) in accord with dictates alien to the slogans invoked. One must of course show indulgence in judging such practices if they are politically necessary, but the evaluator does well to examine options effectively taken, not fictitious images propagated by officials.

(B) *Costs*

It is difficult to evaluate even the purely economic costs of many projects. Educational planners experience special frustration when they attempt to calculate total costs of programs. Invisible costs include the foregone income of students, economic burdens imposed on parents deprived of the labor of children sent to school, and the frustration bred in persons educated beyond the absorptive capacity of a narrow labor market, to say nothing of the damage wrought on family structures or on values cherished by those being educated. Although it is not easy to measure intangibles such as these, it is irresponsible to attach no weight to them as one strives to weigh the benefits of a policy against its true costs.

Students of development have tended to overemphasize the benefits of industrialization and to consider urban marginalization as a lesser evil than rural proletarization. The real terms of comparison, however, are not: what did the peasant leave behind in the Andes or the Aurès, but what have authorities left undone to assure that he has something better than a city slum to come to? What steps have they taken to provide intermediate way-stations between rural life and integrated urban living in decentralized, regional development poles? *Laissez-faire* in regional planning is largely responsible for denying to underdeveloped rurals alternatives other than wretched subsistence on inhospitable land or urban squalor in a few large cities.[29] Government planners and administrators who for electoral or other motives live in the capital often concentrate investment in one or two large cities and leave hinterlands without the equipment needed to stimulate development and absorb part of the unskilled labor fleeing the land. This is but one aspect of the cost problem in development.

More serious is the question of "sacrificed generations." Generations can be "sacrificed" in several ways. If economic development were an absolute value, one could have no scruples about "sacrificing" generations. Throughout history, however, men have lived in conditions far below those objectively demanded by human dignity. To this extent, generations have always been "sacrificed." Their sacrifices can legitimately be prolonged one generation or two while their emancipation is being prepared. During the phase of initial mobilization, of course, consumer goods must be rationed so as to build up infrastructure, provide a pedagogy of solidarity, and increase work input even without appreciable rewards. If this happens, generations are "sacrificed" not in any absolute sense, but in the purely relative sense that their social deprivations are prolonged. There is a different sense, however, in which generations ought not be sacrificed, or deprived of the possibility of achieving true human grandeur. Whether he is poor or rich, a man must never be allowed to become a simple object or a pure means for obtaining social goals. Underdevelopment's great misery clearly dehumanizes man; therefore, some effort

[29] Nevertheless, Latin American slums are not always the frightful pits of degradation they are depicted to be. On the contrary, they often provide a steppingstone upward for recently urbanized men beginning to free themselves from marginalization. On this, cf. William Mangin and John C. Turner, "The Barriada Movement," *Peruvian Times,* July 12, 1968, pp. 16–19.

to meet minimum needs is required. But the most fundamental sacrifice of generations lies in their radical alienation, whether in abundance or misery.

Equally relevant is the degree of servitude to technology resulting from the commitment to economic growth. This question is treated in a later chapter where technological standardization is presented as alien to ecological and cultural diversity. Not standardization but the resulting loss of freedom is the issue here, however. In industrialized countries, serious critics are now asking whether technique is but a cluster of means whose congenital tendency is to transform itself into a universe of ends. Does technology ineluctably create new values which eliminate all other values which resist its symbolic hegemony? If so, does the manner in which technology is transferred from advanced to less-advanced countries minimize or maximize the latter's chances of mastering technique? Do alternate ways exist for making technological transfers which would leave poor countries less vulnerable to the necessitating effects of technology? What are these alternatives and what is required for them to be implemented? Although the present work cannot deal with such questions, they would need to be answered by a fully elaborated development ethic.

Have leaders in underdeveloped countries been led to think (falsely?) that anything less than the most modern technological machinery is no good for them? Is research so conducted that successful adaptation of technologies is truly possible? Or are researchers in less-developed countries kept in bondage to the exigencies of scientific metropoles?

Only very large countries and associations of wealthy countries have the funds needed for conducting mass-scale technological research. And since political life is increasingly conditioned by technical considerations, must technological research and transfer of knowledge be institutionalized so that less-developed countries will not become mere passive obedient servants of technological masters elsewhere?

Robert Theobald [30] warns against assuming that the benefits of development can be obtained in underdeveloped countries without upsetting their most cherished goals. It has been believed, for example, that full (or nearly full) employment is necessary if the purchasing power of the masses is to be improved significantly. Yet, Theobald observes, maximum productivity requires a level of automation and cybernation incompatible with high employment. Must we therefore

---

[30] Robert Theobald, "Needed: A New Development Philosophy," *International Development Review*, March 1964, pp. 21–25.

conclude that a leisure society whose economic security rests on a guaranteed income ought to become a worldwide goal? Is the only alternative a world in which a few high-technology countries enjoy a leisure society and control the export of lower technology to heavily populated areas where low-level human productivity will be relied on to create the abundance of goods which will have been demanded? Citizens of Third World countries feel insulted when they are advised to use machinery which has grown obsolete in industrialized nations. How will they accept the counsel to engage in productive activity based on maximum employment within their own boundaries, if technologically advanced countries themselves move beyond this pattern, which is inefficient, unproductive, and socially regressive? For these and similar reasons, basic questions affecting the maintenance and expansion of technology in developed countries are decisive in all realistic efforts to determine the cost of development policy in the Third World. We may be reaching the point where the only margin of freedom left to mankind for controlling technological determinism will reside in the Third World. It is essential, therefore, that the education of its technologists prepare them to deal critically with these issues. The argument is often made that one advantage of undertaking development now is that a society can profit from the mistakes of those which have trod the same paths before it. This is an illusory benefit unless vigorous and enlightened steps are taken immediately, while there is still time, to assure the Third World of mastery over the very technology it needs in order to overcome its underdevelopment. What is required is an intelligent strategy for skipping certain technological phases traversed by countries already developed. Tanzania is experimenting with one sectorial model for skipping phases. Its effort has centered on devising a general educational system synchronized with the agricultural cycle. Assuming Julius Nyerere's decision to lead Tanzania along the path of agricultural development as a priority, it is a progressive measure to adopt a school system in harmony with the demands of productive farming. Conventional wisdom tends to regard such innovation as a regressive step toward a pre-industrial form of education, but the very opposite is the case: Tanzania's approach is a modern developmental one which skips the phase of an educational framework isolated from functional developmental needs.

(C) *Consequences*

Ethics has a special interest in the consequences of choices. Responsibility and freedom—the twin components of ethics—are indissolubly linked to consequences. The burden of freedom resides in precisely this, that one is accountable for the consequences of his actions. Responsibility also implies that one could freely have produced other consequences. Any retroactive evaluation of development must examine consequences inasmuch as we cannot know beforehand the outcome even of policies which appear sound. Nevertheless, societies have now accumulated more than twenty years' experience in development efforts. What can we learn about success and failure in performance as we scrutinize consequences? We possess enough information about certain problems, particularly those relating to aid, trade, and the brain drain, to formulate some tentative evaluation as to whether policies followed have contributed positively or negatively to development.

This is not the place to review aid practices, but a general sentiment prevails among donors and recipients alike that aid has not lived up to expectations. Were expectations realistic, we may ask? And how has aid in fact been given? According to what criteria? How has it been received? How perceived? How employed? Honest replies to these questions are disappointing. More exhaustive answers to these questions might well lead us to conclude that:

—"aid" must become cooperation, in name and in fact;

—such cooperation should be carried out on a global scale in order to solve priority need problems with the optimum use of resources;

—it is not a welfare state which is desirable for the entire world, but generalized agreement on the social responsibility of all nations for the development of all;

—even palliative solutions to aid problems cannot be found until war expenditures are curtailed. Notwithstanding arguments that war breeds higher employment and greater demand for commodities and services (as well as higher prices), adequate aid funds will not be forthcoming until war expenditures are drastically reduced. Current aid trends have reinforced the practice of applying massive resources to war purposes. United States aid has gone to countries it deems strategically important in the Cold War. The aid programs of the U.S.S.R. have suffered from a similar defect. Much technical assistance has contributed toward transforming military classes in non-developed countries into the vanguard and custodians of technology. Sales of arms (often obsolete) to these countries have produced further distortions. And U.S. public opinion has stubbornly refused to view these questions as parts of a single, total problem. More specifically, the ground rules governing technical aid have been defective and led to domination, humiliation of recipients, waste, harmful demonstration effects. Furthermore, the consequences of tying aid loans to purchasing clauses from donor countries are largely undesirable.

One could analyze in similar fashion trade practices, investment abroad, the brain drain, population policies, agricultural policies, or over-all national plans.

One possible conclusion of such examination is that certain kinds of performances ordinarily termed "development" are in fact "anti-development." They are "anti-development" because they do not contribute to increased life-sustenance or esteem for the neediest masses, nor do they expand freedom from constraints. Rather they reinforce domination and create new servitudes. This is the portrait of what development is not. It must, of course, be completed by a profile of authentic development. To supply this profile is the task of the next chapter.

CHAPTER ELEVEN

The Dimensions of Authentic Development

It is far easier to denounce the failings of developed societies and the dangers inherent in the development process than to specify the components of sound development, an endeavor that courts the pitfall which has dogged utopian thinking throughout the ages. Saint-Simon believed that economic action must be based on love, and that technocrats must be priestly souls, disinterested in power and profit but singularly dedicated to creating a universally just society. According to his disciple Rathenau, "The technician will launch a program which endows a nation with many millions of automobiles, but he will himself travel on foot. He will satisfy men's needs but will know how to dominate his own appetites." [1] But reality teaches otherwise: even ascetic monks do not resist the urge to create new needs for themselves. Moreover, the proliferation of new social and economic opportunities opened up by managerial and technical careers, in rich and poor countries alike, confirms the illusoriness of Saint-Simon's dreams of a technological priesthood. Modern society rewards technical skills in generous economic terms; hence, would-be ascetics do not become industrial managers. This fact instills caution: after all, it may be as

[1] Quoted in Georges Duveau, *Sociologie de l'Utopie* (Presses Universitaires de France, 1961), p. 62.

PART III: *What Kind of Development?*

futile to describe what kind of development ought to exist tomorrow as it was for nineteenth-century Socialists—"utopian" and "scientific" alike—to portray what kind of society they wanted. Nevertheless, the reader of this essay is entitled to ask of the author: what kind of development can be considered "human?" The aim of the present chapter is to reply to this question. My explicit normative referents are the goals and regulative principles of development presented earlier. Before describing the attributes of authentic development, however, I wish to render explicit the theory of needs which is latent in my view of development's proper goals.

A Theory of Needs

For Galbraith, "The final requirement of modern development planning is that it have a theory of consumption . . . a view of what the production is ultimately for—has been surprisingly little discussed and has been too little missed . . . *More important, what kind of consumption should be planned?*" [2] The priorities herewith submitted flow from the value premises which underlie this essay. By definition, any *normative* theory of needs is not empirically verifiable. Neither is it self-evident or assured of immediate approval in all cultures or social classes.

Needs vary even in identical cultural settings. Household budget surveys among low-income groups reveal great variety in the kinds of goods acquired by people enjoying minimal purchasing power. When discussing priority needs, therefore, one can only submit tentative propositions. To the extent that these propositions are valid, they constitute a pedagogy for consumers, not merely a reflection of what people in fact prefer. Such a pedagogy implicitly criticizes the three systems of need-satisfaction now in force: the autarkic subsistence pattern, the free demand and supply system, and the planned centralization system. Each of these, it is evident, has variants; mixed types also exist.

Under autarkic subsistence patterns of need-satisfaction, production aims at satisfying a few relatively undifferentiated needs. Since the general level of material life is low, survival is the effective priority need, although considerable resources are also spent for celebration,

[2] John Kenneth Galbraith, *Economic Development in Perspective* (Harvard University Press, 1962), p. 43.

festivity, and play. When a society's resources are scarce, new economic dynamism is possible only if more resources become available. Accordingly, the subsistence pattern which prevails among underdeveloped populations reveals no sophisticated theory of consumption. Its foundation is the compelling pressure upon all members, except small numbers of privileged individuals, to meet minimum needs. Necessity imposes itself on most people, and few theoretical choices are effectively open to them. Therefore, a *theory* of needs remains superfluous as long as resources remain at the subsistence level.

The second system of need satisfaction—free demand and supply —is practiced in "developed" market societies. The theory of needs operative here declares that those goods and services will enjoy priority whose provision is most profitable. But long-term profitability depends on sustained demand. As a result, demand has to be induced. Within the market system, need priorities are simply those demands which effectively motivate suppliers to keep supplying. Of course, many unprofitable services or goods are also desired by citizens. Most of these, however, upon the default of private producers, are provided by public authorities. In recent years, it is true, and amid relative abundance for large numbers of men, the irrationalities of this system have begun to appear. In practice, it becomes the prime function of consumption to assure continued production, which is itself justified on the grounds that it is necessary in order to keep employment high. High employment, in turn, is assumed to be a requisite of high levels of material living which are, to close the circle, equated with high levels of consumption. Normative judgments about priority needs are meaningless because the system obeys patterns of response which tend to absolutize economic functions. Only by inverting basic concepts and subordinating economic categories to qualitative norms of human life can a theory of needs even appear warranted. It is precisely such a theory of needs which is now called for by responsible social critics within the United States.

Within centrally planned economic systems and their variants, planners decide which goods will enjoy priority. Historically, the criteria of planned economies have usually been to maximize national power and to increase productive capacity itself, in part to "catch up" with advanced capitalist societies and partly to lay the foundations for future improvement in consumption. But questions about goals are not answered satisfactorily in planned economies. Even if productive capacity were boosted enough to supply abundant consumer goods, no explicit standard presently exists in planned economies to set the priorities according to which specific consumer goods ought to be produced.

One basic assumption of this book is that the development of every man is intimately bound to the development of all men. This is why I have postulated universal solidarity as the second regulative principle of development. Granted interdependencies among societies with different levels of development, granted also the widespread consciousness of disparities, no theory of needs can ignore the existence of relative superfluity alongside absolute want. Any sound theory of needs must reject both the wasteful use, and the non-utilization, of resources. One now begins to discern the general contours of priority need-satisfactions. Veblen and, more recently, Boulding rightly insist that economic preferences are by-products of social systems and that the price system or the plan determines preferences just as much as preferences determine prices or plans.[3] Affluent societies face two problems: the first is their inability to "get out of their own skin" and imagine a scale of preferences other than that dictated by their markets or plans. Their second difficulty is how to reconcile subjective need with objective priorities. Whatever be the conceptual problems in defining objective needs, a practical distinction must be made among goods of first necessity, goods which foster human fulfillment, and luxury goods. The generic term "goods" includes services as well as physical objects. "Needs" obviously refers to a requirement that men have these "goods." And, in Scitovsky's words, "The economist can no longer regard his standards as given to him from outside, but must make a judgment of his own what standards to accept within what limitation and with what qualifications."[4] Notwithstanding relativities in need, the ethical theorist, no less than the economist, must try to set standards.

"If people are hungry," writes Galbraith, "ill-clad, unsheltered or diseased, nothing is so important as to remedy their condition. . . . It will be time to worry about leisure, contemplation, the appreciation of beauty and the other higher purposes of life when everyone has had a decent meal."[5] Elsewhere we read that "a striving for self-

[3] Cf. Kenneth E. Boulding, "The Basis of Value Judgments in Economics," in *Human Values and Economic Policy,* ed. Sidney Hook (New York University Press, 1967), p. 72.

[4] Tibor Scitovsky, *Papers on Welfare and Growth* (Stanford University Press, 1964), p. 240.

[5] J. K. Galbraith, *The New Industrial State* (Houghton Mifflin Company, 1967), p. 407.

238

realization, for poetry and play, is basic to man once his needs for food, clothing, and shelter have been met." [6] Such statements mirror a prevalent view—viz., that needs for poetry, play, leisure, contemplation, and celebration can be met only after primary needs have been satisfied. This view is wrong, however. Every human society, no matter how poor, ill-fed, or badly clad, devotes a portion of its meager resources to the satisfaction of non-utilitarian needs: celebration, ritual, artistic expression, and playful activity. On grounds of common human experience, if no other, we must surely conclude that men's primary needs extend far beyond mere life-sustenance.

Creative leisure undoubtedly presupposes a measure of economic security. Nevertheless, even very poor societies devote many man-hours to leisure. Leisure blends with their "productive" activities: singing, dancing, playfulness, and "idle" conversation punctuate the hours dedicated to "work." One must beware of ethnocentrism when he discusses leisure and work in underdeveloped countries. Many writers mistakenly treat leisure as the time left over for pleasurable consumption of goods or services after productive tasks have been accomplished. This image is drawn from mass-consumer society, which surrounds men, in their hours of recreation, with a plethora of things to play with and activities to pursue. Little attention seems to have been given to the richly tapestried unity between work and play which marks traditional societies' mode of daily activity. One consequence of this distorted viewpoint is that primary needs are often conceived in a manner which exaggerates the relative importance of material objects. Accordingly, other goods are conceived as coming later, after all physical needs have been met.

This conception is not totally wrong; but what is valid for analytical purposes proves unsuited to the task of formulating policy. Although clarity of explanation is gained by isolating life-sustenance needs from others, no society should be advised to pursue the satisfaction of survival needs to the exclusion of others. Otherwise stated, human beings cannot be whole unless certain seemingly gratuitous needs are met, even if their primary sustenance needs have not yet been adequately satisfied. Maslow's criteria for determining basic needs are instructive. In his view, a need is basic if:

(1) its absence breeds illness;
(2) its presence prevents illness;

---

[6] "A Call to Celebration," *mimeo,* n.d., distributed by FVO-USCC, Washington, D.C. Author's name not indicated.

(3) its restoration cures illness;

(4) under certain (very complex) free choice situations, it is preferred by the deprived person over other satisfactions;

(5) it is found to be inactive, at a low ebb, or functionally absent in the healthy person.[7]

These standards are deficient in one important respect, however. For Maslow, a mature individual is one who has been largely freed from basic needs and can pursue creative self-actualizing goals, in part by undergoing "peak experiences." But *basic* and *primary* needs must be more sharply distinguished. In Maslow's terms, self-actualization needs are basic—that is, fundamental to man's growth and maturation. Primary needs, on the other hand, refer to minimum thresholds of elementary satisfactions, lacking which the deployment of men's capacities—individual or societal—is impeded. For the student of development it is more useful to classify needs as follows: *needs of first necessity, enhancement needs,* and *luxury needs.* Each of these will now be described and a general principle of priorities among them enunciated.

Before doing so, however, I shall speak parenthetically of pathological needs, which cannot be subsumed under any of these categories. Chief among these are "shibboleth" needs—desires nurtured by slogans and catchwords. Massive armaments, for instance, are not legitimate defense needs, which would fall under the first category—life-sustenance. Rationality is of course surrendered when societies, whether impelled by collective fear, paranoia, or self-deception, apply massive resources to the creation of a kind of "wealth" which can only destroy the very good it seeks to preserve. Arms escalation cannot promote, it can only destroy, security. All expenditures inspired by an exaggerated sense of emulation likewise fall into this category. They are called "shibboleth" needs because, as in the ancient Biblical tale which describes how Gileadites were distinguished from Ephraimites (*Book of Judges,* 12:6), these separate the technological "men from the boys." Expenditures arising from shibboleth needs do not, in any ordinary sense, include ostentation, waste, or luxury—what some authors have called "symbolic modernization." On the other hand, and in quite literal fashion, they give expression to counter-needs. Such counter-needs will be ignored in the ensuing discussion, although

[7] Abraham H. Maslow, *Toward a Psychology of Being* (D. Van Nostrand Co., 1962), p. 20.

it is evident that a rational policy of need-satisfaction is thwarted by the abiding fascination of societies with such alienating "needs" as shibboleths.

(A) *Needs of the First Order*

No mystery surrounds goods in this category—food, clothing, shelter—since all are required for survival. Also included are goods without which protection and security are impossible. Protection is sought against nature and hostile organisms. Security, although quite a relative thing, is based on the general sense that men organized in society *need* to reduce their vulnerability to untoward events and to the passage of time. Thus, in primitive agricultural or pastoral societies, security needs dictate the existence of storage facilities to assure food between harvests, as well as means of transport to enable people to move to new pastures when old ones are exhausted. Other goods are required to facilitate the accomplishment of mandatory tasks by members of society. Hence, fishermen need boats, nets, and bait to engage in their life-sustaining activity and housewives need cooking utensils. Some instruments of production, in short, are themselves goods of first necessity. So are training and education, to the degree that they are required for survival and mutual protection. Adolescent hunters in certain societies are still taught how to shoot arrows and gather honey from trees without being stung; young girls are shown how to weave straw mats on which to place sleeping infants; forest guides must learn how to follow animal trails when rain has rubbed out fresh tracks. Even in rudimentary subsistence societies, some measure of education constitutes a primary need. And primary needs must be met if men are to enjoy the minimum freedom required to satisfy other needs. The dynamics of needs is such "that a new and higher need emerges as the lower need fulfills itself by being adequately gratified." [8] The best way to satisfy higher needs is obviously to gratify primary needs first. This holds as a general principle, notwithstanding the fact that poor societies which are incapable of feeding, clothing, or protecting themselves adequately nonetheless invest resources in expressing their feelings and thoughts, in playing, celebrating, and creating.

As a general rule, major productive energies ought to be devoted to the satisfaction of needs of the first order before attending to the production of goods destined to satisfy other needs.

[8] *Ibidem*, p. 53.

(B) *Enhancement Needs*

All individuals and societies seek to express themselves in various ways: through language, gesture, symbolic activity, silence, and display. Beyond expression, men need to create and to actualize their latent capacities. Therefore, they must have access to those goods which enable them to invent, explore possibilities, and bring their capacities to maturity. Such needs are called enhancement needs because they are not directly ordered to utilitarian functions except insofar as they contribute to expression and creation. Ultimately, of course, creation and expression are themselves *useful* (indeed, *necessary*) to health, growth, and maturity. Nevertheless, they are self-validating ends: it is good for its own sake to be healthy or proficient. Enhancement needs comprise two general categories: what psychologists call actualization needs, and what philosophers, poets, and social theorists term "needs of transcendence." Marcuse defines transcendence as a man's sustained capacity to choose a future which is not the logical outcome or projected sequence of his present. Transcendence is the creation of an alternative to what has to be in virtue of what has already been. Kolakowski is more existentialist and asserts that the only authentic response to the agonizing human condition is a blend of desperation, hope, affirmation of life, and wise skepticism. One must proceed along the thorny path, he says, and engage in a "stubborn struggle with the finiteness of one's own thought." [9] Ultimately, the two main problems of life are freedom and death; and the essence of man's grandeur is to experience the tension—even when his other needs have been "satisfied"—between life and death, between freedom and necessity. Kolakowski scorns all simplistic forms of materialism because they misinterpret the nature of human needs. He thereby joins company with Sartre, Camus, and a host of contemporary philosophers. The relevant point is that "transcendence" is not thought to lie outside man's experience, but is viewed as immanent to his endless quest for meaning and identity. Enhancement needs in this sense are the most intimately "human" needs of all, for man must stretch out beyond himself in order to be human.

For Régis Debray, freeing the present from the past is the central act of revolution.[10] Transcendence thus comes to signify the emanci-

[9] Cf. Leopold Labedz, "Kolakowski, On Marxism and Beyond," *Encounter,* March 1969, pp. 77–88.

[10] Régis Debray, *Révolution dans la Révolution* (Paris: Maspéro, 1967), pp. 13–96. Part I of this book (pp. 13–96) is entitled "Libérer le Présent du Passé."

pation of the future from the present. There is a considerable measure of self-delusion in this vision, for voluntarism can not wish away the social determinisms, admittedly partial and relative, induced by specific choices. Nevertheless, men and societies need to go beyond what they already are in the hope of achieving what they can become. Because they are simultaneously individual organisms and social beings, men need physical objects to test their possibilities. They require goods—freely provided by nature or created by men's economic activity—to give material support to their actualizing and transcending activities. This is not to deny the ability of exceptional mystics or poets to realize themselves through introspection, contemplation, or simple human communion. But in order to have suitable outward settings for such activities, most men require physical goods. Moreover, once these activities become social and not purely personal, *things* and *places* are required even for purposes of expression. Whatever may be the ultimate meaning of human life, it is something more than simple existence. Beyond subsistence, survival, and all useful functions, man in society has an endless range of enhancement needs, the satisfaction of which perfects him, actualizes his potentialities, thrusts him beyond perceived limits and into new environments he himself creates.

After needs of the first order have been met, therefore, the major productive energies of society ought to be devoted to providing those goods and services which best foster the satisfaction of all men's actualization and transcendence needs.

(C) *Luxury Needs*

A twin mystification cripples the ability of most need theorists to reflect soberly on a third category of needs and goods, designated "luxury." Sombart, Veblen, and others have emphasized the economic neutrality of luxury spending and its display function. Of wasteful display and luxury Veblen writes that "In view of economic theory the expenditure in question is no more and no less legitimate than any other expenditure. It is here called 'waste' because this expenditure does not serve human life or human well-being on the whole, not because it is waste or misdirection of effort or expenditure as viewed from the standpoint of the individual consumer who chooses it." [11] Economic theorists often treat the distinction between

[11] Thorstein Veblen, *The .Theory of the Leisure Class* (Mentor Books, 1963), p. 78.

objective and subjective need as unscientific because it involves value judgments which go beyond the simple analysis of preference or demand. Nevertheless, economists themselves must help determine what is "reasonable" expenditure and what is "waste." According to Paul Baran, if society forbids the economy to cater to the tastes of drug addicts, it should logically and rationally overrule consumer preferences, even when expressed with effective purchasing power, if these are foolish, frivolous, or wasteful. Notwithstanding the difficulty of setting objective measures, objective reason and rational judgment, he asserts, ought to guide economic activity. In Baran's opinion, research could ground objective judgments on cultural requirements as well as on biological needs.[12]

Consumer preferences must surely be disciplined if wasteful luxury is not to distort demand curves and thereby lead to the allocation of scarce resources to the satisfaction of low-priority needs. Most development economists, regardless of their theoretical positions, urge underdeveloped governments to avoid waste and ostentation. They might well follow their own advice when recommending productive priorities for their own countries. What is more likely to happen is that they will continue to defend luxury and waste as essential to freedom, as incentives to creativity and useful motors of achievement. To illustrate, the Magazine Publishers Association, which claims to represent "365 leading U.S. magazines," has distributed in recent years a photograph and text of Benjamin Franklin whose theme is: "I have not yet, indeed, thought of a remedy for luxury." A full-page ad instructs us, in Franklin's words, that luxury has no remedy, that it is no great evil, and that the hope of being someday able to purchase luxuries spurs the poor to work harder and to produce more. We are told that the existence of luxuries makes all people happier. The Association also places full-page ads quoting Adlai Stevenson to the effect that the "imaginative genius of advertising" sharpens demand and stimulates improved quality in products; it is, therefore, a major cause of the American standard of living. At present a polarization of views is taking place regarding the merits of widescale luxury spending. On the one hand, detractors of luxury often overlook its contributions to "civilization." On the other, most pleas on behalf of luxury heard in "opulent" societies assume that misery has been abolished and that both waste and luxury represent qualitatively higher levels of developmental achievement than austerity. Both views are unsound: the first

[12] Baran's position is reported in Scitovsky, *op. cit.*, pp. 233–234.

argues too much, the second ignores structural interdependence at work in the world.

It is a mistake to think that luxury always exercises a debilitating effect on human virtue or that it necessarily corrupts men. Historians of culture remind us of the enormous contribution to all civilizations made by seemingly wasteful luxurious expenditures.[13] Moralists, on the contrary, tend to exaggerate the merits of poverty and to over-estimate the dangers inherent in wealth. Yet no one can speak of absolute superfluity or of some ceiling above which each new possession would diminish the existential quality of the owner. Luxury goods can be as noble as the use to which they are put or the spirit in which they are enjoyed. Moreover, the history of great fortune-builders shows that even crass displays of conspicuous waste often lead to the creation, after their author's death, of public monuments to man's exhibitionist capabilities. Ironically, selfishness leads men to build monuments to their own egos; but often what survives is a museum to be visited by a public which ridicules their grandiose pretensions.

Apologists of luxury tend to err at the other extreme by ignoring two important facts, one psychological, the other political. Psychologically, it is a sign of puerility, when not of pathology, for a man to base his identity and his sense of importance on the possession of luxury goods rather than goods which enhance his actualization and transcendence. This is not to deny that grandiosity itself can be a psychologically rewarding posture which demands visible expression. But too frequently its quest is mere compensation for character deficiencies or the unwillingness to grasp the hollowness of a life which does not progress interiorly and spiritually. Toynbee believes that the Gospel injunction "What does it profit a man to gain the whole world and all the riches thereof, if he lose his own soul?" applies to societies as well as to persons. Alienation in abundance is no less possible than alienation in misery. Even if we assume, for the sake of argument, that the pursuit of luxury can be conducted without alienation or pathological compensation, there remains a solid political reason why the large-scale pursuit of luxury is reprehensible: the worldwide consciousness of the intolerability of mass insatisfaction of primary needs. Were all men living on this planet to be adequately fed, clothed, and cured, individuals might perhaps be allowed to indulge in their luxury fanta-

[13] On this, cf., e.g., UNESCO's multi-volume *History of Mankind, Cultural, and Scientific Development;* or Joseph Pieper, *Leisure, the Basis of Culture* (Mentor-Omega Books, 1963).

sies. One suspects that with the passage of time they would grow bored with luxuries, their psychic toys, and begin desiring goods better suited to actualization and transcendence. But in real life, massive wastefulness and luxurious display coexist alongside monumental need. Otherwise stated, a relative superfluity of goods is enjoyed by a minority while the majority suffers from an absolute insufficiency of goods. Political realism and moral objectivity alike dictate new producer priorities.

There is no justification for allowing a few wealthy societies to use a disproportionate share of world resources for the satisfaction of luxury needs while the basic needs of the masses are left unmet. This is a plea not for egalitarianism but for rational priorities. Although developed societies claim to be rational in their social organizations, they are incapable of following the dictates of rationality on a world scale.

A third general principle derived from this analysis condemns as irrational and disorderly the engagement of substantial portions of mankind's production capabilities in luxury goods while the more essential needs of most men remain unsatisfied. Luxury goods can improve the quality of human life for some; but no moral, political, or psychological justification exists for granting luxury needs equal or higher priority than the global satisfaction of survival and enhancement needs.

Of the three categories, enhancement goods contribute most directly to the quality of human life. They help foster community, creativity, and personal fulfillment. Luxury items, on the contrary, are often status goods catering to men's desire to be deemed important. To possess great luxury in the midst of a needy humanity not only heightens one's insensitivity, it alienates him in trivia as well. Luxury obviously offers great psychological advantages; it relieves a man of his sense of inadequacy by providing compensations and allows him to express his wish to appear important or powerful. But men are easily estranged from true greatness if their preoccupation with such psychic toys leads to a fixation rendering them incapable of integral human growth, thanks to the ordered pursuit of goods which promote emotional, intellectual, and spiritual perfection. The possession of insufficient goods produces a dehumanizing condition; conversely, excessive attachment to luxury goods when other men are in dire need and when more important needs are overlooked because of the superior glitter of luxuries is also dehumanizing. It is not, as Scitovsky

246

claims,[14] economic progress which diverts time and energy away from intellectual pursuits or lowers the prestige of learning, but rather irrational need satisfaction.

As Croce put it, the mission of ethics is to create new facts.[15] Development ethics, in particular, must create new producer and consumer priorities in accord with need. The appeal to present structures is no sound rationale for maintaining present trends.

We need not review the complex psychological and anthropological literature on needs in order to derive valid guidelines for development action. The action required is investment in certain kinds of productive capacity. But consumer goods are, in a patent sense, the outcome of productive capacity; and productive goods themselves are "consumed" when they are put to work producing. Consequently, a theory of consumer priorities directly affects investments in productive capacity. For purposes of practical development planning, therefore, three kinds of needs must be recognized: needs of first necessity, enhancement needs designed to foster actualization and transcendence (however conceived), and luxury needs. For each category of needs, there is a corresponding category of goods. Good policy-makers acknowledge the difficulty of measuring with precision the amounts of goods which should be produced. They are likewise aware of vast cultural and idiosyncratic relativities involved in enhancement needs, as well as the flexibility of criteria used to assess luxury needs. Nevertheless, prior urgency clearly attaches to the universal provision of goods of first necessity to all men. Beyond this, a priority of intrinsic importance attaches to the satisfaction of enhancement needs for all. Luxury needs are less urgent than needs of the first order, and less important than enhancement needs. Three explicit policy consequences flow from this position:

(a) All nations, developed and underdeveloped, should concentrate their major economic efforts on providing all men with sufficient goods of first necessity. Existing FAO and UNESCO studies can help experts set quantitative minimum needs in food, housing, health care, education services, and other goods. Production and distribution of essential goods should also constitute the priority target of all regional and international economic policies. In moral terms, any economic system or policy which, in theory or in practice, rejects this priority of

14 *Op. cit.,* p. 209.
15 Benedetto Croce, *Politics and Morals* (Philosophical Library, 1945), pp. 188, 196.

urgency is *structurally unjust:* it violates two of the three regulative principles which govern development efforts. These are the priority of "being" over "having" and the obligation to optimize universal human solidarity. Of course, abrupt radical change in present priorities is not immediately feasible, but this principle supplies a direction for contemplated improvement.

(b) The second priority task of economic effort is to facilitate access for all men to enhancement goods, which directly relate to the fulfillment of their properly human potentialities—intellectual, emotional, cultural, expressive, creative, and spiritual. No universal norms exist, nor are needs static in this domain. For this reason, permanent instruments of popular consultation must be instituted at every level if social planning is to be humane. What I have written elsewhere in this book on the dynamics of value change based on "existence rationalities" operative in diverse societies suggests the lines along which such consultation might be conducted. A normative judgment is made that enhancement needs contribute most directly to human development. In this realm above all others, cultural diversity is to be safeguarded. The further judgment is made that existing patterns of mass-consumer economies are incompatible with the worldwide fulfillment of this category of needs, here deemed to stand highest on a scale of intrinsic importance.

(c) Only after the aforementioned needs are met with some relative degree of adequacy can one justify major economic effort aimed at producing luxury goods, whose contribution to human well-being and human growth is certainly not negligible, but whose disordered use perpetuates misery, condones wastefulness, and legitimizes structurally alienating forces in human society. It is further asserted that their use would be disorderly were they given a higher priority over other, more urgent and more essential goods.

The vested interests of those who benefit from existing structures cannot be wished away. Corrective action, therefore, will be monumentally difficult. No doubt it is utopian to expect immediate change. Nevertheless, if developers genuinely seek a higher standard of living —quantitatively and qualitatively—for all men, the necessary first step is to accept a higher standard of thinking. The embryonic theory of priority needs just elaborated has as its primary purpose to elicit creative research and experimentation in closer accord with this higher standard of thinking. Lebret has diagnosed the issue with remorseless accuracy: "The problem confronting the world is nothing

248

less than the creation of a new civilization. There is a striking contrast between man's desire to prove his worth and his childish ideas of 'going one better' than his neighbor, which he often confuses with being 'better off.' The rich are covetous, desiring more than they need; and this covetousness is rapidly spreading to the poorer peoples. A greedy world can only be a divided world, ethically sordid, heading toward barbarism." [16] All partial efforts at rationality are doomed to fail unless worldwide rationality is instituted in the production and consumption of goods according to valid criteria of priority needs. Perroux has wisely affirmed that "notwithstanding opposing dogmas and systems, East and West have accumulated and preserved a common patrimony of positive knowledge, of ideals, of utopias, and of myths. In the East as in the West politics, when carried to its ultimate consequences, denies constraints. And *economics, thought through to its ultimate consequences, finally negates scarcity.* The myths of a society without constraints and of an economy without scarcity belong equally to East and West." [17]

Scarcity and constraint cannot be abolished, however, unless the need priorities herein outlined are observed. New facts must be created to make reality conform to this norm.

Development's Three Dimensions

Although the evils of present developmental forms are considerable, it must not be supposed that underdevelopment is a blessing. On the contrary, it is because underdevelopment is such a bad condition that societies are prone to choose imperfect models of development.

When famine, disease, and ignorance can be eliminated, it is morally wrong to perpetuate them. And no justification exists for preserving old values if these buttress social privilege, exploitation, superstition, and escapism. Furthermore, men's cognitive horizons ought not be limited to tradition on grounds that new knowledge is troubling. On the other hand, it is foolish to assume that what *has been done* in developed countries in the name of development is necessarily better than what *could be done* in countries presently underdeveloped. The case is not against development, but against the

[16] Louis J. Lebret, *The Last Revolution* (Sheed and Ward, 1965), p. 4.
[17] François Perroux, *La Coexistence Pacifique,* III (Presses Universitaires de France, 1958), 429. Italics mine.

pseudo-development of many contemporary "advanced" societies. Measured against the goals and principles described above, many "developed" countries have achieved not genuine development but mass alienation and pseudo-development.[18]

Three issues crucially affect the quality of life in developed and underdeveloped societies alike. These value questions are now being posed in acute form by social critics in economically developed countries. Although the illusion persists that they are "luxury" questions for poor countries, the very opposite is the case. Massive determinisms are at work in the world's drive toward technological and post-industrial societies.[19] As a result, development itself cannot take place in the world except as a conscious effort on the part of pre-technological societies to overcome vulnerability in the face of these determinisms. Troubling value questions must be answered before new and inhuman determinisms become irreversible. Some observers fear it may already be too late in developed countries and that the worldwide post-industrial society of the future will comprise only two classes of people: the manipulators and the manipulated. The three crucial value questions are: (1) Can world misery be abolished? (2) Is global austerity, imposed and voluntary, necessary? (3) Can cultural diversity be saved in the face of standardization?

These questions derive their importance from the fact that an authentically developed society is something other than the combination of political democracy with industrial society and mass-consumer patterns of economic behavior. Not that political democracy is worthless, but it is illusory in the absence of other freedoms. Moreover, its historical birth in a Western cultural matrix distorts its possible appeal elsewhere. This is also true of industrialization, some measure of which may be necessary in most societies. The real issue is: can societies be free to pursue modes of industrialization in harmony with their own evolving values? One cannot dispel the suspicion that mass-consumer economy represents an intrinsically alienating form of social organization. The major task of development planners in non-industrialized countries may consist, therefore, in devising ways of achieving economic modernity while avoiding the trap of the mass-consumer

[18] A graphic description of what I call "anti-development" in a prosperous society is found in Susan Sontag, "A Letter from Sweden," *Ramparts*, Vol. VII, No. 14 (July 1969), pp. 23–38.

[19] For a comprehensive study of these issues, cf. Radovan Richta and others, *Civilization at the Crossroads: Social and Human Implications of the Scientific and Technological Revolution* (Prague, 1967).

society. Paul Ricoeur fears that "the triumph of consumer culture, universally identical and integrally anonymous, would represent the zero point of a creative culture; what would result is skepticism on a planetary scale, absolute nihilism in the triumph of well-being. One must admit that this peril is at least as great as and perhaps even more probable than that of atomic destruction." [20]

The prevailing imagery of relationships between developed and underdeveloped countries assigns to the former the role of "saving" the latter from misery, disease, and stagnation, thanks to superior technology. At the deepest level, however, the roles may have to be reversed. Perhaps it is "developed" nations which must be "saved" from servitude to means by creative options yet to be made in "underdeveloped" societies as they struggle to "modernize" in a human mode. In truth, the agonizing value questions which perplex developed countries—questions regarding ends and the quality of human existence— lie at the heart of the underdeveloped countries' choice of their own futures. Third World developers must understand that their drive toward development poses the identical value questions now faced by developed societies. If they fail, they thereby lose their chance of achieving a humane form of development for themselves. Furthermore, the dangers of global war, ecological suicide and total standardization can be offset only if sound answers to these value questions are found in the Third World. Clearly implied is the possibility that value questions raised in developed and underdeveloped countries alike may be generated by a contradiction between wanting both material development and a good society. Accordingly, normative inquiry into the good life and the good society is meaningless unless it is conducted in worldwide terms. The query must evidently be rooted in history and contemporary reality, not in mere logic or ritual. To pose it in modern terms is to acknowledge but not to acquiesce in a world in which technology holds sway, in which widening disparities between rich and poor grow increasingly abhorrent, in which political and economic domination remains a stubborn fact which cannot be wished away, in which challenges to old meanings assume traumatic proportions. Despite great progress in the realm of means and instruments, modern men have regressed in the domain of ends and of meaning. Pre-modern leaders must grasp this because the pervasiveness of means threatens to make all ends obsolete even within their own socie-

[20] Paul Ricoeur, "Civilisation Universelle et Cultures Nationales," *Monde Uni*, No. 57–58 (January 1961), p. 20.

ties. Now that Third World consciousness is alerted to the dangers of cultural imperialism, the slim hope exists that perhaps somewhere in that world a new wisdom can be fashioned. Yet pressing material needs must be quickly met. The answers given to these basic questions reveal, at least in general terms, what constitutes a "human" form of development. My own replies to the three questions are presented in these pages. First, I contend that development policy ought to aim at abolishing misery, not at obtaining affluence. Second, that large-scale austerity must be practiced in advanced countries as well as in premodern ones. Third, that cultural diversity needs to be actively pursued as a counterweight to the powerful forces of standardization inherent in modernization processes.

(A) *Eliminating Poverty, Not Obtaining Affluence*

The authors of Pakistan's twenty-year perspective plan warn that "massive improvement will still leave living standards far below the level of developed countries. It will, however, eliminate poverty and ensure that at least the basic minimum of necessities of life are available to everyone." [21] Leaders in underdeveloped countries delude themselves if they set their sights on "catching up" with today's economically advanced nations. If the oracle at Delphi could speak once again, its message to the Third World would be: "Do not try to match economic levels of countries already developed, you are not going to make it." This is doubtless a hard saying, and it must not be delivered unless accompanied by two additional messages. The first is: "Don't complain; those who have 'made it' are only now beginning to taste the bitter fruits of dehumanizing affluence. You are the lucky ones." The second, and more important, message is: "The developed world has no moral right to transmit the first two messages unless it practices austerity itself." It is sheer cynicism to recommend austerity to others unless one assumes it himself. Seen through the eyes of underdeveloped societies, the rich world is one of the major obstacles preventing them from "making it." Realists know that even if all the exploitative activity of rich nations, classes, and interest groups could be suppressed in an instant, the cruel equation of development would still read: the poor masses will not "make it." Nevertheless, by and large, it is the rich who have tampered with the poor man's desire mechanisms and made him want to "make it." This is why rich socie-

[21] Cited in *Government of Pakistan, The Third Five Year Plan* (1965–1970), May 1965, p. 18.

ties and classes must tamper with their own desire mechanisms—this time to moderate acquisitive desires, not to arouse them—if they expect others to reverse the forces they themselves have set in motion. One may say of the modern dream of affluence what Claudel wrote of woman: that she was created to awaken desires she cannot satisfy. The "affluence" image of the good life may already be irreversible in many underdeveloped lands. Development economists are privately fond of declaring that "Poor countries have not had the image of affluence shoved down their throats; they are hell-bent on getting it." Galbraith puts it somewhat more elegantly: "No other social goal is more strongly avowed than economic growth; no other test of social success has such nearly unanimous acceptance as the annual increase in the Gross National Product. And this is true of all countries, developed or undeveloped; communist, socialist, or capitalist. . . . Similarly, it is now agreed that ancient cultures—India, China, and Persia —should measure their progress toward civilization by their percentage increase in G.N.P. Their own scholars are the most insistent of all." [22]

Yet it is a serious mistake to judge civilization, or even development, in terms of G.N.P. *Affluence for the masses is impossible except on terms demeaning to underdeveloped societies themselves.* Realism dictates that a more modest goal be set: the elimination of misery. The terms are demeaning because, according to the inner logic of technological progress, poor masses can achieve abundance rapidly only if countries at the leading edge of the technological revolution concentrate their productive potential on producing essential consumer goods for everyone in the world. By using automation and cybernetics massively, this would be possible. But human labor would become largely superfluous in the process. Nevertheless, if the satisfaction of humanity's priority needs were pursued with the seriousness and urgency with which men wage wars or explore space, abundant goods for all men could quickly be produced. The weakness of this hypothesis lies in the unrealistic assumptions it makes, namely:

(a) that the rich world is willing to harness its productive forces to meet the world's priority needs;

(b) that poor nations can accept, without damage to their dignity, being mere beneficiaries, and not creative agents of their own development; and

(c) that such a course can be followed without thereby transform-

[22] Galbraith, *The New Industrial State,* p. 173.

ing the human race into a gigantic social-engineering laboratory.

Nevertheless, these are the assumptions which would have to be realized in order to achieve worldwide affluence in any foreseeable future. But these conditions are at once offensive to the dignity of underdeveloped people and incompatible with values now prevailing in the rich world. They are also morally repugnant in terms of the future of the human race itself, for all men would be reduced to the status of mechanical actors in a global "bread and circuses" culture. The only agrument which recommends this measure is its technical feasibility. Of course, it is also technically feasible to destroy all life on the planet, through radiation or germ warfare!

If we reject, as we must, this alternative, we are forced to conclude that *inhuman poverty cannot be wiped out unless the world as a whole sets out to eliminate poverty, not to obtain affluence.* The dynamisms unleashed by the unrealistic quest of affluence instead of moderate levels of material well-being breed forms of determinism, exploitation, and social privilege which are abhorrent to the world's poor. Indeed, the limited affluence we now witness in the world is itself the consequence of *not* subordinating private gain to social good, of *not* limiting acquisitive desires for the sake of preserving the capacity for value integration in periods of change, of *not* accepting the responsibilities dictated by the demands of solidarity, of *not* respecting ecological balances in nature. Given present population trends and densities (and all imaginable alternative projections), affluence for the few is the only form of affluence possible, unless we choose the alienating "Santa Claus" model of affluence for all described above. But affluence for the few—for rich countries or rich classes in poor countries—is precisely what the Third World has rejected! To pursue the dream of universal affluence, therefore, is to condemn most men to cruel frustrations and to exacerbate the same traumatic inequalities the Third World already finds so repugnant.

What of the argument that the total supply of goods can become virtually infinite, thanks to vanguard technology? In terms of strict material possibilities, this is perhaps true. It is no less true, however, that technological power is vested in the hands of small numbers of men and organizations whose values, loyalties, and interests prevent them from consenting to use that power to provide affluence for all. Even more fundamental is the intolerable human and ecological price exacted to achieve affluence in this mode. The world would become a social arena in which a few manipulators would "provide" for vast hordes of manipulated men, all of whose needs, emotions, and fantasies would have to be socially engineered. At length even the manipulators would grow disenchanted, since they will have been transformed into mere machines for satisfying the needs of others, while preventing these others from asserting their humanity. The basic error lies in thinking that affluence for all is an unqualified good. Sensitive critics have recently begun to reflect on the dehumanizing effects of mindless affluence. This is certainly not a propitious time for men to commit themselves *en masse* to compulsive consumption. Durkheim, Freud, and others have taught us that civilization is impossible in the absence of social constraints on desire. For poor countries, survival itself is at stake. Unless they mobilize their populations around an attainable image of material improvements, acquisitive desires will spread through society in a manner which will ineluctably breed destructive individualism and multiply insoluble conflicts. Whatever economists may say about the social utility of greed at the level of individual entrepreneurs or of social categories within a mobile system, it is sheer nonsense to expect the mass populace in a society to endure perpetual frustration in order to reward the greed of a few. The recent outbreak in East Pakistan against the privileged treatment afforded West Pakistan is a mild example of the kind of explosion I have in mind. The central target of development efforts in the world's poor nations must be to abolish poverty, not to chase after a will-o'-the-wisp universal affluence. Such affluence is both unattainable and undesirable. The gap between rich and poor will reach intolerable proportions, however, unless moderation of desires in underdeveloped countries finds its counterpart in nations already developed. Imposed austerity in the first must be matched by voluntary frugality in the second.

(B) *Voluntary Austerity in Developed Countries*[23]

Where poverty, however grim and degrading, is the lot of the masses, as in India or Egypt, it is not noteworthy since the fate of few is otherwise. Indeed, dominant belief systems in these societies provide a *rationale* for poverty which is consoling to many. But it is no longer possible to view world poverty except as a disgrace. If poverty is to be wiped out in underdeveloped lands, austerity must be *imposed*. Auster-

---

[23] I have borrowed here from an earlier essay. Cf. Denis A. Goulet, "Voluntary Austerity: The Necessary Art," *The Christian Century*, Vol. LXXXIII, No. 23 (June 8, 1966), pp. 748–752.

ity is not a pleasant word; it is an even harsher reality. Nevertheless, where no rational austerity policy exists in an underdeveloped country, misery is by that very fact imposed on all who do not enjoy privileged positions. Not to impose equitable austerity on a developing nation is to condemn its underprivileged masses to a degrading form of austerity whose only beneficiaries are privileged classes and foreign interests. The underdeveloped condition itself is a kind of austerity imposed on unwilling human beings. If the abolition of poverty is one proper goal of the development effort, national austerity must be imposed. Not any kind of austerity will do, however. Valid austerity entails the acceptance of privation in order to overcome some crisis, enhance one's future position, or achieve greater equity in the distribution of goods. This is qualitatively different from that form of austerity which is the by-product of social injustice, permissive entrepreneurship which rewards those who are most astute at making profits, and the failure to mobilize energies around urgent collective tasks. Genuine austerity within poor countries is the refusal to waste, to practice ostentation, or to allow potential resources to lie idle out of inertia. Such austerity combats underdevelopment and marginalization, whereas *laissez-faire* austerity perpetuates them. At the symbolic level there is, to paraphrase Kierkegaard, an infinite qualitative difference between suffering deprivation because one has no voice in his destiny and undergoing deprivation as the price one pays to free himself from inertia and structural backwardness. It is the difference between Haiti and Cuba!

The principle of austerity is acknowledged readily enough in underdeveloped countries, although political obstacles to its implementation are enormous. Furthermore, arms expenditures prevent many countries from establishing sound priorities in their budgets. Perceptive leaders are sensitive to the unnecessary cruelty involved in requiring additional labor and sacrifice from poor peasants and workers without granting them visible rewards in the form of necessary consumer goods. Thus, there is no simple formula for setting the exact measure of austerity to be recommended in non-developed lands. Nevertheless, the greatest obstacle may lie elsewhere: how to introduce *voluntary* austerity in countries already developed. One major difficulty is that the need for collective austerity and personal frugality is not so apparent as it is in poor countries. Notwithstanding its unattractive visage, however, voluntary austerity is vital to the moral health of prosperous societies.

Homeopathy is not confined to medicine, it applies to ethical life as well. There is, in addition to qualitative cures for the ills of quantitative societies, a therapy of quantity. As in every treatment of like by like, the crucial problem is dosage. Against the ailment of compulsive consumption, voluntary austerity in the use of material goods is prescribed for those who hunger after fullness of good rather than mere abundance of goods. Societies court tragedy when they produce men who have leisure time but are bereft of the leisure spirit. Without leisure spirit, leisure time is the breeding ground of alienation in triviality. Men in want possess too little to become human, but satiated men, on the contrary, are prevented from becoming human because they possess too much. Notwithstanding pious disclaimers to the contrary, *to be* has come to mean, in developed countries, *to have*. Patriotism and social duty enjoin men to want more so that the national productive apparatus can be fed without interruption. As it does in non-developed countries, austerity in rich lands calls upon men to forgo immediate gratification for the sake of some greater good. Once general affluence has become possible, however, austerity cannot be imposed; it must be voluntary. Various motives can lead one to practice it. Thus, there is the poverty of the ill-tempered, the embittered, or of the unyielding devotees of an outdated ethic of frugality for its own sake. Others seek compensation because, in the words of Lawrence Lipton (in *The Holy Barbarians*), they "wooed the bitch goddess Success with panting breath and came away rebuffed." What is required, on the other hand, is independent and voluntary austerity. These qualities differentiate it from imposed austerity. Unlike the imposed variety, voluntary austerity produces no severe physical hardship and it begins only after basic needs have been satisfied. As for the physical objects possessed, voluntary austerity in affluent lands might well correspond to abundance in underdeveloped societies. Whereas austerity is an absolute condition for survival in poor areas and a harsh requirement of their economic development, the opposite is true in rich countries. There it is the fruit of individual choices, not the inescapable by-product of existing social organization. Because it is freely chosen, voluntary austerity risks being false and hollow. Many who practice it succumb to the temptation to be play-acting, as did Marie-Antoinette when she played the peasant girl at her Trianon "farm cottage." The difference between genuine and sham austerity is as great as that between Marie-Antoinette and a real peasant maid. A second pitfall of optional poverty is that those who engage in it can

257

easily transform their righteousness into self-righteousness. The truly poor man, on the other hand, is immune to this temptation. Rarely can he escape his plight, and as he struggles to escape the clutch of his own misery, his alternatives are usually confined to resigning himself to his lot in life or denouncing (probably in vain) those responsible for it. Whoever assumes poverty voluntarily, on the contrary, is protected in dire moments by his talents, his earning capacity, perhaps even by the Social Security Act! Yet, in spite of all its dangers, voluntary austerity is essential. Why is this so? What arguments recommend its large-scale practice within developed regions?

Throughout history poverty, not misery, has been freely embraced by men, individually and collectively, for religious reasons. For some religions the *raison d'être* of voluntary poverty is a nihilistic condemnation of earthly goods. More frequently, however, the basic *rationale* is to teach men detachment from things in preparation for total self-awareness or unencumbered union with Absolute Good. Without doubt, such asceticism has always been practiced only by tiny minorities. Nevertheless, as Bergson has observed (in *The Two Sources of Morality and Religion*), the values attached to it become diluted, as it were, "for the rank and file of mankind into a general indifference to the conditions of daily existence. There was for one and all an absence of comfort which to us is astonishing. Rich and poor did without superfluities which we consider as necessities." For centuries Christianity has drawn inspiration from its mystical poet of voluntary poverty, Francis of Assisi. Meanwhile Zen clings to the lesson of its great masters: "Above, not a tile to cover the head; below, not an inch of ground for the foot." My purpose here is not to examine poverty in its religious manifestations, although its voluntary practice in history has generally been linked to such forms. Development is my concern, and voluntary austerity is dictated by two compelling human reasons of crucial importance to the success of world development.

The first reason is freedom: men must free themselves from slavery to their own desire mechanisms. In order to do so, individuals living in societies which goad them to consume relentlessly must freely deprive themselves of certain material objects, even when these are useful and well within reach of their purchasing power. They must assert, not conceptually but by their actions, the primacy of their persons over things and over forces which insistently violate their faculties of desire. A high wall needs to be erected against the strategy employed by profit-seekers who, backed by dollars and brains, employ psychology's findings to seduce men into spending, accumulating, wasting, and throwing away. Voluntary austerity is manifestly alien to the deep psychological inclinations of the developed world. Even the Soviet Union has climbed aboard the "goulash and television bandwagon" and Marxist writers in developed countries wish to expunge the word "austerity" from their permanent vocabulary.[24] Not surprisingly, therefore, increasing numbers of people in developed lands drift unwhimperingly toward insignificance, fettered to their tyrannical consumer functions. This uncritical pursuit of affluence breeds novel forms of dehumanization. It is not always an overt or painful form of alienation; it is often well disguised, well fed, and even well bred. The best description one can give is that it legitimates for entire societies what Pascal called *divertissement,* the dissipation of men's energies in trivial diversions. My argument is that men must exercise voluntary austerity in the use of goods as a necessary, though insufficient, measure to resist the thralldom of consumer servitudes. Deliberate acts must be performed and positive resistance offered to the forces of compulsive consumption; otherwise men in developed lands are doomed to a life of generalized boredom wherein everything amuses them, but nothing interests them. They will gain an ever widening range of increasingly insignificant choices. Marginal utility will have been transcended, and new desires will appear faster than the disenchantment which comes from discovering that the objects of desire, once possessed, bring no abiding satisfaction. Voluntary austerity is one of several instrumentalities for de-mythologizing technology; it is necessary if men are to learn a modicum of detachment from technology itself. Perhaps they can learn to abandon their idolatry of productive technology only by growing indifferent to its most visible benefits: consumer goods. The human capacity to assert mastery over technology is one of the central issues in development. As Ellul explains, "Men must be convinced that technical progress is not humanity's supreme adventure, but a commonplace fabrication of certain objects which scarcely merit enthusiastic delirium even when they happen to be Sputniks. As long as man worships Technique, there is no chance at all that he will succeed in mastering it." [25]

Unless citizens at large as well as leaders in developed countries

[24] V.g., cf. Roger Garaudy, *Le Problème Chinois* (Paris: Seghers, 1967), pp. 222–227. Garaudy has confirmed orally to me his rejection of "austerity" as an appropriate component of Socialist humanism.

[25] Jacques Ellul, "The Technological Order," in the book of the same name edited by Carl F. Stover (Wayne State University Press, 1963), p. 26.

gain mastery over technology, whatever is technically possible will become actual. As one observer facetiously put it, "when enthusiasts get busy on a feasibility study, they invariably find that it is feasible!" [26] Technology tends to transform itself into a self-justifying end. There is ample reason to fear that advanced countries, faced with rapid population growth and mass poverty in the Third World, will employ the most efficient technology available to keep the Third World "under control," or will prove unable to resist the temptation to become elitist dispensers of development's benefits for the entire world. Under both hypotheses, authentic, self-promoting development will have been destroyed. This is why the practice of voluntary austerity in rich countries is crucial to sound development in the world: it acts as a safeguard against absolutizing technology in ways injurious to human autonomy.

There is a more essential link, however, between voluntary austerity and world development: a bond of solidarity must be forged between the privileged and those upon whom austerity is imposed. Unless one has psychologically "tuned in" on the wavelength of the poor, he cannot imagine even vicariously what it means to be under-developed. This is especially true of technicians working abroad; they cannot hope to gain ready acceptance in underdeveloped settings unless they practice voluntary austerity in judicious fashion. Others, too, need to become aware of what deprivation means. Of course the danger of play-acting is great: unless practice springs from inner conviction, voluntary austerity is little more than fastidious moral masturbation. Therefore, it must be founded on internal detachment from egocentric pursuits and on active respect for others. Social and political activists further demand that it be efficacious. Before seeking efficacy, however, the practice must acquire authenticity. This it cannot do unless it is free, for only then can it begin to make its adepts aware of the grim asperities of underdevelopment. Privilege builds psychological walls of incomprehension, and men must be able to peer over these walls if they are to discover reality. Although it must remain free, austerity should nonetheless be severe enough to awaken the man who practices it to the true dimensions of hardship outside his own world of sufficiency.

Imposed austerity, moreover, will not be accepted globally unless its subjects are convinced that their state of underdevelopment does

[26] Lord Ritchie-Calder, "Polluting the Environment," *The Center Magazine,* May 1969, p. 8.

not single them out as exclusive victims of deprivation. Austerity has many dimensions and, taken in isolation, it offers no solution to problems. *At best, it is a psychological prelude to the invention of true solutions.* Voluntary austerity may eventually prove insufficient; if so, imposed austerity might then be theoretically required in rich countries. If it is imposed, however, it will create and generalize a kind of consciousness which cannot foster solidarity except in some paternalistic, guilt-laden mode. The ethical significance of the choice resides in staying the contagion of greed. If it were widely practiced in the rich world, on the other hand, voluntary austerity might help to reduce wastefulness, release the stranglehold of advanced economies over underdeveloped ones, and render disinterested financial cooperation possible. Above all, it would impel men to greater collective responsibility and fraternal community. Psychologically speaking, freely embraced austerity can lead to greater equanimity in the face of want and abundance alike. Intelligent and courageous self-denial is the first step a slave of desires takes to emancipate himself from hidden and overt persuaders. Modern man's attitude toward death could likewise undergo profound transformation, thanks to detachment from things. A greater willingness to consider the consequences of one's death with regard to his possessions may be a salutary protection against irrational accumulation while others perish, as against the inconsiderate despoiling of the environment one must perforce leave to his successors on the planet. Material objects undeniably bring great psychological, emotional, and other satisfactions to men far beyond the boundaries of sheer necessities. But the viciously circular automatisms of acquisitiveness must be shattered if men are not to grow insensitive to absolute want in others. For, in Ellul's words, "Money, which enables one to secure for himself what material progress offers (in truth, what is desirable in virtue of what is most vile in man), has ceased to be an economic value and has become a moral value. . . . We must destroy the primacy of money, relegate economic activity to a second place, and apply brakes to technical progress." [27]

It is also worth noting that voluntary austerity and the elimination of needless waste and superfluous consumption do not constitute economic regress, but rather progress. The major economic effect of widespread voluntary austerity would be to bring levels of production into line with conscious choices of individuals and societies. Such

[27] Jacques Ellul, *L'Homme et l'Argent* (Paris: Delachaux et Niestle, 1954), p. 20.

261

practices would also contribute to halting the trend toward absolute quantification of human conduct.

Two important political questions must be asked: (1) Can widespread social effects result unless austerity is practiced by large numbers and unless personal convictions generate political action? (2) Granted that general acceptance is unlikely, must some means be devised to induce or force people to practice it? At the deepest level, these are unanswerable questions which can be asked only in societies whose members are the victims of technological idolatry. Ultimately, the problem is neither institutional nor organizational. What is needed is not some "movement" on behalf of voluntary austerity so that people will be impelled to practice justice and solidarity toward less-favored others. No solution could be worse than mounting a Madison Avenue selling campaign in reverse. Were this done, inner liberation from the tyranny of alienating possessiveness would be reduced to the status of a gimmick. Austerity means nothing if it becomes a mere fad or a new "in" thing to do in a society already disdainful of discretion. Westerners hypnotized by efficiency desperately need to discover the power of non-efficient solutions to problems which transcend efficiency. Consequently, whether it has overt political repercussions or not, voluntary austerity is self-validating simply because it is gratuitous and human. To engineer its diffusion by social manipulation or to reduce it to being simply a political instrument designed to salve rich men's consciences or give them a better image *vis-à-vis* the Third World is absolute sham. One need not conclude, however, that personal witness cannot be contagious, or that non-efficiency is sterile.

The contrary may prove to be the case: were it to achieve sufficient scope—provided it grew organically and were not imposed from without as a neo-Pavlovian reflex—voluntary austerity could change the political face of the earth and radically transform relations between rich and poor countries. Above all, it would make imposed austerity more palatable to poor countries obliged to tighten their belts if they are to develop successfully. Given men's acquisitive instincts and emulative propensities, poor nations will accept imposed austerity on the required scale only if rich nations themselves choose freedom and fraternity over sordid abundance. Realism dictates that rich nations and governments become less egocentric in their trade relations with unequals. Privileged societies and classes can no longer adopt with impunity political stances which are repugnant to the poor. These have grown tired of being despised and going hungry. Development poses to the world universal value questions regarding the use of goods. Without massive austerity, imposed and voluntary, human concern for the genuine needs of other men cannot survive.

This recommendation is patently utopian; it cannot take effect if present trends and attitudes continue. But in a world grown irrational in its totality although each of its parts is supremely rational, it is the only realistic path. To imagine that anything less can solve the agonizing tension between having enough and having too much is sheer illusion. To propose this utopian measure, however, is clearly no gesture of optimism, for there is little likelihood that men will accept hard solutions. They are more likely to continue searching for palliatives. Because of their near-incorrigible tendency to do so, one can only be pessimistic.

(C) *The Defense of Cultural Diversity*

Development processes release social forces whose cumulative effect is to standardize tastes, behavior, and institutions. Many observers fear that worldwide development will produce cultural homogenization. Others argue, on the contrary, that full standardization is impossible because societies have divergent histories and even now strive arduously to establish new identities. To them cultural diversity, not standardization, seems inevitable. Without assuming either that diversity is doomed or that it is indestructible, I submit that the promotion of cultural diversity must become a general objective of development planning. This position flows from the reply to three questions: (1) Is cultural diversity good? (2) Why is it good? (3) Which standards determine whether specific diversities are worthy of preservation or can be sacrificed?

No satisfactory answer is possible if one accepts total relativity and the equivalence of all cultural variables. As Talcott Parsons explains, "one cannot be a radical cultural relativist who regards the Arunta of Australia and such modern societies as the Soviet Union as equally authentic 'cultures,' to be judged as equals in *all basic* respects. Our perspective clearly involved evolutionary judgments—for example, that intermediate societies are more advanced than primitive societies, and modern societies, though not discussed in this volume, are more advanced than intermediate societies. I have tried to make my basic criterion congruent with that used in biological theory, calling more 'advanced' the systems that display greater generalized adaptive capacity." [28] Parsons' position about generalized adaptive capacity

[28] Talcott Parsons, *Societies, Evolutionary and Comparative Perspectives* (Prentice-Hall, 1966), p. 110.

is refuted by Dubos' arguments, presented later. Moreover, it leaves unanswered the question of knowing whether there are, as Kluckhohn puts it, "fairly definite limits within which cultural variation is constrained by pan-human regularities in biology, psychology, and the processes of social interaction." [29] Hence, the problem is how to avoid both the historicism of absolute relativists and the ethnocentrism expressed by Parsons. Of course no thinker can totally free himself from his particular cultural matrix of rationality. And there is no objective sense in which statements about the merits of uniformity or diversity can be rendered fully compelling. Nonetheless, several questions need to be answered.

One of these asks if cultural diversity is good. On principle, the reply is affirmative, for several reasons. The first concerns social identity. Much as individuals seek recognition of their incommunicable personal worth, so do societies assert themselves as culture carriers of unique value. It is their unshared peculiar characteristics which differentiate them most sharply from others and to which they cling most tenaciously. Some traits, it is true, are secondary or trivial. Others are more central, because they express collective human experience in a special mode. Prodigal nature fosters great diversity among all organic species, thereby enhancing the beauty of the universe. Likewise with men: no single society can reflect all the achievements of which men are capable in their institutional creation. The basis of cultural diversity as a value, therefore, is simply that the human potential is too rich to be expressed adequately in a single form. Only blind parochialism can make men wish to eliminate this multi-faceted existential wealth from the planet in the name of efficiency or to obey the demands of standardization.

There is an even stronger reason, however, for regarding cultural diversity as a positive good: the human species' capacity for adaptation. Biologists and ecologists alike warn that the human organism will be stunted and many of its potentialities atrophied if its adaptive powers are, for long periods of time, challenged exclusively or predominantly by over-specialized artificial environments. All projections point to a very high degree of concentration of the world's population in cities. By 1990, according to some estimates, more than half of the world's population will reside in cities of 100,000 inhabitants or more. The drive toward dense urbanization, social mobility based on occupa-

[29] Clyde Kluckhohn, "Universal Categories of Culture," in *Anthropology Today,* ed. A. L. Kroeber (University of Chicago Press, 1965), p. 507.

tional function, uniform socialization based on values of efficiency, manipulative rationality, and the objective equivalence of human experiences, is presently occurring in a manner which emphasizes almost exclusively man's special adaptive capacities to identical artificial environments. One consequence of such over-specialization is that man's general capabilities are being genetically debilitated. This trend places in doubt the merit of existing patterns of developmental processes. What is needed in its stead is a systematic and imaginative effort to promote diversity. Not only must surviving cultures be aided to adjust on their own terms to the impingements of proffered change, but systematic restraints must likewise be placed on the homogenizing tendencies operative in the "forces of modernization." This implies that standards used by many developers must be revised. They must reject the assumption that mass urbanization in densely populated large cities is the only developmental alternative to subsistence in stagnant rural areas. As suggested above, new inquiries must be made into viable strategies of primary, secondary, and tertiary poles of development.[30]

A similar problem arises regarding "linguistic assimilation" of underdeveloped rural populaces to the *lingua franca* of an entire nation, a burning issue in Andean countries, many African nations, and India. To presume that linguistic uniformity fosters development may be a form of blindness which overlooks the special incentive structures operative in differentially marginalized populations. Above all, it tragically ignores one profound wellspring of change: a population's desire for cultural esteem. It would be unpardonably cruel, therefore, to elicit development efforts by placing on human groups conditions tantamount to their cultural annihilation.

One further justification exists for promoting diversity in the face of rapid development trends: to enhance the global quality of life. When American Indians are exterminated by frontier settlers, when Montagnard tribesmen are humiliated by the Annamite majority in Vietnam, and when Harratin ex-slaves in the southern Sahara are maligned by the Arab majority, the general quality of human life suffers diminution. Irreplaceable positive values are wiped out in two domains. First, victims are rendered socially impotent and prevented from flowering culturally. In extreme cases they are decimated. Second, the cul-

---

[30] This is discussed by J. P. Baillargeon and others in "Le Rôle des Pôles dans le développement," *Développement et Civilisations*, No. 5 (January 1961), pp. 31–53.

tural aggressors demean themselves in the very process of demeaning others and thereby lower their own human quality. This is a familiar tale: the torturer destroys himself as he vents his fury on his victim. Some cultural traits, it is true, are doomed to disappear with modernization. Perhaps entire societies will lack survival value and vanish before the onslaught of industrialization. Sentiment is surely a foolish guide in such matters. Hence there is no warrant for adopting a "museum-piece" outlook on economically backward cultures, no valid reason for preserving in artificial societal mausoleums every folkloric vestige or cultural curiosity. Many picturesque and perhaps even some functional values will have to give way to standardized tastes and behavior. But men's creative imagination needs to be taxed far beyond present bounds if they are to invent a variety of forms to express diversely the values they now so blithely standardize in their pursuit of development. Adaptation to peculiar local conditions can be as truly innovative as original creation. Full opportunities must be afforded backward countries to actualize what Keynes called the "possibilities of things." This goal is unattainable, however, unless the peculiarities of these countries are respected.[31] We lack clear universal directives to help us decide which diversities are worth preserving and which can be sacrificed. Rational discernment in this delicate area is itself a major function of a developmental wisdom which must govern choices in such realms as research, planning, policy formulation, political mobilization, and education. Unless societies foster distinct cultures, their members cannot develop the self-consciousness and pride demanded for full creativity. That cultural diversity is a precious value indispensable to over-all human growth cannot be demonstrated. The contrary assertion, that standardization is a greater good, is refuted only by appealing to the general sense of peoples in history, to the survival of multiple traditions, and to every society's declared interest in preserving a specific identity. The general judgment in favor of diversity is founded on the principle of biological adaptation presented above. No single culture incarnates every important human value; diversity *alone* can generate a wide variety of value constellations. Even if it were possible to reduce all men to a single homogeneous pattern, it would still be *desirable* to foster diversity.

Survival and the preservation of identity are largely dependent upon what Claude Bernard called the "constant internal environment

[31] On this, cf. Alexander Gerschenkron, *Economic Backwardness in Historical Perspective* (Harvard University Press, 1962), p. 29.

of each species." Interior stability is doubly necessary in the face of great changes in the outer environment. Modern genetics suggests, moreover, that man uses only 10 to 15 percent of his genetic potential: "All the other genes are depressed, do not manifest themselves, through all sorts of mechanisms that have their origin in the environment." [32] It is precisely because environmental stimuli are essential to the actualization of man's latent potential that diversity of such stimuli needs to be safeguarded, especially as these stimuli impinge on the young. Therefore, in Dubos' words, "the future of our civilizations depends precisely upon our ability to recognize and cultivate diversity." We may state with reasonable assurance that the latent potentialities of human beings have their greatest chance of becoming fully actualized in a diversified environment which provides great varieties of stimulating experiences, especially to the young. Cultural forms sift out the dominant stimuli offered to the young. High societal and biological specialization doubtless confer upon organisms the advantage of great efficiency. But, in the long run, specialized efficiency is a source of weakness. History tells of once-powerful societies enjoying high specialization which have not survived drastic changes in their conditions. Specialization prevents them from adapting rapidly to changing conditions of survival and function. The same phenomenon has occurred in animal life: highly specialized and powerful animals have disappeared, to be replaced by much weaker and less "efficient" species. Quite apart from philosophical or esthetic considerations, therefore, valid reasons derived from biology, psychology, and pedagogy can be found for guarding against technological standardization. Identical life-styles and behavioral patterns must be carefully avoided as ever more societies move toward development. Adaptability for purposes of survival and for the rich expression of a wide range of potentialities requires diversified environments, both external and internal. Consequently, different kinds of societies and symbolic systems must be allowed to flourish. There must also be variation in life-styles and scale of human organizations, in their rhythms of activity and their densities.

Recent discussion has centered on the common traits possessed by all "industrial societies" regardless of their political or ideological sys-

---

[32] In these paragraphs I am utilizing ideas presented by René Dubos in "The Potentialities of Man," an address delivered at the Tenth National Conference of the U.S. National Commission for UNESCO, Kansas City, Mo., November 17, 1965.

tems. Unless planners safeguard environmental and cultural diversity, massive uniformities will continue to impose themselves throughout the world as power lines are laid in its open spaces, as tractors and mechanical harvesters supplant rudimentary farm implements, as food processing and packaging are disseminated, as airports, highways, supermarkets, and drugstores continue to spring up in remote hinterlands. In a word, the external environment of the entire world runs the risk of becoming too homogeneous.

If societies achieve mastery over technological processes, however, they can withstand a considerable degree of standardization in external conditions without losing their uniqueness. The crucial point of defense is to resist the homogenization of social mores and life-patterns. Dubos cites the case of Indian tribes in the American Southwest to illustrate the principle that even under similar physical environments, different societies can achieve quite different kinds of civilization. "The Hopis live a sedentary and agricultural existence in crowded adobe settlements, carefully husbanding the scarce water to raise a few crops. In contrast, the Navajos move their immense reservation from one isolated family hogan to another, maintaining painfully a pastoral type of culture based on the herding of sheep and goats. Here we see how human beings have the ability to impose on their environment a pattern of their own choice. Man in some way is the product of his environment, but he can also take advantage of his environment to create a pattern of life of his own choice." This capacity is not without its proper explanation. Unlike other organisms, man can respond to stimuli in a manner which transcends the mere stimulus. In most cases his responses are determined less by the direct effects of the stimuli on his body than by the symbolic interpretation and the vision of goals that he relates to the stimulus. Behind the façade of external similarities, therefore, the important dimension is the realm of meaning man attaches to what takes place about him. Although consumer patterns may acquire great uniformity, or look-alike industrial plants fill every empty landscape, different societies remain possible because the meaning and relative importance attached to these outward realities can vary. One notes with interest remarks made by the Italian novelist Alberto Moravia several years ago upon returning from a trip to the Soviet Union. He had meditated for the first time on the intimate nexus linking a society's spiritual values to the material objects with which it surrounds itself. Moravia concluded that it is catastrophic for any system of production to eliminate variety in consumer goods. More significantly, he discovered that variety can symbolize, in addition to wastefulness, prodigality, or even the liberation of the person, the affirmation by a people of its creative spirit. "The borderline separating the work of art from a product of handicraft," he writes, "or from the product of light industry cannot be traced with certitude. One can even affirm in this regard that the identical creative spirit lies at the origins of a monument, a novel, a rug or a crystal vase. On the other hand, we can locate the exact dividing line between these objects and a tractor, a truck or any other product of heavy industry. In the former category what is expressed with more or less talent is taste, artistic sense, and imagination; whereas in the latter what is revealed is rational utility. The former objects manifest the profound diversities in traditions, national genius, and particular characters. The second category, on the other hand, is based on the precepts of universal necessity." [33] This text suggests the great cultural importance attaching to a society's choices of the consumer goods it will produce, whether by personal artistry, handicraft, or light or heavy industry.

Raymond Aron argues that humanity will not necessarily be unified even if industrial society is universally implanted. A unified humanity would exist only if, in addition to common means and material conditions of life, societies adopted a single philosophy of life, a common esthetic vision or style of expression.[34] Whatever one may say about economic or political "convergence," however, he cannot extrapolate to the realm of cultural convergence. Some fear that preferences, attitudes, and behavior are being ineluctably standardized in the very processes of development. Nevertheless, societies having diverse histories, traditions, and identities bend seemingly impersonal institutions to their own fancies. Hence, Japan has industrialized while devising employment patterns within industry, particularly in techniques of high-level manpower recruitment, which bear a distinctively Japanese stamp. The important issue, ultimately, is this: the possibility of cultural diversity needs to be safeguarded by deliberate policies. Perplexing questions arise when it must be decided which cultural peculiarities are to be allowed and which eliminated when these interfere

33 Alberto Moravia, *Un Mois en U.R.S.S.* (Paris: Flammarion, 1958), p. 165. Cited in Bernard Cazes, "Galbraith ou du Bon Usage des Richesses," in *Cahiers de l'Institut de Science Economique Appliquée*, No. 111 (March 1961, Series M), p. 47.
34 Cf. Raymond Aron, ed., *Colloques de Reinfelden* (Paris: Calmann-Levy, 1960), p. 89.

with development.

Although economic and social development are not absolute values, it does not follow that they cannot enjoy precedence over certain other values. Indeed, certain well-entrenched cultural values and practices not only impede development, but cause positive harm to men. By general admission, infanticide, slavery, and chattel marriage are incompatible with human rights. One is not guilty of ethnocentrism, therefore, if he regards such institutions as expendable. Thus, Gandhi could anticipate with equanimity the future abolition of the sacred cow as a parasitical vestige which could no longer be tolerated in a nation grown conscious of its economic backwardness and the alarming protein deficiencies of its population. The African practice of accumulating cattle herds as prestige symbols may likewise constitute a form of cultural diversity which is doomed to disappear. Nonetheless, there are no facile solutions in these matters. Many Indian villagers might, if consulted, vote to keep their sacred cows even at the price of living on a starvation diet. Similarly, African farmers might choose not to slaughter their animals for food or transform pasture lands into agricultural plots. Yet where the general level of life-sustenance is extremely low or precarious, as in India, responsible leaders are justified in imposing solutions even when these are contrary to the expressed value preferences of people. A parallel situation prevails during epidemics; health authorities do not hesitate to impose such stringent measures as quarantine, compulsory vaccination, food rationing, and curtailment of physical contact. When the evil to be cured is serious, drastic measures are justified. Most of the time, however, the incompatibility between specific practices and urgent development needs remains hidden.

Development economists often ask what they should do about local customs which get in development's way. No sensitive change agent is blind to the traumatic effects of the "bull-in-the-china-closet" approach to local customs. Nevertheless, persuasive campaigns are sometimes necessary, even if they are unpopular. Even a champion of local participation in decisions like Danilo Dolci does not retreat from vigorous measures. Rather he fights relentlessly to induce people to abandon their local customs when these produce harmful effects. He respects local *people,* but not their alienating local practices.[35] One

---

[35] For detailed examples, cf. Danilo Dolci, *Waste* (Monthly Review Press, 1964), *passim.* Dolci castigates superstition masquerading as religion when people pray for rain instead of installing electric motors to pump water from wells, or when farmers waste manure because it "dirties" the land.

solution to the problem is to be found in the *procedures* adopted in the conduct of value research, of mobilization, of pedagogy for purposes of planning and implementation, and of a critical evaluation of consequences once processes have been launched. No valid general assumption that all local values must either be kept or sacrificed appears possible. This is why permanent debate engaging all interested parties and bearing on values, practices, and costs is an integral component of sound planning. Difficulties arise in reconciling the exigencies of improved life-sustenance with proper regard for a population's esteem needs. But horizons of knowledge can be expanded and communities which formerly possessed a relatively static outlook can begin to perceive that their old values do not shield them from seductive alternate ways of life. True alternative choices do not lie merely between keeping the old and accepting the new. Rather, novel combinations of the new and the old, as yet undetermined, must be tried. The central issue is control over destinies. Will "new" values simply be imported and superimposed? Or will they be proposed for ratification after dialectical interaction with old values has occurred, thereby assuring that the final shape taken by a society's new values is the fruit of that society's own maturation? Which values ought to be preserved and which sacrificed for the sake of modernization? No answers exist except those which emerge from vital processes of critical reflection. The main flaw in present practice has been the premature assumption of incompatibility between old and new values before the old have been fully explored in their latent, as well as their overt, dimensions.

I have asserted that rich societies must practice austerity so as to gain freedom from technology's determinisms. A strategy which optimizes cultural diversity can likewise help decelerate technology's onward march. Restraints on technology are required in underdeveloped and developed nations alike if men are not to become powerless to use technology as a means for reaching humanly defined ends. The mobilization of people in underdeveloped lands to resist technological determinism is tactically sound if it appeals to the preservation of cultural values already cherished. Thus, a road would not be built between village A and village B, let us say, if villages C, D, and E risk having their way of life completely traumatized as a result. At the very least, the communities affected must have a decisive voice in such decisions. The identical issue, interestingly enough, lies at the heart of social discontent within developed countries: the powerlessness of people affected by decisions made in the name of "progress" to assess the relative benefits and harmful effects of those decisions. This observation confirms the view of many students of development that the basic question is not modernization, improved standards of living, levels of industrialization, or even the rapidity of change, but rather the degree of control men can wield over their destinies. Roland Colin correctly insists that "henceforth there is but a single battle on behalf of development which concerns rich industrial societies as well as poor agrarian societies. *There is no longer any country which can pretend to consider itself developed, that is, humanly developed.* The real problem for us, *underdeveloped nations all of us,* is to find ways and means of building new models of culture within which men can be equally responsible and equal participants. The ancient Communist myth takes on the appearance of a stimulating Utopia: Americans quite as much as Soviets, French as much as Chinese, Indians no less than Latin Americans will grow increasingly aware that the problem of problems is and will be the assumption by each man of his share of collective responsibility." [36] Culture, therefore, not economics, technology, or politics, is the primordial dimension in development. And the central problem of culture is not its content but the degree of control men can exercise over the speed, direction, and modality of cultural evolution. Accordingly, the defense of cultural diversity assumes the character of an option in favor of the "little" man over elites, of collective value creation over the mere acquisition of development's benefits or the imposition of ethnocentric models. If it is to be a humane operation, development must encourage and stimulate cultural diversity. This is its general normative concern as it elicits varied specific responses to precise culture dilemmas.

These remarks do not adequately solve the agonizing value dilemmas posed by conditions of differential development and vulnerability. I believe, nonetheless, that one cannot supply more specific answers to normative questions such as these without becoming doctrinaire or irrelevant.

The burden of this chapter has been to answer the question: what kind of development? The answer is: development in accord with certain priority needs, development marked by general austerity and wisdom in the use of goods whether these are scarce or abundant, and development which fosters cultural diversity in the face of standardizing forces.

[36] Roland Colin, "Trois Révolutions pour le Développement," *Développement et Civilisations,* No. 36 (December 1968), p. 4. Italics mine.

CHAPTER TWELVE

World Resources and Priority Needs

Ecological Control

For practical purposes, if not in theory, planet earth can be treated as a closed system. Inputs of energy are still received from outer space and men can leave earth for short periods by carrying a fabricated life-support system with them. Nevertheless, in the words of one ecologist, "the constraints of the biosphere are those of a closed system. Until the twentieth century, men and nations could act as if the system were infinite. But now that possibility is gone forever." [1] A new condition has been created which leaves human institutions ill-adapted to treating the planet as *Spaceship Earth*.[2] For the first time in history, survival, health, and creativity require that major human efforts be devoted to protecting the "dynamic stability" and the regenerative powers of the world's ecological systems. Technology has so altered the cosmos that it is no longer possible for natural balances to reestablish themselves independently of human intervention. Develop-

---

[1] Lynton Keith Caldwell, "An Ecological Approach to International Development: Problems of Policy and Administration," p. 44. This is the final chapter in a forthcoming book, to be edited by John P. Milton.
[2] Title of a book by Barbara Ward (Columbia University Press, 1966).

ment processes pose with special acuity the problem of man's total relationship to other organisms and to his global environment. Development is an important ecological problem in both senses of the word "ecology": (a) biology, dealing with relations between organisms and their environment, and (b) sociology, concerned with the spacing of people and institutions and resulting interdependencies. The preservation of life and the quality of society are equally at stake.

Development experts purport to act rationally when exploiting nature for economic purposes. Many experts believe that such rationality has enabled the "developed" world to reach the summit of material achievement and that, consequently, this rationality ought to be diffused throughout the world. A recent statement by the chairman of OECD's Development Assistance Committee is typical in this regard. According to him, global development "strategy should promote feelings of *capacity to dominate one's environment* and to improve one's economic and social position." [3] Scientific knowledge endows men with the power to dominate their environment. But it does not confer the wisdom needed to avoid violating that environment beyond repair. The laws of technological progress for its own sake and of quick results (for profit or in order to meet social need) militate against duly weighing ecological considerations in development decisions. Industrialization models derived from the economic history of Britain, the United States, Japan, and the Soviet Union establish no precedents to policy-makers for incorporating the exigencies of ecological health into their policy formulation. The United States has, in its march toward "modernity," condemned millions of acres of arable soil to wind and water erosion, destroyed numerous animal and vegetable species, irresponsibly depleted vast forest and mineral reserves, and created huge artificial environments in which the atmosphere, troposphere, stratosphere, and water systems have become seriously polluted.

In the nineteenth century such procedures were merely wasteful and scandalous: they constituted no direct threat to life in the biosphere, that zone of the earth's crust, waters, and atmosphere wherein living organisms must subsist. To pursue technological advance without ecological wisdom in the twentieth century, however, is to threaten life itself on this planet, or, at the very least, to diminish vitality so greatly as to inflict irreparable genetic damage on all living organisms.

[3] Edwin M. Martin, "A Global Strategy for Development," *The OECD Observer*, No. 36 (October 1968), p. 15. Italics mine.

The social, psychological, and political forces which impel societies to seek rapid development through mass technology tend to subordinate ecological health to short-term benefits fraught with dangers to the health of the cosmic environment. Ecological health presently centers around two relationships between living beings and environment: dynamic stability and ecological renewal. Ecological stability is not static; on the contrary, it is the on-going capacity of an environmental system to compensate for all injurious disturbances it suffers. Since our world system is for all practical effects closed, a pathological state results if interference goes beyond the limits of compensation or adjustment. Ecological renewal, in turn, signifies the absolute necessity of preserving or reconstituting elements required for vitality. Large-scale thermal pollution is one example of damaging the capabilities of ecological renewal even in large bodies of water. Similarly, once a certain threshold of radioactivity is reached, nothing can arrest contamination of the air men breathe, the food they eat, the liquids they drink, and the genes they transmit to their offspring. Given technology's present state, to subordinate ecological health to resource exploitation—even for urgent development purposes—is to risk destroying the very possibility of life on earth. Even if damage does not extend this far, ecologically irresponsible development will create social densities, conflictual intensities, and determinisms which signify the death of precious human qualities. Caldwell warns that "Modern development, when based on inadequate diagnosis, is dangerous *because* of the likelihood that it will achieve results of some kind. It may fail to achieve its objectives, but incur costly and damaging consequences in the process. Conversely, it may attain its goals, but the attainment may entail an ecological backwash and unforeseen side-effects, some of which may be harmful. Ecological disasters in development may coexist with technical successes. The gross national product of a developing country may increase simultaneously with a diminution in the actual quality of life for most of its people and a foreclosure of future opportunities." [4] In short, the basic forces at work in development obey criteria incompatible with ecological health and renewal. What are these criteria? And what hazards to sound ecology are posed by current development practices?

These can be grouped in five major categories:

[4] Lynton Keith Caldwell, *op. cit.*, p. 9. I wish to acknowledge my debt to Professor Caldwell in these pages. Cf. his recent book, *Environment: A Challenge for Modern Society* (Natural History Press, 1970).

(1) ungrounded optimism founded on prior development success;

(2) the fragmented state of development decision-making;

(3) an inadequate perception of the developmental task itself;

(4) the circular relationship existing between development concepts and development machinery; and

(5) the operation of political structures which uncritically favor quick results.

Without examining each in detail, it suffices to note that sound ecological policy demands the coordination of many long-term measures which rarely gain precedence over short-term considerations. Successful leaders usually strive to develop quickly without much regard for environmental consequences. Economic considerations tend to assume compelling persuasiveness notwithstanding their long-term effects on resources or ecological balance. The uncritical assumption prevails that more goods for society means greater good for all. Development agents, moreover, respond to internal pressures placed on them by planning, aid-giving, or aid-receiving agencies as well as to the need felt by most political leaders to produce results for their constituents. Perceptions of developers and people at large must change at two distinct levels if sound decisions are to be made. These are the concept of dominating nature or "using" resources, and the primacy of quantitative inputs in the planning process. Inasmuch as the second question has received detailed treatment in an earlier chapter, present remarks are confined to the dangers inherent in the notion of mastering nature which prevails in the West.

Biblical injunctions upon man to "subjugate" nature, Greek rationalism, the Roman engineering mentality, and the post-Enlightenment mystique of technological progress have all reinforced Western man's disposition to transform nature to suit his own ends in the belief that he could do so with impunity. And although eminent scientists like Bertrand Russell and Albert Einstein profess a quasi-mystical reverence for the cosmic mysteries, the dominant spirit of scientists and technologists has been to cajole, pressure, or even violate nature so as to extract from her those practical secrets which empower men to use resources and harness nature's forces to the satisfaction of their wants. African and Asian societies, on the other hand, have throughout their recorded history cultivated an attitude of non-interference with nature. This choice has led to lesser achievement than the West in realms of productivity, utilitarian invention, and material levels of life. So long as Western societies were tapping unspoiled and seemingly inexhaustible resources, the ecological ravages wrought by their Faustian[5] interference with nature could proceed unnoticed or remain within tolerable bounds. This is no longer the case, however, and a serious attitudinal problem ensues. To overcome it, development leaders must learn to distrust their own profound impulse to manipulate environment. This is no plea for inertia, stagnation, or the sacrifice of gains already made, but a summons to reflect on the consequences of man's interventions at crucial points of the cosmic eco-system. Men would have to possess a clear synthesis of all their fragmentary knowledge in order to appraise correctly the possible, or probable, disruptive effects of their technology. This synthesis is precisely what they lack; and no further progress in analytic science or statistical correlations can supply it to them. Modern man, in effect, is playing God, all the while remaining fundamentally ignorant of the boundaries of his own knowledge. Pascal's bewilderment in the face of "the infinitely small and the infinitely large" has its twentieth-century counterpart in the incapacity of experts to explain the basic elements of reality, as well as the larger interdependencies operative in known planetary systems. What is advocated, therefore, is not that man abandon science, technology, or the effort to develop, but that he subordinate these to ecological values without which development becomes a destructive process. Even when development programs are of limited scope, the conceptual framework in which they are planned ought to be comprehensive. In earlier chapters I have urged comprehensiveness in the domain of values and meaning—all that relates to man's "internal environment" in the two senses mentioned above: biological relationships between organisms and their environment, and sociological spacing of people and institutions in networks of interdependency. Within such a comprehensive perspective, demographic problems are seen in their *ecological,* rather than their properly *economic,* dimensions.

This is not to imply that demographers and economists err in stressing the importance of the rate of population growth over its sheer magnitude.[6] Rather, it is to state that the question of *optimum* popu-

[5] Cf. Lawrence Lee, *The American as Faust* (Boxwood Press, 1965).

[6] Cf., e.g., Stephen Enke, "Politico-Economic Global Systems: Slowing Population for Development as an Example," p. 17: "it is not the absolute size of a nation's population that concerns economic welfare so much as the *rate* at which it changes." This unpublished MS. dated January 1969 will appear in a forthcoming book to be published by the University of California. Also Goran Ohlin, *Population Control and Economic Development* (Paris: OECD, 1967), p. 57: "By and large, however, size seems to be of subordinate impor-

lation for the world or any unit thereof can be settled only with reference to biological and sociological ecology. Even assuming, for argument's sake, that enough food, housing, and education could be provided for all men while avoiding economic catastrophe, it would still be necessary to limit the total number of people living in the world. This is true for several reasons: eventual shortage of space, depletion of resources, the incompatibility of a high birth rate with a low mortality rate, the physical impossibility of maintaining present birth rates for long periods of time, and the pressure of time on underdeveloped countries. The world simply cannot wait a century for its population to stabilize itself. Were present trends to continue, India's population density would equal Manhattan's in less than a century. If India's 1951 birth rate and its mortality rates projected for 1986 were to continue for 1,200 years, the total weight of the Indian population would exceed that of the earth's total mass, an obvious impossibility.

The authors of these projections, A. J. Coale and E. M. Hoover, are forced to conclude that either the birth rate must drop or mortality rates must increase. They argue that, in the long term *and independently of the revenue level,* high reproduction cannot coexist with low mortality.[7] Geophysicist H. Brown[8] has calculated, by extrapolating current trends for 5,000 years, another set of impossibilities. (Fifty centuries in the life of man are very little compared to the hundred or two hundred centuries of hominid's prior history.) At present rates, says Brown, all known food sources on earth would be consumed by the end of this century. Let us suppose, however, that science became so ingenious that men learned how to transform rock itself into food. By the year 2700 all the earth would have been consumed. Assuming still further, always for purposes of illustration, that science found a way of utilizing other planets as food. This would help little, for by the year 3200 all the planets would have been eaten. Brown pushes

---

tance. Neither the present nor even the future size of population constitutes a major economic problem—after all, we can say with certainty that a transition to lower growth rates will come in the next century no matter what is done to encourage it now. The real problem is the excessive rate of growth which impedes the process of modernization. This problem is no less acute in sparsely settled African or Latin American countries than in the most crowded regions."

[7] Coale and Hoover are quoted with approval in Pierre Pradervand, "La Course Démographie-Développement Economique," *Développement et Civilisations,* No. 36 (December 1968), p. 7.

[8] H. Brown, *The Challenge of Man's Future* (Viking Press, 1954). Cited in Pradervand, *op. cit.,* p. 7.

his hypothetical case even further: let us assume that science could transform the sun itself into food. By the year 3700 the sun would also have been eliminated. These wild speculations do not stop here, but the central point is clear: quite apart from economic considerations,[9] the world cannot indefinitely support either present growth rates or the absolute population which these rates prefigure. Demographic balance is required for the ecological survival of the planet. Moreover, the quality of human life is directly affected by population thresholds much lower than the absolute impossibilities just evoked. One sociological consequence of speedy population growth is an unmanageable increase in the size and density of cities, an important by-product of which is social disorganization. As mentioned above, by 1990 more than 50 percent of the entire world population (estimated to number approximately six billion by then) will inhabit cities of more than 100,000 inhabitants. This gigantic social transformation can lead to deterioration in the quality of human life and to serious disruption of sociological and biological balances. One is forced to conclude that unchecked demographic increase would produce irreversible ecological disturbances. The stabilization of world population is, therefore, necessary for ecological regeneration. And man cannot afford to wait until such stabilization arrives as a by-product of economic development!

Nor can we escape the general conclusion that world ecological control is urgently needed. Such control must, of course, embrace many spheres of activity other than population control. It will be necessary to limit the amounts of radioactivity allowed to circulate in the atmosphere, the troposphere, and the stratosphere. New problems of preventive medicine and of environmental regeneration will arise once space travel becomes commonplace. Urgent need already exists for international control over oceans, polar regions, and artificial weather programs. These are but a few of the domains[10] wherein long-range protection of the regenerative powers of eco-systems must take precedence over resource exploitation or technological applications even for legitimate development purposes. Civilizations reveal the nature of their goals and values in the environmental conditions they create. As

[9] And these are grave enough; cf. Ohlin, *op. cit.*, ch. IV. Also George C. Zaidan, "Population Growth and Economic Development," *Finance and Development,* March 1969, pp. 2–9.

[10] For others, cf. "Environment and Society in Transition," Program of Conference (October 6–11, 1969) sponsored jointly by the American Geographical Society and the American Division of the World Academy of Art and Science.

they reflect on the irreparable damage caused by heedless optimism, ecologists warn that inadvertent side-effects of development on the stability and self-renewal capabilities of the biosphere threaten to make earth unfit for life unless development is pursued with proper regard for environmental consequences. Caldwell is right: "the development process itself—whatever its scope or complexity—is inherently ecological. It is a process of purposeful change in the systematic interrelationships of living and inanimate things as they have evolved and continue to evolve in a biosphere dominated by human society." [11] Some environmental disruption is unavoidable, but harmful effects can be minimized by careful planning and judicious ecological research.[12] Planning and study will not suffice, however; they must be accompanied by legal controls over practical activities so as to promote salutary ecological practices and prohibit harmful ones. Only a worldwide system of control and enforcement has a realistic hope of dealing with the problem.

The United Nations has grasped the importance of ecological health. UNESCO held a conference in 1968 on the rational use and conservation of the biosphere. Later that year the U.N. General Assembly voted to convene a conference on the human environment in 1972. Yet something more than discussion is required. Even for purposes of theoretical clarification, greater enlightenment may come from the application, even in a single sphere, of sound principles of world ecological management. This is the reason why recent proposals such as that for a world ocean regime assume such enormous importance.[13] The principle of global responsibility to prevent ecological catastrophes and to promote the optimum use of new resources for the benefit of those whose needs are greatest—to the exclusion of warlike purposes or purely commercial exploitation—must be demonstrated in action. This is true in all problem areas just mentioned. Practical regimes of the seas, of the atmosphere, of space, of polar regions, of river systems, and of the entire planet need to be worked out in detail. In a word, much imaginative model-building will have to take place. Clearly, the ethician's task in all this is not to design the

11 Caldwell, "An Ecological Approach . . . ," p. 4.
12 On this, cf. Luther J. Carter, "Development in the Poor Nations: How to Avoid Fouling the Nest," *Science*, Vol. CLXIII (March 7, 1969), pp. 1046–1048.
13 Cf. Elisabeth Mann Borgese, *The Ocean Regime*, Occasional Paper, Vol. I, No. 5 (October 1968), Center for the Study of Democratic Institutions. Also, *Pacem in Maribus: Ocean Enterprises,* a Center Occasional Paper, 1970.

model himself but to establish its norms. In a broader sense, world ecological control is but the prerequisite for making optimum use of resources.

The Requirements of Optimum Resource Use

Optimum use of world resources, both actual and potential, aims at providing basic necessities to all men. A second priority is the multiplication, for the benefit of all men, of those goods which facilitate human expression and creativity. The third priority is the production of luxury goods or services. Mankind's ultimate business is to maximize wisdom and love in a variety of communitarian modes. Nevertheless, simply to meet basic needs in food, clothing, and shelter for all of mankind's needy is a monumental task.

Enormous resources still idle must be harnessed to the satisfaction of global needs. Technology must be applied on a grand scale, for instance, if rivers on every continent are to provide water for irrigation and electric power instead of causing floods or serving as channels along which precious waters flow wastefully out to sea.[14] According to a recent estimate, the world's food output from lands already cultivated could be trebled or quadrupled.[15] Moreover, hundreds of millions of dwellings need to be built before the inhabitants of Calcutta and other burgeoning capitals of poverty can find decent shelter. Optimum exploitation of resources, or *"mise en valeur"* as French planners call it, is imperative. Unless resource use is improved massively and quickly, population increase will nullify productive gains.

"Optimum" is a relative term whose referents can be identified as the goals of development and its regulative principles. Taken together, these criteria rule out waste, ostentation, needless luxury production, and the irresponsible extraction of non-replenishable resources. They likewise impose rules of solidarity designed to assure allocation to the neediest groups in society before those already supplied are allowed to waste or display. In Crosland's words, "The highest rewards are inordinately high—far higher than any civilized person should want or

---

[14] On this, cf. Danilo Dolci, *Waste* (Monthly Review Press, 1964), pp. 338–346, entitled "Waste of Water in Menfi." For a scholarly treatment of the water problem, cf. Jean Labasse, *L'Organisation de l'Espace* (Paris: Hermann, 1966), pp. 33–70.

[15] Cf. Goran Ohlin, *Population Control and Economic Development* (OECD, 1967), ch. III, "Is the Population Problem a Food Problem?"

need; and the lowest are inhumanly low—far lower than any civilized person should have to endure." [16] The problem is absolute misery at the bottom of the scale, not inequality. Consequently, improvement should be sought for the masses at the bottom of the income scale even if this leads to relative hardship for minorities at the top. It is of course senseless to lower the top echelons of the scale, regardless of the absolute position of those at the bottom. Differential incentives are a useful regulating principle assuring efficiency and high productivity; they must neither be eliminated injudiciously nor treated as sacrosanct.[17] Hence two questions arise: Should development aim at an egalitarian society? And can the development needs of the world's poor be adequately met out of the mere increase in productivity and total wealth? Stated differently, the question is whether existing wealth must be divided equally in order to be divided justly and should the poor become agents of the wealth-producing machinery and share in decisions as well as in future gains? Much polemic literature on the "gap" between rich and poor nations is simplistic. World development cannot result solely from redistribution nor from the overflow of newly created wealth from the top down to the bottom. If all existing wealth were instantly redistributed, misery would still survive in the world. What is worse, underdeveloped marginals would not be changed qualitatively into agents of their own welfare. Moreover, no conceivable reform, revolution, or cataclysm could render such redistribution possible. The solution must, clearly, lie elsewhere. The incorporation of underdeveloped marginals into new productive dynamisms has been proposed above, but this cannot take place rapidly enough under present arrangements for producing wealth and disseminating technology. As long as privileged classes or nations continue to regard the emancipation of the world's poor as the fruit of productivity gains alone or mere increases in GNP, without altering present arrangements governing access to resources or shattering the nexus between productive capacity and purchasing power, rapid worldwide development remains impossible. *Neither the redistribution image nor the salvation-by-growth image is adequate to the problem.* Only massive restructuring of production priorities, allied to major changes in the distributive norms governing wealth, skills, and

[16] C. A. R. Crosland, *The Conservative Enemy* (New York: Schocken Books, 1962), p. 28.
[17] For an example of increased income differentials introduced by Socialist workers, cf. Branko Horvat, "Planning in Yugoslavia," in *Development Plans and Programmes* (Paris: OECD, 1964), pp. 149–165.

access to resources, can produce universal development. These major changes in the world's economic, political, and cultural systems are prerequisites of development. Idle resources must be put to use and wasted resources must be exploited wisely. This, in a word, is optimum *mise en valeur*.

Efforts must also be made to change the outlook of developed countries regarding the rate of their own economic and technological growth. Unless, for one or two generations, the rich accept reconversion of their economic and research facilities to meet priority needs of the world's poor, the latter cannot achieve development. More than foreign aid (money, food, or technical experts), the Third World needs a commitment from the rich world to moderate its *new development gains* until basic necessities have been provided for all in the world. Rich nations and classes are not asked to redistribute their wealth, to lower their standard of living, or to remain stagnant, but to practice on a world basis a principle they repeatedly urge upon governments of underdeveloped countries—namely, to meet the urgent and important needs of poorer classes even at the cost of not giving new privileges to those already advantaged. During one or two generations, "advanced" countries will have to temper their acquisitive desires in order to abolish underdevelopment in poor nations. These in turn must practice great austerity. Since the possession of relative superfluity alongside massive absolute want among men is dehumanizing both for those who have too much and those who have too little, the course now prescribed will improve the quality of life in developed as well as in underdeveloped societies. It may help restore wisdom in the use of goods in accord with the first regulative principle of development with its twin injunctions: man must have enough in order to be more, and the fullness of human good is more than mere abundance of goods. The proposal is also designed to give substance to the two other regulative principles: optimum solidarity, and the widest scope for persons to become authentic human agents of their own development. Unless institutions are overhauled, these goals will remain unattainable. A world plan, new patterns of world financing, a world technical pool, and an institution for altering the values of the developed countries are minimum requirements.

(A) *World Plan*

Where need is pressing and wealth scarce, economic rationality imposes planning as a strict necessity. If, moreover, local national and trans-national plans are to be successfully coordinated, world planning is essential. A major task of any plan is to harmonize efforts aimed at solving problems in diverse sectors, locales, and levels of performance. This suggests a special reason why a world plan is necessary: Underdeveloped countries are vulnerable to influences which operate outside their boundaries but which nonetheless decisively condition their chances of success. Their own efforts at rationality in meeting priority needs must be supported by world structures which foster human creativity and promote resource use based on need priorities. At this point, however, it may be useful to open a parenthesis regarding the absorptive capacity of the Third World.

Some have argued that development aid ought not be given to the poor equally, or to those who need it most, but to those with the greatest ability to use it best—that is, to those with the highest absorptive capacity.[18] This recommendation ignores the historical fact that the chasm between developed and underdeveloped groups has resulted from the operation of this very principle in the past. Wealth and power have been granted to those best capable of using them and of making them serve their ends. Sharp polarization between advanced and depressed areas is the product of the largely unconscious workings of this rule in the past. Nothing is more ill-advised, in present circumstances, than to erect it consciously into a rule. One thing such a measure cannot do is abolish world underdevelopment. On the contrary, it increases the rewards of those societies which can "make it" to the inner circles of a competitive reward system where nominal "equality of opportunity" masks structural inequalities. But we may close this parenthesis and return to the need for a world plan.

For many years Perroux, Myrdal, Tinbergen, and Lebret have urged the adoption of a world plan. In the absence of satisfactory general mechanisms, the Center for Development Planning, Projections and Policies of the United Nations has engaged in preliminary exercises clearing the way for truly international planning machinery. Moreover, developers in growing numbers agree that international development policy, in Tinbergen's words, "should show an improvement in the distribution of world incomes, that is, a more rapid growth of incomes per head in the developing nations than in the developed countries. Incomes per head in the developing countries should certainly have a growth-rate of 4 per cent per year, which

18 V.g., Neil H. Jacoby, *The Progress of Peoples,* Occasional Paper, Center for the Study of Democratic Institutions, Vol. II, No. 4, June 1969, p. 19.

means that the growth of total incomes of many countries must be at 7 per cent per year." [19] Certain policy decisions ought to be made nationally, others trans-nationally, still others worldwide.[20] Although economic policy is its special province, Tinbergen declares that development planning is concerned in principle with "the whole economy and even with a considerable part of society" and that "the basis of qualitative planning is the theory of welfare economics." [21] This statement can be misleading, however, inasmuch as the ideal goal of world planning is not to create a worldwide welfare state. We must go, as the title of Myrdal's book suggests, *Beyond the Welfare State*. Nevertheless, the historical dependence of economic thought on the categories of welfare economics is incontestable.

Tinbergen pleads for a worldwide indicative plan. By definition, such a plan is not imposed but serves as a guideline for the activities of diverse institutions such as governments, corporations, unions, families, etc. Among expected benefits are the avoidance of duplication in national planning, the coherent supply of market-analysis materials to business, and a major contribution to the establishment of an international order needed, he writes, "instead of the junglelike behavior of national governments." [22] Other putative advantages are: to specify the aims of international economic policies, and to exert pressure on developed countries to accept greater burdens in removing the stigma of underdevelopment from the world. The task of such an indicative world plan is to formulate a world development strategy expressed both qualitatively and quantitatively. The chief practical aims are the growth of production and incomes and the distribution of growth among the countries of the world and among social groups. Growth and distribution figures must be allocated among various industries and sectors. At the risk of arbitrariness, Tinbergen quantifies targets, urging a 7-percent annual growth rate for underdeveloped countries. Population growth may lower this rate to 4 percent per capita, although targets vary in accord with varying demographic rates, initial income levels, and resource availabilities. Tinbergen believes that, in the effort to narrow the gap between the rich and poor

[19] Cf. Jan Tinbergen, *Development Planning* (McGraw-Hill, 1967), ch. 13, "The International Planning Organization," pp. 188–199. A more thorough examination of the problem is given by this same author in "Wanted: A World Development Plan," in *International Organization*, ed. Richard N. Gardner and Max F. Millikan, Vol. XXII, No. 1 (Winter 1969), pp. 417–431.

[20] Tinbergen, *Development Planning*, p. 196.

[21] *Ibidem*, p. 194.

[22] *Ibidem*, p. 211.

nations, we must not undertake to reduce the growth rate (averaging about 3 percent yearly in recent years) of developed countries, on grounds that this is probably impossible and perhaps even harmful to underdeveloped countries themselves.[23] I contend that, on the contrary, were productive capacities of rich nations oriented toward satisfying the priority needs of the world, national growth rates might continue to grow substantially, although such growth might not be registered in national statistics of the rich countries themselves. Part of the growth rate registered inside the developed countries would comprise goods and services transferred on a non-profit basis to needier countries. Productive capacity would not be lowered but channeled to other priorities, many of them public and even trans-national. The statistical measurement of the latter would credit the underdeveloped country benefiting from it. The theoretical basis for such a procedure is not traditional welfare economics, but rather Perroux's concept of the economy of *gift*.[24] More will be said of this later. What is worthy of note is that growth in advanced countries will have to undergo changes in its composition, moving away from wasteful or superfluous consumer goods in the direction of goods designed to satisfy the first and second categories of needs described above. *Added value* would be transferred to needy societies and recorded as growth in their national statistics. Recipient nations might then aim, as Tinbergen proposes, at a growth rate of 7 percent per year by their own efforts, not counting what they receive.

Unless some version of the Perroux scheme is adopted, underdeveloped countries may prove unable to reach even the 7-percent goal for autonomous effort set by Tinbergen. Too much of the world's resources, of its technological expertise, and of its efficient productive capacity is engaged in producing goods of low priority. Yet the mode in which goals are pursued is as crucial as the material obtention of the goals.

Tinbergen concludes his valuable essay by describing the procedures needed to conduct world planning. After conceding that his

[23] Tinbergen, "Wanted: A World Development Plan," p. 418. A similar argument is made by J. M. Albertini, "Economie Mondiale et Coopération des Peuples," in *Economie Mondiale, Economie des Hommes* (Economie et Humanisme, 1963), p. 79: "Face au besoin des pays sous-développés, les pays industriels ont un devoir d'expansion."

[24] Perroux has developed his theory of the economic gift in *Economie et Société, Contrainte, Echange, Don* (Presses Universitaires de France, 1963). A briefer treatment is found in his *L'Economie du XXIème Siècle* (Presses Universitaires de France, 1964), pp. 372–396.

outline is but a rough sketch, he calls for immediate further action, affirming that "the difficulties are not unsurmountable." I believe, however, that they are unsurmountable unless major institutional changes are made. The reconversion of world financing structures is one such change.

(B) *World Financing*

To financial experts belongs the task of outlining the rudiments of a new world financial strategy. Only qualified experts can state in specific terms the functional equivalent, for the domain of financing, of a world plan. Detailed policy recommendations at many different levels will be required. Conflicting goals must sometimes be sought. Thus, a wise policy of international payments can produce results which run counter to anti-inflationary measures taken in a given underdeveloped country. Only bold thought and experimentation hold out any hope for success in reconciling these and other tensions. Balance-of-payment problems, import subsidies, development loans, the quantity and terms of financial flows, convertability, and absorptive capacity—these are some of the massive problems which challenge innovative financial authorities. What is here asserted is simply that development presupposes the overhaul of present world financial structures and the creation of new instititions formally designed to meet the world's priority development needs. As is the case with planning, current financial practices, however deficient, are not totally devoid of strategic points at which innovation is possible. One indication is Professor N. T. Wang's belief that "A breakthrough in development finance is, therefore, more likely to come about by probing alternative sources of finance from the developed countries than by repeated pleas from the developing countries. This means that the problems of the developed countries themselves must be faced squarely." [25]

The erection of UNCTAD into a permanent commission is another sign of a growing awareness among developers of serious failings in present structures. Trade lies at the heart of international financing problems: indeed, trade and financing are inseparable both in their mechanisms and in their effects. New trade schemes aimed at overcoming structural inadequacies in world market systems are, therefore, an important contribution to the solution of the international financing problem. The proliferation of multilateral and international

[25] N. T. Wang, "New Proposals for the International Finance of Development," *Essays in International Finance,* No. 59 (April 1967), p. 7.

financing institutions is further evidence of a groping search for solutions outside the confines of traditional efforts. Nevertheless, anything less than the reorganization of development financing in its totality and on a world level, in harmony with a world development plan, is mere palliative. Ordinary banking rules are not adequate to the problem any more than are the automatic workings of supply-and-demand forces within the economy. In the realm of finance no less than in that of productive capacity, new institutions, procedures, and methods are required to meet global priority needs in a mode which optimizes resource use and frees distributive mechanisms from the rigidities and inequities attendant upon present structures of financial power and control. Quite as urgently as world planning, comprehensive world development financing is required so as to promote world order, minimize waste and duplication, and channel capital and credit to priority uses. The precise nature of financial reconversion, it is evident, cannot be defined by the ethician. Its desired shape can perhaps be inferred only remotely from proposals already advanced by experts in these matters.[26] What now appears certain, however, is that mere palliatives will not suffice; nothing less than a total reconversion of institutions will do.

No less essential than world planning and the recasting global financing institutions is the creation of a world technical pool.

(C) *World Technical Pool*

A torrential "migration of minds" or "brain-drain" occurs because skilled men gather where rewards are greatest, not necessarily where such men are most needed. If the world's human resources are to be utilized in accord with sound priorities, new mechanisms must be devised for attracting trained personnel to perform priority tasks where their skills are in urgent demand. Neither the demand system of the international market nor the application of nationalistic norms has proved satisfactory: a world technical pool must be created. Earlier in this book I advocated the internationalization and professionalization of technical cooperation. The aim of recommendations made there is

---

[26] Cf., e.g., *The Horowitz Proposal: Selected Documents,* UNCTAD, E/Conf. 46/C.3/2, April 6, 1964. Also André Philip, "Des Transformations de Structure dans les Pays Industrialisés Sont Indispensables" (pp. 80–88); Jacques Blanchet, "L'Aide financière Internationale en question" (pp. 29–32); and Michel Virally, "Le Cadre Juridique International du Développement—vers une Charte Internationale du Développement" (pp. 70–79), all in *Développement et Civilisations,* No. 32 (December 1967).

to reduce ethnocentrism in the dispensation of technical cooperative aid. The world technical pool presently under discussion, however, is a far more ambitious enterprise. It represents for human resources the analogue of total mobilization of world productive facilities in order to meet global development needs. I believe a world technical pool could become possible long before world government comes into existence. Within national boundaries, governments now employ fiscal and other incentives to induce men within states or localities to contribute to the over-all economic well-being *of the nation.* These practices need to be adopted on a worldwide scale. Initially, perhaps, this could be tried on a voluntary basis. Consequently, it is not accurate to visualize all engineers, chemists, pharmaceutical researchers, or fertilizer experts as employees of a single worldwide agency. What is contemplated, on the contrary, is that each important technical sector and unit of production would assume certain responsibilities transcending national boundaries and in accord with general directives in force throughout the world for conducting research, for supplying services, and for producing goods on a non-commercial basis. This proposal is one implication of the structural economic gift mentioned earlier. Perroux informs skeptical readers that, as here employed, the term "gift" signifies neither philanthropy nor charity but rather capital transfers made without the usual compensations—that is, interest payments or direct reimbursement. The altruistic motives which are sometimes operative in human exchange constitute untapped resources in the world. Perroux adds, *"Capital transfers without compensation seem destined to become a procedure which is not exceptional and, of necessity, a school for solidarity. They will necessarily lead to the exploitation of a layer, which still lies dormant and sterilized nowadays, of altruistic motives which it is perfectly unjustifiable not to use economically."* [27]

Authentic economic gifts are to be distinguished from apparent gifts. As examples of the former, Perroux cites the donation by all French coal miners after World War II of one day's work in order to procure one bag of coal for each political deportee. The social purpose of donors was to offer help in a period of extreme penury, without anticipating or expecting any *quid pro quo.* Relief shipments to victims of natural catastrophes are likewise of this nature. Perroux also mentions a Swiss organization which, between 1944 and 1948, engaged in "saving unfortunates for the good of humanity" by provid-

[27] Perroux, *L'Economie du XXième Siècle,* p. 373.

ing needed material and services. Other instances include the activities of U.N.R.R.A. during the years 1943–1946, when 80 percent of assistance took the form of gifts "pure and simple" and was financed by quota contributions totaling 1 percent of the revenue of member states.[28] Numerous other transfers, however, although they are designated as gifts, contain an economic calculus. In these cases, concessions are always made for the sake of increasing profit (usually in the future), improving efficiency, or obtaining political advantages. Judged in the light of this criterion, the Marshall Plan was not a strict economic gift, since the donor, to a large extent, sought to prevent the Communist subversion of Europe. Moreover, anticipated economic consequences also entered into the giver's calculus. But it is now time, says Perroux, for theorists to make room in their theories and policy recommendations for the economic resource and mode of exchange known as the gift.

Perroux, wishing to expand the scope of gift transactions, urges the creation of an International Support Center,[29] subsidized by monies diverted away from arms expenditures and by funds contributed proportionately by those benefiting from earlier subsidies. The proposal is cited here merely to illustrate the principle of the economic gift. This is not the place to analyze in detail the implications of the proposal. What is relevant to the ethics of development, however, is the formal recognition that altruistic dispositions in men and collectivities constitute a genuine *human resource* which needs to be mobilized and utilized according to properly *economic* criteria of rationality. The world technical pool described in these pages is presented merely as one possible example of just such a use. And worldwide economic rationality may well prove impossible without it.

According to Albertini, "When we analyze the development of countries now industrialized, we notice that they have been equipped in all cases thanks to what are, in effect, gifts."[30] These gifts have taken various forms: fiscal exemptions, war indemnities, and unredeemed bonds. Nevertheless, gift-giving has its own peculiar drawbacks and suitable techniques; perhaps new codes of practical jurisprudence are required.

I have proposed that all technical units and sectors, including those

---

[28] These examples are found in *ibidem,* p. 374.
[29] *Ibid.,* 376ff.
[30] Albertini, "Economie Mondiale et Coopération des Peuples," *op. cit.,* p. 76.

privately owned, be made to accept responsibility for producing some goods and providing services (primarily research) on behalf of those in greatest need. This procedure is doubly necessary inasmuch as underdeveloped nations lack the capacity to engage in costly research. The brain-drain could become less catastrophic for them than it now is if contributions by emigrating experts were eventually to find their way back to the experts' country of origin in the form of useful information, advice, or invention. No deductive or speculative model-building can serve for devising precise mechanisms whereby such a scheme should operate. The aim of these lines is limited: to suggest how urgent a world technical pool has become and how illusory is any global policy which ignores this requirement. Technical knowledge is at present the single most valuable resource existing in the world. The creation of a technical pool upon which those in priority needs may draw is a major instrument for institutionalizing the principle of cooperation with a view to optimizing efficiency. It must be apparent to the reader that the corps of developers outlined in Chapter Eight is simply one component in a larger strategy. The technical pool here advocated is one element in that broader strategy. Public and private personnel alike will contribute assigned quotas of goods and services to the pool. These "quotas" will be determined by the world plan. The difficulty of instituting such arrangements must not blind us to this important truth: that it is unrealistic to expect solutions to the chronic shortage of skills in underdeveloped lands from anything less than a world technical pool. The creation of such a pool is, therefore, a key ingredient in an over-all policy of institutional reform aimed at optimizing chances for successful world development.

As with planning and financing, realistic strategy dictates that innovative efforts be grafted onto what already exists. Radically new recruiting procedures in the United Nations and other international organizations could begin to generate progress in the proper direction. Governments themselves, moreover, as well as foundations and research organizations, can provide special incentives for their own and other experts who *donate* their time and talents to the pool. Transnational training programs might be redesigned so as to impose commitments on visiting scholars or technicians to labor for the pool whenever they leave their needy country in order to improve their education elsewhere or to use superior research facilities. Private firms now agree to pay taxes in *specie;* they must be induced to provide goods and services to this world technical pool. Although the idea is simple in principle, precise working modalities are yet to be invented through multiple experiments by qualified creative experts.

(D) *The Cultural Revolution in Developed Countries*

The institutional changes just outlined can take place only if *developed countries* radically alter their value systems. The value changes demanded of them are as revolutionary as those which underdeveloped countries must undergo. Spokesmen from rich countries and classes recognize the necessity incumbent upon their poor counterparts to adopt new attitudes and motives which contradict "traditional" ones. They defend this plea for change in the name of "modernization." Yet these same spokesmen are loath to admit that their own values impede the achievement of global development founded on the satisfaction of priority needs, the creation of universal solidarity, and the optimum participation of all men as agents of their own growth. The dominant values and institutions of developed countries or classes contradict, to a considerable degree, the regulative principles of sound world development. They obey no sound priority system of need-satisfaction. Instead they reinforce particular interests, and tend toward the creation of a world technocratic oligarchy which monopolizes all important decision-making. For these reasons, a revolution of values within developed nations is urgent: unless it takes place, universal development cannot occur.

There are no quick formulas or easy short-cuts for obtaining this end. It is evident that the perpetuation of Cold War attitudes in industrialized nations, with its attendant waste of resources on armaments and emulative prestige projects, is a major obstacle to development. No less apparently, the value systems of mass-consumer societies based on profit and social competition are also dissonant with the integral development just outlined. Notwithstanding its importance and urgency, voluntary austerity in advanced nations remains impossible unless large numbers of citizens acquire a revolutionary new conception of relationships between goods and the good life. Crises in education, the revolt of oppressed minorities, youthful alienation, and generalized boredom among the "successful" are signs that complacency has been shattered. Acknowledging the ills of contemporary developed societies is the first step toward discovering that these societies rest on the shifting sands of false values. It is likewise encouraging to note that social scientists now deal more forthrightly than in the past with development's normative issues and reject the "value-free" illusion which has held sway for so many decades.

Developed societies and privileged classes must reconvert their institutions and values in order to create conditions without which the painful changes required of underdeveloped societies will be thwarted. Otherwise stated, a cultural revolution must take place in the world's "advanced" countries if the cultural and political revolutions needed in the Third World are to bear fruit.

Mankind's religious spokesmen have at times raised their official voices and attempted to speak with moral authority to the rich of the world, in the hope of "converting" them to greater political altruism, justice, and concern for equity. Typical pronouncements of this sort are the Papal encyclical *Populorum Progressio* and official reports addressed to the World Council of Churches and to the Pontifical Commission of Justice and Peace.[31] Such declarations, however, have little impact. Documents like *Pacem in Terris* or *Populorum Progressio* have no doubt encouraged those engaged in Christian-Marxist dialogue and stimulated others to reflect on the ethical requirements of development. The encyclical on development, in particular, has received favorable comment from Marxists, Muslims, secular humanists, and others.[32] Nevertheless, the world needs something other than sermons from moral pedagogues. As I have written elsewhere, "no major ethical system or world religion has clean hands; historically, all have condoned structures favoring the creation and perpetuation of underdevelopment. As a result, none can speak out with unblemished authority from a universal moral platform." [33] To a considerable degree, churches and moral authorities in developed countries have contributed to the problem by entering into connivance, partial at least, with colonialism. They have shared in the cultural disdain of weaker partners and international privilege systems.[34] One consequence of these historical interventions is that no ethically irreproachable vanguard or prophet of the worldwide cultural revolution exists. Like all true vanguards, this one too will have to be secreted by the world

---

[31] V.g., the report entitled *World Development: The Challenge to the Churches,* Beirut, Lebanon, April 21–27, 1968.

[32] Cf. v.g., Jean Suret-Canale, "Réformer Fondamentalement les Structures pour Faire un Monde de Tous les Hommes," and Mohammed Said-Al-Attar, "Nous Saluons ce Grand Texte Historique," both in *Développement et Civilisations,* No. 30 (June 1967).

[33] Denis A. Goulet, "Ethical Issues in Development," *Review of Social Economy,* Vol. XXVI, No. 2 (September 1968), p. 111.

[34] This is analyzed in J. da Veiga Coutinho, "The Church and the Third World," *Cross Currents,* Vol. XVII, No. 4 (Fall 1968), pp. 435–450.

society now in ferment. The growing sense of identification with the cause of the Third World among revolutionary students in all developed countries is one sign that a new universal consciousness is in gestation. But before this sign can be translated into institutional reality, profound mutations must occur in the advanced world's educational, media, and incentive systems.

Developers in growing numbers now confess that world underdevelopment reflects a basic value crisis affecting developed and underdeveloped societies alike. Only by simultaneously altering men and institutions can solutions be found. The four institutional reconversions outlined in these pages are not a comprehensive program, but merely an augury of the scope of changes needed. Indeed, a new international legal order is also mandatory. Even if world government does not come to pass, innovations in this direction appear possible.[35] Various international legal sub-orders already exist, as well as a variety of mediating standards and rules which differ according to the characteristics of the specific parties involved. These can and should be used as springboards to more fundamental changes. The crux of the problem, however, remains the *manner* in which innovations are made. Since adequate solutions are not instantly possible, many gains will have to be realized incrementally, or step-by-step. Accordingly, it is essential to distinguish two qualitatively different types of incremental change.

Two Forms of Incrementalism

The development norms outlined in these pages can be implemented only if world institutions are radically changed. In minimal terms, the institutions in need of basic reconversion are those which govern access to resources—including human knowledge and research capabilities—and the central decision-making regarding resource use. Strategic priority must therefore be given to world planning, to new global financial arrangements, and to the creation of a worldwide technological pool. None of these three objectives is remotely feasible,

[35] This is a major theme in the work of Argyrios Fatouros, "International Law and the Third World," *Virginia Law Review,* Vol. L, No. 5 (June 1964), pp. 783–823. Cf. also his "Comments on International Law and Economic Development," *Proceedings of the American Society of International Law,* 1966, pp. 18–22, and several unpublished papers by the same author. Among these are: "Participation of the New States on the Fusion of National and International Affairs" and "A Note on the Process of Legal Change in Present-Day International Society."

however, unless deep and far-reaching attitudinal changes take place in the public opinion of developed countries. This is why a new pedagogy of values is postulated as a prerequisite to the reconversion of world institutions. Only scant mention has been made of further changes which are no less necessary but which deal less directly with resource use for development purposes. Chief among these, of course, is the creation of a new world legal order.

In the case of all institutions discussed, major progress is not realizable by abrupt mutation, or by any single revolutionary program or combination of programs. Many obstacles must be removed before final implementation is rendered possible. The existence of numerous practical constraints leads us to pursue much change via a series of cumulative steps. Of course, revolutionary new beginnings are often desirable; more rarely are they feasible. The burning question is: Can deep social mutations be obtained by a series of incremental steps? Or are incremental measures necessarily and always mere palliatives?

What appear to be identical measures are at times mere palliatives, whereas in different circumstances they expand possibilities for future change. That is to say, there exist two contrasting kinds of incrementalism: the one palliative, the other creative.

Palliative measures obstruct basic change because they lull people into believing that gradual amelioration is an adequate response to fundamental problems. As time passes, however, palliatives always worsen the condition they set out to improve. The reason is that they give birth to hopes they cannot satisfy or tinker with failing social mechanisms, thereby postponing treatment until the disease becomes incurable. Creative incremental measures, on the other hand, breed new possibilities for subsequent radical change, although at the moment of adoption they appear quite modest. Such measures contain a latent dynamism, however, which propels society beyond immediate problem-solving toward new possible futures. John Wilkinson aptly remarks that the "potential energy of a rock that has been sitting on top of a hill for a million years is harmless to anyone. Only when its energy can be made kinetic by some random push can it cause a new situation to arise." [36] Like energy, contemplated social changes enjoy a greater or lesser potential for generating major transformation. Any

---

[36] John Wilkinson, "The Revolutionary Potential," paper delivered at the Center for the Study of Democratic Institutions, January 17, 1969, p. 1. An abbreviated version of this paper has appeared in *The Center Magazine*, March 1969, pp. 72–76.

serious strategist of induced change must learn to discern which measures have a merely palliative potential, which a creative potential. All potential social energy has to be kineticized. Of course, not all consequences of any given measure can be assessed before the fact. Randomness or serendipity can transform "safe" concessions into explosively revolutionary instrumentalities. Nonetheless, sensitive change agents are not totally bereft of criteria for assessing the change potential contained in contemplated moves. These criteria are both subjective and objective in nature.

Many revolutionists reject violence as an acceptable means, but have nonetheless lost faith in the capacity of existing political institutions to produce in piecemeal fashion the structural changes they seek. Whenever they feel compelled to resort to what appear to be incremental tactics, they always do so in the hope that modest moves today will open the door to more radical mutations tomorrow. Consequently, their specific recommendations can only be evaluated in the light of their agents' intentions. An illustration may help. We may suppose that Country A favors the creation of an international ocean regime having sole authority over all seabeds and committed to using the ocean's resources exclusively for peaceful developmental purposes. Let us further assume that Country A embraces such a scheme because it sees it as a step in the direction of abolishing national sovereignties and creating world government. That country's leaders may reach the practical judgment that the cause of world government is advanced if world control over the oceans can be established before sovereign nations acquire uncontested rights over them. In this case, the measure is not merely palliative: subjectively at least, it is perceived as capable of creating new leverage for a more basic institutional change to come later.

An identical ocean regime, however, may be advocated by Country B for opposite reasons. Country B may abhor the idea of world government and the disappearance of national sovereignty. Nevertheless, the country wishes to prevent use of the ocean floor by powerful nations who might use it for warlike purposes or engage in commercial exploitation to the detriment of poorer nations. Relative to the final goal, world government, B's support of an international ocean regime must be considered a mere palliative. Incrementalism is at work in both cases, but a subjective criterion helps us discern whether the measure constitutes palliative or creative incrementalism.

One can argue with some plausibility that proponents of radical change do well to present any measures they publicly advocate in the guise of modest problem-solving moves. By so doing, the argument goes, they disarm the fears of those who mistrust their ulterior subjective intentions. I do not wish to debate this point, however. What seems more important to me, even in political terms, is to inquire whether any *objective* criterion exists for discriminating between incremental steps which are mere patchwork and those which genuinely expand future possibilities.

Thinkers like Denis Gabor affirm that palliative solutions to social problems, however attractive or structurally adequate they may appear at the time of adoption, inevitably worsen the very ills they set out to cure.[37] According to Gabor, non-palliative measures, on the contrary, if programmed in a computer designed to isolate the consequences of a contemplated course of action, can be shown in projected games dealing with futuribles (i.e., future possibles) to result in better conditions. The opposite is also true: palliatives, if played out, will make matters visibly worse. If this is true, it becomes possible to distinguish palliative from creative incremental measures *without appealing to subjective or to ideological norms.* For the true believer in a free-enterprise economy or in Marxist Socialism, there is of course a simple putatively *objective* criterion of discernment: the degree to which the measure envisaged strengthens or weakens the preferred system. Great wisdom is doubtless required of the programmer if he is to assess all relevant variables adequately in his computer-programming exercise. Nevertheless, if Gabor is right, it may become possible to judge the change potential of prospective measures according to some scaled coefficient of kinetic social-transformation value.

I judge the institutional changes advocated in this work to be creative, not palliative, incremental measures. The standard of values in the light of which this judgment is made is a notion of universal development which meets priority needs and which fulfills men integrally and in a non-elitist mode. The measures advocated are incremental insofar as they do not suffice by themselves to generate such development. They are more than palliatives, however, because they reduce obstacles impeding authentic development and create new possibilities of moving toward the eventual achievement of such development.

[37] Information supplied to the author by Denis Gabor in a private conversation May 8, 1969, following discussion of several Gabor papers at the Center for the Study of Democratic Institutions. These papers were entitled: "A New Anthropology"; "The Mass University"; and "Fighting Existential Nausea in the Technological Society."

Why are palliative solutions to social ills so pernicious? Because they do not root out the causes of ailments but merely tamper with symptoms. In political terms, they are calculated to "buy off" potential agents of profound change with social bribes, in the form of visible benefits. Yet, how development is obtained determines whether men are liberated or alienated: the manner is as important as the matter! The benefits of development could probably be obtained in some elitist, technocratic, oligarchic mode. They might even be gained under the ostensible banner of greater freedom and democracy. Behind the scenes, however, would lurk deterministic forces manipulating mass opinion and desires. To achieve the benefits of development at the cost of sacrificing human freedom and critical intelligence is to negate the very good life and good society development seeks to produce. Palliative measures may solve problems or settle issues; they cannot foster the vital qualities which are the terminal goals of development itself.

Anything less than a major change in the world's institutions is a palliative to the evils of world underdevelopment. The crucial task, therefore, is to devise bold creative measures which are also feasible. Ultimately, development is not an "art of the possible" but rather an art of creating new possibilities. Critical debate over the ethics of development is but a preliminary step. It merely sets the normative boundaries of what must be made possible if development's global promises are not to be betrayed. In the contemporary world, however, these promises have often been betrayed. Countless social reformers despair of all forms of incrementalism and feel drawn to an alternate solution, revolutionary violence. We must now turn our attention to the disturbing ethical problems posed by the use of violence as a means of righting social wrongs. This is the task of the following chapter.

CHAPTER THIRTEEN

Despair's Dilemma:
Ethics and Revolution

Social scientists frequently define revolution so broadly that it includes any far-reaching change in men's outlook, behavior, self-image, or life-style. Hence, they speak of technological, educational, and sexual revolutions. More precise definitions are required, however, for purposes of analysis. Anthropologist Eric Wolf sees revolution as the "process by which varying components of the middleman layer and of the peasantry are mobilized and brought into contact with each other." [1] Fanon views it rather as a method by which the oppressed man severs the umbilical cord that binds him to exploiters and thereby heals his psyche by a renovative act which purges him of his inferiority.[2] Revolution, in Camus' work, means the construction of universal human justice after revolt has overthrown injustice. Finally, Régis Debray asserts that the direct aim of revolution is to conquer central political power in order to build socialist society.

Indeed, revolution is a special kind of total warfare engaging the violence of arms, economic rationing, manpower impressment, and manipulative propaganda. Its aim is to seize political power and

[1] Eric R. Wolf, "Reflections on Peasant Revolution," Carnegie Seminar, Indiana University, April 3, 1967, *mimeo,* p. 10.
[2] Frantz Fanon, *The Wretched of the Earth* (Grove Press, 1966), *passim.*

thereafter proceed to alter the rules of collective decision-making. At least on principle, modern ideologies of social revolution reject elitist modes of decision-making: it is always "the people" who must come to wield power.

This view is the antithesis of that described in *The Statesman*. There Plato imagined that "the government of human beings was originally government by gods. In their control of the world things improve as if they were wound up on a spindle to achieve a high tension and power control. Then at a certain point the gods decide that they will let this unwind, and this is the period when human beings take over. After this happens, human beings become worse and worse at the art of government, until finally government degenerates into a kind of chaos, anarchy, tyranny, and so forth. When it gets bad enough, the gods decide they will take over again, and so they begin— perhaps through a man—to wind up the process again, and it begins to improve." [3]

As used here, however, the term "revolution" designates the illegal seizure of the central organs of political power, with the declared aim of instituting new, or restoring old, arrangements for governing society, especially in its economic and political spheres, on behalf of all the people.

The special kind of radical change known as revolution creates a dilemma for the human conscience because it admits the possibility of using direct physical violence. A revolutionary situation poses alternative choices of such a nature that men cannot always avoid committing serious evil, regardless of their option. During many centuries, when faced with moral perplexity, men were instructed by moralists to set their consciences to rest by choosing the lesser evil. But this answer is useless in the case of contemporary revolutionary situations because one cannot weigh on the same scale two opposite categories of evils—the first, present and unbearable, the second, future and unpredictable. The future is unpredictable precisely because all revolutions go through a stage at which they must reconsider and perhaps even deny their original aims and set new aims in the light of lessons learned during the revolution. A true revolution is always a profoundly shattering experience in which the people who revolt get re-educated as profoundly as the people against whom they are revolting.

[3] Scott Buchanan, *On Revolution: A Conversation* (Center for the Study of Democratic Institutions, 1962), pp. 1–2.

The Ethical Dilemma

Heated debate continues to rage over the morality of revolutionary violence as a means of obtaining desired social changes such as development. Many observers contend that there is no moral justification for attacking established legal orders and destroying whatever fragments of justice or social values may be embodied therein. They argue that revolutions never achieve their original purposes, or that if social improvement follows the overthrow of unjust regimes, the price paid is exorbitant. Advocates of this position counsel patience, therefore, in the face of social evils. They want change only through gradual measures: persuasion, legislation, perhaps even decentralized non-revolutionary violent confrontations among competing interest groups.[4]

Others retort that the highest moral act is to engage in revolutionary activity, using violence if necessary. The central organs of governmental power must be seized, illegally if need be, in order to provide social reformers with the leverage they need to institute deep changes in institutions governing the distribution of power, wealth, and access to decision-making in society. Revolutionaries consider both their cause and their choice of means to be supremely moral since they contribute to the creation of social values which are more human than those presently existing. As righteously as their adversaries denounce them, revolutionaries condemn champions of the existing order as immoral, inhuman, and irresponsible.

No single ethical strategy for dealing with revolutionary situations can be fully acceptable, however. Men who give their allegiance to identical value systems often make contradictory practical judgments as to the political choices open to them. This is why there are Christian revolutionaries and anti-revolutionaries, just as there are Marxists who endorse and Marxists who oppose guerrilla warfare. Ethics has always been concerned with alternative decisions which are genuinely *possible* to men, never with what is inevitable or beyond their reach. For this reason Jacques Ellul's views on the ethical worth of political decisions raise special difficulties. According to him, a political act cannot be *just* if it has already become *necessary*. He holds

---

[4] On the latter point, cf. Albert O. Hirschman, "The Contriving of Reform," ch. 5 in *Journeys Toward Progress* (Anchor Books, 1965), pp. 327–384.

that "once circumstances evolve and solutions get progressively eliminated, the freedom of the player diminishes at each step and finally there remains but a single solution which imposes itself of necessity. It becomes necessary [i.e., inevitable] and we may say that in all such cases, the solution is the expression of the greatest measure of force and *never* of justice. In politics a solution imposed by necessity is never a just solution. [For the French government] to grant the Moslems [of Algeria] genuine political participation and a decent economic statute was not necessary in 1954; it was just." [5] If we interpret this text literally and assume revolutions to be necessary in the sense of having become inevitable, we can neither place moral strictures nor confer moral approval on them. The crucial point, of course, is how necessity is defined: Is it the inevitability arising from conditions which eliminate all other options? Or is it the only course open to us if a given objective has already been willed? If the situation is so evil that oppression, privilege, stagnation, and exploitation have bred total despair, revolution is necessary in the first sense. Yet when one waits this long, revolution may well have become hopeless. Perhaps the most it can then accomplish is to allow the victim a final chance to assert his manhood. Revolution thus becomes a symbolic redemptive act by which men purge themselves of passive complicity in the destruction of their own humanity. The case is analogous for societies as well: they too may undertake even suicidal resistance to oppressors merely to bear final witness to their sense of worth. Nevertheless, revolutions for the construction of a new social order are not of this sort: their advocates are always convinced they can win. As Sorel put it, only the man who is convinced that his cause will ultimately triumph can be a genuine revolutionary. Or, in Che Guevara's words, "intensive popular work must be undertaken to explain the motives of the revolution, its ends, and to spread the incontrovertible truth that victory of the enemy against the people is finally impossible. *Whoever does not feel* this undoubted truth cannot be a guerrilla fighter." [6]

Every social ethic except principled and heroic non-violence can present to its adherents logical options either in favor of revolutionary violence or against it. The decisive factor seems to be the relative importance attached by subjective evaluators to present evils weighed

[5] Jacques Ellul, *L'Illusion Politique* (Paris: Robert Laffont, 1965), pp. 190 ff.
[6] Che Guevara, *Guerrilla Warfare* (Monthly Review Press, 6th printing, 1967), p. 22.

against the probable chances of improvement in some conditional future. As a result, every ethic except supreme non-violent heroism places men in a distress situation in the face of revolutionary conditions, for it is impossible to follow one course of action to its ultimate consequences without betraying certain ethical values. The reason is that once inhuman conditions reach a certain point, there exists no fully moral manner of eliminating evil, of attenuating it, or even of tolerating it. In quite literal terms, an ethical dilemma is posed. The logic of these situations may be summarized as follows:

(a) Development and other desirable social changes are sometimes impossible to obtain under prevailing ground rules governing change. Therefore, it is possible, at least on principle, to defend revolution as a morally valid course of action.

(b) No infallible way exists, however, of knowing whether non-revolutionary means could produce desired social change in a given situation or not. Historical precedents are never fully conclusive, since each situation contains unique, unpredictable elements. Consequently, any judgment will be heavily subjective and incommunicable to others except in terms of some ideological, political, or other form of persuasion. Inherent in such mobilization, however, is the danger that subjects will be manipulated as objects, and that all facts or interpretations thereof discordant with the aims of mobilization will be suppressed or distorted.

(c) Even when it is morally justified to launch revolutionary action, its main actors can never exercise full control over the totality of means which inevitably become "necessary" in the conduct of that action. This is also true of non-revolutionary courses of action (or inaction) which, in certain circumstances, ineluctably lead to complicity with the institutionalized violence perpetrated by the reigning order.

(d) Every ethic, therefore, whether of revolution or anti-revolution, involves moral compromises.

(e) Consequently, each ethical agent must choose the cause for which he will compromise, and in his choice of means he must draw a line beyond which he will not compromise. The locus of that line depends ultimately on his conception of the human person and of society, and on the moral quality of his goals. There is, of course, a monumental difference between commitments to historical goals and to trans-historical goals. Each commitment produces its special effects on the pursuit of developmental tasks. Yet in both cases the final moral judgment passed on revolution or non-revolution cannot be based on the commitment's putative effectiveness or its alleged necessity, but must rather be based on the totality of values served by ends and means alike.

Conflicting antecedent biases as to the moral worth of revolution can be found in diverse social systems. Within capitalist and self-styled "free democracies" the general presumption is that revolution is immoral, destructive, politically regressive, and subversive of humane goals. Inside Socialist countries, on the other hand, revolution—provided it is not directed against established Socialism—is assumed to enjoy *prima facie* moral legitimacy. The fact seems to be, however, that all social systems merely institutionalize different forms of violence against human beings. This is why it is possible for judiciously selected revolutionary counter-violence to be more acceptable, in certain cases, than passive non-resistance in the face of institutionalized violence. In other circumstances, the use of revolutionary violence may constitute, as Celso Furtado warns,[7] political regression and the negation of personal and social values. Both these biases stand in need of correction. Sociologists like Orlando Fals Borda, Camilo Torres, and Irving Louis Horowitz perform a useful service by explaining that to label revolutionary activity as subversive, insurgent, destructive, and illegal is itself an exercise in persuasive definitions at the service of interests wedded to the preservation of privilege and domination. Similarly, the use of terms like reactionary, imperialist, and exploitative is often a pretext used by revolutionaries for casting moral aspersions on courses of action incompatible with their own interests.

Notwithstanding the complexity of these problems, clear options can and must be made in specific cases regarding the justice of revolutions against authority for the sake of instituting a new social order. Nevertheless, these options always contain elements of subjective evaluation. They are not amenable, therefore, to formulation in a binding set of prescriptions valid for all other situations. To illustrate, the Vietnamese revolution conducted by the National Liberation Front, and assisted by the regular forces of the People's Republic of North Vietnam, is a just insurrection. This does not mean, however, that every tactic or claim of the NLF is just. Nor must we conclude that every American, Australian, or South Vietnamese participating in

[7] Celso Furtado, "Brazil: What Kind of Revolution?" in *Economic Development: Evolution or Revolution?* (D. C. Heath, 1964), p. 38.

counter-insurgency is acting immorally. These men may be acting in accord with their own priority goals and their moral principles. I believe these principles to be wrong. Nevertheless, for purposes of persuasion, I can only adduce evidence to suggest that the humane goals they profess in their ethic are negated by the anti-revolutionary strategy they pursue.

Ethical dilemmas arise only because revolutions can be good as well as bad. One reason why there is much confusion over their ethical merits is that revolutionary doctrines often base their ethical justification on necessity. Most moralists instinctively tend to regard violent revolution as something dangerous, possibly even very harmful. But, they argue, men are sometimes so cruelly victimized that they must revolt against their rulers in order to defend their humanity. The rapid evolution in Camilo Torres' thought illustrates this tendency. Speaking as a priest in 1963, Torres condemned violence on the grounds that it was incompatible with Christian morals. Within three years, however, he publicly declared that "the people do not believe in elections. The people know that legal paths have been exhausted. The people are in a state of despair and are resolved to risk their lives so that the next generation of Colombians will not be slaves. . . . Every sincere revolutionary has to acknowledge that armed combat is the only alternative that is left." [8]

A recent publication of the National Council of Churches proceeds in a similar vein when it asks: "Is it lawful for the Christian actively to participate in revolutionary movements that may resort to violence, in cases where the goal of social transformation *does not appear viable by any other means,* but which is indispensable from the point of view of social justice and human well-being?" [9] Once again the plea is made, this time by insinuation, to condone violence because there is no other way.

If in any absolute sense, however, there are no other alternatives, there can be no moral dilemma. No one is morally obliged to do what is impossible. If social justice is truly unattainable except through revolutionary violence, men cannot be morally bound to resort only to futile or inefficient non-violent means. Furthermore, it should be recalled that what ethics condemns is the use of "intrinsically bad"

[8] *Camilo Torres,* in the Collection *Sondeos,* No. 5 (Cuernavaca: CIDOC, 1966), pp. 116, 374.

[9] "A Theological Reflection by Latin American Christians on Violence and Non-Violence," *Latin American News Letter,* National Council of Churches, No. 66 (December 1967), p. 9.

means, even in the pursuit of acceptable ends. Yet, throughout history, moralists have condoned such acts as police coercion, defensive war, and military assistance given to embattled allies. Thus, they have never treated violence as an intrinsically bad means. Although many contemporary ethicians condemn atomic, bacteriological, and chemical instruments of violence as inherently evil, these are hardly the weapons used by insurgents! One is prompted, therefore, to ask moralists: "Why have you not always preached that revolutionary violence is unequivocally good? According to your own principles, it has to be good because it is not intrinsically bad and you yourselves say that it is sometimes the only option *possible*." Dilemmas have been created because moralists appeal to ethics, which presupposes freedom, in their effort to justify revolution while uncritically pleading necessity, which is the antithesis of freedom. We need to clarify, however, what is meant by freedom and necessity. Ellul, in the text cited earlier, contends that no political solution can be just if it is necessary, since it is not free. He argues that in delicate political matters justice depends primarily on the moment at which decisions are taken, not on their author's lofty conception of justice, on his good intentions, or on the particular political line he follows. "A decision must be reached," he says, "before irreparable acts have been committed, before public opinion has been aroused. . . . When a situation is nascent, it is not *necessary* to intervene; consequently, the act runs the risk of seeming gratuitous. . . . A just solution can in fact be found only in the freedom of the decision-maker who has a gamut of solutions and possible combinations before him. Once circumstances evolve and solutions get progressively eliminated, the freedom of the actor diminishes at each step and finally there remains but a single solution which imposes itself of necessity." [10]

Ellul's point is that the passage of time eliminates certain theoretically possible choices. Besides, there can be no *justice* in the fullest sense if political agents allow a decision which *ought to be made* (because it is morally right) to be postponed until such time as it can no longer be made at all, or can be made only in circumstances which reduce the agent's power to control all the moral consequences of the action taken. Even if an alternative becomes necessary, in Ellul's sense that no other solution remains possible, varying degrees of internal endorsement of the imposed course of action can be made by the moral agent. At times this internal moral freedom may consist in nothing more than saying: "I accept this great evil because I cannot

[10] Ellul, *op. cit.*

avoid it, and any other possible course of action risks producing greater evil."

Regardless of the precise qualifications needed to interpret Ellul's statement realistically, it remains true that theorists of revolution have created a moral dilemma for themselves by arguing the justice of their cause on grounds of its necessity. When defending revolution they have sought ethical justification on grounds of necessity or inevitability. But if revolution has truly become inevitable or necessary in absolute terms, it is already too late to erect proper safeguards against absolutizing its means, against betraying the justice and brotherhood of its cause in the name of strategic efficiency. The problem arises because revolutionaries can always legitimately argue that realism posits strategic efficiency as a *moral* requirement of *good* revolutionary action. Even the Christian Gospel warns men against building a tower unless they can finish it, or launching a war unless they can see it through. Such ethical thinking is able to provide suitable arguments to justify launching a revolution, but is powerless to impose effective limits on violence or the abuse of personal rights in the prolonged conduct of revolutionary warfare.

When appealed to uncritically, determinism or necessity nourishes the good conscience and the dilemma of decision-makers: their good conscience, because they justify revolution as inevitable, their dilemma because they cannot fully control revolution. By its very nature, revolutionary action forces men to tread paths whose destination is unknown. Its goals must change within its own processes as participants get perpetually re-educated to a truth yet to be revealed. One can perhaps "free the present from the past," as Debray hoped, but who will free the future from the present? And how does one reply to the objections posed by Djilas—namely, that "throughout history there have been no ideal ends which were attained with non-ideal, inhumane means, just as there has been no free society which was built by slaves. Nothing so well reveals the reality and greatness of ends as the methods used to attain them. If the end must be used to condone the means, then there is something in the end itself, in its reality, which is not worthy." [11]

If it takes itself too seriously, revolution ends up loving a man who does not yet exist. "But the man who loves a living being," warns Camus, "if he loves him truly, can only accept to die for that living being, not for a man who does not live yet." [12]

---

[11] Milovan Djilas, *The New Class* (Praeger, 1957), p. 162.
[12] Albert Camus, *The Rebel* (Vintage Books, 1956), p. 96.

Revolutionary programs move men to action and sacrifice by denouncing the injustices they suffer in their flesh and blood. Yet they risk perpetrating new injustices on that same flesh in the name of an idealized man who lies at the term of history. This is why, if it wishes to be human, revolution must accept relativity. As Camus concluded, revolution's "universe is the universe of relative values. Instead of saying, with Hegel and Marx, that all is necessary, it only repeats that all is possible and that, at a certain point on the farthest frontier, it is worth making the supreme sacrifice for the sake of the possible." [13] Perhaps revolutions can be moral—and therefore liberating—only if they do not pursue victory at any cost.

The virtue of antagonists in revolutionary situations resides largely in their choice of means, since, in the last analysis, the ends of all combatants are in some sense good. At its deepest level, the debate is over two competing acts of faith. Any revolution strives to wed political power to humanitarian love. The crucial question is: Must love bow in submission to power because it is unable to triumph in the real world? Or will power accept love's gentle yoke in recognition of its own impotence to serve human purposes? Fanon's faith commands him to believe "that only violence pays. . . . The exploited man sees that his liberation implies the use of all means, and that of force first and foremost." [14] At the opposite pole, Thomas Merton professes faith in love: "the non-violent resister is persuaded of the superior efficacy of love, openness, peaceful negotiation and above all of truth. For power can guarantee the interests of *some men* but it can never foster the good of *man*. Power always protects the good of some at the expense of all the others. Only love can attain and preserve the good of all. Any claim to build the security of *all* on force is a manifest imposture." [15]

The option in favor of one or another of these conflicting faiths transcends mere rational discourse on the ethics of violence, and in both cases the believer falls into an "ethics of distress" situation. This means that no matter what he chooses, he cannot fully predict or control the moral outcome of his options. Revolutionary violence perpetrated in the name of justice can easily become repression under the banner of "eliminating counter-revolutionaries" or "saving the revolu-

---

13 *Idem,* p. 290.
14 Fanon, *op. cit.,* p. 48.
15 Thomas Merton, *Blessed Are the Meek: The Christian Roots of Nonviolence* (Fellowship of Reconciliation Reprint, July 1967), p. 7.

tion." Conversely, non-revolution chosen for the sake of fear or love can just as readily pave the way for the greater violence of desperate victims. No one can avoid risking the subversion of moral values which are precious to him, and if he is lucid his conscience is in distress. Lucidity is indeed essential; so is advertence to the ambiguity of the word "necessity." Marx calls class struggle an historical necessity. Even when "enlightened" exploiters carry out reforms, they unwittingly deepen class antagonisms and prepare the day of ultimate violence. The history of all class societies moves ineluctably toward conflict, says Marx, and human freedom consists in ratifying history's dialectics ahead of history's apocalyptic deadline. He believes that people create their own history—not arbitrarily, but by yielding to the pressure of conditions.

For Ellul, on the other hand, necessity signifies the failure to meet freedom's deadline and the resulting loss of moral options. Not that it is wrong to start a revolution, but once revolutionaries launch their action, they have no leverage left with which to counter revolution's tendency to subordinate purity of goals to efficiency of means. The revolutionary is forced by the very dialectics of polarization to parody Christ: "he who is not with me is against me." Ultimately, insurgents and counter-insurgents alike need every citizen and "cannot afford to let him remain neutral." [16] Under both kinds of necessity, ethics falls into distress, becoming in the process either impossible or superfluous.

Christian Ethics in Distress

Much has been written in recent years on the possibility of formulating a Christian ethic of revolution applicable to Latin America. There is some analogy here with new trends in Vietnam and elsewhere in Asia where reflection has centered on reinterpreting Buddhism to make of it a viable political and social ethic. Within China itself Mao has invoked non-Confucian ethical values derived from variant value systems (Taoism and Buddhism) in his revolutionary pedagogy of the masses. It is, of course, always possible in given historical circumstances to elaborate an authentically Christian, Buddhist, or Muslim justification for participation in revolutionary violence. By the very fact that a "religionist" owes his ultimate allegiance to trans-historical or

[16] David Galula, *Counter-Insurgency Warfare: Theory and Practice* (Praeger, 1964), p. 76.

other-worldly values, however, he may enjoy less tactical freedom in drafting his ethic of participatory violence than others—Marxists, existentialists, or positivists—whose ultimate goals reside totally within history. Therefore, it is perhaps delusory for Christians, while remaining faithful to their own ethic, to imagine that they can achieve as high a degree of political efficiency in revolutionary situations as do Marxists. Particularly in the short term (let us say, one, three, or five years), Christians may be strategically "handicapped." When one conducts guerrilla operations, notwithstanding the high moral plane on which he justifies all his acts, he may sometimes find it debilitating to entertain moral scruples about killing "innocent" people or weighing too diligently the consequences of a destructive course of action. More than others, Christians are required to obey the logic described by Camus: "Does the end justify the means? That is possible. But what will justify the end? To that question, which historical thought leaves pending, rebellion replies: the means." [17] Participation in revolutionary violence places the Christian actor in a fundamentally ambiguous posture, in a veritable "ethics-of-distress situation." In such a situation, unless one bears heroic witness to absolute love and nonviolence, he cannot avoid making moral compromises regardless of which course he adopts. This dilemma causes moral distress in him. There are, accordingly, many possible expressions of a responsible, free, authentic Christian ethic. One particular form of the ethic of commitment to social justice leads Camilo Torres to take part in guerrilla warfare. Or it leads Bishop Helder Câmara of Recife in Northeast Brazil to preach social revolution through non-violent means.

Although fewer constraints on a revolutionary's choice of means and tactical modes flow from the inner logic of Marxist ethics than from Christian ethics, these very constraints may prove to be a long-term blessing. Whatever be the tensions under which a Christian revolutionary (or anyone professing allegiance to trans-historical goals) must perforce operate, his own faith forces him to accept limits. He must respect the inviolability of the human person and the supremacy of the means in the combat, and accept the risk of failure. In the long run, says Camus, "that is the only attitude that is efficacious today." [18] This apparent paradox need not dismay Christians inasmuch as they profess to believe Christ's words: "unless the grain of wheat fall to the ground and die, it cannot bear fruit." It may well be true that in political life, as much as in personal spiritual endeavor, the pursuit of

[17] Camus, *The Rebel,* p. 292.
[18] *Idem.,* p. 292.

310

justice is ultimately more efficacious than Machiavellian expediency.[19]

It is illusory to think that there exists a Christian ethic of revolution; there are only multiple attempts by Christians to interpret complex issues in ethical terms. Many such efforts have foundered on the shoals of the "just war" theory. According to this doctrine, a war is just if it meets the following criteria:

(a) War must be declared by legitimate authority.

(b) The cause must be just. This has usually been interpreted to mean self-defense or helping a beleaguered ally under attack.

(c) Leaders waging war must preserve a right intention. Their goal must remain peace, not war; reconciliation, not vengeance; equity, not conquest.

(d) Only lawful means are permitted. That is, means must be morally indifferent or inherently good. This criterion urges moderation in destruction and advocates "proportionality" between damage inflicted and benefits obtained. The principle of licit means obviously assumes some operational difference between combatants and noncombatants, and knowledge of what constitutes a good or bad instrument of violence.[20]

These principles were revised some years ago to fit revolutionary situations in Latin America. Thus adapted, the code reads as follows:

(a) It must be certain that legitimate authority has lost its mission —that is, become tyrannical or incapable of administering the common good.

(b) All peaceful means must be exhausted before revolutionary violence is lawful.

(c) Revolution's anticipated "good" effects must outweigh the harm it causes.

(d) Revolutionary leaders must entertain reasonable hope of success.

(e) No intrinsically evil means can be employed.

(f) It is forbidden to exacerbate the pre-revolutionary situation in order to precipitate the outbreak of violence.[21]

I shall not here undertake to refute this teaching point by point, but these criteria, even refurbished to apply to revolution, overlook cer-

---

[19] This is the theme of Jacques Maritain, "The End of Machiavellianism," *The Range of Reason* (Charles Scribner's Sons, 1953), pp. 134–165.

[20] This summary of the "just war" theory is drawn from P. R. Regamey, *La Conscience Chrétienne et la Guerre* (Cahiers Saint-Jacques, n.d.), pp. 31–40.

[21] Based on Gerardo Claps Gallo, "El Cristiano Frente a la Revolución Violenta," *Mensaje,* No. 115 (1963), p. 142.

tain hard political realities. Let us take the first principle: Who will judge whether or not legitimate authority has lost its mission? A majority of voters? But what if voters represent only a minority of citizens? A revolutionary party composed of a tiny minority? Who has given it a mandate to speak for the body politic? The masses? A particular class? Through what mechanism can this judgment be tested, according to what rules?

As for exhausting all peaceful means, the second principle, what does a budding revolutionary group do if it expects to be wiped out unless it conceals its opposition to the ruling elite until it is ready to engage in combat at a propitious strategic moment? And who can predict a revolution's possible "good" or "bad" effects? How does one gauge a "reasonable" prospect of success? Several competing revolutionary groups in Angola[22] have now been fighting the Portuguese for ten years, and victory still seems far off. Nevertheless, if we are to believe Ho Chi Minh, the revolutionary who perseveres to the end is certain to win. Indeed, it took the Algerians many years to win their own battle.

Why belabor the point? The "just war" theory fails to come to grips with the psychological and political realities of revolutionary situations; it is worthless.

What of some Christian form of situation ethics? At first glance, there seems to be much to recommend this approach: it is quite often hardheaded. But it provides no norms other than purely subjective ones for evaluating objective situations. Nevertheless, a man's ideology, class interests, occupational bias, heredity, and environmental conditioning, to say nothing of his personality characteristics, go far toward inclining him to violence or non-violence. Can social conscience truly be formed, therefore, if the ultimate appeal is to subjective persuasion? At best, the direction such a position can take is that of moral ambiguity. Niebuhr correctly stated in 1932 that "the struggle for social justice in the present economic order involves the assertion of rights, the rights of the disinherited, and the use of coercion. Both are incompatible with the pure love ethic found in the Gospels. How, then, do we justify the strategy of the 'class struggle'? We simply cannot do so in purely Christian terms. There is in the absolute sense no such thing as 'Christian socialism.' " [23]

[22] For one view, cf. John A. Marcum, "Three Revolutions," *Africa Report,* November 1967, pp. 8–23.

[23] Reinhold Niebuhr, "The Ethic of Jesus and the Social Problem," *Contemporary Moral Issues,* ed. Harry K. Girvetz (Wadsworth, 1963), p. 315.

The Gospels contain no ethic of the *status quo* and no ethic of revolution. All ethical positions taken by men in their personal life, as in political affairs, compromise Jesus' "pure love principle." Yet there is no need to assume that pure love is meant to be an ethical norm. Christianity urges the dynamics of love, but love's demands cannot adequately be expressed either in juridical or in ethical terms. Jesus advocates love of enemies, eschatological hope in God's defense of the victimized, the sacrifice of one's rights for the sake of brotherhood, not as *moral laws* but as a *spiritual ideal* which will constantly thrust us *beyond ethics* and beyond the "realistic" dictates of political or personal wisdom. The worst moral distress for a Christian is, indeed, to be forced to recur to violence in his defense of important human values. Distress means that he is not free to work on behalf of love without, at least tentatively and temporarily, professing his impotence to love, to forgive, or to transmute his earthly despair into eschatological hope. It is no weakness of Christianity or bankruptcy of the Gospel that breeds this distress; it is man's condition in history. Were man more than human, he could create goodness, justice, and freedom for all men without having to destroy these values in those he calls enemies, perhaps even in himself. If revolutionaries did not live in history, they could "free the present from the past." Yet, destruction never leaves the destroyer unscarred and free to build anew with a blithe heart and a clear conscience. Like ecclesiastics and politicians, revolutionaries cannot avoid compromises. I. F. Stone warns that "for the Revolution, as for the Church, the world is full of snares and pitfalls: the unavoidable minimum of intercourse with things-as-they-are, the need for trade to earn one's bread . . . and the logic of statecraft which demands weapons, technology, compromise and duplicity. With the assumption of temporal power, the Revolution, like the Church, enters into a state of sin." [24]

Revolutionary situations place men in an ethical dilemma whose only issues are heroism or compromise. One may, of course, try to escape distress by fleeing reality or by abdicating ethics, but these are pseudo-solutions. Nevertheless, even the man who cannot rise to heroism is morally obliged to avoid escapism; and if he wishes to be moral, he can never resign himself either to the determinisms of violence or to the passive complicities of non-violence. Neither violence nor non-violence can be absolute; total non-violence is connivance

[24] I. F. Stone, "The Legacy of Che Guevara," *Ramparts,* December 1967, p. 21.

with the violence of exploiters, whereas total violence is the rationalization of evil and the absolutization of history's relative values.

The Travail of Marxist Ethics

As far back as 1850 Engels wrote that "the worst thing that can befall a leader of an extreme party is to be compelled to take over a government in an epoch when the movement is not yet ripe for the domination of the class which he represents, and for the realization of the measures which that domination implies. What he *can* do depends not upon his will but upon the degree of contradiction between various classes, and upon the level of development of the material means of existence, of the conditions of production and commerce upon which class contradictions always repose. What he *ought* to do, what his party demands of him, again depends not upon him or the stage of development of the class struggle and its conditions. . . . Thus he necessarily finds himself in an unsolvable dilemma. What he *can* do contradicts all his previous actions, principles, and the immediate interests of his party, and what he *ought* to do cannot be done. In a word, he is compelled to advance the interests of an alien class, and to feed his own class with phrases and promises, and the asseveration that the interests of that alien class are its own interests. Whoever is put into this awkward position is irrevocably lost." [25]

As sadly as any purist Christian, Engels laments the betrayal, not of Gospel love, but of proper class interests. Like contemporary Christians, he sees his elite in the grip of an insoluble ethical dilemma. Along with Ellul, Engels defines political ethics as a function of time, the moment in the history of class struggle, and not of right objectives or lofty and sincere personal goals. Reluctantly he concedes that revolutionary leaders must lie and manipulate men. "Whoever is put into this awkward position is irrevocably lost!"

Marx in turn regarded violence as an historical necessity flowing from class structures; its use posed no special problem of principle. Yet Marx did not state clearly which principles of action ought to inform working-class ethics. His second great omission, in the words of Alasdair MacIntyre, concerns "the morality of socialist and com-

[25] Friedrich Engels, "The Peasant War in Germany," in Lewis S. Feuer, ed., *Marx and Engels: Basic Writings on Politics and Philosophy* (Anchor Books, 1959), p. 435.

munist society. He does indeed speak in at least one passage as though communism will be an embodiment of the Kantian kingdom of ends. But he is at best allusive on this topic. The consequence of these two related omissions is that Marx left later Marxists room for interpolation on this point. What he could not have foreseen is what would be interpolated." [26] Bernstein, believing that socialism could not arrive in the near future, tried to restore an absolute Kantian type of labor-class morality. Nevertheless, Kautsky condemned Bernstein's appeal to a categorical imperative as a regression to precisely the kind of abstract morality above class and above society which Marx had tried to eliminate. His own solution, however, proved little more than crude utilitarianism.

More recently, the special problems arising in Marxist revolutionary societies have compounded the confusion which prevails among Marxist ethical thinkers. Times have indeed changed. There is something anachronistic in much revolutionary rhetoric; the hard realities are very different from revolutionary clichés. How does one create new managerial and scientific cadres to replace old oligarchies and foreign personnel? How will revolutionaries in power inspire and organize the hard work of an illiterate mass over many hungry years? As I. F. Stone puts it, "For after the music of Revolution dies down, everybody still has to go to work." [27] Even if one concedes that the goal of guerrilla warfare is the conquest of political power, what does one do with political power after his revolution is successful? Is the successful revolutionary inevitably trapped, as Engels feared, by the objective conditions of history's moment?

The history of successful revolutions does not leave one very optimistic as to the genuine possibility that revolutionary governments can maintain an open-ended attitude toward the future. The mobilization of the oppressed by the use of a pedagogy whose central themes are class struggle and the suppression of exploiters almost unavoidably elicits, engenders, or reinforces simplistic allegiances to a dogmatic utopianism ill-prepared to be self-corrective after power has been gained. Mannheim alludes to the dangers of requiring men to draw a blank check on their future:

"The dangerous fallacy in the communist argument is that its champions promise to pay for every inch of lost freedom in the inter-

[26] Alasdair MacIntyre, *A Short History of Ethics* (MacMillan Company, 1966), p. 214.
[27] Stone, *op. cit.,* p. 21.

315

mediary period of dictatorship with an undated check on a better future. . . . Once a dictatorial system, whatever its social content, seizes the educational apparatus, it does everything to obliterate the memory and need of free thought and free living; it does its utmost to transform free institutions into tools of a minority." [28]

To this day, Djilas' query about means and ends has not been met satisfactorily by Marxists. The Communist "leading edge"—Garaudy, Althusser, Adam Schaff, Ernst Fischer, Machovek, and others— welcomes dialogue. Some Communist thinkers have even debated the possibility, in Marxist terms, of dissociating religious alienation from social alienation. And Kolakowski makes a valiant attempt to over-come the dilemma by professing "the doctrine of total responsibility of the individual for his deeds and of the amorality of the historical process. In the latter we avail ourselves of Hegel; in the former of Descartes." [29] By and large, however, Marxist ethics remain in a state of disarray and raises more questions than it can answer. China's cultural revolution, in particular, seriously undermines the assumption of all revolutionaries since 1789—namely, that a radical act of violence will burst open the door to a better society. In the words of one editorialist (*The Economist,* January 14, 1967, p. 99); "It is this belief that Chairman Mao has now finally and perhaps decisively put in doubt. . . . What is needed, and what he has set himself to achieve, is perpetual revolution—to be precise, a regular succession of up-heavals, following each other at intervals of a generation or less. He believes that nothing short of this will keep the original revolutionary impetus alive." Yet Mao is accused of heresy by the Holy Office of Marxist orthodoxy and he is challenged within China itself by many of his old Yenan revolutionary comrades. Even if Mao is proved right, as is quite possible,[30] why should downtrodden men sacrifice their all for a revolution that itself needs to be discarded every fifteen years?

[28] Karl Mannheim, *Freedom, Power and Democratic Planning* (London: Routledge & Kegan Paul, 1951), p. 28.

[29] Leszek Kolakowski, *Toward a Marxist Humanism* (Grove Press, 1968), p. 141.

[30] Cf. "Comments by Michel Oksenberg" in *China in Crisis,* ed. Ping-Ti Ho and Tang Tsou, Vol. I, Book 2 (University of Chicago Press, 1968), p. 496: "Second, it is possible that if Mao even partially succeeds, historians will record the years 1965–67 in China as a period of high social mobility, when the gains of the revolution were consolidated and when a young elite educated under Communist rule began to shape the nation's modernization effort. If this young elite, steeled in the turmoil fostered by Mao, remains committed to such values as self-sacrifice, national achievement, and individual initiative, the effects of the Cultural Revolution may yet prove to be compatible to the demands of industrialization."

Can an unending *remise en question* become a permanent way of life for a whole nation?

The present travail of Marxist revolutionary ethics is merely a symptom that ancient doctrinal certitudes are being eroded by the relativities of political life. Even wily old Togliatti, leader of the Italian Communist Party, complained before his death that Communists were incapable of recognizing the new forms of alienation they had generated in their own societies.

The Moral Stance of Revolutionaries in the United States

Underdevelopment is a chronic state of violence. This is the reason why the adoption of a gradualist path to social improvement may entail much complicity with violence. Revolutions also lead to violence. The first form of violence is expressed in inhumanly high birth and death rates, degrading poverty, ignorance, and non-participation in significant decisions affecting the lives of countless men. Support given to a more visible and militant form of violence, revolutionary activity, likewise involves the loss of life. It may, nonetheless, prove to be a more ethically sound position than passive complicity in privilege structures which perpetuate injustice and that impersonal, anonymous, and disguised form of violence known as underdevelopment. The problem needs to be diagnosed in terms of a choice not between violence and non-violence—since even the non-violent position allows violence to exist—but between different kinds of violence and different degrees of human complicity with it. "Developed" observers tend to argue that violence is too high a price to pay to obtain development. What they choose to ignore is the high price paid by underdeveloped peoples to remain underdeveloped.

Industrialized countries need to revise their policies *vis-à-vis* social revolutions in other lands, perhaps even in their own. The United States has been singularly deficient in its attitude toward radical change elsewhere. Its chief official aim has been to maintain intact global interests incompatible with indigenous reform and development efforts in much of the Third World. Conceptual rigidity at home, allied to a Manichaean view of social systems in conflict, has reinforced the good conscience of Americans and confirmed their desire to "domesticate" the world's development efforts. Despite critics within the nation, the United States has officially rejected the proposition that its own posture is an important ingredient of the underdevelopment problems in the world. Consequently, it is unrealistic to expect significant change in U.S. dealings with the Third World unless its own internal values are themselves revolutionized. The nation's response to its own internal value crises, however—to anti-war dissent, to claims of blacks for genuine self-determination, to regional and sectorial poverty in the midst of affluence—has been crude and inflexible.

Consequently, there is little ground for optimism regarding a new vision of revolution elsewhere. Nevertheless, the U.S. does badly need a new policy toward revolution abroad. Heilbroner has argued that the only constructive course to follow "is a policy of neutrality toward the revolutionary movement—though not ceasing to differentiate between revolutionary regimes that we can actively support and those that we cannot. Such a policy . . . would call for an immediate halt to military aid to reactionary regimes and for a cessation of clandestine activity against revolutionary movements. Second, it would require an acceptance of some form of revolutionary nationalist social-ism as the political and economic order most suited to guide many developing nations in their desperately hard initial stages of change. Third, it would permit the continuation of humanitarian programs of food and medical aid, as well as technical assistance of a non-military kind, for all governments, revolutionary or not, provided that reasonable standards of international behavior were met." [31]

Among the reasons why it is so difficult to induce change in the United States is the wide acceptance of the view that change must be peaceful in order to be legitimate. This is an indefensible attitude when it is recalled that the "humanistic" values of liberty, equality, and respect for persons have been won at the cost of brutally violent social upheavals in Western societies themselves. Harvard historian Barrington Moore rejects the placid view of history: "For a Western scholar to say a good word on behalf of revolutionary radicalism is not easy because it runs counter to deeply grooved mental reflexes. The assumption that gradual and piecemeal reform has demonstrated its superiority over violent revolution as a way to advance human freedom is so pervasive that even to question such an assumption seems strange. In closing this book I should like to draw attention for

[31] Robert L. Heilbroner, "Making a Rational Foreign Policy Now," *Harper's,* September 1968, p. 70.

the last time to what the evidence from the comparative history of modernization may tell us about this issue. As I have reluctantly come to read this evidence, the costs of moderation have been at least as atrocious as those of revolution, perhaps a great deal more.

"Fairness demands recognition of the fact that the way nearly all of history has been written imposes an overwhelming bias against revolutionary violence. Indeed the bias becomes horrifying as one comes to realize its depth. To equate the violence of those who resist oppression with the violence of the oppressors would be misleading enough. But there is a great deal more. From the days of Spartacus through Robespierre down to the present day, the use of force by the oppressed against their former masters has been the object of nearly universal condemnation. Meanwhile the day-to-day repression of 'normal' society hovers dimly in the background of most history books." [32] The Third World can achieve social justice and development without major violence only if "developed" countries freely relinquish their privilege and domination. Since this is unlikely to happen, it is hypocritical for the developed world to stifle social revolution in the Third World, or to exploit indigenous revolutionary forces for the sake of ideological victories in the Cold War. Advanced countries fear to allow "underdeveloped" nations to develop on their own terms lest the moral bankruptcy of their own vaunted development be bared to the world. This fear explains the need felt by developed countries, capitalist and communist alike, to "domesticate" development efforts throughout the world in subordination to their own interests.

Without romanticizing revolutionary violence, one can acknowledge its capacity for institution-building. Camilo Torres describes how years of *"la violencia"* in Colombia radically transformed the social institutions of rural inhabitants: "We can say that violence has constituted the most important socio-cultural change in Colombia's peasant localities since the Spanish conquest. Through the agency of violence, rural communities have been integrated to a process of urbanization in the sociological sense, with all the elements which this implies: division of labor, specialization, socio-cultural contacts, socialization, mental receptivity to change, the awakening of social expectations and the utilization of methods of action for the purpose of achieving social mobility through channels not provided by existing structures." Furthermore, violence has established the systems which are neces-

[32] Barrington Moore, Jr., *op. cit.*, p. 505.

sary for structuring a rural sub-culture, a peasant class, and a pressure group made up of this same class and having a revolutionary character. Torres concludes, however, that "violence has brought all these changes about through pathological channels and disharmoniously with respect to the process of the country's economic development." [33]

One obtains much the same picture as he examines revolution in Algeria, Viet Nam, China in the days of the Long March, or Cuba. Whatever be one's allegiances regarding revolutionary movements, one fact is undeniable: these movements are a powerful tool for re-structuring societies in many of the patterns allegedly required for "modernization" or "development." But the United States must do more than simply alter its attitude toward revolutions within the Third World: it must create domestic conditions allowing native revolution-aries to solve their ethical dilemmas.[34]

Many of the well-known general criteria of a pre-revolutionary sit-uation exist in the United States. Large numbers of citizens seek to change the country's basic institutions; they despair of obtaining these changes through legal channels; they are sufficiently organized to con-stitute a political force; they are actively accelerating the polarization of opinion without which revolutions cannot get off the ground; and there is a hardening of resistance in the face of these demands.

There are two kinds of revolutionary consciousness in the United States: that of blacks and that of youthful white radicals. Black revo-lutionary consciousness is very similar to that of the Third World. American blacks are conscious of being economically and politically exploited by privileged groups and they know that others enjoy a dis-proportionate share of the rewards yielded by social effort. What is worse, their self-esteem and dignity have been crushed. It is not sur-prising, therefore, that black militants find in the writings of anti-colonialist spokesmen like Fanon and Ho Chi Minh rich fodder for a "pedagogy of the oppressed" suited to their needs. And Malcolm X has formulated a political rationale for the stirrings of the black soul. By moving the debate from the arena of "civil" to that of "human" rights, and by liberating black self-expression from the "domes-

---

[33] Camilo Torres, "La Violencia y los Cambios Socio-Culturales en las Areas Rurales Colombianas," in *Camilo Torres,* Collection *Sondeos* No. 5 (Cuernavaca CIDOC, 1966), p. 174. Further details on the institution-building role of "la violencia" are found in Orlando Fals Borda, *Subversion and Social Change in Colombia* (Columbia University Press, 1969), *passim.*

[34] The following paragraphs are based on Denis Goulet, "The Troubled Conscience of the Revolutionary," *The Center Magazine,* May 1969, pp. 43–50.

ticated" vocabulary of religion (Christianity and Islam), Malcolm invested his people with the mantle of champions of universal justice. He ripped off the masks behind which an innocent society basked in its good conscience. After Malcolm, whose diagnosis of U.S. society as racist was later confirmed by the Presidential Commission's Report on Civil Disorders, whites can no longer dismiss the voices of James Baldwin, LeRoi Jones, and Stokely Carmichael as mere strident, raucous irrationality. By exposing the pathology of American society to public view, Malcolm has provided legitimacy to the counterpathology of Black Power on grounds of homeopathy.

The black revolutionary is almost a pure type of Camus' universal rebel. His rebellion is aimed at one who, until now, was incapable of even entertaining the notion that he was an oppressor. The ethical dilemmas black revolutionaries must face have been spelled out above. They must decide for which cause they will compromise, and trace out the lines beyond which they cannot compromise. The cause is clear: liberation of the black man. Nevertheless, debate continues around the form liberation shall take: a separate state, a nation within a state, or some other model. The instrumental boundaries, too, are fuzzy: Martin Luther King's means are not those of Eldridge Cleaver. Notwithstanding deep and bitter divisions among black groups, however, advocates of non-violence and of violence increasingly acknowledge one another as "brothers." The boundary question is largely a domestic one among blacks and offers scant leverage to hostile whites desirous of exploiting internal differences among blacks to their own advantage.

The revolutionary consciousness of young white radicals is different. Unlike anti-colonialists or oppressed groups in underdeveloped lands, white U.S. radicals are a privileged group thrashing out against an impersonal enemy which robs them of their very being. White radical students share with black dissidents, it is true, a sense of powerlessness over their own destiny, since they are alienated from substantive decision-making affecting their own activities and aspirations. In this respect at least, their grievances are like those of blacks. Nonetheless, the basic complaint of white revolutionaries is different. They rebel, not because they are deprived, but because of what their exploiters wish to share with them. In this sense, theirs is a metaphysical revolt: a profound rejection of what is because it chokes off what can be. It is not its past or its present that radical youth contests, but its future. More precisely, it says a resounding "No" to the future which society is preparing for it. Its revolutionary consciousness is no doubt profoundly sensitive to the ethical injustice of racism, poverty, war, underdevelopment. But, above all, youth is discovering that it has been declared the heir of a social fortune it does not want. This discovery has been made at the murky level of self-identity and its central message is that men are being trodden underfoot not by having too little, but by having too much. To use Erich Fromm's phrase, American youth has learned that "affluent alienation" can be as dehumanizing as "impoverished alienation." The cause of that alienation is the irrationality of a total system each of whose parts is supremely rational. The only posture of self-defense left is revulsion: to spit out the whole rotten mess. Ultimately, it may prove irrational to be a radical revolutionary in the U.S. But this is no deterrent, since it is also irrational *not* to be a revolutionary! All depends on the matrix of rationality from which one draws his images of where reason stops and where will picks up. To some extent, every revolution is fiercely voluntaristic. But in a very special sense the revolution of U.S. youth is structurally voluntaristic: will is the only instrument it has left with which to challenge the Molochian voracity of a system which is exasperatingly "rational."

Although it is true, as many observers remark, that it is a revolution of bored men (*acedia* now becomes a sociological category!), I do not believe that this is its most essential note. It is, above all, a guilt-laden revolt, because rebels can ordinarily relate their own privations to those suffered by all the underprivileged in time (history) and space (the contemporary world). Today's American youth, however, is an envied and privileged minority. This is why nothing so painfully galls a white radical as to be told by black militants that "you can afford to be against the system, because you're living off it." The very suggestion that a revolutionary is parasitical is a blow to one who seeks identification with a class which has always challenged the right of exploiters to be parasitical. The young, of course, deny that they are parasites. And in some mysteriously deep way they are right: it is those who are most "productive" in society who are the parasites, those who live off the "capital" of Western society's residual Greek wisdom, Christian personalism, and Enlightenment rationality.

Nevertheless, youthful white radicals in the United States suffer from unconscious guilt over the fact that they cannot visibly assume before the world the posture of economic self-sufficiency. It is indeed humiliating for revolutionaries to have to depend on Daddy's money or on friends within the system to pay the bills. This is true even if in most cases their revolutionary activity is confined to their student years. U.S. revolutionaries could enjoy the sympathy of numerous groups throughout the world who also have a stake in the success of internal revolution in the United States. This potential foreign support is ambivalent, however, because serious disruption of the U.S. system could lead to military adventurism whose chief victims might be other nations.

It is sometimes imagined that the U.S. is a powerful and sophisticated social system with no vulnerable nerve centers, points of weakness which could collapse in the face of a relatively minor assault and lead to disruption of larger parts of the system. Whatever may be the outward appearances of strength, the American Goliath has feet of clay. One needs only to recall the chaos produced in New York City by the "blackout." To this day, the precise cause of the power failure has not been determined. And it could happen again! Another sign of vulnerability, trivial perhaps but suggestive nonetheless, is the incapacity of the New York Stock Exchange to handle its voluminous paperwork except by closing down periodically for a few days in order to "catch up." Besides, as bank clearing operations and innumerable other procedures vital to the system become increasingly centralized and computerized, the possibility grows that a well-planned tactical assault—conducted by men having intimate knowledge of computers and information-processing—on such a "nerve center" could produce the kind of disarray on which revolutions thrive. One need not suppose, therefore, that revolution could succeed in the U.S. only "by accident" or thanks to a serendipitous random stroke of guerrilla genius. Thus far the main factor operating in favor of the social system has been the profound immaturity of the revolutionaries themselves.

It is puerile to call for power and confrontation when what is needed is a politico-technological equivalent of guerrilla warfare. Confrontation and shouted demands for power are calculated to evoke responses at precisely those points where the establishment is strongest. There is nothing startling, however, about the inability of U.S. revolutionary groups to devise a valid indigenous formula of action. This has been the common difficulty faced by most revolutionary groups. Mao nearly lost his entire army before learning the lesson that an "orthodox" popular front with the nationalist Kuomintang was unworkable. Even Guevara made the mistake of thinking he could export Cuba to Bolivia. It is out of desperation that U.S. revolutionists have looked to foreign models. They have yet to find their own; and unless they do, they are easy game. The wielders of legitimacy in this country unconsciously grasp this, I believe. One wonders whether they truly consider dissent and obstruction to be a serious threat to the foundations of American political and social institutions. Establishment spokesmen no doubt warn against the dangers posed by "guerrilla warfare" on campuses. But the question remains: do they fear that the whole house of cards will come tumbling down, or simply that their own role in the game is under assault? The question remains open. The purpose of these pages is not to diagnose or prognosticate, however, but to analyze the ethical dilemma faced by white revolutionaries in the United States.

Generally speaking, they are unable to answer the two crucial questions: for what cause will they compromise, and where do they draw the line beyond which they will not compromise? By their own admission, the cause has not been defined: it must be born through the process itself. Furthermore, most young radicals refuse to draw a line, because they wish to be purists. There is a noble logic to their demand for absolute purity: they have too often seen revolutionary objectives pulverized in the mill of accommodation. And they simply reject the idea that one must get his moral hands dirty. In every combat, it is true, evil creeps in, but the only respectable human decision is to refuse all compromise in advance. When one decides to keep his hands clean, he will resist being swept along by the tide of circumstances and will constantly weigh, before every choice, the degree of corruption it entails. Yet many young revolutionaries are purists as regards concessions to the "system" while remaining pathetically naïve about the compromises demanded by their own revolutionary posture. But one simply cannot dismiss the possibility that Sartre may be right and that it is in fact impossible for a revolutionary to keep his hands clean. The reason is that counter-power corrupts quite as much as power itself. And it may even corrupt absolutely!

Italian author Guido Piovene once compared the United States to a huge digestive system. All kinds of abrasives can be introduced into it. But, like the oyster, it has an infinite capacity to secrete social gastric juices which transform the rough stones of dissent into smooth pearls of conformity. If this is true or even half true, American revolutionists face an impossible task. Pre-emption or co-option may turn out to be their ineluctable destiny. Whether they reject the system, drop out of it, or fight it to the death, they will be making useful contributions to its functioning. Their only role would then be to manifest to the world the troubled conscience of revolutionaries—and of counter-revolutionaries!

No honest man can feel very secure about communicating moral enlightenment to others regarding the ethical dimensions of revolution. The advice given by Domenach deserves to be heeded: "Carry on your revolution if you wish: in the extreme case, wage your war if you wish. But stop preaching someone else's war. When the moment comes to take up guns, then let the intellectual resort to arms, but not to words which place bullets inside guns at a distance! . . . What weight can we give to the bad conscience which preaches peace and justice without forging the means to establish them?" [35]

Regardless of the ethical strategy adopted, one is ceaselessly haunted by Camus' words: "Violence is at the same time unavoidable and unjustifiable." [36] This is why revolution as a strategy for development leads to dilemma. In developed and underdeveloped settings alike, it places moral agents in distress.

[35] Jean-Marie Domenach, "Un Monde de Violence," in *Violence, Recherches et Débats* (Paris: Desclée de Brouwer, 1967), p. 37.

[36] Albert Camus, "Réponse à E. d'Astier" in *Actuelles I* (Paris: Editions de la Pléiade), II, 355, cited in Thomas Merton, "Terror and the Absurd: Violence and Non-Violence in Albert Camus," August 1966, *mimeo*, p. 23.

CONCLUSION

The Cruel Choice

Development processes are both cruel and necessary. They are necessary because all societies must come to terms with new aspirations and irresistible social forces. Yet the choices they face are cruel because development's benefits are obtained only at a great price and because, on balance, it is far from certain that achieving development's benefits makes men happier or freer.

Moreover, development has always been and remains a harsh process. While it was developing, England experienced proletarian agonies, colonialist expansion, and wars over trade. The United States, in turn, underwent labor violence, immigrant sufferings, slavery, Civil War, the annihilation of native populations, and economic depression. Even today, after development has supposedly been won, the nation is prey to widespread social alienation. Development in the Soviet Union has likewise exacted heavy tribute in the form of massive purges, ideological coercion on a grand scale, rigorous compression of consumer demands, and troubled foreign policy.[1] Yet the options faced by today's low-income countries are even more cruel. Leaders endure schizophrenic cultural tensions and proud nations are thrust into a humiliating dependence on foreign economic and political agents. Neutral countries are propelled against their will onto the Cold War stage, helpless to chart their destinies because others, stronger

[1] On the last point, cf. Alexander Gershenkron, *Economic Backwardness in Historical Perspective* (Harvard University Press, 1962), ch. 6.

than they, will brook no alteration in the strategic balance of power.

As income gaps between rich and poor widen, as debt-servicing becomes ever more onerous to the Third World, and as the fabric of internal politics is everywhere rent by further conflicts, it becomes manifest that development choices are indeed cruel. This is so precisely because the demand for development's benefits cannot be silenced. There are, says W. Arthur Lewis, two reasons for this: death control takes place more quickly than birth control, and consumer wants multiply faster than productive capacities.[2] Indian economist Jagdish Bhagwati adduces several other reasons why "the need for a higher growth rate in the underdeveloped areas has become inescapable." [3] The imagination of the Third World has been aroused by the rapid entry of the Soviet Union into Great Power status. Ex-colonies seek equal status with politically mature nations and know that demands must be backed up by economic muscle. And nationalist sentiment seeks to nourish itself internally with visible development gains. Finally, political and humanitarian reasons dictate that the world at large give at least lip-service to the cause of development for all.

The major task faced by developers everywhere is to fashion institutions which will allow men to transform their drive for economic and social development into a liberating enterprise. This implies, of course, that the benefits of development are often obtained in a manner which is alienating rather than liberating. At the global level the needs of all men must be met according to a twofold order of priorities—of urgency and of importance. I have insisted throughout this book that first priority must go to the satisfaction of life-sustenance needs for all, the second to providing goods which enhance human expression and creativity, and the third to luxury goods. Other central development goals are the creation of world solidarity without domination, the fostering of cultural diversity and ecological health, and the assertion of human freedom in the face of multiple determinisms generated by economic and technological processes. Although many development problems must ultimately be solved on a planetary scale, it is no less necessary to find appropriate strategies for application within diverse types of developed and underdeveloped nations, as well as for the conduct of trans-national exchanges of goods,

---

[2] W. Arthur Lewis, *The Theory of Economic Growth* (Richard D. Irwin, 1955), final chapter. Reproduced in B. Okun and R. W. Richardson, eds., *Studies in Economic Development* (Holt, Rinehart & Winston, 1962), p. 490.

[3] Jagdish Bhagwati, *The Economics of Underdeveloped Countries* (McGraw-Hill, 1966), p. 35.

of information, and of personnel.

Reflection on the dynamics of world development resurrects in dramatic fashion and on an unprecedented scale ancient questions about the good life and the good society. It is the differential ability of societies, classes, and interest groups to master the forces that affect them which gives rise to the concept of "vulnerability" as the key to understanding underdevelopment and promoting development. This is why stronger partners in relationships must be led or forced to offset the structural vulnerability of weaker interlocutors by being themselves rendered politically, economically, and culturally vulnerable. The object is to create conditions favorable to reciprocity, the only valid basis for cooperation in a non-manipulative mode. Only thus can the shock of underdevelopment be overcome and conditions conducive to the achievement of professed goals established. In the present book I have attempted to identify certain broad goals common to all development efforts: increased life-sustenance, esteem, and freedom for all. I have also delineated, in tentative fashion, some governing principles and general requirements of ethical strategies in development. Three such principles are the subordination of goods to the good, the universalization of solidarity through conflict, and optimum sharing by the populace in decision-making. These normative principles can neutralize the tendency of planners to reach decisions in an elitist manner. As illustrations of how specific criteria might work, I have outlined strategies for non-elitist planning, worldwide technical cooperation, and induced value change.

Current patterns of development thinking have been sharply criticized on the grounds that genuine development is neither mere mass-consumption nor impersonal technological efficiency, but rather a new cultural dynamism characterized by men's mastery over their acquisitive desires in a regime of austerity where this is necessary, of abundance where this is possible. Cultural diversity and ecological health must also be actively defended. A number of far-reaching structural changes have been advocated as necessary to the creation of new patterns of development. Among these are a world plan, global development financing, a world technical pool, and a new pedagogy of values for developed countries. Most important of all, the cultural revolution needed in underdeveloped countries cannot bear fruit unless a cultural revolution also takes place within developed countries. Otherwise, structural obstacles to world development will be kept in place by those in power, who will continue to domesticate the Third World.

328

Nevertheless, the desired changes are unattainable except over long periods of time and after much conflict. Furthermore, no single revolutionary program or series of programs can prove adequate to the problem. Therefore, many such changes must proceed by incremental steps. There is a basic qualitative difference, however, between palliative incrementalism and gradualism which creates new possibilities. Some of the criteria for distinguishing creative from patchwork solutions to social problems have been outlined. My conclusion is that to accept palliatives is to court disaster. The difficulty arises from the fact that the required changes go too deep: it will not do simply to improve the present mechanisms of development planning or technical assistance. Nevertheless, these changes are unlikely to occur quickly—innumerable political and psychological obstacles stand in the way. Consequently, certain measures—which may appear to be palliatives but are not—appear necessary. Under certain conditions, however, described in Chapter Twelve, such incremental measures may help create new possibilities and prove acceptable. The crucial point is to distinguish creative steps from palliatives which delude people into thinking problems have been met when in fact they have only been disguised. It has nonetheless been recognized that incremental steps are often not enough. This opens the doors of possibility to violent revolution. An attempt is made in the final chapter to characterize the nature of ethical dilemmas posed by revolutionary conditions. The conclusion is reached that violence in some form is inevitable, but that no appeal to historical determinism can justify abdicating moral responsibility. Furthermore, complicity with evil and violence is the common temptation faced by gradualists and revolutionists alike.

The normative strategies recommended in this work open up new possibilities. They tend, taken singly and cumulatively, to render possible the kind of international, national, regional, and local structures required for authentic development. In this category are such measures as the establishment of world planning and financing, ecological control agencies, new procedures for inducing value change, the establishment of a trans-national corps of developers, and the institution of large-scale voluntary austerity within developed areas so as to render imposed austerity more palatable to underdeveloped societies.

As explained earlier, the term "ethics" when used in a context of development, refers to the degree of freedom and responsibility men can conquer in the face of worldwide ecological, symbolic, and social forces which exercise strong deterministic pressures. Two basic ethical questions have been raised: what *kind* of development is human? and *how* must such development be obtained? The major ethical issue is how to achieve development's authentic benefits without destroying, in the process, men's capacity to act freely. Because it is rooted in contemporary history, which is dominated by mass technology and global interdependence, development ethics can impose neither a utopia nor a "contented cow" society. Rather, it must accept endless risk-taking and a maximum commitment to liberation of the oppressed and responsibility for all. François Perroux rightly terms world development a "grand design." But who can bring grandeur to the designers themselves? Neither specialists nor an army of juxtaposed specialists can do so. Wisdom can come only from "the people." Moreover, the aspiring generalist who does not gain his wisdom through the *praxis* of dialectical historical experience is doomed to fail. Development is both a dialectical process and an ambiguous adventure. In final analysis, therefore, it will be whatever conscious men will make of it. But development's victims must first liberate themselves from the structures of vulnerability.

And men cannot fashion sound development unless they first engage in disciplined normative reflection and transform ethics into a "means of the means" transfusing other instrumentalities—planning, technical transfers, and efficiency systems—into liberating agencies. Failing this, development's blind forces will make men into their own image: process without goals, power and abundance without freedom.

There would be one minor consolation in such a world, however. Cruel choices would no longer exist. Indeed, all choices, cruel and benign, would have been consigned to oblivion.

APPENDIX I

The Terms "Ethics" and "Development"

Ethics

Since the time of early Greek philosophers, the term "ethics" has meant for Westerners the reflective study of what is good or bad in that part of human conduct for which men have some responsibility. Contemporary ethical theories focus, it is true, on how to explain the "oughtness" in human experience, whereas older viewpoints centered more directly on how man could best live and act so as to reach his final objective. Nevertheless, as a recent historian of ethics has explained, "This contrast between the older and the modern viewpoints is a matter of different emphases and not an absolute shift in the meaning of ethics." [1]

Among contemporaries the dominant ethical stress is placed upon the body of norms regulating action, with little critical examination of the ends themselves. Many observers view ethical choices as no different from empirical statements about alternative ways of reaching the same objective. Goals themselves, however, can be endowed with different moral qualities. As Aristotle wrote centuries ago, some ends are good because they are intrinsically noble, others because they are useful, others still because they are pleasurable. Accordingly, Morris Ginsberg does well to remind us that "reason has not only a regulative but a constitutive function in relation to the ends of action. A rational ethic must assume that there is such a thing as rational action, that intelligence has a part to play not only in cognition, but volition. . . . It is concerned also with the relative worth of the different ends in relation to the costs involved in attaining them, and this task it cannot fulfill adequately without inquiry into the basic human needs and grounds of our preferences and choices." [2]

Ethical thinkers acknowledge of course the existence of utilitarian, emotional, esthetic, and other values. Without being reducible to any of these, or seeking to assimilate them, ethics judges them all by appealing to norms of "oughtness" which are neither initially given nor self-evident. On the contrary, these norms are perpetually conditioned historically,

[1] Vernon J. Bourke, *History of Ethics* (Doubleday, 1968), p. 8.
[2] Morris Ginsberg, *On Justice in Society* (Penguin Books, 1965), p. 29.

socially, psychologically, culturally, and biologically. Indeed, as Alasdair MacIntyre has written, "moral concepts change as social life changes" and "one key way in which we may identify one form of social life as distinct from another is by identifying differences in moral concepts." [3] The norms themselves, therefore, must be subjected to rational critique and judged in the light of other values. By reason of their "oughtness," ethical norms can exist only where freedom and accountability are found. The very possibility of ethics is annihilated if full determinism or irresponsibility prevails.

Ideally, development ethics plays several roles:

—It teaches men by making them critically aware of the moral content of their choices.

—It coerces them to the extent that it commands good, and forbids bad, action.

—It gives exploiters a bad conscience and exploited victims rational grounds for revolting against their lot.

—It builds institutions inasmuch as norms must be embodied visibly in rights, duties, and laws.

Because of its insertion in shifting historical processes, development ethics cannot be based on any Kantian imperative or fixist natural law. Ultimately, development ethics is the pursuit by man's intelligence of leverage to act with varying degrees of freedom and responsibility in a universe where multiple and complex determinism and irrationalities operate. The very possibility of ethics is conditioned by a prior possibility of freedom and accountability. It must be noted, however, that the accountability here invoked need be only to man himself; it does not presuppose (nor, on the other hand, need it exclude) any extrinsic source of morality.

Throughout this work the term "ethics" is employed to mean those conditions of knowledge and will men require in order to exercise a genuine choice of ends or of means. Some of these conditions are manifestly cognitive—men must know certain things. Others are structural: men must not be fully determined by the social forces which impinge on them. All are deeply subjective, since they are grounded on diverse levels of self-awareness. Freedom, of course, cannot be treated in a vacuum; it is always freedom for something. Were it otherwise, there could be no "oughtness" and no ethics in freedom itself.

Development

In purely economic terms, "development" has come to mean the capacity of a national economy whose initial condition at some point in time is relatively static to sustain an annual increase in its gross national product at a rate ranging perhaps from 3 percent to 7 percent or more, while altering the structure of its product and its employment so that a declining proportion of both is generated by agriculture, whereas an increasing proportion is provided by secondary and tertiary sectors. Monetary flows are likewise important: the outflow of hard currency for imports and expenditures abroad must not be substantially higher than the inflow of hard currency into the country from investments, loans, grants, and

[3] Alasdair MacIntyre, *A Short History of Ethics* (MacMillan, 1966), p. 1.

remittances. Certain economists stress the ability of a nation's government to execute its budget in such wise as to eliminate deficits and control inflation. Certain indicators can be preferred to others, but any economic assessment is meaningful only if indicators are viewed as components in a series (usually based on comparable annual statistics) manifesting a trend. Relativity is further compounded, however, by the general acceptance of non-economic "social" indicators of development: gains in literacy, schooling, health conditions and services, provision of housing, and the like.

In the present study, however, I have used the term "development" more broadly to include political and cultural as well as economic and social goals. My main emphasis is placed on the ethical demands of the development experience. Moreover, the same term—"development"— designates simultaneously two realities: a terminal *condition* and a *process* by which successive approximations to this allegedly desirable condition are made. Terminal state is not to be construed statically here, but merely as embodying levels of living more acceptable than earlier ones. I accept the postulate that new levels of material wealth may possibly be required to provide support for the attainment of certain values by individuals, groups, and societies. "Development" as here employed thus covers the entire gamut of changes by which a social system, with optimal regard for the wishes of individuals and sub-systemic components of that system, moves away from a condition of life widely perceived as unsatisfactory in some way toward some condition regarded as "humanly" better. These changes may be gradual or mutational. And if they are to qualify as "development," some degree of calculation must be present on the part of society's influential decision-makers regarding optimum speeds at which change ought to proceed and minimal costs be paid. It matters greatly, of course, which values *ought to be* fostered in the effort to obtain a "humanly better" life. In fact, everyone who defines development makes an explicit or implicit option regarding several basic values. Among these are the degree of mastery to be exercised by persons over things, the level of critical awareness to be judged desirable in different categories of human agents, the optimal sharing of power to make decisions, and the destruction of particularistic interests in favor of wider reciprocity and solidarity. Certain quantitative improvements (in food, in real income, in suitable educational services, in increased life expectancy, etc.) are clearly necessary to improve the quality of life. Nevertheless, the most important elements of development are not subject to quantitative measurement. Diverse ideal models of the good society exist; attitudes vary toward material benefits and the relation of these to personal wisdom, enlightenment, harmony, and other values. Development must be gauged by the values a society itself, or some member thereof, deems to be requisite for its health and welfare. This evaluation requires careful attention to differential abilities to produce wealth but also to less visible capacities such as that of processing information and providing "meaning" to life itself. In this sense at least, development can be described as the "maturation," "humanization," or "qualitative ascent" of human societies.

Some writers distinguish social change from development, alleging that development is induced change whereas other changes are not induced. This distinction is faulty, however. Although "development" is doubtless induced change of a certain sort, many other social changes are also induced. Moreover, underdeveloped societies undergo many changes which are not induced by themselves and they harvest unplanned effects even of their conscious efforts to induce change. For still another reason, "development" may be an unsuitable word to describe the deliberately induced change which is the object of plans and programs. Many societies are not developing at all in spite of plans and programs. Moreover, the gap between developed and underdeveloped is widening and all credible forecasts indicate that it will continue to widen.

Historically, the word "development" was coined by spokesmen from "developed" areas to characterize efforts by others which they often implicitly presume to be aimed at imitating their own accomplishments and achieving their own status. This supposition is evidently not completely unfounded. Nevertheless, it overlooks significant realities in underdeveloped countries themselves, where there has been considerable resistance to development.

Among alternative terms proposed, "modernization" enjoys special favor among social scientists from "developed" countries. Yet it has the same undertones as "development": the notion of catching up, of getting up to date, of achieving parity with those already developed. Although it cannot be denied that much imitation takes place in the Third World, the central question is whether the concept of imitation gets to the heart of what occurs in the process of development. Certain authors have suggested names like "contemporaneity" or "maturation." Contemporaneity suggests three related notions: (a) an attempt by a society to live consciously in its own historical time; (b) the recognition that this time is not fully of its own making and that there is a necessitating character to contemporary history as it affects the Third World; and (c) the will to achieve some measure of control over its own destiny on the presupposition that the same forces which have unleashed the determinism can also be utilized to free men from some of their servitudes. The term "contemporaneity" implies, therefore, both a qualified acceptance and a profound rejection of modernity. The value questions it raises are not answerable except with reference to initial situations encountered by specific Third World countries in the total world context, and to the degree of leverage they can obtain in pursuing their chosen objectives in history.

Specialized definitions of development need not be totally incompatible with more comprehensive terms such as maturation and contemporaneity. "Economic," "social," and "political" development are simply methodological constructs adopted within specific disciplines to study aspects of a change process which they "abstract" from a total reality which comprises, beyond facts, meanings and symbols. In this work the context usually suggests whether by "development" I meant "economic growth plus social change" or "human ascent" or "maturation" in a broader sense.

APPENDIX II

The Ethics of Power and the Power of Ethics

Power is the effective influence or ability of an individual or group to modify the conduct of others in some desired manner. Unless one participates in decisions, he lacks the power to affect their outcome. Political power is the form of power which most closely approximates the pure definition. Not surprisingly, therefore, Lasswell judges that "the concept of power is perhaps the most fundamental in the whole of political science: the political process is the shaping, distribution, and exercise of power." [1] It is through political power that one can influence decisions affecting the whole society. Although it is not the only relevant value in politics, power is obviously crucial. The present book is an attempt to influence development decisions otherwise than through power—namely, by appealing to certain normative values. It may be instructive, therefore, to inquire into the relationship between ethical norms and political power.

Such inquiry is needed because development "prescriptions" of another order—economic plans—have frequently been "shelved" [2] by political leaders. Like a development plan, development ethics is useless unless it can be translated into public action. By public action is meant action taken by public authority, as well as actions taken by private agents but having important consequences for the life of the public community. The central question is: How can moral guidelines influence the decisions of those who hold power?

In order to reply, one need not study elite recruitment or mobility patterns, analyze modalities of interest aggregation, or postulate ideological reasons why power is exercised in one mode or another in given circumstances. On the other hand, he must discuss the purposes and limits of power. As Irving Louis Horowitz has written, "The study of power is the beginning of sociological wisdom—but the essence of that wisdom is that power resides in men. Hence the existence of power is a less significant area of study than the human uses made of power. Men define power; they are not necessarily defined by it. This, at any rate, is

[1] Harold D. Lasswell and Abraham Kaplan, *Power and Society* (Yale University Press, 1965), p. 75.
[2] Brazilians use a picturesque term for referring to a report which is shelved. They say it has been "engavetado"—i.e., buried in a drawer.

the liberating task of the social sciences."[3] Where power is badly used within underdeveloped countries, the blame does not rest primarily on the personal deficiencies of rulers. In most cases the problem is structural: society is so organized that only the representatives of certain interests enjoy access to the wealth, culture, contracts, information, and influence without which decisions cannot be made. Consequently, meaningful policy changes cannot be brought about simply by "throwing the rascals out" because those who replace them may emerge from the same structures and represent identical interests. This is why revolutionary theorists like Guevara and Debray perform a useful service by reminding us of the importance of "subjective conditions" in pre-revolutionary situations. Nevertheless, there is a threshold below which "objective conditions" impede structural change or lessen the speed at which even non-revolutionary change can occur.

We should, above all, reject a narrow exegesis of the dictum that "politics is the art of the possible." The formula usually postulates given limits of possibility within which power can be exercised. The range of possibilities is assumed to be definable only in terms of interests consonant with a *status quo*. Implicitly, therefore, any politics which moves outside these borders is branded as "utopian" or "subversive." Yet in underdeveloped societies, sacred verities are challenged and established orders are being increasingly denounced as iniquitous. Hence, the range of the possible becomes as wide as the imagination of the viewer; politics, in turn, becomes the "art of redefining the possible." In the domains of technology, communication, information-processing, and behavior, innovation is the rule rather than the exception. Realism dictates, therefore, that in the arena of development decisions, political arts likewise become innovative.

Political "development" is generally defined as a political system's capacity to process new and expanding demands (treated as "input") and to produce a widening array of decisions, rules, policies, and adjustment mechanisms ("output"). Missing in this perspective, however, is the explicit recognition that *even efficient power* is no self-validating, consummatory end. Power clearly exists for a purpose beyond the legitimization of particularistic interests or the arbitration among conflicting aggregate demands. In the language of the ancients, politics is concerned with the rational management of power in the service of society's common welfare. Without doubt Plato and Aristotle, like other ancient political theorists, delineated the "common good" uncritically in terms of particularistic social interests. Worse still, their undialectical "idealism" led them to assume that their own normative thought was genuinely universal. One major consequence of the demystification begun by Machiavelli and completed by Marx is to rule out in definitive fashion all prescriptive politics formulated in ideal terms and divorced from his-

[3] Irving Louis Horowitz, ed., Introduction to *Power, Politics and People: The Collected Essays of C. Wright Mills* (Ballantine Books, 1963), p. 11. The same case is made by John Pincus in *Trade, Aid and Development* (McGraw-Hill, 1967), p. 14: "Yet ethical considerations, uncomfortable though they may be in a power-centered world, are underlying elements of North-South economic relations. If there were no ethical issues involved, then the present situation would be quite satisfactory from the North's viewpoint; aid could even be reduced."

torically conditioned structures. Nevertheless, Marx himself stubbornly refused to accept existing power categories as givens or to condone Hegel's glorification of state power as the incarnation of the Absolute. On the contrary, he denounced all existing political power as radically immoral because it represented minority interests, not a common good. He wanted in its place a form of power incarnating the *majority interests* of proletarians considered as the latent bearers of *universal human values*. The central tenet of this normative view of political power is that power is justified by its use and that, ultimately, the only valid use of political power is the construction of some societal goal which transcends the mere aggregation of particular goods.

Therefore, normative strategies elaborated by ethicians should not be regarded by developers as mere velleities born of moral passion over the indignities wrought on mankind's poor by heartless wielders of power. They ought rather to be seen as frontiers of new political possibilities. Within this perspective, development ethics has four distinct although related functions: evaluative, critical, pedagogical, and normative. Ethical judgments can influence the observable course of events according as they are formulated by men who wield effective power in society or by those who lack such power. In terms of immediate results, of course, ethical norms are empirically influential only if they are acted upon by persons having power. Nevertheless, even persons deprived of power may influence decisions if they can persuade or pressure power-holders to accept their ethical judgments as effectively normative. More significantly, however, strong discontent with rulers' norms on the part of the ruled, allied to good organization by the latter, plays an indirect normative role in decision-making. Even when ethical judgments cannot influence decisions directly or indirectly, they may exercise other valuable functions in society.

Evaluation

All societies are inextricably caught up in interlocking social, technological, and ecological processes whose meaning and consequences must be judged in the light of several criteria. One important criterion is the degree of necessity imposed on human societies by these processes. Multiple determinisms impinge on all human affairs. But the determinisms inherent in development processes have special characteristics which are deeply imbedded both in history and in men's historical consciousness. It is plausible to argue that every determinism is dehumanizing so long as it remains just that. And the danger of dehumanization varies according as it affects rich or poor nations. The dehumanization of poor nations, classes, and persons is not due solely to conditions of inherited misery or to uncritical acceptance of modernization, but also to the deterministic character of the world's economic and political systems. These systems severely limit options in domestic and international policy. Certain uses of power render men powerless to control or even to understand the processes affecting them. This is why existing norms governing power decisions need to be evaluated according as they increase or lessen historical determinism. Alternative norms governing the use of power need to be constructed as possible models. The consequences anticipated from these alternatives must be evaluated in a prospective, probabilistic mode.

337

Many categories of people, even within a single society, may carry out such evaluation: those who themselves wield power, those devoid of power but in agreement with the effective norms of the power elite, those lacking power while in (greater or lesser) disagreement with the operative norms of rulers. In all cases, some explicit articulation of ethical norms is required if evaluation is to be made. It is in this sense that ethical judgments have an evaluative function.

Critical role

Criticism is closely allied to evaluation. When based on formal ethical constructs, it can render those who hold power as well as those who are held by power critically aware of the value-meaning and consequences of the mode of power exercised in their society. Especially for development ethics, prevailing modes of power cannot be assumed to be just or inevitable. Freedom to contest power verbally and symbolically and to oppose it by actions is therefore a necessary requisite for the responsible use of political power. Critique is manifestly dialectical. If those in power reject ethical critique, those without power will find in the directives provided by the rejected ethic the basis for the legitimacy they need to validate their opposition to that power.

Pedagogical role

Development ethics is also eminently pedagogical and in some cases it may successfully "educate" leaders holding effective influence. Even if it fails to do so, however, it may still educate those who are led. As here understood, education is closely allied to self-awareness. If underdevelopment is viewed not as a morally neutral phenomenon, but as the by-product of certain forms of "development" and of domination, it follows that the task of a normative theorist is to articulate an ethic capable of serving as a pedagogy of the oppressed in case it is rejected as pedagogy by the oppressors. The very refusal by rulers to accept as normative a development ethic based on the need for all men to have enough in order to be fully human, on universally expanding solidarity, and on maximum popular decision-making is a powerful force accelerating the growth of consciousness in a hitherto culturally passive populace.[4]

Normative role

What is meant by the normative role of ethics is that rulers may exercise political power constructively with a view to implementing desired values. They must usually do so in the face of resistance. And though it is commonly assumed that ethics plays a normative role only when those having influence translate prescriptions into action, it is also

[4] On this cf. Paulo Freire, *Pedagogy of the Oppressed* (Herder and Herder, 1970); also the same author's *Cultural Action for Freedom,* Harvard Educational Review and Center for the Study of Development and Social Change, Monograph No. 1, 1970.

true that ethics provides norms to counter-elites engaged in the critical and evaluative activities mentioned above.

Indeed, all development policy devised by political leaders (as distinct from policy formulated by planners, advisors, international administrators of assistance programs, and the like) is a "mix" of diverse commitments: a commitment to capture or hold power, a commitment to reach certain economic objectives, and some degree of adherence to value goals (of leaders themselves, of particular groups, of a nation, of a category of people whose existence must be "wished" into existence).

The ethical perspective on development presented in this work may prove more or less compatible with value commitments in specific countries. A few examples will illustrate the point.

Case #1

This ethic is clearly incompatible with the commitments to maintenance in power one finds in Spain, Paraguay, or South Africa. This development ethic cannot play its normative function among leaders in these countries; therefore, it will have at best a critical, evaluative, and pedagogical function.

Case #2

C. Wright Mills[5] argued years ago that the power to make important national and international decisions in the United States is so totally concentrated in political, military, and economic institutions that other institutions (religion, education, the family) are shaped by what he calls the "big three." If he is right, the ethic here proposed can become normative only if pressures are built up—domestically and internationally —sufficient to "force" the United States to act against its own "best interests" as presently conceived.

Case #3

Some Socialist nations have ideological commitments incompatible with the ethic here advanced. If their power elite chooses to optimize ideological orthodoxy over the achievement of professed development goals, it follows that the ethic cannot function as normative *within* those societies. It may, on the other hand, operate *critically* inside other Socialist societies so as to accelerate movement away from ideological rigidity. The evidence suggests that this phenomenon has occurred in the decentralization of economic planning in Yugoslavia in response to practices followed inside the Soviet Union.[6]

The main point of this note is not the obvious one that normative thought is largely irrelevant if it is not accepted and implemented by political power. What I wish to emphasize instead is that normative thought, if rejected by wielders of power, becomes a powerful critical and pedagogical tool in the hands of those who are ruled by power. This is tantamount to telling today's rulers that, given contemporary levels of awareness, consciousness, and sophistication, victims can be pushed (or manipulated) only so far before they will seek to destroy the oppressor,

[5] In Horowitz, ed., *op. cit.,* p. 27.
[6] Cf. Branko Horvat, "Planning in Yugoslavia," *Development Plans and Programmes* (OECD, 1964), pp. 149–166.

even if their act is suicidal. To disregard norms, *on the pretext that these are incompatible with the present concerns of those who exercise power*, is unrealistic. Only a critical regard for norms, even norms which challenge interests and power itself, can, in strictly political terms, modify the frontiers of the possible.

The use of power is always fraught with uncontrollable and unpredictable consequences. My contention is simply that the *responsible* use of power leads to consequences which are more controllable and beneficial than its irresponsible use.

By themselves, rich nations are powerless to assure the development of the Third World. They can, nonetheless, effectively impede that development. Leverage for achieving development must be created, above all, within underdeveloped nations themselves. Third World domestic forces must be aggregated so as to pressure those who hold power to accept the development thrust from below or be replaced by others who will do so. For it is indeed true, as Lipset has written, that the *"only effective restraint on the power of the dominant class is counter-power."* [7] Moreover, Third World nations will also seek to aggregate their trans-national group interests to increase their collective bargaining strength in the face of the Rich World and thus gain effective leverage on power decisions. These measures presuppose at some point ethical justification for the conferral of legitimacy. Even before the Third World achieves power, it is aided in its understanding of the issues by the pedagogical and evaluative functions of development ethics. In rich and poor societies alike, only those having power can apply normative prescriptions. This is true in the international arena as well. Consequently, no ethic can appear "realistic" to those who wield power if it contradicts their narrowly defined interests. Nevertheless, it is possible for men to wield power so as to promote a common welfare above narrow interests. It is also possible for those with narrow interests, provided they are lucid, to prefer survival to maintaining brute domination by power alone.

The existence of poverty in the midst of affluence is no mystery. Poverty and affluence are polar realities, mutually supportive of each other. This polarity is ineradicable within a competitive framework. Even in societies generally characterized by affluence and political democracy, poverty is maintained by the choices the poor make or are caused to make. The poor themselves are transformed into accomplices of the very system which keeps them poor. In worldwide terms, as John Seeley has written, "the system of external poverty, i.e., the existence and perpetuation of relatively poor or 'underdeveloped' nations, reinforces and necessitates the system of internal poverty that supplies the motive to produce the defence of the 'developed' system. Absolutely, planes of living can move up, internally and externally—as they have—without any real attack on poverty and its problems, which are relative." [8]

It is likewise with power: the powerful can seduce the weak into complicity with the system whereby they are held in servitude. Even if the political power of Third World countries increased in absolute terms, the problems of world domination might grow worse in relative terms if the power they had newly gained simply made them more acutely

[7] Seymour Martin Lipset, *Political Man* (Anchor Books, 1963), p. xxiii.

[8] Cf. John Seeley, *The Americanization of the Unconscious* (Science House, 1967), p. 283.

conscious than before of the frustrations attendant upon being deprived of power to affect substantive international decisions.

The main lesson to be drawn from the interplay between power and normative values is that power without legitimacy must ultimately perish. Conversely, legitimacy must be based on perceived ethical merit in order to endure. Therefore, responsible power accepts the obligation to be normative, whereas irresponsible power arms its enemies by refusing to be normative. Indeed, it is foolish to trust power alone. As he reflects upon his struggle with the Mafia in underdeveloped Sicily, Danilo Dolci argues that "Anyone with genuine revolutionary experience knows—and must admit—that in order to change a situation one must appeal, whether explicitly or tacitly, to moral rather than material considerations, for they take precedence. . . . Revolutionary action is, therefore, also that which helps to evolve a new sensitivity, a new capacity, a new culture, new instincts—human nature remade." [9]

[9] Danilo Dolci, "Mafia-Client Politics," *Saturday Review,* July 6, 1968, p. 11.

APPENDIX III

Research on Value Change

In Chapter 9, I have outlined a strategy for inducing value change. The purpose of this appendix is to describe a method for conducting research on such changes. In both cases procedures have been derived from the concepts of vulnerability and existence rationality which are central to the view of development presented in this work.

As a general concept, "value" embraces all attitudes, judgments, affects, and behavioral preferences to which conscious subjects attach the note of "oughtness." When men experience important technological innovations, new patterns of demonstration effects, and other impingements on their habitual sensibilities, their old values are profoundly disturbed. For this reason the study of value change is important to developers.

Yet such study is a delicate matter inasmuch as research itself tampers with values.[1] A second problem arises because many change agents assume development's values to be unequivocally good and conclude that pre-existing values ought not to stand in their way. Such an instrumentalist approach fails to see development as a relative good, itself subject to judgment in the light of prior values. Finally, most strategies for inducing value change have uncritically assumed that "modernizing" elites ought to be the main agents of change. The research strategy outlined below challenges these assumptions.

Research and Action Modes

Underlying much empirical research is the belief that all social realities are amenable to "objective" study: investigators, it is asserted, can stand outside a reality and observe it without altering it, much as a spectator watches a football game. But "spectators" at a game influence players,

[1] On this, cf. Clyde Kluckhohn and others, "Values and Value-Orientations in the Theory of Action," in *Toward a General Theory of Action*, ed. Talcott Parsons and Edward A. Shils (Harper Torchbooks, 1962), p. 408: "perhaps the most provocative idea which emerged from our discussions of research problems is the hypothesis that when one studies values directly, the values are changed by the process of study itself. . . . Thus the mere focusing of attention upon value-problems changes the problems. In so far as this hypothesis is correct, *the values we discover are in part a function of the research approach.*" Italics mine.

who testify that a stadium full of enthusiastic fans modifies their performance. Investigators in many social situations engage in participant-observation.[2] Nevertheless, participation is usually subordinated to observation and the demands of research. It is observation, not participation, which enjoys priority. This stance proves inadequate in cases where commitment is indispensable to gain understanding of the motivational dynamics at work in certain societies. Merely observing the routine of a Zen monastery, for instance, will never enable one to "understand" the spiritual meaning of Zen. To do so one must "let go" intellectually and suspend the ordinary canons of rational judgment. Likewise with the student of revolutionary guerrilla movements: crucial moments arise when he cannot maintain an observer's posture because to refrain from action is to impede the success of that action. One finds countless examples of the same phenomenon. I have explained in Chapter 2 why and how one ought to make himself vulnerable, even in the conduct of research. But field investigators are generally ill-prepared to accept the principle of vulnerability and they feel "uncomfortable" when "participation" interferes with "observation." Their approach is a stumbling block, however, to the realistic study of value change in contexts of development. A further difficulty arises from the opinion which the population under study has of the agency sponsoring the research.[3] Even when a sponsor's credentials are not tainted, the special knowledge possessed by a researcher can intimidate a population.[4] The inadequacy of conventional research on values is unmasked. Research on values is generally described as an activity carried on *in the study mode*. The truth is, on the contrary, that such study is a special kind of interference exercised *in the action mode*.

Efforts to induce value changes among populations constitute an overt action mode. In most instances these inducements are by-products of technological or educational innovations, themselves treated as though they were value-neutral and beyond criticism in value terms. Thus, artificial insemination will be introduced on grounds that it will improve the quality of stock and, eventually, increase productivity of meat, milk, or hides. This practice, however, can have profound repercussions on the life-view operative within a given symbolic system. And again, agents of progress easily assume that pre-modern viewpoints on life are obsolete or irrelevant. Nevertheless, the long-term consequences of treating life as an "object" with which technology can tamper at will may be far more detrimental to human development than the "archaic" view so blithely rejected by "modernizers." This does not mean that technological

[2] On participant-observation, cf. Arthur J. Vidich, "Participant Observation and the Collection and Interpretation of Data," *The American Journal of Sociology*, Vol. LX, No. 4 (January 1955), pp. 354–360. Also Florence R. Kluckhohn, "The Participant-Observer Technique in Small Communities," *The American Journal of Sociology*, Vol. XLVI, No. 3 (November 1940), pp. 331–343; and Howard S. Becker, "Problems of Inference and Proof in Participant Observation," *American Sociological Review*, Vol. XXII, No. 6 (December 1958), pp. 652–660.

[3] For one particularly dramatic case study, cf. Irving Louis Horowitz, ed., *The Rise and Fall of Project Camelot* (M.I.T. Press, 1967).

[4] Gypsies interviewed by the author refused to speak to anyone with a written document (in this case, a questionnaire) in hand. It was necessary to devise a mnemonic scheme of "trigger words" to obtain replies.

innovations such as artificial insemination are necessarily wrong or harmful. The example nonetheless warns against treating values instrumentally —that is, as mere obstacles to achieving objectives uncritically assumed to be good.

The equation has to be inverted: it is development itself which must be viewed instrumentally. A human community's values—seen not as an immobile deposit, but as a vital tissue of perceptions and symbols which supply meaning to life and human activity—should be the primary referent. If some particular developmental change—the introduction of fertilizer, let us say, the use of electric motors to pump water from a well, the erection of a factory, the building of a clinic, or the construction of a road—is seen by a population itself to be compatible with its image of desirable societal life, then such an innovation may be regarded as good. Consequently, open debate on values must precede technological innovations. Such a procedure will not impede or retard progress. This would be so only if traditional value systems were inherently static and hostile to change. But, as I have argued in Chapter 9, traditional value systems are capable of considerable change if innovations are presented to them as improving life-sustenance or expanding esteem and freedom for the populations concerned. Such presentation cannot result from the ethnocentric assessment of a society's value system. By definition, premodern value systems do give primacy to values which characterize modern societies: material achievement, punctuality, productivity, efficiency, and deliberately provoked exponential increase in acquisitive desires. The simple fact that "modern" men are richer and more powerful than "traditional" men is no argument for the superiority of their values. This is manifest now that "developed" countries are beginning to experience deep value crises generated in their own societies by the uncritical pursuit of a narrow model of a better life. Chronic malnutrition and high mortality rates are doubtless dehumanizing evils which ought to be abolished; and abolition requires the application of technology and "modern" techniques. What is crucial, however, is that the people affected be helped to become fully conscious of the value implications inherent in proposed innovations. Since many "modernizing" agents are so unconscious of values implicit in their supposedly "neutral" tool-kit of instruments of progress, they are not qualified to judge how value change should be induced in a population. Worse still, biases in favor of empiricism, objectivity, and allegedly neutral observation suggest that dominant patterns of social-science research cannot deal adequately with the value perceptions of those for whom underdevelopment is a vital experience. Alternate strategies must be sought.

An Alternative Approach

The philosophy underlying a little-known approach to the study of values is derived from experiments in community development, educational planning, and politicization of urban and rural masses in several African countries, the Middle East, and Latin America. The author of this approach is Georges Allo, who overtly links the study of values to their alteration. His mode of insertion combines research pedagogy with mobilization; the emphasis is placed on perceiving value changes— including heightened consciousness of pre-existing values—as the result of dynamic interplay among multiple tensions. The basic assumptions of Allo's approach are the following:

—All formulations used in studying values need to be made in the language and symbols of those being studied.[5]

—Value studies must focus on integrated patterns of total value orientations in a human community.

—Total integrated patterns of value cannot be obtained if people are treated as *objects* of observation or interrogation. They must be associated to the process of studying their own values in their capacity as *subjects* or active judges of the study undertaken.[6]

—Images and conscious profiles of themselves held by individuals and groups express their values more adequately than descriptions, measurements, correlations, or classifications dealing with their economic activity, political life, kinship structure, or intra-societal roles.

—Members of developing societies, while under study, should be allowed to appraise the value changes they are undergoing or which can be anticipated.

—Empirical research procedures used by cross-cultural social disciplines must be allied to modes of reflection which are both philosophical and phenomenological. This reflection should be conducted jointly by researchers and members of a culture, if the distortion produced by fragmentation of value patterns is to be minimized.[7]

—Fruitful generalizations about values and scaled needs can be gained only from permanent disciplined exchange among representatives of many value systems in the process of being challenged by "modernity."

Allo[8] strives for generality by deliberately provoking confrontations among varying diagnoses of total value profiles. Comparison and confronta-

[5] The same recommendation is made by Hadley Cantril in his defense of "self-anchoring" scales. Cf. *The Pattern of Human Concerns* (Rutgers University Press, 1965), ch. 3.

[6] F. S. C. Northrop expresses a parallel concern. Cf. "Cultural Values" in *Anthropology Today,* ed. A. L. Kroeber (University of Chicago Press, 1953), p. 678.

[7] In this connection, Philip E. Jacob and James J. Flink in "Values and Their Function in Decision-Making," *The American Behaviorial Scientist,* Vol. V (May 1962), No. 9, Supplement p. 9, explain that "the phenomenological approach has the particular advantage for social research of avoiding at least one major opening for the injection of observer's bias into the analysis: the analyst makes no attempt to structure his inquiry according to a preconceived value scheme."

[8] Georges Allo has described progress on his work in several articles: "Research on Values at the Crossroads of Modern Civilization," a brochure printed in English and French by IRFED (Beirut, 1961); "La Recherche de l'IRFED sur les Valeurs et les Civilisations," *Développement et Civilisations,* No. 13 (March 1963), pp. 104–108; "La Recherche de l'IRFED sur la Rencontre Moderne des Civilisations," *Développement et Civilisations,* No. 14 (June 1963), pp. 113–116; "L'Evolution des Valeurs dans une Civilisation," *Développement et Civilisations,* No. 20 (December 1964), pp. 78–87; IRFED VEC *Bulletin de la Recherche No. 5* (Beirut, May 1963), an appraisal of the eighteen-month trial run on research in the Middle East; "Révolution des Valeurs," *Economie et Humanisme,* No. 160 (May/June 1965), pp. 3–10; "Les Valeurs dans la Rencontre Moderne des Civilisations," *Développement et Civilisations,* No. 23 (September 1965), pp. 80–87; "Pourquoi le Développement Exige un Dialogue Entre Civilisation," *Développement et Civilisations,* No. 35 (June 1968), pp. 61–66.

tion, he believes, generate dynamic syntheses of value systems as they undergo evolution. His aim is to focus attention on dynamic (not static) value profiles and to learn what happens to these profiles when they are challenged by altered conditions. Much light is obtained by eliciting joint "brainstorming" by researchers and participants over how to react, in value terms, to such challenges. Knowledge generated by such an approach can help planners, educators, and technicians to appraise the cost in value sacrifices of their own recommendations. More importantly, this approach allows communities to participate actively in choosing the speed and direction of their own value change in accord with their preferred images of development. Thus, the "pulse-taking" operation advocated by Allo prior to social-science study of values reflects his concern to devise a method which reduces manipulative and elitist biases. Values experienced by individuals or groups are easily distorted unless empirical scientists derive their hypotheses and instruments of study from the "pre-scientific and non-objective total experience of the population studied." Consequently, sound research procedure ought to allow individuals and communities under study to aid in the elaboration of research tools employed to study them. Direct attention is given to the value dilemmas engendered by development. Accordingly, a wide array of phenomenological instruments is employed in order to obtain kinds of data which objective indices cannot supply.

Several principles advocated by Allo appear valid in any method for studying value change in a developmental setting. What seems to be required is a procedure wherein research is allied to a pedagogy aimed at helping a populace achieve heightened self-awareness of its value dilemmas, and to devise a strategy for inducing value changes desired by the people themselves. The illusory objectivity of the detached spectator must be abandoned in favor of a new form of participation which operates neither in the pure mode of intervention nor in the pure study mode. By conducting this exercise, it is hoped that theoretical clarification can be gained, that the population affected will both educate and be educated by the outside elements confronting it, and that an acceptable form of mobilization of energies on behalf of developmental tasks will be discovered. The most significant feature of this new mode is *the principle of normative sequence.*

Experienced values are easily distorted unless those who study them derive their hypotheses and research instruments from a holistic view of these values in their pre-scientific human setting. Scientific fragmentation is inappropriate in this special domain because, by definition, values refer to *evaluational* totality as well as to *valuational* fragments. When he "evaluates," a subject situates his values in an over-all framework of standards he deems important. In order to do this, he must posit a reflective act and refer, at least implicitly, to a total pattern of meaning and worthwhileness. When he merely "valuates," on the other hand, a man does not engage in this reflective action, nor does he make a critical, or judgmental, reference to his total universe of standards. To "valuate" simply means that he makes a selective preference, to which he joins some judgment about the suitability of the preference and of the object of preference. Therefore, values contain an essentially subjective component and one cannot reduce values to mere objects of study. Accordingly, any procedure used to study values must respect the nature of values as integral and integrative. Otherwise stated, one cannot examine the values of an individual or society validly unless he understands the relative position of all of that individual's or society's values in their totality. Abstraction and analysis are not thereby outlawed, but they become legitimate only at the right "moments" in a given sequence. The goal of a comprehensive research sequence is to achieve permanent evaluative synthesis of dynamic value profiles and to capture the meaning of the evolution undergone by these profiles. The stages in this process of permanent synthesis are the following:

(A) *Preliminary Synthesis*

The investigator solicits from the "natural" elites in a community and from popular spokesmen having no influence beyond their limited kinship or affective circles their view of what their total human existential situation is, what it means, and what it ought to be. Information is also obtained as to which changes are affecting them, how society's members assess these changes, what is their perception of issues lying outside the purview of their daily concerns, and what degree of relevance or interest they impart to these issues. In order to harvest such "testimonies," an investigator must insert himself deeply and over long periods of time in the environment studied. More importantly, he must establish relations of confidence with informants. Confidence comprises both "trust" and the willingness of interlocutors to "confide" or divulge intimate thoughts. From this "pre-reflection," so named because it precedes systematic empirical study, a researcher obtains preliminary global notions of what is valuated and what is evaluated by a populace.

(B) *Systematic Observation*

Under ideal conditions, systematic observation should take place at four different levels. The first is that of primary groups or sub-systems constituting natural units of daily life. General observation can be conducted, for instance, on all aspects of life in a village or among an itinerant tribe. A second arena of observation is some sector of activity such as work, recreation, worship, family relations, or the like. A third realm is the cultural system, whether it be the belief system (cognitive values), the set of norms, patterns of interaction, or the total network of social forces affecting cohesion and disruption. A fourth level is that of "world-view" or philosophy of life.

Social-science disciplines play a major role in these studies. But, according to Allo, areas of study must be chosen and hypotheses derived from the psychic universe revealed to investigators in this first step of the research sequence. This global first approach is the matrix from which empirical research orientations are to flow.

(C) *Reflective Synthesis*

The third stage in the process is the elaboration of a reflective, critically conscious synthesis by the research team. The team ought to include members of the society under observation as well as trained investigators from outside. Those who have "taken the pulse" of the populace in Stage A and conducted systematic study at any of the four levels in Stage B must confront their findings as a group. The purpose of these comparative elaborations of the "meaning" of what has been found is to

347

begin formulating a reflective synthesis of the value universe of the human group under study. This synthesis is not naïve, as it was in Step A; it is formulated at a more explicit level of consciousness than the earlier one. Moreover, it is elaborated only after the investigators themselves have impinged on the consciousness of the population. The elements of this new systematization are drawn from findings obtained in prior stages, examined in the light of all available secondary documents or relevant parallel studies. Inasmuch as diverse interest groups, classes, partisans, and ideologies are represented, the reflective value syntheses which result are necessarily varied. This diversity itself is viewed as desirable, and each partial synthesis is made to confront all the others in order to test the critical survival value of each and to probe inductively for possible generality, partial or total.

(D) *Feedback to Populace*

The final stage of the normative sequence consists in resubmitting the critical syntheses obtained in Stage C to the informants who provided the naïve synthesis in Stage A. The choice of appropriate terms and symbols evidently depends on prolonged interaction between the research team and a representative portion of the interested populace. Initial informants may reject the synthesis elaborated, correct it, accept it tentatively as a new outlook to be considered in the growing self-awareness of their own values and value evolution, or, again, endorse it, with or without reservations. It is likewise conceivable that they will not understand it, in which case further pedagogical action is required for purposes of clarification.

The research team never arrogates to itself the right to interpret the problems of the native populace, which preserves the final veto over the value synthesis elaborated. This synthesis states what existing value constellations are, it interprets the significance of challenges posed (or proposed) to these constellations, and it explores alternatives in the face of probable evolution.

The normative sequence just outlined launches a dynamic process of permanent synthesis among values held, values proposed, values newly chosen. Underlying the whole endeavor is the belief that social science can best formulate testable hypotheses regarding value change after a pre-reflection or global approach has been conducted. The findings of social-science research are afterward subjected to a treatment which is not merely abstract or analytical, but critical and "dialogal" in nature. Finally, all knowledge obtained is tested in the crucible of pedagogical action, itself fraught with consequences in the realm of mobilization.

Since this embryonic method is still in its experimental phase, one cannot easily judge its merits. The Allo effort is itself a by-product of the desire to overcome limitations inherent in empirical methodologies. To empiricism are added three new sources of light: experiential observation and testimony, philosophical critical discourse, and transposition of "reflective" findings into a language acceptable to interested populaces, no longer treated as "objects" of study but themselves transformed into active "subjects" of a total enterprise which is simultaneously research, pedagogy, and mobilization.

The primary significance of Allo's experiment, however, is not methodological but epistemological. His views on the respective roles of philosophy and social science are contained in the following lines drafted by

348

Allo at my request. They are drawn from an unpublished memorandum dated October 25, 1967, and written in French.

Allo on the Roles of Philosophy and Social Science in Values Research

1. Everything originates with living reality. But living reality comprises men, families, localities, regions, and nations which, like all human realities, are *wholes*. That is to say, these are realities made up of complex elements assembled in a living unit. I have spoken of what lives because a living reality engages in spontaneous activity even before it becomes the object of any consciousness or of any mental representation by the one who has knowledge of it.

This is the reason why I advocate a first step which is an effort to develop consciousness. This is what you have correctly termed a "pre-reflection" when you situate it with reference to scientific investigation.

2. *Two kinds of knowledge* will exercise themselves on this vital reality, brought to a state of clear consciousness.

a. *Scientific knowledge* will seek to analyze, discipline by discipline, all components and laws. What distinguishes these disciplines one from the other is the specificity of their point of view.

b. *Philosophical knowledge* is essentially an *interrogation made to understand one's own life* and *to situate oneself in existence*. What is at stake here is to find meaning for one's existence—that is to say, a significance and an orientation for oneself and for one's group.

It should be emphasized that these two modes of cognition are born in the same soil, the same humus, and both directly. That is to say, both are born in the vital experience. It is sometimes thought that philosophic knowledge intervenes only at a later moment and in the wake of conclusions already reached by science. The very contrary is true: one is first of all imbued with a philosophy of life, the philosophy one has received from his culture and which inspires him without his even knowing it. Or it may be that he has developed a more personal philosophy of life, conceived by himself. The two processes (scientific and philosophic cognition) are simultaneous, but they are not parallel because they can never merge. Although they are distinct one from the other in essence and procedures, they illuminate each other mutually. Let us simply assert, in summary, that philosophy, in its critical aspect, grounds and situates diverse types of knowledge in the knowledge of total reality. Thanks to its precise analyses of reality, science supplies to philosophical reflection a knowledge of reality which is far more extensive and richer. Nevertheless, it remains true that philosophical reflection already exercises itself on the primary data supplied by common sense, and that great philosophical geniuses have reached summits even in periods when sciences were still rudimentary.

As a final step in our approach to human reality, I recommend an interdisciplinary reflection. What I mean by interdisciplinary is dialogue around a single reality among spokesmen for all points of view interested in this reality. Interdisciplinary reflection cannot operate in a vacuum, however; it must focus on some concrete reality. It must not be conceived as a simple juxtaposition of results obtained through diverse scientific analyses. If one reflects on this, he sees that material juxtaposition is no more possible than is the juxtaposition of different photos of the same monument *taken from different angles*. What we can do in this connection is to look at the photos, one after the other, and mentally refer them each time to the same monument. Hence, all particular points of view are referred to the identical reality. In the context of our present interests, the reality under discussion is a human whole: a man, a family, a locality, etc. . . .

It is at this point that we reach the heart of the matter: what relations can possibly be established between scientific and philosophical knowledge? Before answering this question, one must have correctly understood the specificity of philosophic cognition.

Let us merely say here, by way of summary, that a human totality, even when it is experienced only implicitly, is not so easy to grasp as one might initially suppose. This complex reality includes elements of interiority and exteriority, and it is not immediately perceptible to the senses. It needs to be reconstructed, beginning with all the detailed viewpoints we may have obtained of it, and, moreover, rediscovered in its internal unity. The mind is able to do this only by stepping back, not only from all external data, but also from itself. This is the only instrument it has for capturing the interior dimensions of man. The mind achieves this by turning upon itself, and by reflecting upon the situation which it first experiences without explicit consciousness of self and of the meaning of that situation. Afterward it proceeds to a constant shuttling back and forth between itself and the surrounding reality, and the surrounding reality and itself. Its purpose is to see wherein it differs and wherein it resembles this reality—for example, in that it itself exists. On this basis the mind tries to extract a few important components of man. This type of reflection is the philosophical process.

Dialogue on man is established in satisfactory terms when it takes place between reflection on man conducted at these two levels, the positive level of science and the reflexive level of philosophy. These two types of discipline absolutely need each other, and this in two directions, because their contributions are reciprocal.

If, however, dialogue between scientists and philosophers is to be possible and fruitful, *all* must have attempted to make *a first global approach* to the reality to be studied. This approach is at once prescientific and pre-philosophic. And is the same for all. It is an approach which is not specialized but *"existential"* in the sense that one tries to engage in it with everything that he is: intelligence, sensitivity, affectivity —in a word, with his entire experience. This experience is doubtless limited: each one's experience is always situated in a given place, it is conditioned and subjective. Nevertheless, it is a first attempt to draw near to a totality and it brands a man with a sense of the whole which he ought never lose thereafter. This approach is rich because it is vital. Afterward it behooves scientific reflection to control all the elements of this totality which lie within its capabilities. And philosophical reflection should make a twofold use of findings for its own elaboration: findings seen as a vital whole, and as analyzed by scientific disciplines.

On this common foundation and on all specialized studies undertaken from this point will be built all interdisciplinary work, properly speaking. I see it as *a journey along a common path*. No participant tries to persuade others of the conclusions of his own science or philosophy, but each accepts to retrace in the presence of others the description of his own personal formulation. As they listen to him, others begin to perceive better than before how to relate their viewpoint to that of others; new perceptions enter into play and critiques are formulated. At the end of the road, what will have been achieved is a better approach to a human reality which is perennially so complex and so unified.

One of the advantages of this procedure is to impress on each and all how much distortion is caused by any fragmentary approach to reality.

One final remark: I myself am working only on one aspect—the dialogue between different levels of cognition. It is, nonetheless, indispensable that men of action play a role in the dialogue, inasmuch as the desired objective is to act. Practitioners, too, must make the same initial effort to approach the global reality I have described above.

This is the direction my research is taking. I have thought it necessary to retrace its steps here. *To content oneself* simply with extracting from my data a few hypotheses utilizable by a social scientist is to disfigure these data. The reason is that my research formulates its own hypotheses at another level, one which is not immediately transposable into social-science research hypotheses. Moreover, to insist on looking first of all for hypotheses is to miss the whole point of the problem, which is *primarily a problem of epistemology*—that is, of critical study of different types of human cognition. All sciences, social sciences like the rest, must first consent to question their own assumptions in terms of a critique of knowledge and of the requirements of action.

For my part, I absolutely refuse to dispense with this sequence of operations, lest I fall into the serious trap of completely bypassing the real problem—namely, the kind of collaboration to be established among all modes of knowing with a view to orienting development in the most human way possible.

I fully appreciate the reservations that scholars, in the name of scientific rigor, make in the face of any social philosophy which is obsolete today and *even* with regard to philosophical systems as such. This is why I advocate no system, but simply an attitude of philosophical interrogation which leads me to attempt to rehabilitate a register of thought which is indispensable and in which we are constantly engaging. Indeed, man cannot prescind from a certain signification and a certain orientation of his life. He should, however, engage in this activity more consciously.

If one familiarizes himself with this register of thought, I believe he will acquire flexibility of mind and a sense of men's real possibilities. What I mean by this is that development, like every human action, is a project, a human project. And in this realm men can never attain total demonstrability or verificability. Man moves forward in accord with what he thinks is best; he relies on the judgments of others as much as on his own. He takes advantage of the multiplicity of viewpoints and agrees to engage in dialogue, while forever maintaining the most unremitting subjection to what is real.

Having said this, I remain extremely open to the need to enter, with as much detail as possible, into problems of methodology, especially in social sciences.

Index

absorptive capacity, 284, 287
abundance: of goods, 90, 123,
    128, 223–224, 257, 283; mis-
    placed, 105, 134
acculturation, resistance to, 195
achievement orientation, 83–84,
    207
actualization, 91, 94, 124–127,
    189, 219, 225, 245–246
Africa, 31, 42, 56, 72, 79, 157,
    270, 276, 278n
African socialism, 62–63
aid, 66–69, 77–78, 104, 171–186,
    233–234
Albert the Great, 4
Albertini, Jean-Marie, 290
Algeria, 48, 83, 146, 320
alienation: of abundance, 105,
    216, 322; in misery, 105, 216,
    322
Alliance for Progress, 66, 78, 175
Allo, Georges, 344–349
amoral familism, 203
animation, 150
anti-development, 189, 215–225
Antoine, Pierre, 135
Antoninus of Florence, 4
Apter, David, 3, 211
Aquinas, Thomas, 4
Arendt, Hannah, 91
Aristotle, 3, 99, 336
Aron, Raymond, 38–39, 104, 124–
    125, 269

Ashby, Sir Eric, 56
Asia, 42, 70–72, 276
austerity: imposed, viii, 121, 137,
    201, 252; voluntary, viii, 121,
    137, 252, 255–263, 283, 292
Austruy, Jacques, 108
autarkic subsistence pattern of
    need-satisfaction, 236–237

Baldwin, James, 321
Bandung Declaration, 44
Banfield, Edward, 244
Baran, Paul, 244
Barr, Stringfellow, 181
Bergson, Henri, 258
Berle, Adolph, 7
Bernard, Claude, 266
Bernstein, Eduard, 315
better life (good life), 10, 42, 87–
    95, 130, 136–137, 251–253,
    333
Beyond the Welfare State
    (Myrdal), 285
Bhagwati, Jagdish, 180, 327
Bidney, David, 86, 87
Bolivia, 44–45
Boulding, Kenneth, 179, 181, 238
Brand, Gert, 176
Brazil, 24, 43, 57–59, 61–62, 93,
    154, 157, 225, 228n
Brown, H., 278–279
Browne, Robert, 85
Buddhism, 309

355

budget, 77–78
Buganda, 211
Buron, Robert, 182

Caillot, Robert, 161–164
Caldwell, Lynton Keith, 216, 275, 280
Caló, 200
Câmara, Helder, 29, 310
Campos, Roberto, 154
Camus, Albert, 9, 222, 242, 299, 307–308, 310, 321, 325
capitalism, 39
Carmichael, Stokely, 321
Castro, Fidel, 31, 40, 46, 117, 226
change, 14–16, 36–37; ego-focused image of, 190–191, 201, 207; group-focused image of, 190–191, 201, 207; induced, 188–192, 208–212, 333–334; resistance to, 204–205. *See also* value change
Charter of Algiers, 31, 72–73, 151. *See also* UNCTAD
Chia T'o-fu, 62
Chile, 43
China, 34, 45, 48–49, 55, 69, 172, 221, 309, 320; cultural revolution in, 316; existence rationality strategy in, 211–212; goals of, 62; ideological mobilization in, 208; normative strategy of development in, 117–118; populism in, 116, 147; use of elites in, 151
Christianity, 4, 11, 133, 258; and revolution, 309–314
Chrysostom, John, 4, 133
Cleaver, Eldridge, 321
Coale, A. J., 278
Colin, Roland, 173–174, 273
collective responsibility, 135, 145–146
Colombia, 140, 319
colonialism, 15, 30, 42, 45, 107–108
Communist Manifesto, 6–7

competition, 98, 102
conflict, 106–107, 136, 141–142
consciousness, Third World, 25–26, 28–32, 42–51
consensus, 141
consultations in development planning, 160–164
consumption, 122, 128–138, 206–207, 236–249
Costa Pinto, L. A., 50
costs of development, 229–232
Croce, Benedetto, 247
Crosland, C. A. R., 281
Cuba, 40, 45, 46, 48, 49, 117, 226, 256, 320; reversed country-city population flow in, 72, 147
cultural diversity, 263–272
cultural revolution, viii, 26, 105, 292–294
cultural "seduction," 17
cultural universals, 87
culture of poverty, 23
Curle, Adam, 56
Cyprus, 63
Czechoslovakia, 146

Darwin, Charles, 98
Debray, Régis, 242, 299, 307, 336
de Castro, Josue, 131
dehumanization, 337
demonstration effects, 10, 17, 25, 42, 45, 74–76, 88, 134, 210, 219, 342
demosocracy, 150
Descartes, René, 316
desires, 74–77, 121–122
determinism, 14–16, 54, 115, 128, 173, 221–222, 250, 332, 334, 337
developers, 178–186, 276
development, definitions of, 14, 19, 96, 165, 332–334
de Vries, Barend A., 32–33
dialectical materialism, 8
dialectics, 97–108
dissensus, 141
Djakarta, 80n

Djilas, Milovan, 307, 316
Dolci, Danilo, vii, 84, 270, 341
domestication of development, 15,
    27, 34, 45, 68, 107, 120, 142,
    175, 317
double standard, 113–114, 140
Dubos, René, 194, 264, 267–268
Dumont, René, 224
Durkheim, Emile, 255
Durrell, Lawrence, 55

ecology, 273–281
economic: independence, 112;
    progress, 155–156
economics, development of, 3–8,
    10
economy, progressive, 155–156
efficiency, 144, 220–221
Einstein, Albert, 276
elitism, 144–152, 161, 174
Ellul, Jacques, 173, 259, 261, 301,
    306–307, 309, 314
empathy, 23–28. *See also* psychic
    empathy
Engels, Friedrich, 131, 314–315
England, 40, 103, 326
enhancement: goods, 246, 248;
    needs, 242–243, 247
"enough" goods, 128–138
esteem, viii, 89–90, 113, 118, 119,
    125, 130
ethics: definition of, 331–332;
    development, vii–x, 3–12, 18–
    19, 114–116, 119–120, 232,
    247; as means of the means,
    116; normative role of, defined,
    338–339; of power, 335–341;
    and revolution, 310–317
ethnocentrism, 11–12, 28, 32, 49,
    53, 55, 224, 239, 264, 289
ethocracy, 150
Europe, 103
evaluation of norms, 337–338
existence rationality, vii, viii, 150,
    188–212, 342; inner limits of,
    191, 194; outer boundaries of,
    191, 194

existentialism, 8, 9, 310, 351

Fals Borda, Orlando, 107, 304
False Start for Africa (Dumont),
    224
Fanon, Frantz, 102–103, 299, 308
feedback, 348
Fichte, Johann, 99
formation-information, 162
France, 48, 226
free demand and supply, 237
freedom, viii, 91, 113, 118, 125,
    130, 332
Freire, Paulo, 43
Freud, Sigmund, 98, 222, 255
Freyssinet, Jacques, 39
Fromm, Erich, 91, 105, 134, 215,
    322
fullness of good, 90, 128, 223, 257,
    283
Furtado, Celso, 61, 91–92, 100,
    115, 127, 304

Gabon, 48n
Gabor, Denis, 297
Galbraith, John Kenneth, 89, 132,
    142, 236, 238
Gandhi, Mohandas K., 130, 133,
    270
Gellner, Ernest, 56
Ghana, 34, 62–63
gift, economy of (Perroux), 286,
    289–290
Gilson, Etienne, 10
Ginsberg, Morris, 331
goals, 60–95; order of priority
    among, 123–127
Goodman, Paul, 223
Group of 77, *see* Charter of Algiers
Guevara, Che, 302, 323, 336
guilt, 135–136
Gypsies, 93, 195–208

Hagen, Everett E., 89, 144, 145,
    168, 217
Haiti, 256
Harbison, Frederick, 124

357

Heckscher, August, 218
Hegel, Georg Wilhelm Friedrich,
  99–100, 102, 104, 316, 337
Heilbroner, Robert L., 5, 7, 29,
  105, 318
Heraclitus, 121
Hersch, Jeanne, 125
Hervé, Pierre, 120
"Hiding Hand," 34–37
Hirschman, Albert O., 34–35, 37,
  190, 209–210
historical materialism, 100
Hong Kong, 48–49, 118
Hoover, E. M., 278
Hopi Indians, 268
Horowitz, Irving Louis, 304, 335–
  336
human ascent, 333, 334
human promotion, 155–156
Hungary, 146

illusion of omniscience, 154
images, 138
improvidence, 206–207
income redistribution, 71, 79–80,
  106, 137
incrementalism, 294–298
India, 40, 55, 64–65, 112
Indonesia, 34, 49
Industrial Revolution, 39
industrialization, 39, 41, 96–97,
  118, 274
innovation, 41, 103, 143, 158,
  165, 166, 189, 191–192, 342,
  344
institutionalization, 114
intelligent love, 157
International Support Center, 290
investment, 29, 79, 155, 165, 230
Israel, 146, 147–148
Itaparica, 57–59, 89

Japan, 63, 65, 90, 211, 269
Jevons, William Stanley, 6
Johnson, Lyndon B., 67
Jones, LeRoi, 321
"just war" theory, 311–312

justice, 72, 116, 135, 143

Kant, Immanuel, 99, 315
Kapital, Das (Marx), 7
Kaplan, Abraham, 150
Kaufmann, Walter, 99
Kautsky, Karl, 315
Keane, Robert, 1644 trial of, 5
Kennan, George, 125
Kenya, 47, 63
Keynes, John Maynard, 6, 266
Kierkegaard, Soren, 256
King, Martin Luther, Jr., 321
Kluckhohn, Clyde, 264
Koestler, Arthur, 55
Kolakowski, Leszek, 242, 316
Kubitschek, Juscelino, 225

Lasswell, Harold D., 150, 335
Latin, America, 31, 33, 42, 64,
  66, 71–72, 77–79, 175, 230n,
  278; elites in, 148
Lebanon, 157
Lebret, Louis J., x, 52, 131, 134,
  137, 167–168, 180, 183–185,
  248–249, 284
Le Corbusier (Charles Edouard
  Jeanneret), 218
legitimization, 114
Lerner, Daniel, 43, 187
le Sinto, Lick, 90
Let's Join the Human Race
  (Barr), 181
Lévi-Strauss, Claude, 223
Lewis, W. Arthur, 92, 327
Libya, 228n
life-sustenance, viii, 87–88, 113,
  118, 125, 130
Lin Yutang, 221
Lipset, Seymour Martin, 340
Lipton, Lawrence, 257
Luddites, 103

Macao, 48–49, 118
Machiavelli, Niccolò, 336
MacIntyre, Alasdair, 314–315,
  332

Madrid, 80
Magazine Publishers Association, 244
Malaya, 74
Malaysia, 63
Malcolm X, 151, 320–321
Malthus, Robert, 6
Mannheim, Karl, 179–180, 315
Mao Tse-tung, 46, 117, 309, 316, 323
Marcel, Gabriel, 24
Marcuse, Herbert, 51, 97, 242
marginals, 72, 118, 136, 192–208, 265, 282
Marshall, Alfred, 6, 137
Marshall Plan, 290
Marx, Karl, 6–7, 98, 99, 100, 106, 216, 222, 309, 314–315, 336–337
Marxism, 9–11, 46, 120, 141, 297, 310, 314–317
Maslow, Abraham, 120, 126, 135, 219, 239–240
materialism, 218–219
M'Ba, 48n
Meiji Restoration, 211
Melman, Seymour, 148
Mercier, L. S., 219
Merton, Thomas, 308
Middle East, 72, 79
Mill, John Stuart, 6, 7
Miller, Henry, 143
Millikan, Max, 64–65
Mills, C. Wright, 217, 339
mise en valeur, 281, 283. *See also* optimum resource use
mobilization, 43, 114, 116, 156, 189–190, 201–202, 208, 344, 346
modernization, 14, 41, 50, 96–97, 138, 189–190, 204, 334; resistance to, 41, 119
Moore, Barrington, 107, 318–319
moral philosophy, 3–12, 18–19
Moravia, Alberto, 268–269
Mumford, Lewis, 87, 88, 138
Muslim, 309

Myers, Charles A., 124
Myrdal, Gunnar, 30, 64, 77, 79, 112, 131, 134, 284, 285
myths, 42, 80–81, 173, 209

National Council of Churches, 305
National Liberation Front, 304
national sovereignty, 33–34
nationalism, 108, 111–113, 121
"natural law" morality, 8, 10
Navajo Indians, 268
Needler, Martin, 68
needs, 236–249; enhancement, 242–243, 247; of the first order, 241, 247–248; luxury, 243–247; self-actualization, 240, 242; shibboleth, 240
Nehru, Jawaharlal, 28
Niebuhr, Reinhold, 312
N'Krumah, Kwame, 34, 62
normative humanism, 215
normative sequence, principle of, 346–348
normative strategies, 12, 111–122, 329, 337
norms, 81–83, 140, 332, 340
Nyerere, Julius, 211, 232

observation, systematic, 347
occult compensation, 117
optimum: centers for innovation, 166; consultation, 164–165; governmental and administrative structures, 229; participation in decision-making, 121, 123, 144–152, 283; population, 277–278; resource use, 280, 281–294; speeds, 333
options, 227–229, 337
Organization for Economic Cooperation and Development, 172, 274
Ouled Sidi-Aissa, 83
Ouled Sidi-Cheikh, 83
over-abstraction, 156–157

Pacem in Terris, 293

Pakistan, 63, 79, 255
palliatives, 233, 295–298
Paraguay, 339
pariah entrepreneurs, 197
Paris, 145
Parsons, Talcott, 263–264
participation: optimum, in deci-
    sion-making, 121, 123, 144–152,
    283; survey, 161–164
Pascal, Blaise, 117, 259, 277
paternalism, 25, 45, 47, 52, 55–56,
    172–173
pathology of normalcy, 220
Peace Corps volunteers, 31, 216
"pedagogy of the oppressed," 43
Perroux, François, 34, 138, 156,
    165, 178–179, 249, 284, 286,
    289–290
Philippines, 79
pilot projects, 210
Piovene, Guido, 324
Plague, The (Camus), 222
planned centralization, 237–238
planners' occupational hazards,
    154–161
planning, ix, 16, 54, 61–65, 153–
    169, 206–212; priorities, 125–
    126, 154, 176, 177, 247–249
Plato, 3, 98–99, 300, 336
Poland, 146
pole, development, 41, 104, 165–
    166, 265
politics, 336
Pontifical Commission of Justice
    and Peace, 293
population policies, ix, 277–279,
    285
populism, 116, 117, 144–147
Populorum Progressio, 293
Portugal, 63–64, 117
positivism, 8–9, 10, 310
"possibilities of things," 266
poverty, 23–30, 252–255, 340
power, 19, 335–341
Prebisch, Raúl, 28
professionalization of developers,
    179–186

psychic empathy, 43, 187, 191,
    197
psychic mobility, 191–192

Rathenau, Walter, 235
reciprocity, viii, 37, 52–53, 55
*Report on the World Social Situa-
    tion, 1967,* 70–73
resource use, 280, 281–294
responsibility, 135, 145–146
revolution, 299–325, 336; cultural,
    viii, 26, 105, 292–294; of rising
    expectations, 36, 102
revolutionaries, 42, 46–47, 140–
    141, 296
revolutionary violence, 300–325
Ricardo, David, 6
Ricoeur, Paul, 251
Rondônia, 24
Rose, Stephen, 107
Rouda, Vando, 202
Russell, Bertrand, 128, 276

sacrificed generations, 230–231
Sahara Bedouins, 93
Saint-Simon, Claude Henri, 235
Salazar, Antonio de Oliveira, 117
Sartori, Giovanni, 149
Sartre, Jean-Paul, 9, 100, 242
scapegoat theory, 30, 40, 135
Scitovsky, Tibor, 238, 246–247
Seeley, John, 340
Senegal, 48, 226–227
Senghor, Leopold S., 145, 172
seringueros, 24
servitude to technology, 231
shadow plans, 160
shibboleth needs, 240
signification, 166
Silvert, Kalman, 111–112
Smith, Adam, 6, 223
Socialism, 209
Socialist countries, 46, 117, 208–
    209, 304, 339
Socrates, 3
solidarity, 123, 138–143, 238, 283
Sombart, Werner, 243

Sorel, Georges, 302
South Africa, 339
South Asia, 79
Soviet Union, 28–29, 69, 172, 226,
 227, 233, 259, 326, 327, 339
space, man's triumph over, 13, 17–
 18
Spain, 197–202, 339
standardization, 127, 138, 263–272
Statesman, The, 300
Steere, Douglas, 220
Stone, I. F., 313, 315
strategic (raw) materials, 67–68
stratification, 18, 101
"subversives," 142
Sukarno, 34, 49
superfluity of goods, 132–138
Sutton, F. X., 96–97
synthesis, 99; preliminary, 347; reflective, 347–348

Tagore, Rabindranath, 143
Taiwan, 118
Tanzania, 49, 211, 232
Taoism, 117, 309
technical: assistance, 170–186,
 224; cooperation, ix, 170–186;
 transfers, 171–186
technological mastery, 36, 259–
 260
technology, 10, 143, 231–232
Teilhard de Chardin, Pierre, 124
Thailand, 79
Theobald, Robert, 231
Theory of Moral Sentiments
 (Smith), 6
time: man's triumph over, 13, 17;
 as a constraint on development,
 225
Tinbergen, Jan, 158, 160, 167,
 284–287
Togliatti, Palmiro, 317
Torres, Camilo, 140, 304, 305,
 310, 319
traditionalism, 211–212
transcendence, 242–243, 245–246
transfer of motivations, 173

*Two Sources of Morality and Re-
 ligion, The* (Bergson), 258

U Nu, 28n
UNCTAD (United Nations Conference on Trade and Development), 44, 48, 72–73, 105, 287.
 See also Charter of Algiers
United Nations, 172, 280; Center
 for Development Planning, Projections and Policies, 284; documents, 69–73; Progress Reports,
 70
United States, 31, 33, 66, 103, 216,
 220, 226, 227, 233, 326, 339;
 Agency for International Development, 66–67; aid to Vietnam, disruptive effects of, 30n;
 attitude toward radical change,
 317–320; blacks in, 36, 49, 90,
 135, 141, 320–321; reliance on
 underdeveloped world's raw
 materials, 67–69; revolutionary
 consciousness in, 320–325; white
 radicals in, 321–325
Universal Declaration of Human
 Rights, 69–70, 181
urbanization, 71–72, 79, 94

Vaizey, John, 56
value change, ix, 81–85, 157–161,
 171, 188–212, 270–271, 292–
 294, 343; research on, 342–351
values, 49–50, 86–91, 116–117,
 331, 333, 342; normative, 81–
 85, 335; significative, 81–85
Van der Post, Lauren, 219
Veblen, Thorstein, 132, 238, 243
Vietnam, 30n, 304–305, 320
violence, 300–325
voluntarism, 46
Votaru, Lionel, 202
vulnerability, vii–ix, 23–25, 38–
 39, 51–57, 142, 342; Third
 World structural, 46, 103, 113

Wang, N. T., 287

war expenditures, 233, 256
waste, 56, 115, 176, 182, 243
wealth: redistribution, 106, 137;
  superfluity of, 132–138
Wealth of Nations, The (Smith), 6
Weil, Simone, 11
Weill, Eric, 11
Weisskopf, Walter, 217
welfare disparities, 70–71
Wilkinson, John, 295
Wilson, George, 3

Wolf, Eric, 299
world: financial strategy, 287–288;
  legal order, 295; ocean regime,
  280, 296–297; plan, 283–287;
  technical pool, 288–292
World Council of Churches, 293

Yugoslavia, 146, 339

Zofio, 80

Denis Goulet

Denis Goulet has lived and worked with the slum dwellers of Madrid, cannibals in the Amazon region, Gypsies in southern Spain and Bedouins of the Algerian Sahara. These rare experiences have given him remarkable insights into the psyches of the people of the Third World. An earlier book, *The Ethics of Development* (in Spanish and Portuguese), has become known in Latin America as a pioneer inter-disciplinary work. Mr. Goulet is currently a Fellow at the Center for the Study of Development and Social Change in Cambridge, Massachusetts, where he lives with his wife and two daughters.